STUDIES IN ANCIENT ORIENTAL CIVILIZATION • No. 49

THE ORIENTAL INSTITUTE OF THE UNIVERSITY OF CHICAGO

Thomas A. Holland, Editor

with the assistance of Richard M. Schoen

A CRITICAL STUDY OF THE TEMPLE SCROLL FROM QUMRAN CAVE 11

MICHAEL OWEN WISE

THE ORIENTAL INSTITUTE OF THE UNIVERSITY OF CHICAGO

STUDIES IN ANCIENT ORIENTAL CIVILIZATION • No. 49

CHICAGO • ILLINOIS

Library of Congress Catalog Card Number: 90–61248

ISBN: 0–918986–63–X
ISSN: 0081–7554

The Oriental Institute, Chicago

TABLE OF CONTENTS

FOREWORD

This book is an entirely revised form of my dissertation, which was accepted by the department of Near Eastern Languages and Civilizations of the University of Chicago in June, 1988. It is a great pleasure to thank here those who guided and aided the work of the dissertation. My advisor was Norman Golb; he introduced me to the study of the Dead Sea Scrolls in Hebrew, and taught me the value of questioning every assumption. He shared generously of his knowledge and insights during the course of my work, and I owe him a large debt of gratitude. Dennis Pardee was the dissertation's second reader; he taught me much about Northwest Semitic Philology in the course of my graduate studies, and was never too busy to stop and talk about problems involved with my research. My third reader, W. Randall Garr, raised important questions and contributed much to the substance of the thesis. His concern with the manner of its presentation helped me to smooth out many rough spots, and to think about the writing task in a new light. I can only hope that the rewriting which has taken place in transforming the dissertation into a book has taken it somewhat further along the path on which he started me. The administration of Trinity College, Deerfield, Illinois helped me to make substantial progress early in the dissertation with a Reduced Load Grant in the fall of 1986. I hereby record my appreciation for their generosity and encouragement, especially that of the dean, Robert Baptista.

Although I have discussed portions of this book with numerous scholars, I wish to single out two persons in particular, James A. Sanders and Philip R. Davies, for their help. Professor Sanders more than once went out of his way to encourage this young scholar in general, and I am thankful to him for his willingness to spend time discussing specific aspects of this study, and for his helpful comments. Professor Davies read the entire manuscript and raised numerous questions, the contemplation of which has, I believe, aided me in improving the work substantially. Of course, none of these scholars is responsible for any of those errors or infelicities which have doubtless escaped even their critical eyes to survive into the work in hand. That responsibility is mine alone; whatever credit is due, however, must be shared with them.

I wish to thank Janet Johnson, then Director of the Oriental Institute, for accepting this book for publication. Thanks are also due to Thomas Holland, the Publications Coordinator of the Oriental Institute Publications Office, and his assistant Richard Schoen, for their careful preparation of a sometimes difficult manuscript.

Finally, my wife Cathy encouraged and supported my every effort during the research and writing first of the dissertation and then of the book, and it is no exaggeration to say that without her those efforts would have been neither possible nor worthwhile. She is truly עזר כנגדי, and to her I dedicate this work as a small token of my love and gratitude.

Michael O. Wise
30 April 1990

ix

LIST OF FIGURES

LIST OF TABLES

LIST OF ABBREVIATIONS

ACP	*Annuaire du College de France*
AEPHE	*Annuaire. École Pratique des Hautes Études*
AESC	*Annales Économies Sociétés Civilisations*
AfO	*Archiv für Orientforschung*
AJBI	*Annual of the Japanese Biblical Institute*
AJSR	*Association for Jewish Studies Review*
Ant.	Josephus, *Antiquitates Judaicae*
BA	*The Biblical Archaeologist*
BAR	*Biblical Archaeology Review*
BASOR	*Bulletin of the American Schools of Oriental Research*
BDB	Brown, Driver and Briggs, *Hebrew and English Lexicon of the Old Testament*
BH	*Buried History*
BHS	*Biblica Hebraica Stuttgartensia*
BiO	*Bibbia e Oriente*
BJ	Josephus, *Bellum Judaicum*
BK	*Bibel und Kirche*
BLE	*Bulletin de Littérature Ecclésiastique*
BM	*Beth Mikra*
BO	*Bibliotheca Orientalis*
BSER	*Bulletin de la Société Ernest-Renan*
CB	*Cultura Bíblica*
CBQ	*Catholic Biblical Quarterly*
CRAIBL	*Académie des Inscriptions et Belles-Lettres: Comptes Rendus des Séances*
DJD(J)	*Discoveries in the Judaean Desert (of Jordan)*
DSS	*Dead Sea Scrolls*
DTT	*Dansk Teologisk Tidsskrift*
EB	*Estudios Biblicos*
ED	*Euntes Docete*
EI	*Eretz Israel*
ET	*Expository Times*
ETh	*Evangelische Theologie*
ETL	*Ephemerides Theologicae Lovanienses*
ETR	*Études Théologiques et Religieuses*

FO	*Folia Orientalia (Kraków)*
GKC	Gesenius, Kautsch and Cowley, *Gesenius' Hebrew Grammar*
HAR	*Hebrew Annual Review*
HS	*Hebrew Studies*
HTR	*Harvard Theological Review*
HUCA	*Hebrew Union College Annual*
IEJ	*Israel Exploration Journal*
IMJ	*Israel Museum Journal*
JAAR	*Journal of the American Academy of Religion*
JAOS	*Journal of the American Oriental Society*
Jastrow	M. Jastrow, *Dictionary of the Targumim*
JBL	*Journal of Biblical Literature*
JJS	*Journal of Jewish Studies*
JLA	*Jewish Law Annual*
JNES	*Journal of Near Eastern Studies*
JQR	*Jewish Quarterly Review*
JSJ	*Journal for the Study of Judaism*
JSOT	*Journal for the Study of the Old Testament*
JSS	*Journal of Semitic Studies*
JTS	*Journal of Theological Studies*
KK	*Kirke og Kultur*
LBH	Late Biblical Hebrew
LM	*Lutherische Monatschrift*
LXX	The Septuagint
MB	*Le Monde de la Bible*
MH	Mishnaic Hebrew
MT	Masoretic Text
NJ	New Jerusalem
NRT	*Nouvelle Revue Théologique*
NT	New Testament
NTT	*Nederlands Theologisch Tijdschrift*
OS	*Oudtestamentische Studiën*
PAAJR	*Proceedings of the American Academy of Jewish Research*
PAPS	*Proceedings of the American Philosophical Society*
PEGLBS	*Proceedings of the Eastern Great Lakes Biblical Society*
PEQ	*Palestine Exploration Quarterly*
RB	*Revue Biblique*

RBI	*Rivista Biblica Italiana*
RBL	*Ruch Biblijnyi i Liturgiczny*
REJ	*Revue des Études Juives*
RHR	*Revue de l'Histoire des Religions*
RO	*Rocznik Orientalistyczny*
RQ	*Revue de Qumran*
RSLR	*Rivista di Storia e Letteratura Religiosa*
RSR	*Recherches de Science Religieuse*
RSRs	*Revue des Sciences Religieuses*
RStR	*Religious Studies Review*
SA	*Sciences et Avenir*
SBH	Standard Biblical Hebrew
SBL	Society for Biblical Literature
SE	*Science et Espirit*
SH	*Spiegel Historiael*
ScH	*Scripta Hierosolymitana*
SJOT	*Scandinavian Journal of the Old Testament*
SR	*Studia Religioznawcze*
SR/SR	*Studies in Religion/Sciences Religieuses*
TDNT	*Theological Dictionary of the New Testament*
TDOT	*Theological Dictionary of the Old Testament*
ThSt	*Theological Studies*
TM	Torat Ham-Melekh
TPQ	*Theologisch-Praktische Quartalschrift*
TS	Temple Scroll
TSt	*La Terre Sainte*
TT	*Tidsskrift for Teologi og Kirke*
TvT	*Tijdschrift voor Theologie*
VT	*Vetus Testamentum*
Yadin I-III	Y. Yadin, *The Temple Scroll*, 3 vols.
ZAW	*Zeitschrift für die Alttestamentliche Wissenschaft*
Zion	*Zion. A Quarterly for Research in Jewish History*
ZKT	*Zeitschrift für Katholische Theologie*

Abbreviations of the names of biblical books and Qumran texts follow the systems employed in the *Journal of Biblical Literature*, as listed in the "Instructions for Contributors," volume 107 (1988): 579-96.

1

THE TEMPLE SCROLL: PREVIOUS WORK
AND THE PRESENT STUDY

Introduction

The Temple Scroll (TS) is a confident sphinx still awaiting its Oedipus. It requires the construction of a vast temple whose details accord with neither the biblical nor any other known Israelite or Jewish temple. Its compiler frequently quotes from the Hebrew Bible, especially from Deut, but in so doing, he intentionally omits the name of Moses where it appears in the biblical text. The effect is to make the TS seem a direct revelation from God. The scroll includes a Festival Calendar which mandates hitherto unknown festivals, sacrifices, and festal regulations. The riddle of the temple plan and the meaning of the other puzzling phenomena of the TS have now engaged scholars for over twenty years. Nevertheless, after two decades of study of this longest of the Dead Sea Scrolls (DSS), no consensus has emerged on the principal questions. Who composed the TS, and for what purpose; how and when was it done?

These questions are so tightly intertwined that it is impossible to consider any one of them in isolation from the others. Still, the most fundamental concern is clearly to determine the scroll's sources. Without at least a basic comprehension of the scroll's literary composition, there is little hope of a successful inquiry into the other areas. One must start with source criticism, only turning to questions of provenance, date, and purpose when some progress has been made in that endeavor. Such is the object of this investigation. By applying critical techniques developed in biblical studies—but strangely underexploited by DSS research—this study seeks to loose the knots of the salient questions which the TS poses. To provide a proper context for this analysis, I first briefly review the two decades of research on the TS, giving some consideration to each major area of investigation. In view of the aims of this study, however, primary emphasis is on previous approaches to the scroll's composition, provenance, date, and purpose.

The First Decade of Research

Prepublication Notices and Studies

The TS has been known since 1960, but it was not until June 1967 that Yigael Yadin was able to acquire it.[1] Several months later, in October, Yadin announced the acquisition at an archaeological convention.[2] Because of publication lag-time, however, it was not this announcement which first supplied scholars with details of the discovery, but the preliminary report which appeared simultaneously in *The Biblical Archaeologist* and the *Comptes Rendus* of the Académie des Inscriptions et Belles-Lettres.[3]

Since Yadin had only four months to study the scroll, it is remarkable that many of the final conclusions of his later analysis of the TS are already present in this preliminary announcement. Based on paleographical analysis, Yadin dated the copy of the scroll to the second half of the first century B.C.E. or the beginning of the first century C.E., while conceding that the composition of the original could be "perhaps a little earlier."[4] As to provenance, Yadin believed the scroll was sectarian; its author was an Essene.[5] Because the tetragrammaton appears in the scroll in ordinary Aramaic square script (instead of the earlier Hebrew script), and God is depicted speaking in the first person, Yadin deduced that the sect regarded the scroll as Scripture.[6] In his view its author would be more accurately described as an editor, who grouped legal materials now scattered throughout the Pentateuch to produce a book which harmonized apparent discrepancies. This editor also drew eclectically from the biblical descriptions of the tabernacle, First Temple, and Ezekiel's Temple to fabricate a new temple plan.[7] Finally, Yadin's conclusion that the scroll's calendar was the solar calendar of 1 (Ethiopic) Enoch and other texts of the Second Temple period also appeared in the preliminary report.[8]

Several years later Yadin republished this preliminary report, making only minor changes in wording.[9] The most significant change concerned the dating. Where the first report had read,

---

1. The most detailed account of the fascinating and sometimes even dangerous effort to acquire the scroll is found in Yadin's semi-technical book, *The Temple Scroll: The Hidden Law of the Dead Sea Sect* (London: Weidenfeld and Nicholson, 1985) pp. 8–55. For additional details, which Yadin could not reveal in his lifetime, see H. Shanks, "Intrigue and the Scroll: Behind the Scenes of Israel's Acquisition of the Temple Scroll," *BAR* 13 (1987): 23–27.

2. Y. Yadin, "מגילת המקדש," [The Temple Scroll] in *Jerusalem Through the Ages: The Twenty-Fifth Archaeological Convention October 1967* (Jerusalem: Israel Exploration Society, 1968), pp. 72–84.

3. Y. Yadin, "The Temple Scroll," *BA* 30 (1967): 135–39. The French report was "Un nouveau manuscrit de la Mer Mort: 'Le Rouleau du Temple,'" *CRAIBL* (1967): 607–16.

4. Yadin, "Temple Scroll," p. 136.

5. Ibid., p. 137.

6. Ibid., p. 136.

7. Ibid., pp. 136 and 139.

8. Ibid., pp. 137 and 138.

9. Y. Yadin, "The Temple Scroll," in *New Directions in Biblical Archaeology*, eds. D. N. Freedman and J. C. Greenfield (Garden City: Doubleday, 1971), pp. 156–66. At about the same time two condensations of

"... indeed there are good reasons for placing the date of composition perhaps a little earlier," the new publication rephrased, "... indeed there are good reasons for placing the date of composition at the end of the second century B.C.E."[10] With this statement the essential elements of Yadin's views on the TS were in place.

On the eve of publication of the *editio princeps*, Yadin once again gave a preliminary report. Here the basic perspectives were unchanged, the report only reflecting the greater detail and nuances resulting from a decade of study of the scroll.[11]

Based on the article in *Biblical Archaeologist* and its French counterpart, notices of the discovery of the TS soon appeared in German,[12] French,[13] Italian,[14] Spanish,[15] Dutch,[16] and other European languages.[17] Few of the authors of the notices were specialists in DSS study, and even fewer manifested any skepticism about Yadin's ideas on the scroll.

Between these publication notices and the appearance of the *editio princeps* in 1977, Yadin occasionally revealed additional information about the scroll in studies devoted to ancillary topics. He published TS 64:6b–13a, on the crucifixion of political criminals, in an attempt to elucidate a crux in 4QpNah.[18] His ideas on the relationship between these two texts were

this article appeared: *Encyclopedia Judaica,* s.v. "Temple Scroll," and "What the Temple Scroll Reveals," *The Daily Telegraph Magazine,* July 19, 1968, pp. 15–17. Another adaptation appeared in Dutch, "De Tempelrol," *SH* 4, (1969): 203–210, but it did not contain the crucial changes in wording.

10. Yadin, "Temple Scroll," *New Directions,* p. 158.

11. Y. Yadin, "Le Rouleau du Temple," in *Qumrân: sa piété, sa théologie et son milieu,* ed. J. Carmignac (Paris: Duculot, 1978), pp. 115–20. Ironically, this preliminary report appeared after the publication of the *editio princeps.*

12. G. Wilhelm, "Qumran (Tempelrolle)," *AfO* 22 (1968–69): 165–66; W. Baumgartner, "Eine neue Qumranrolle," *Universitas* 23 (1968): 981–84.

13. E. M. Laperrousaz, "Presentation, à Jérusalem, du plus long des rouleaux-actuellement connus-provenant du Qumrân," *RHR* 174 (1968):113–15; H. de Saint-Blanquat, "Le nouveau manuscrit de la Mer Morte," *SA* 257 (1968): 582–89, esp. 585–89; A. Caquot, "Information préliminaire sur le 'Rouleau du Temple' de Qumrân," *BSER* 22 (1973):1, 3–4.

14. P. Sacchi, "Scoperta di un nuovo rotolo in Palestina," *RSLR* 3 (1967): 579–80; P. Colella, "Nuovi manoscritti del Mar Morto," *RBI* 16 (1968): 214–15; J. M. Keshishian, "Il più lungo manoscritto del Mar Morto," *Sapere* 59 (1968): 60–63; L. Moraldi, *I manoscritti di Qumran* (Turin: Unione Tipografico-Editrice Torinese, 1971), pp. 733–36.

15. F. Sen, "El nuevo Manuscrito del Templo," *CB* 25 (1968): 173–74.

16. K. R. Veenhof, "Een nieuw handschrift van de Dode Zee: De 'Tempelrol'," *Phoenix* 14 (1968): 186–88.

17. A. Andreassen, "Tempel-rullen," *KK* 73 (1968): 262–67; J. Chmiel, "Nowe rekopisy z Qumran," *RBL* 22 (1969): 302–303, and T. Scher, "A kumráni Templomtekercs," [The Temple Scroll from Qumran] *Világosság* 9 (1968): 636–37. For an overview of the perforce limited Eastern European studies on the Temple Scroll, not covered in detail here, see Z. J. Kapera, "A Review of East European Studies on the Temple Scroll," in *Temple Scroll Studies,* ed. G. J. Brooke (Sheffield: *JSOT* Press, 1989), pp. 275–86.

18. Y. Yadin, "Pesher Nahum (4QpNahum) Reconsidered," *IEJ* 21 (1971): 1–12.

widely influential.[19] An article on Essene views on marriage and divorce excerpted TS 57:17–19, which interdicts royal polygamy and divorce.[20]

The *Editio Princeps* and Other Yadin Publications

When Yadin published the TS in a three-volume edition,[21] many felt that the ten-year wait since its discovery was at least partially justified. He provided a detailed introduction to the text, a transcription and concordance, indexes, and a volume of plates (with a supplement). The work included discussions on physical aspects of the scroll, its festivals, offerings, temple and temple city, laws, date, and status.[22]

Where Yadin touched on areas he had discussed in the prepublication reports, his views were virtually unchanged. He reiterated his opinion that the author was essentially an editor whose purpose was to harmonize discrepancies in the Pentateuch. The text he worked with was practically identical to the Masoretic text (MT). Therefore, where biblical quotations in the scroll differed from the MT, Yadin thought the changes must be intentional, reflecting polemics with sects of the author's day. His ideas on the date of the scroll's composition were likewise unchanged.

In 1983 Yadin published an English edition of the TS.[23] He made many substantial changes in the text of volumes 1 and 2, including the adoption of over fifty new readings in the scroll. Because of these changes, and its fourteen pages of *addenda et corrigenda*, the English edition is the *editio maior* of the TS.[24]

19. See the immediate favorable response by A. Dupont-Sommer, "Observations nouvelles sur l'expression 'suspendu vivant sur le bois' dans le commentaire de Nahum (4Q pNah II8) a la lumière du Rouleau du Temple (11Q Temple Scroll LXIV, 6–13)," *CRAIBL* (1972): 709–20, and the literature cited in M. Horgan's discussion, *Pesharim: Qumran Interpretations of Biblical Books*, Catholic Biblical Quarterly Monograph Series, no. 8 (Washington: Catholic Biblical Association of America, 1979), pp. 158–62. For a discussion of the relationship between 4Q Pesher Nahum and the TS, see chapter 4, below.

20. Y. Yadin, "L'attitude essénienne envers la polygamie et le divorce," *RB* 79 (1972): 98–99. See the rejoinder by J. Murphy-O'Connor, "Remarques sur l'exposé du Professeur Y. Yadin," *RB* 79 (1972): 99–100.

21. Y. Yadin, ed. מגילת המקדש [The Temple Scroll], 3 vols. and supplementary plates (Jerusalem: Israel Exploration Society, 1977).

22. Surprisingly for a major publication, the work was not widely reviewed. For reviews, see J. Baumgarten, *JBL* 97 (1978): 584–89; D. Flusser, *Numen* 26 (1979): 271–74 and *Immanuel* 9 (1979): 49–52; and J. Maier, *ZAW* 90 (1978): 152–54. B. Levine's, "The Temple Scroll: Aspects of its Historical Provenance and Literary Character," *BASOR* 232 (1978): 5–23 is a review article.

23. Y. Yadin, ed., *The Temple Scroll*, 3 vols. and supplementary plates (Jerusalem: Israel Exploration Society, 1983). For reviews, see X. Jacques, *NRT* 107 (1985): 603–605; J. Milgrom, *BAR* 10 (1984): 12–14; L. Schiffman, *BA* 48 (1985): 122–26; M. A. Knibb, *The Society for Old Testament Study Book List 1986* (Leeds: W. S. Maney & Son, 1986), pp. 138–39; J. A. Fitzmyer, *CBQ* 48 (1986): 547–49; F. F. Bruce, *PEQ* 118 (1986): 76.

24. References in this study will be to the English edition unless otherwise specified.

Two years later Yadin published a distillation of the contents of volume 1 of his scientific edition.[25] This book included excellent color photographs of the scroll at various stages of the unrolling process, and helpful diagrams of the architectural elements of the TS. For these reasons it is of interest even to specialists.

The Second Decade of Research

Translations and General Studies

Soon after Yadin published the *editio princeps,* translations of the scroll appeared.[26] Caquot published a French translation complete with notes and a thorough introduction.[27] Maier wrote a short monograph on the TS, which included a German translation and copious notes.[28] Other scholars produced annotated translations in Spanish[29] and Polish.[30] A small but important portion of the scroll was translated into Dutch.[31]

General surveys of the DSS and Second Temple Judaism began to include the TS in their purview. Most, such as those by Soggin,[32] McNamara,[33] and Davies,[34] followed Yadin's views closely. Writing somewhat later than the others, Cohen was more critical of Yadin's

25. See note 1, above. For reviews, see S. Goranson, *BA* 47 (1984): 127; L. Schiffman, *BAR* 11 (1985): 12–14; M. A. Knibb, *Book List,* p. 139; and F. García-Martínez, *JSJ* 17 (1986): 124–25.

26. In addition to Yadin's own translation of the TS into English in his English edition of the scroll, one should note that the recently published third edition of G. Vermes, *The Dead Sea Scrolls in English* (Sheffield: *JSOT* Press, 1987) includes a translation of the TS on pp. 128–58.

27. A. Caquot, "Le Rouleau du Temple de Qoumrân," *ETR* 53 (1978): 443–500. Now see also idem, "Rouleau du Temple," in *La Bible: écrits intertestamentaires,* eds. A. Dupont-Sommer and M. Philonenko (Paris: Éditions Gallimard, 1987), pp. 61–132.

28. J. Maier, *Die Tempelrolle vom Toten Meer* (Munich: Ernst Reinhardt, 1978).

29. F. García-Martínez, "El Rollo del Templo," *EB* 36 (1978): 247–92.

30. W. Tyloch, "Zwój swiatynny," [The Temple Scroll] *Euhemer* 27 (1983) no. 3 (129): 3–20; 28 (1984) no. 1 (131): 3–24; 28 (1984) no. 2 (132): 11–28; 28 (1984) no. 3 (133): 9–27.

31. TS 56:12–57:21. See B. Jongeling, "De 'Tempelrol,'" *Phoenix* 25 (1979): 84–99, and A. S. van der Woude, "Een Gedeelte uit de Tempelrol van Qumran," in *Schrijvend Verleden: Documenten uit het oude Nabije Oosten Vertaald en Toegelicht,* ed. K. R. Veenhof (Leiden: Leiden Terra, 1983), pp. 387–91. According to Kapera, "Review of East European Studies," p. 283, a Russian translation of the scroll should appear in the series *Teksty Kumrana,* under the charge of K. B. Starkova.

32. J. A. Soggin, *I manoscritti del Mar Morto,* Paperbacks civiltá scomparse 22 (Rome: Newton Compton, 1978), pp. 60–61.

33. M. McNamara, *Intertestamental Literature,* Old Testament Message vol. 23 (Wilmington: Michael Glazer, 1983), pp. 136–40.

34 P. R. Davies, *Qumran* (Grand Rapids: Eerdmans, 1982), pp. 27, 83–86, 95–96, and 103. See also the surveys by G. Vermes, *The Dead Sea Scrolls: Qumran in Perspective,* rev. ed., with the collaboration of P. Vermes (Philadelphia: Fortress Press, 1977), pp. 54–56 and M. Delcor and F. García-Martínez, *Introduccion a la literatura esenià de Qumran* (Madrid: Ediciones Cristiandad, 1982), pp. 187–206.

views, arguing that the scroll might not be a sectarian creation, and might be of much earlier date than the late second century.[35]

A number of general introductions came out soon after מגילת המקדש. These works made no pretense of taking an independent stance on the major questions involved with the TS. Their only purpose was to mediate Yadin's work to the interested general reader who was unable to read the original.[36] Various authors produced more technical introductions for scholars who were not specialists in DSS studies.[37]

In addition there appeared various general and serial studies which dealt not with the entire TS, but with several important aspects in a single article. In "Le Rouleau du Temple de Qoumrân," Caquot studied cols. 1–15 of the scroll, concentrating in particular on the ceremony of priestly investment (מלואים).[38] Delcor wrote a series of articles concerned with the *explication* of the scroll.[39] Luria pondered the location of the temple of the TS, and the identity of the mercenary soldiers the Hasmoneans hired during their wars of conquest (a question involved with the interpretation of TS 57).[40] Brooke authored a study in which he attempted to draw connections between various passages in the TS and the archaeology of the site of Qumran.[41] It would seem far too early for such attempts, however, given the uncertainties of

35. S. J. D. Cohen, *From the Maccabees to the Mishnah* (Philadelphia: Westminster Press, 1987), pp. 151, 184, 191, and 212. Because he did not specify a date, it is not possible to compare Cohen's view with those of others maintaining a very early dating, such as Stegemann. See the discussion on dating below.

36. See F. Manns, "Nouveautes en Librairie au subject de Qumran," *TSt* (March-April 1978): 74–75; M. Broshi, "Le Rouleau du Temple," *MB* 4 (1978): 70–72; G. Garner, "The Temple Scroll," *BH* 15 (1979): 1–16; and A. Caquot, "Le Rouleau du Temple," *MB* 13 (1980): 34–35.

37. The most widely cited of these studies is by J. Milgrom, "The Temple Scroll," *BA* 41 (1978): 105–20. See also Delcor in *Dictionaire de la Bible, Supplement* vol. 9; B. Jongeling, "Tempelrol"; H. A. Mink, "Præsentation af et nyt Qumranskrift: Tempelrullen," *DDT* 42 (1979): 81–112; A. S. van der Woude, "De Tempelrol van Qumrân (I)," *NTT* 34 (1980): 177–90; idem, "De Tempelrol van Qumrân (II)," *NTT* 34 (1980): 281–93; D. Dimant, "Qumran Sectarian Literature," in *Jewish Writings of the Second Temple Period,* ed. M. Stone (Philadelphia: Fortress Press, 1984), pp. 526–30; T. Elgvin, "Tempelrullen fra Qumran," *TTK* 1 (1985): 1–21; and E. Shürer, *The History of the Jewish People in the Age of Jesus Christ (175 B.C.-A.D.135),* rev. by G. Vermes, F. Millar, and M. Goodman (Edinburgh: T&T Clark, 1986), vol. 3.1, pp. 406–20.

38. A. Caquot, *ACF* (1977–78): 577–80.

39. M. Delcor, "Explication du Rouleau du Temple de Qoumrân," *AEPHE* 90 (1981–82): 229–35; *AEPHE* 91 (1982–83): 257–64; and *AEPHE* 92 (1983–84): 245–51. See also Delcor's consideration of an interesting problem in the scroll in "Réflexions sur l'investiture sacerdotale sans onction à la fête du Nouvel An d'après le Rouleau du Temple de Qumrân (XIV 15–17)," in *Hellenica et Judaica: Homâge à Valentin Nikiprowetzky,* eds. A. Caquot, M. Hadas-Lebel, and J. Riaud (Leuven-Paris: Editions Peeters, 1986), pp. 155–64.

40. B. Z. Luria, "הערות למגילת המקדש," [Notes on the Temple Scroll] *BM* 75 (1978): 370–86.

41. G. Brooke, "The Temple Scroll and the Archaeology of Qumran, Ain Feskha and Masada," *RQ* 13 (1988): 225–38.

the site's archaeology, and the still poorly understood interconnections between, and history of, the various scrolls found in the caves nearby.[42]

Textual Studies

Because the TS weathered the centuries rather poorly—indeed spending the better part of a decade deteriorating while wrapped in a shoe box—reading the scroll, especially its early columns, has never been easy. Extraordinary efforts have been made to recover the text. Aside from Yadin, Qimron has been the foremost scholar in this regard. After Yadin had published the Modern Hebrew edition of the scroll, Qimron obtained access to the MS in the Rockefeller Museum. His examination of the scroll led to the publication of two important articles, in which he suggested many new readings.[43] The English edition later adopted many of them. Subsequently, Qimron made further suggestions for new readings in cols. 14, 20–21, 32, 37–38, 50, 58, and 60–61.[44] In a more problematic study, Mink attempted a restoration of col. 3, which is nearly completely lost.[45]

Another aspect of textual studies has been the examination and reconstruction of other copies of the TS. Scholars have often been unsure precisely how many copies exist. Yadin himself was somewhat unclear on this point.[46] Although estimates have ranged as high as eight copies,[47] it is virtually certain there are no more than two MSS of the TS altogether, including the main copy.[48] The second copy of the TS has been dubbed 11QTS[b], and consists of

42. For trenchant though brief comments on the archaeology of the site—for which no final excavation report has ever appeared—see P. R. Davies, "How Not to Do Archaeology: The Story of Qumran," *BA* 51 (1988): 203–7.

43. E. Qimron, "New Readings in the Temple Scroll," *IEJ* 28 (1978): 161–72; and "מן העבודה במלון ההסטורי" [From the work on the historical dictionary] *Leshonenu* 42 (1978): 136–45.

44. E. Qimron, "שלוש הערות לנוסח של מגילת המקדש," [Three notes on the text of the Temple Scroll] *Tarbiz* 51 (1981): 135–37; "הערות לנוסח מגילת המקדש," [Notes on the text of the Temple Scroll] *Tarbiz* 53 (1983): 139–41; "Further New Readings in the Temple Scroll," *IEJ* 37 (1987): 31–35, and "Column 14 of the Temple Scroll," *IEJ* 38 (1988): 44–46.

45. H. A. Mink, "Die Kol. III der Tempelrolle: Versuch einer Rekonstruktion," *RQ* 11 (1982–84): 163–81. Mink's is a valiant effort at recovery, but his methodology is flawed. After determining the probable length of the missing lines based on the longest still preserved, he turns to the Bible. There he considers all verses which touch upon the context of the missing portion in the scroll. He chooses that which most nearly fits the length requirement. The flaw is that he has assumed that the author has quoted the biblical text verbatim, when in fact the Temple Source, of which col. 3 is a part, virtually never does so. See chapter 3, below. One fruit of his effort, however, is the reading in 3:3 of the word מיסים ("forced contributions"). This reading is preferable to Yadin's מיסביב (surrounding), which assumes both a scribal error and unusual orthography.

46. Yadin I, p. 8.

47. H. Stegemann, "'Das Land' in der Tempelrolle und in anderer Texten aus den Qumranfunden," in *Das Land Israel in biblischer Zeit*, ed. G. Strecker (Göttingen: Vandenhoeck & Ruprecht, 1983), p. 168 note 21.

48. These can be ennumerated as follows: (1) 11QTemple, as edited by Yadin; and (2) 11QTSb, discussed below. We cannot include the scroll represented by the fragments 43.366, as I will demonstrate in chapter 2. Certain 4Q fragments in J. Strugnell's allotment, which he has mentioned in a letter partially published

approximately thirty-five fragments. Van der Ploeg discussed them at a scholarly conference in 1977 under the rubric of "Apocryphal Leviticus."[49] In his opinion, these fragments were of little importance, save for a few textual variants from the main copy.[50] He subsequently gave them to his student van der Bogaard.[51] Unfortunately the resulting study did not succeed in recovering from the fragments all possible information.[52]

Study of these thirty-five fragments has resulted in the discovery of several new manuscript joins, which in turn elucidate the main copy. Mishor joined 36*:3 to 36*:2, lines 9–12.[53] Van der Bogaard and Qimron independently joined 38*:1 with the tiny fragment 40*:12.[54] I have proposed joining 38*:1 with 37*:1 col. II, lines 12–18.[55] The latter two joins enable a fuller reconstruction of the festival of wood offering (col. 23).

The TS provides a wealth of information for the science of biblical text criticism, because it quotes so profusely from the biblical books.[56] In a preliminary survey of the scroll Tov decided that its text aligns itself with neither the MT nor the LXX.[57] An interesting variant in

---

by B. Z. Wacholder in *The Dawn of Qumran: The Sectarian Torah and the Teacher of Righteousness* (Cincinnati: Hebrew Union College Press, 1983), pp. 205–6, were taken by Wacholder to be a copy of the scroll, the earliest known. But evidently they are not such. Stegemann has seen the fragments, which E. Puech is editing, and says that they "come from a late second-century [*sic*] B.C. copy of an expanded text of Deuteronomy, evidently differing from the text of the Temple Scroll." (Stegemann, "Is the Temple Scroll a Sixth Book of the Torah—Lost for 2,500 Years?" *BAR* 13 (1987): 35, n. 4.) It is just possible that a third very fragmentary copy exists, only six broken lines long; see J. van der Ploeg, "Les manuscrits de la Grotte XI de Qumrân," *RQ* 12 (1985–87), p. 9. Mink's arguments in "The Use of Scripture in the Temple Scroll and the Status of the Scroll as Law," *SJOT* 1 (1987), pp. 23–24, are belied by a reconstruction of 11QTSb. See my article in note 55, below.

49. See the discussion in J. van der Ploeg, "Une halakha inédite de Qumrân," in *Qumran: sa piété, sa théologie et son milieu,* ed. J. Carmignac (Paris: Duculot, 1978), pp. 107–14. Recently A. S. van der Woude has recognized and published another fragment of this copy in "Ein bisher unveröffentlichtes Fragment der Tempelrolle," *RQ* 13 (1988): 89–92.

50. So the discussion in J. van der Ploeg, "Les manuscrits," p. 9.

51. L. van der Bogaard, "Le Rouleau du Temple: quelques remarques concernant les 'petits fragments,'" in *Von Kanaan bis Kerala,* eds. W.C. Delsman *et alia* (Kevelaer: Butzon & Bercker, 1982), pp. 285–94.

52. Van der Bogaard did not attempt to reconstruct the MS of 11QTSb, a process which greatly elucidates a number of crucial portions of the main copy. I intend to discuss this approach in detail elsewhere.

53. M. Mishor, "עוד לנוסח של מגילת המקדש," [Once more on the text of the Temple Scroll] *Tarbiz* 48 (1978): 173.

54. Qimron, "הערות," p. 140, and Bogaard, "Remarques," p. 289.

55. M. O. Wise, "A New Manuscript Join in the 'Festival of Wood Offering' (Temple Scroll XXIII)," *JNES* 47 (1988): 113–21. On col. 23 see also B. Jongeling, "A propos de la colonne XXIII du Rouleau du Temple," *RQ* 10 (1981): 593–95.

56. See E. Tov, "The Nature and Background of Harmonizations in Biblical Manuscripts," *JSOT* 31 (1985), p. 18 and notes 50–51.

57. E. Tov, "מגילת המקדש ונוסח וביקורת נוסח המקרא," [The Temple Scroll and biblical text criticism] *EI* 16 (1982): 100–11. Not surprisingly this conclusion accords with Tov's position on the interrelationships among the so-called manuscript families—the MT, the LXX, and the Samaritan Pentateuch. He argues that no families as such existed, since they cannot be typologically differentiated in the way that, e.g., New Testament manuscript families are. See his writings detailing this approach, e.g., *The Text Critical Use of*

col. 64 of the scroll has led another scholar to reevaluate the significance of several medieval LXX manuscripts.[58]

Finally, in a study devoted to the origin of the DSS, Tov identified the TS as sectarian, based on the scroll's orthography and language. He made it an important element in his argument, dubious on several grounds, that the scrolls of Cave 4 represent the real Qumran library.[59]

Linguistic Studies

In this area of research on the scroll, Qimron has again made strong contributions. In "לשונה של מגילת המקדש" he dealt with questions raised by its phonology, morphology, and orthography.[60] In "למלונה של מגילת המקדש" he collected diagnostic lexical items from the scroll,[61] hoping to narrow the dating of the text and to improve understanding of Second Temple language usage. Brin and Ben-Hayyim subsequently added to this linguistic material.[62]

Alongside these general linguistic studies, there have been numerous studies of single words or phrases in the TS. Among the more helpful contributions has been Nebe's examination of the puzzling word אדשך in col. 41:16. He demonstrated that it is probably a Persian loan-word meaning "a certain quantity."[63] In another helpful note, Thorion discussed the reason why the TS replaces the biblical phrase אשני חיל ("men of war") with the synonymous גבורי חיל למלחמה in col. 57:9.[64] The same author elsewhere considered the tendency of the TS to replace the biblical כי with אם in conditional sentences.[65] Qimron

---

the Septuagint in Biblical Research (Jerusalem: Simor, 1981). Although one must respect the views of this accomplished text critic, in the case of the TS my impression is that the scroll is very often in agreement with the LXX against the MT where these versions differ. See tables 1 and 2 below.

58. L. Rosso, "Deuteronomio 21,22: Contributo del Rotolo del Tempio alla valutazione di una variante medievale dei Settanta," *RQ* 9 (1977): 231–36. See chapter 4 for further discussion of this variant.

59. E. Tov, "The Orthography and Language of the Hebrew Scrolls Found at Qumran and the Origin of those Scrolls," *Textus* 13 (1986), pp. 31 and 56. Tov's study is flawed by his nondiscrete categorization of the scrolls with mixed "Qumran" and "non-Qumran" forms, the lack of consideration given to the possibility of scribal modernization, and the inadequate treatment of the question of whether and to what degree the DSS may reflect spoken dialects. In addition, he ignores literary critical studies bearing on the origin of the DSS.

60. [The language of the Temple Scroll], *Leshonenu* 42 (1978): 83–98.

61. [Concerning the lexicon of the Temple Scroll], *Shnaton* 4 (1980): 239–62.

62. See G. Brin, "הערות לשוניות למגילת המקדש," [Linguistic notes on the Temple Scroll] *Leshonenu* 43 (1979): 20–28, who compares a phenomenon in the TS to the language of the Tannaim, and Z. Ben-Hayyim, "ישנים גם חדשים מן צפוני מדבר יהודה," [Old and new from the hidden treasures of the Judaean Desert] *Leshonenu* 42 (1978): 278–83, who adds to the material of Qimron's 1978 article.

63. G. W. Nebe, "אדשך 'Mass, Abmessung' in 11Q Tempelrolle XLI, 16," RQ 11 (1982–84): 391–400; see also his "Addimentum zu אדשך in 11Q Tempelrolle," *RQ* 11 (1982–84): 587–89. He suggests a pronunciation *ʾaddasak*.

64. Y. Thorion, "Zur Bedeutung von גבורי חיל למלחמה in 11QT LVII, 9," *RQ* 10 (1979–81): 597–98. For a consideration of his argument, see chapter 4, note 8, below.

65. Y. Thorion, "Die Sprache der Tempelrolle und die Chronikbücher," *RQ* 11 (1982–84): 423–26.

elucidated the difficult כוננה (kōnᵉnāh) at 33:14.[66] Baumgarten offered an alternative understanding of 60:2 which may shed light on the scroll's concept of tithing.[67] Rokeah showed that in the TS כפר ("cover, atone") has taken on a new or broader meaning, and is sometimes equivalent to התיר ("loosen, free; permit").[68]

It is more difficult to embrace Eisenman's view of the difficult word בלע (in the Bible usually the root means "swallow") which appears at 46:10. Applying an allegorical and associative method of interpretation, he argued that the term is a circumlocution for "the Herodians." In the context, however, this suggestion runs against the grain of ordinary usage.[69] Similarly too clever was Callaway's treatment of the problematic ארביה in TS 24:8.[70] He suggested that Yadin's reading was faulty, and that a better reading would be ארבחיה. This attempt to read an Aramaic form including an (unattested) prothetic ʾaleph appears unnecessarily drastic over against Milgrom's idea that the strange root is simply a metastasized form of אבר ("limb").[71] In these situations the more banal the suggestion, the more likely it is to be correct. Also unpersuasive was Thorion's suggestion that חטא in the TS meant not "sin" but "dangers."[72] He apparently did not perceive the idealistic tone of the text at this point.[73]

In addition to these studies, which focused on the TS, several broader linguistic studies have drawn much of their data from it.[74]

Studies of the Calendar and Halakha

The religious calendar presupposed by the TS, which it may be possible to derive from cols. 13–30 and 43, has proved to be a matter of controversy. As noted above, Yadin felt that the calendar reflected in the scroll was the 364-day calendar familiar from Jubilees and Ethiopic Enoch. The substance of his argument was based upon the regulations governing the first-fruit festivals. The TS mandates three such festivals, separated from each other by periods of fifty days. Yadin's position depended upon a certain interpretation of the counting formulas used to

---

66. E. Qimron, "כוננה = כלי מכלי המזבח," ["Konenah" equals "a vessel from the altar vessels"] *Tarbiz* 52 (1982–83): 133.

67. J. Baumgarten, "Critical Notes on the Non-literal Use of Maʿăśēr / Dekatē," *JBL* 103 (1984): 249–51.

68. D. Rokeah, "הערת השלמה למאמר הערות אסיוח," [Postscript to the article "Essene Notes"] *Shnaton* 5–6 (1982): 231.

69. See R. Eisenman, *James the Just in the Habakkuk Pesher* (Leiden: Brill, 1986), pp. 87–94, and "The Historical Provenance of the "Three Nets of Belial" Allusion in the Zadokite Document and BALLʿ/BELAʿ in the Temple Scroll," *FO* 25 (1989): 51–66.

70. P. Callaway, "ʾBRYH [sic] in the Temple Scroll XXIV, 8," *RQ* 12 (1985–86): 269–70.

71. J. Milgrom, "Further Studies in the Temple Scroll," *JQR* 71–72 (1980): 89.

72. Y. Thorion, "Zur Bedeutung von חטא in 11QT," *RQ* 10 (1979–81): 598–99.

73. See chapter 4, note 10, for a more detailed evaluation of Thorion's argument.

74. See Y. Thorion, "Die Syntax der Präposition B in der Qumranliteratur," *RQ* 12 (1985–87): 17–64; T. Thorion-Vardi, "Die Adversativen Konjunktionen in der Qumranliteratur [sic]," *RQ* 11 (1982–84): 579–82; idem, "ʾt nominativi [sic] in the Qumran Literature," *RQ* 12 (1985–87): 423–24; and idem, "The Personal Pronoun as Syntactical Glide in the Temple Scroll and in the Masoretic Text," *RQ* 12 (1985–87): 421–22.

describe these festivals and the understanding that the word שבת in the formulas meant "Sabbath."[75]

Levine countered with a different view, based on a (theoretically) equally viable understanding of the key term שבת.[76] According to him it meant "week." If this interpretation were correct, the calendar of the TS need not be that of Jubilees. To this argument Milgrom responded that indeed both meanings for the crucial term were possible, but that the phrase שבע שבתות תמימות ("seven full šabbatōt") resolved any ambiguity. The explicit reference to the Sabbath in this phrase showed that it meant seven whole weeks, each week ending with a Sabbath. For Milgrom Yadin's position was vindicated.[77] Sweeney subsequently reconsidered all the arguments and agreed with Milgrom that Yadin's position was correct.[78]

Baumgarten and Vanderkam have more recently returned to the matter of the calendars of the TS and Jubilees. Baumgarten[79] asked whether the pentecontad sequence of harvest festivals in the TS necessarily presupposes the Jubilees calendar, and concluded that it does for three reasons. First, he argued that the description of the lifting of the Omer places it after the seventh day of Passover, not the first as in the "Pharisaic"[80] system. His second reason was that the sequence of pentecontad extrapolations for the new wine and oil festivals must have begun on a Sunday. Finally, he claimed that the esteem in which the scroll was held at Qumran is inexplicable if it were felt to side with the Pharisaic view on the Omer. None of these arguments are particularly compelling. Vanderkam was more convincing when he pointed out that the basis of Yadin's position was not the TS alone, but the relationship of the scroll to a tiny calendrical fragment which reads "on the twenty-second day of it [the sixth month] is the feast of oil." Vanderkam concluded, "The only ancient Jewish calendrical system which could both accommodate the calendrical specifications of the ... [TS] and locate the oil festival on 6/22 ... is the 364-day arrangement of Jubilees."[81] This latest contribution to the issue of the calendar underscores the fact that the TS calendar is problematic, and that further attempts to define its relationship to the Jubilees calendar may be expected.

Perhaps the promise of the TS to contribute to a better understanding of Second Temple Judaism is most clearly adumbrated in halakhic studies. The first fruits have already been offered. Altshuler reacted to Yadin's suggestion that Josephus' Essene upbringing influenced him in his work on the *Antiquities*. Yadin had noted that in the third and fourth books of that work, Josephus had categorized the laws of the Bible according to subject, and argued that the

---

75. Yadin I, pp. 116–119.

76. B. Levine, "Aspects," pp. 7–11. L. Schiffman supports Levine's view in "The Temple Scroll and the Systems of Jewish Law in the Second Temple Period," in *Temple Scroll Studies*, p. 244.

77. J. Milgrom, "'Sabbath' and 'Temple City' in the Temple Scroll," *BASOR* 232 (1978): 25–26.

78. M. Sweeney, "Sefirah at Qumran: Aspects of the Counting Formulas for the First-Fruits Festivals in the Temple Scroll," *BASOR* 251 (1983): 61–66.

79. J. Baumgarten, "The Calendars of the Books of Jubilees and the Temple Scroll," *VT* 37 (1987): 71–78.

80. Baumgarten holds the view that the rabbinic system, on which his argument is based, was the same as that of the earlier Pharisees.

81. J. C. Vanderkam, "The Temple Scroll and the Book of Jubilees," in *Temple Scroll Studies*, p. 214.

historian's knowledge of the TS influenced his classificatory scheme.[82] But Altschuler proved in a detailed table that "not even one of the topical units in AJ could owe its editorial structure to the TS."[83]

Several scholars have written halakhic studies commenting on the contents of the TS *seriatim*. In "Studies in the Temple Scroll," Milgrom considered two of the scroll's particularly important ideas.[84] First, he noted that the tribe of Levi never appears in a ritual in concert with the other tribes in the Bible; it does in the TS. He saw this innovation as a polemical protest against the Wicked Priest (Jonathan Maccabee), who had usurped the high priesthood and displaced Zadokites.[85]

Milgrom also sought to explain the scroll's purificatory scheme. He showed that in the Temple City, all impurities led to banishment. At least two ablutions would be required before readmittance. The unclean person would become clean by stages, passing from טומאה (uncleanness) through חול (profane) to קודש (holy). In subsequent articles Milgrom dealt with such topics as the Temple furnishings, the priestly prebends, and the function of the portico in the inner court.[86]

Maier also commented on various halakhic aspects of the scroll. He saw at least two of its traditions as especially ancient: the first fruit ceremonies for wine and oil, and the stricture against eating tithes on "work days."[87] Lehman has authored several helpful articles comparing some of the TS halakhot with those of later Jewish sources.[88]

Perhaps the most intensive research on the halakha of the scroll has been focused on its purity laws. García-Martínez discussed the scroll's generalization of the traditional Temple and

82. Y. Yadin, מגילת המקדש (1977) 1:62, 93–94 and 305.

83. D. Altschuler, "On the Classification of Judaic Laws in the Antiquities of Josephus and the Temple Scroll of Qumran," *AJSR* 7–8 (1982–83): 1–14. The quotation is on p. 11. It is worth noting as well that it is very questionable whether Josephus had a detailed knowledge of Essene doctrine. The relevant passage, *Life* 10–12, indicates that he spent only a short time among them, and was not sufficiently attracted to their views to become an Essene himself. For a convincing interpretation of the passage, see S. N. Mason, "Was Josephus a Pharisee? A Re-examination of Life 10–12," *JJS* 40 (1989): 31–45.

84. J. Milgrom, *JBL* 97 (1978): 501–23.

85. Ibid., p. 503.

86. J. Milgrom, "Further Studies in the Temple Scroll," *JQR* 71 (1980): 1–17; 89–106; and "הערות למגילת המקדש," [Notes on the Temple Scroll] *BM* 24 (1979): 205–11. See also Milgrom's "The Qumran Cult: Its Exegetical Principles," in *Temple Scroll Studies*, pp. 165–80.

87. J. Maier, "Aspekte der Kultfrömmigkeit im Lichte der Tempelrolle von Qumran," in *Judische Liturgie: Geschichte-Structur-Wesen* (Freiburg: Herder, 1979), pp. 33–46. In connection with Maier's view on "work days," see my discussion in chapter 3. I agree that this is a very old tradition, but my approach is textual.

88. M. Lehman, "The Temple Scroll as a Source of Sectarian Halakhah," *RQ* 9 (1978): 579–87. See also his slightly expanded Hebrew version, "מגילת המקדש כמקור להלכה כתתית," [The Temple Scroll as a source of sectarian halakha] *BM* 25 (1979–80): 302–9. A second study is "אשת יפת תואר והלכות אחרות במגילת המקדש," [The beautiful woman and other halakhot in the Temple Scroll] *BM* 114 (1988): 313–16 (of which an English version appeared, "The Beautiful War Bride [יפת תאר] and Other Halakhoth in the Temple Scroll," in *Temple Scroll Studies*, pp. 265–72).

priestly purity to the city and people respectively.[89] Sharvit considered the major DSS and their ideas on cleanness and uncleanness, including the TS. He saw a particular connection between the TS and the Damascus Covenant (CD), because unlike the other scrolls these two are concerned with purity in worship, and have a number of legal positions in common. On the whole, he concluded, the major purity innovation of the DSS is to attach ceremonial uncleanness to moral wrongs, such as murder or theft, to a much greater degree than biblical law.[90]

In an article entitled "The Pharisaic-Sadducean Controversies about Purity and the Qumran Texts," Baumgarten examined the TS to see how its laws line up in these controversies.[91] He found that they often agree with the "Sadducean" position. Therefore, he concluded, the term צדוקים (Sadducee/Zadokite) must designate more than one sectarian group in rabbinic literature. Milgrom pointed out that certain Second Temple Jews regarded the corpse-contaminated person as analogous to the leper, using as his evidence the TS. In order for such a person to remain in his city, he had to undergo ablutions.[92]

Schiffman published one of the most important halakhic studies of the TS.[93] He compared the laws of festal sacrifice in the TS with those of Jubilees, noting not only agreements and disagreements, but also the exegetical method underlying the legal positions. He could find no evidence in Jubilees for several of the major TS festivals, including the yearly ordination of the priests and the ceremonies of new wine and new oil. His conclusion: "There can be no possibility ... of seeing the sacrificial codes of Jubilees as based on those of the Temple Scroll."[94] Finally, Baumgarten has contributed useful studies of the tithing laws in the TS.[95]

89. F. García-Martínez, "El Rollo del Templo y la halaká sectaria," in *Simposio Bíblico Españōl,* eds. N. F. Marcos, J. T. Barrera, and J. F. Vallina (Madrid: Editorial de la Universita Complutense, 1984), pp. 611–22.

90. B. Sharvit, 'טומאהוטהרה לפי כת מדבר יהודה," [Uncleanness and purity according to the sect of the Judaean Desert] *BM* 26 (1980): 18–27. Sharvit's unexamined assumption that all these scrolls have a common provenance renders the study somewhat less useful.

91. J. Baumgarten, *JJS* 31 (1980): 157–70.

92. J. Milgrom, "The Paradox of the Red Cow (Num. XIX)," *VT* 31 (1981): 62–72. The relevant TS portions 49:16–17 and 50:10–14.

93. L. Schiffman, "The Sacrificial System of the Temple Scroll and the Book of Jubilees," in *SBL 1985 Seminar Papers,* ed. K. Richards (Atlanta: Scholars Press, 1985), pp. 217–34.

94. Ibid., p. 233. Note that Vanderkam, "Temple Scroll and Jubilees," sees the two texts as more in accord on sacrificial law than does Schiffman, but similarly concludes that they derive from a broader tradition, not the same small circle. I discuss the relationship of the TS to Jubilees in more detail in chapter 3. In regard to halakhic studies, see also Schiffman's study, "Exclusion from the Sanctuary and the City of the Sanctuary in the Temple Scroll," *HAR* 9 (1985): 301–20. Cf. also J. Baumgarten, "The Exclusion of Netinim and Proselytes in 4Q Florilegium," *RQ* 8 (1972): 87–96, reprinted in idem, *Studies in Qumran Law* (Leiden: Brill, 1977), pp. 75–87.

95. J. Baumgarten, "The First and Second Tithes in the Temple Scroll," in *Biblical and Related Studies Presented to Samuel Iwry,* eds. A. Kort and S. Morschauer (Winona Lake: Eisenbrauns, 1985), pp. 5–15, and idem, "The Laws of ʿOrlah and First Fruits in the Light of Jubilees, the Qumran Writings, and Targum Ps. Jonathan," *JJS* 38 (1987): 195–202.

Studies of the Temple Plan

The architecture of the TS has been the basis of a number of comparative studies.[96] Although some authors have disagreed with various aspects of Yadin's architectural reconstruction of the temple,[97] discussion has primarily centered on three problems: the purpose and structure of the so-called "staircase tower," the relationship between the stipulations in the TS for a latrine outside the city and Josephus' *Betso*, and the connection between the TS court layout and that of Ezekiel.

What was the function of the staircase tower of TS 30–31? According to Smith, it was an element of the Essene sun-cult.[98] Smith connected the tower to a famous statement in Josephus' *Bellum Judaicum* (*BJ*) that may reflect Essene sun-worship, buttressing his argument with extensive documentation for the existence of sun worship in Palestine generally. Milgrom challenged Smith's interpretation of the evidence, but did not attempt another.[99] Although his thesis seems unlikely to be correct, Smith's points are thought-provoking—in spite of the fact that the TS says nothing explicit in support of his idea, and apparently condemns solar worship.[100]

Other studies have considered whether the TS description of the tower may illuminate the difficult Mishnah passages on the מסבה ("staircase"). Magen examined the Mishnah texts and concluded that the usual reconstructions of this architectural element were faulty. He then reconstructed it as a separate structure at the northwestern corner of the Herodian Temple, on the analogy of the TS description.[101] But Patrich has convincingly refuted Magen and offered a superior interpretation of the texts.[102] According to his arguments, the TS offers no parallel to the מסבה of Middot.

---

96. Comparative studies include J. Maier, "The Architectural History of the Temple in Jerusalem in the Light of the Temple Scroll," in *Temple Scroll Studies*, pp. 23–62, J. Barker, "The Temple Measurements and the Solar Calendar," in idem, pp. 63–66, and M. Delcor, "Is the Temple Scroll a Source of the Herodian Temple?," also in *Temple Scroll Studies*, pp. 67–90.

97. Thus H.A. Mink, "Tempel und Hofanlagen in der Tempelrolle," *RQ* 13 (1988): 273–86, and the fascinating discussion in P. B. Bean, "A Theoretical Construct for the Temple of the Temple Scroll," (M. Arch. thesis, University of Oregon, 1987), esp. pp. 265–363.

98. See M. Smith, "Helios in Palestine," *EI* 16 (1982): 199*–214*; and idem, "The Case of the Gilded Staircase," *BAR* 10 (1984): 50–55.

99. J. Milgrom, "Challenge to Sun-Worship Interpretation of Temple Scroll's Gilded Staircase," *BAR* 11 (1985): 70–73. Milgrom has adopted Magen's explanation for the function of the tower as nothing more than a means of access to the roof of the temple. This explanation is itself not without problems, however; on some difficulties with Magen's approach see the study by Patrich below.

100. Cf. TS 51:15–21.

101. I. Magen, "המסבה או בית המסבה של המקדש," [The staircase or the house of the staircase of the temple] *EI* 17 (1984): 226–35.

102. J. Patrich, "The Mesibbah of the Temple According to the Tractate Middot," *IEJ* 36 (1986): 222. He concludes,

> The entire hypothesis has no textual basis ... and is an erroneous interpretation of Middot ...
> The mesibbah mentioned in the Mishnah cannot possibly be interpreted as a stairtower. The

In two early studies, Yadin held that the TS prescription for a latrine in col. 46 was consonant with Josephus' description of the Gate of the Essenes and the *Betso*.[103] He suggested that the Essene Gate be located at the southwestern corner of the "First Wall." (Earlier scholars had located the gate in the southeastern corner.) In accordance with the TS commandment, which places the latrine to the northwest of the city, he placed the *Betso* at a northern locus of the western stretch of the First Wall.[104] Some scholars have found Yadin's ideas persuasive, though they have slightly altered his proposed location for the *Betso*.[105]

Another consideration for scholars has been the relationship between the temple plans of the TS and Ezekiel 40–48. On the assumption that the two are closely related, Busink suggested that the third court of the TS be construed not as an outer court, but as representative of the city of Jerusalem.[106] Also working on the assumption of this close relationship, Maier sought to clarify portions of the prophet's temple description.[107] The assumption of a detailed relationship between these two sources is, however, dangerous. Attempting to reconstruct one on the basis of the other is a very uncertain venture.[108]

The Scroll and the New Testament

Since their discovery the Dead Sea Scrolls have served as an important source of information on the first century Palestinian milieu. New Testament (NT) scholars have turned

---

　　path described in the Mishnah from the entrance of the mesibbah to the entrance of the upper
　　chamber adds up to only a 180° turn.

　　This shape is in contrast with the angular spiral staircase of the TS.

103. Many scholars believe that Betso is simply a transliteration of the Hebrew terms בית צואה meaning "house of waste." See Yadin, "שער האסיים בירושלים ומגילת המקדש," [The Essene Gate in Jerusalem and the Temple Scroll] *Qadmoniot* 5 (1972): 129–30; an English version of this article appears in *Jerusalem Revealed: Archaeology in the Holy City 1968–1974,* ed. Y. Yadin (Jerusalem: Israel Exploration Society, 1975), pp. 90–91. On the city in general see Yadin's "The Holy City of the Temple Scroll," in *Temples and High Places in Biblical Times,* ed. A. Biran (Jerusalem: Hebrew Union College-Jewish Institute of Religion, 1981), p. 181.

104. Note, however, that the map which accompanied Yadin's studies located the latrine only some 200 m distant from the city, not 1.5 km, as his interpretation of the TS text requires.

105. E.g., R. Riesner, "Essener und Urkirche in Jerusalem," *BK* 40 (1985): 71–74. Riesner located the Betso nearer the southwest corner of the Upper City than had Yadin. J. A. Emerton was not persuaded by Yadin's interpretation; see "A Consideration of Two Recent Theories About Bethso in Josephus' Description of Jerusalem and a Passage in the Temple Scroll," in *Text and Context: Old Testament and Semitic Studies for F.C. Fensham,* ed. W. Claassen (*JSOT* Supplement Series 48; Sheffield: *JSOT* Press, 1988), pp. 100–1. Obviously, this entire discussion depends on the identification of the requisite part of the TS as an Essene composition.

106. T. A. Busink, *Der Tempel von Jerusalem von Solomon bis Herodes,* 2 vols. (Leiden: Brill, 1970–80), 2:1424–26. Busink's logic was as follows: since the middle court of the TS has the same dimensions as the outer of Ezekiel's two courts, that which is outside the "middle court" is the city.

107. J. Maier, "Die Hofanlagen im Tempel-Entwurf des Ezechiel im Licht der 'Tempelrolle' von Qumran," in *Prophecy: Essays Presented to Georg Fohrer on his Sixty-Fifth Birthday,* ed. J. A. Emerton (Berlin: de Gruyter, 1980), pp. 55–67.

108. See below, chapter 3.

to the scrolls for help on linguistic, historical, and theological problems. With the publication of the TS, reevaluation of many earlier studies will be necessary.[109]

One NT problem into which the TS has afforded new insight is the Matthean divorce texts, which Fitzmyer has reexamined in the light of TS 57:17–19 and CD 4:12–5:14.[110] The crux in the NT texts is the so-called "exceptive clauses." Matt generally denies the possibility of divorce at 5:32 and 19:9, but qualifies his prohibition by adding the phrases παρεκτὸς λόγου πορνείας ("apart from a matter of *porneia*") and μὴ ἐπὶ πορνείᾳ ("except for *porneia*") to the two verses, respectively. Central to the understanding of these clauses is whether they represent the *ipsissima verba Iesu*. Hitherto an argument against this possibility had been the absence of any first century Palestinian evidence for "absolute" prohibition of divorce. Now with the discovery of the TS, argued Fitzmyer, such evidence exists; the clauses are likely to be genuine words of Jesus. Another problem with the Matthean texts has been the meaning of πορνεία. According to Fitzmyer, the TS, with CD, strengthens the contention that it means "intercourse within forbidden degrees of kinship."[111] In addition to Fitzmyer's, several other studies of the texts in Matt have referred to the TS.[112]

Scholars have invoked the several first fruit festivals of the scroll to explain other NT difficulties. Brooke was puzzled by the combination in Mark 2:18 and parallels of the οἶνος νέος ("new wine") with the idea of fasting. TS 19–21, describing a festival of new wine, suggested to him that Jesus' words referred originally to this occasion. Later tradition forgot the true context, and reinterpreted the "new wine" as a reference to the Gospel.[113] Beckwith responded, however, that the TS occasion was a feast and not a fast, effectively undercutting Brooke's parallel.[114]

109. For general comments see P. Lapide, "Die Nachbarn der Urgemeinde," *LM* 17 (1978): 273–75, and G. J. Brooke, "The Temple Scroll and the New Testament," in *Temple Scroll Studies*, pp. 181–200.

110. J. A. Fitzmyer, "The Matthean Divorce Texts and Some New Palestinian Evidence," *ThSt* 37 (1976): 197–226.

111. Fitzmyer's reasoning was as follows. Because πορνεία is used in the LXX as a translation of the Hebrew זנות, the question has been the possible meanings of the latter. In the Hebrew Bible, the term means "harlotry" and "idolatrous infidelity." Based on the TS and CD 4:20 and 5:18, Fitzmyer argued that it had expanded its meaning in the postbiblical period to include "intercourse with close kin." It is not clear, however, that this is the correct interpretation of the term at CD 5:18, and the use of זנות in published portions of another DSS, 4QMMT, to describe priestly intermarriage with women of nonpriestly families also seems difficult to reconcile with Fitzmyer's conclusions. The term זנות may rather have a more general connotation, "improper marriage." On MMT see note 183 below.

112. See J. Mueller, "The Temple Scroll and the Gospel Divorce Texts," *RQ* 10 (1980): 247–56; A. Vargas-Machura, "Divorcio e indisolubilidad del matrimonio en la sgda. escritura," *EB* 39 (1981): 26–27; B. Brooten, "Konnten Frauen im alten Judentum die Scheidung betreiben?" *ETh* 42 (1982): 78–79; and C. Schedl, "Zur Ehebruchklausel der Bergpredigt im Lichte der neu gefundenen Tempelrolle," *TPQ* 130 (1984): 362–65. For a study of related New Testament texts on marriage in the light of the TS, see A. Ammassari, "Lo statuto matrimoniale del re di Israel (Dt 17,17) secondo l'esegesi del 'Rotolo del Tempio,'" *ED* 34 (1981): 123–27.

113. G. Brooke, "The Feast of New Wine and the Question of Fasting," *ET* 95 (1984): 175–76.

114. R. Beckwith, "The Feast of New Wine and the Question of Fasting," *ET* 95 (1984): 334–35.

Another question concerned with "new wine" (but involving a different Greek term, γλεῦκος) arises in Acts 2:13 and 15. Why does Peter mention new wine at the time of Pentecost? Pentecost is associated with the Jewish festival of Weeks, which celebrated the harvest of new grain, not new wine. Fitzmyer has explained, in the light of the TS festival of new wine, that Luke, a non-Palestinian, may have unwittingly confused Palestinian traditions. Luke was uncertain about what occurred at the time of the first fruits for new wine, and mixed in allusions associating it with the Pentecost of new grain.[115]

Other studies applying new perspectives from the TS to the NT considered the relevance of col. 64 to the matter of crucifixion,[116] duodecimal symbolism in the NT and the TS,[117] the Qumran מבקר ("overseer or visitor") vis-à-vis the Christian office of bishop,[118] apocalyptic elements in the TS,[119] and the identity of the New Testament "Herodians."[120]

Book Length Studies

In the second decade of TS study, two scholars in addition to Yadin have written monographs on the scroll. Although strictly speaking this is not a topical category, it is expedient to consider these volumes separately. The first, by Wacholder, was entitled *The Dawn of Qumran: The Sectarian Torah and the Teacher of Righteousness*.[121] The work was very widely reviewed, in part because of the intrinsic interest of its theses, and in part because of the potentially revolutionary implications of its argument.[122]

---

115. J. A. Fitzmyer, "The Ascension of Christ and Pentecost," *ThSt* 45 (1984): 434–37.

116. J. Massyngberde Ford, "'Crucify him, crucify him' and the Temple Scroll," *ET* 87 (1976): 275–78; and M. Wilcox, "'Upon the Tree'-Deut 21:22–23 in the New Testament," *JBL* 96 (1977): 85–99. See also the discussion of TS 64 in chapter 4, below.

117. J. Baumgarten, "The Duodecimal Courts of Qumran, Revelation, and the Sanhedrin," *JBL* 95 (1976): 59–78; and P. Dion, "Le 'Rouleau du Temple' et les Douze," *SE* 31 (1979): 81–83.

118. B. E. Thiering, "Mebaqqer and Episkopos in the Light of the Temple Scroll," *JBL* 100 (1981): 59–74.

119. H. Stegemann, "Die Bedeutung der Qumranfunde für die Erforschung der Apocalyptik," in *Apocalypticism in the Mediterranean World and the Near East: Proceedings of the International Colloquium on Apocalypticism,* ed. D. Hellholm (Tübingen: J. C. B. Mohr, 1983): 515–16.

120. Y. Yadin, "Militante Herodianer aus Qumran," *LM* 18 (1979): 355–58.

121. B. Z. Wacholder, *The Dawn of Qumran: The Sectarian Torah and the Teacher of Righteousness* (Cincinnati: Hebrew Union College Press, 1983).

122. For reviews, see P. Callaway, *JAAR* 53 (1985): 133–34; J. H. Charlesworth, *RStR* 10 (1984): 405; J. Cook, *BO* 41 (1984): 708–11; C. Coulet, *RSRs* 59 (1985): 271; P. R. Davies, *ET* 95 (1984): 155–56; idem, *PEQ* 117 (1985): 79–80; idem, *JSOT* 31 (1985): 128; M. Delcor, *BLE* 85 (1984): 81–83; D. Dimant, *Zion* 41 (1986): 246–50; J. A. Fitzmyer, *TS* 45 (1984): 556–58; R. P. Gordon, *VT* 35 (1985): 512; K. Kida, *AJBI* 10 (1984): 101–104; A. R. C. Leaney, *JTS* 35 (1984): 493–97; J. Lust, *ETL* 60 (1984): 152–53; R. P. R. Murphy, in *The Society for Old Testament Study Book List 1984* (Leeds: W. S. Maney & Son, 1984): 139–40; J. Nelis, *TvT* 24 (1984): 180–81; M. Nobile, *Antonianum* 59 (1984): 662–64; D. Pardee, *JNES* 48 (1989): 40–41; A. Paul, *RSR* 74 (1986): 129–48 *(inter alia)*; G. Rinaldi, *BO* 26 (1984): 62; J. Sanders, *JAOS* 105 (1985): 147–48; H. C. Schmidt, *ZAW* 98 (1986): 316–17; K. Smyth, *ETR* 60 (1985): 292; R. Suder, *HS* 26 (1985): 373–76; J. C. VanderKam, *CBQ* 46 (1984): 803–4; idem, *BA* 48 (1985): 126–27; G. Vermes, *JJS* 37 (1986): 268; and A. S. van der Woude, *JSJ* 17 (1986): 120–24.

Wacholder's basic theses are as follows. The TS is a new Torah (hence 11QTorah), written by a certain Zadok. This man, a pupil of the famous Antigonus of Socho, was also the Teacher of Righteousness. Zadok wrote the scroll about 200 B.C.E., then "discovered" it a few years later, an event to which CD 5:2 alludes. The astronomical and luminary portions of 1 Enoch antedated and influenced 11QTorah. But all the most important DSS—CD, the Discipline Scroll (1QS), and the War Scroll (1QM), even Jubilees (here identified as of Qumranic origin)—followed the scroll and depend on it heavily. The scroll's temple plan influenced the Jewish historian Eupolemus in his description of the temple of his day. Expatiating these ideas, Wacholder traced the history of the Qumran sect using Qumranic, rabbinic, and Karaite literature.

Unfortunately, many of Wacholder's arguments suffer from a misunderstanding of perhaps the single most important passage in the TS, 29:2–10—a misunderstanding which led him to a false logical antithesis. To Wacholder, "it seems quite inconceivable, after the author's repeated insistence on its eternity, that the sanctuary was to be merely temporal."[123] Again, he asked, "how could God have promised to dwell in a newly designed sanctuary 'forever' (לעולם) and in the next clause limit His dwelling there merely 'until' (עד) the day of the blessing?"[124] Wacholder apparently did not perceive that the scroll connects the term "forever" in 29:7 not with the sanctuary (מקדש), but with God's presence ("I will be theirs forever"). Consequently he faced a chimerical antithesis between the temple whose construction the scroll commands, and that which God will create.

Attempting to resolve this antithesis, Wacholder concluded that the two temples were one and the same, and that the scroll's single temple would be created by God in the eschaton. Yet this solution fails to explain the purpose and many phenomena of the scroll, as even Wacholder was constrained to admit.[125] Reading the text so it would support this interpretation also necessitated occasional philological legerdemain on Wacholder's part, such as his insistence that עד in 29:9 (normally "until" in such contexts) meant instead "while."[126] And his misunderstanding skewed his analyses of the literary relationships between the TS and the other major scrolls.

Added to this, central elements in his basic theses proved to be broken reeds. The idea that Zadok "discovered" the new Torah, and that this book is the one which CD 5:2 describes as "the hidden book of the Torah" (ספר התורה החתום), is vital to Wacholder's position; but his

---

123. Wacholder, *The Dawn of Qumran,* p. 23.

124. Ibid.

125. Thus he says on p. 27,

> After revealing the divine prescriptions for the erection of the sanctuary and the observance of its ritual ... the author says in 29:9 that God himself shall create it. How can this promise be reconciled with the multitude of details recorded in the book's commandments? I have no answer to this question ...

126. On this point see especially the review by van der Woude (cited in note 122), p. 120. P. Callaway, "Exegetische Erwägungen zur Tempelrolle xxix,7–10," *RQ* 12 (1985–86): 97–98, has agreed with Wacholder that עד here cannot mean "until." In my view his study, like Wacholder's, misunderstands the true significance of 29:2–10. See my discussion of the portion in chapter 6.

clever exegesis of CD is unconvincing. A much better explanation of that passage is at hand.[127] Wacholder also misread the numbers of CD 1:5–10. As a result, he placed the Teacher of Righteousness at the beginning, not the end, of that text's "twenty year" period. This error vitiates the entire chronology of his reconstruction. Another apparent weak link in his arguments was his integration of rabbinic elements, which according to one reviewer "do not easily support his thesis."[128]

Finally, Wacholder's methodology was sometimes naive or questionable. For example, when conducting an exegesis of key DSS passages, he virtually never took cognizance of literary critical work on those passages. Often he did not really argue his points; rather, casting a sidelong glance at the evidence, he simply stated his conclusions. At key junctures, his arguments depended on lacunae in the texts he was comparing with the TS, which he simply restored in a way which dovetailed with his reading of the scroll.[129]

Yet along with its faults, Wacholder's work contained many brilliant insights, and ultimately served a useful heuristic purpose.[130] Exposing the weakness of many received truths, it forced people to rethink the question of Qumran origins. Further, Wacholder turned much scholarly thinking on the scroll away from Yadin's mundane interpretation and in the direction of the ultramundane, a shift of profound importance.

The second book length work, Maier's *Die Tempelrolle vom Toten Meer,* came out first in German, and then in an expanded English edition.[131] The book was well received, although reviews have generally not been substantive.[132] It provided English readers with an alternative

---

127. See J. VanderKam, "Zadok and the SPR HTWRH HHTWM in Dam. Doc. V, 2–5," *RQ* 11 (1982–84): 561–70. Wacholder has continued to argue his position in "The 'sealed' Torah versus the 'Revealed' Torah: An Exegesis of Damascus Covenant V,1–6 and Jeremiah 32,10–14," *RQ* 12 (1985–87): 351–68, but without new or convincing arguments.

128. H. W. Basser, "The Rabbinic Citations in Wacholder's '"The Dawn of Qumran,'" *RQ* 11 (1982–84): 549.

129. E.g., his discussion of 4QFlorilegium on p. 95, and his comparisons of Eupolemus' temple description with that of the scroll on pp. 65–76. M. Delcor, "Le temple de Salmon selon Eupolémos et le problème de ses sources," *RQ* 13 (1988): 270–71, has a similar critique of Wacholder's attempt to connect the temple Eupolemos describes with that of the TS, but ultimately his rejection of Wacholder's analysis comes about by reason of his dating of the scroll—Delcor accepts Yadin's dating to the reign of John Hyrcanus, making the TS a generation too late for Eupolemos.

130. A consideration of Wacholder's arguments should take cognizance of the prepublication paper written by his student, J. Kampen, who helped Wacholder research his book. The article is "The Temple Scroll: The Torah of Qumran?" *PEGLBS* 1 (1981): 37–54.

131. J. Maier, *The Temple Scroll,* trans. by John White (Sheffield: *JSOT* Press, 1985). For the German work, see note 28 above.

132. For reviews (including reviews of the German original), see J. A. Emerton, *VT* 37 (1987): 242; G. Fohrer, *ZAW* 91 (1979): 150–51; F. García-Martínez, *JSJ* 17 (1986): 108–9; M. A. Knibb, *The Society for Old Testament Study Book List 1986,* p. 126; J. Lust, *ETL* 62 (1986): 190; R. North, *Biblica* 61 (1980): 116–17; J. Oesch, *ZKT* 103 (1981): 200–1; H. Schmid, *Judaica* 34 (1978): 187–88; G. Vadja, *REJ* 138 (1979): 443; G. Vermes, *JJS* 37 (1986): 130–32 *(inter alia)*; and A. S. van der Woude, *JSJ* 10 (1979): 106. The substantive reviews are M. Sweeney, *HS* 28 (1987): 189–91, M. O. Wise, *JNES* 48 (1989): 40–41, and D. P. Wright, *BA* 52 (1989):45.

translation to Yadin's, one which was often more idiomatic.[133] Included with the translation was a helpful outline of the TS contents, and notes even more copious than in the German work. In Maier's view, the TS "interweaves utopian and realistic" elements.[134] One of the realistic elements, in the sense that the author actually intended to build it, was the temple plan.

Maier saw many cultic prescriptions as part of Zadokite traditions antedating Antiochus IV, and suggested that major elements of the scroll might be pre-Hasmonean. His principle difference with Yadin concerned the architectural plan of the TS. Whereas Yadin held to the "minimalist" position on certain unstated measurements, Maier held the "maximalist" view.[135]

Literary Studies

Studies examining literary aspects of the TS, or comparing the scroll to other Second Temple literature, have been numerous. Dimant relied on the TS to explain obscure symbolism in the portion of 1 Enoch known as the "Vision of the Beasts."[136] In another study, Rokeah examined the relationship between the TS and certain texts from the Mishnah and Josephus.[137]

Betz wrote an interesting, if rather speculative, study of Honi the Circlemaker, building up a portrait of the man from the Talmud and Josephus. He argued that the portrait depicts a man willing to die rather than see the people sin. On a certain occasion Honi was unwilling to pray for God's intervention against the king Aristobulus because he regarded such a prayer as blasphemous. Thus he died rather than do something which, according to TS 64:6–13, was worthy of crucifixion. But Betz stopped short of saying that Honi knew the TS, indicating only that he knew an interpretation of Deut 21:22–23 similar to the scroll's.[138]

Several literary studies have dealt with the scroll's ideology or theology. Finkel drew attention to its basic theological stance, which he believed identical to that of the Pentateuch:

---

133. There were occasional lapses, however, such as at 32:15, where Maier (and Yadin) overlooked the partitive meaning of *mdm* "some of the blood," and 35:8, where Maier did not catch the change in subject with *wqdštmh*, "and you (m. pl.) shall sanctify."

134. Maier, *Temple Scroll*, p. 59.

135. On this see esp. idem, pp. 91–101. For a discussion of their views, see Mink, note 97 above.

136. D. Dimant, "ירושלים והמקדש בחזון החיות (חנוך החבשי פה–צ) לאור השקפות כת מדבר יהודה" [Jerusalem and the temple in the "Vision of the Beasts" (Ethiopic Enoch 65–70) in the light of the influences of the sect from the Judaean desert] *Shnaton* 5–6 (1982): 177–93. Dimant asked why there is no tower—which in this portion of Enoch equates with the temple—in certain parts of the vision. Clearly, the author of Enoch thought that God was with Israel at those times. Her answer came from an equation established using the TS: the City of the Temple equals the Temple equals the Camp of Israel (of the wilderness wanderings).

137. D. Rokeah, "The Temple Scroll, Philo, Josephus, and the Talmud," *JTS* 34 (1983): 515–26. This article is a considerably revised and enlarged version of the Hebrew article, "הערות אסניות," [Essene notes] *Shnaton* 4 (1979–80): 263–68.

138. O. Betz, "מותו של חוני-חוניו לאור מגילת המקדש מקמראן," [The death of Honi-Honyo in the light of the Temple Scroll from Qumran] in *Jerusalem in the Second Temple Period,* eds. A. Oppenheimer, U. Rappaport, and M. Stern (Jerusalem: Yad Izhak Ben Zvi / Ministry of Defense, 1980), pp. 84–97.

both are concerned with exploring the presence of God.[139] Stegemann sought to show that the TS describes a utopian land surrounded by nameless enemies, with a central temple in an unnamed place. In his view the scroll takes pertinent portions of the Pentateuch, mainly from Deut, and "intensifies" them. This procedure applies not only to various heathen customs, which are forbidden to the inhabitants of the land, but also to the strengthened relationship between the temple and the norms for holiness and purity in the temple city.[140] Thorion noted that TS 59:9 ("until they fill up the full measure of their guilt; afterwards, they will repent") is a statement—centuries before the idea's expression in the Talmud—of the belief that redemption would come only after the time of the most wicked, unbelieving generation.[141] Callaway examined the implications of the TS for the canonization of the Torah, and concluded that because of its revelatory stance it was written at a time when no set canon yet existed.[142]

Several scholars have turned their attention to the scroll's literary use of the biblical text. Brin devoted two studies to various aspects of the question, including the relation of the several festival descriptions to the biblical portions describing those or analogous occasions, and the discussion of the false prophet.[143] In "The Temple Scroll and Higher Criticism," Kaufman explored whether it would be possible, relying only on literary criticism, to reconstruct the biblical sources behind the TS. This attempt could serve as a "check" on modern literary criticism of the Pentateuch, since in the case of the TS, we actually possess the earlier texts used by the document (i.e., the Bible). His conclusion was sceptical: "The very complexity and variety of ... patterns makes higher criticism a dubious endeavor."[144]

Source Criticism of the Temple Scroll

In the two decades since the discovery of the TS, very few scholars have bent their efforts to the source criticism of the scroll—a striking situation if it is true that many of the questions involved with the scroll ultimately depend on such an analysis. It is all the more surprising since the possibility that the TS might be a composite text has been acknowledged from the beginning. Dupont-Sommer observed in remarks appended to the initial preliminary report in 1967:[145]

---

139. A. Finkel, "The Theme of God's Presence and the Qumran Temple Scroll," in *God and His Temple: Reflections on Professor Samuel Terrien's 'The Elusive Presence: Toward a New Biblical Theology,'* ed. L. Frizzell (South Orange, New Jersey: Seton Hall University, [1983]), pp. 39–47.

140. H. Stegemann, "'Das Land' in der Tempelrolle und in anderen Texten aus dem Qumranfunden," in *Das Land Israel in biblischer Zeit,* ed. G. Strecker (Göttingen: Vanderhoeck & Ruprecht, 1983), pp. 154–71.

141. Y. Thorion, "Tempelrolle LIX, 8–11 und Babli, Sanhedrin 98a," *RQ* 11 (1982–84): 427–28.

142. P. R. Callaway, "The Temple Scroll and the Canonization of Jewish Law," *RQ* 13 (1988): 239–50.

143. G. Brin, "המקרא במגילת המקדש," [The Bible in the Temple Scroll] *Shnaton* 4 (1980): 182–225, and "Concerning Some of the Uses of the Bible in the Temple Scroll," *RQ* 12 (1985–87): 519–28.

144. S. Kaufman, "The Temple Scroll and Higher Criticism," *HUCA* 53 (1982): 29–43. The quotation is from p. 42.

145. A. Dupont-Sommer, in Yadin, "Un nouveau manuscrit," p. 618 (see note 3 above).

... il semble ... que la rouleau qui est en nos mains ... juxtapose des documents, de ouvrages divers, que la copiste aurait rassamblés en un même rouleau, mais dont chacun peut avoir été rédigé à des dates plus ou moins sensiblement differéntes.

Yadin himself admitted the possiblity of diverse origins for different parts of the scroll in his address to the Twenty-Fifth Archaeological Convention in the same year.[146] He repeated this acknowledgment in the *editio princeps,* saying, "It is very possible that certain portions of the scroll were composed earlier, and that some of the traditions incorporated in it are of much earlier origin."[147] But throughout his analysis he proceeded as though the scroll were of unitary origin, and his discussion was always of "the author." To date, the only source-critical study of the entire TS has been that of Wilson and Wills.[148]

To determine where the documents underlying the present form of the scroll begin and end, these authors relied on three major criteria: content, the use of the divine referent, and variation of nominal and verbal forms. They concluded that five separate sources underlie the TS, as follows:

1. The "Temple and Courts" document: 2:1–13:8; 30:3–47:18

2. The "Festival Calendar" document: 13:9–30:2

3. A "Purity Collection": 48–51:10

4. The "Laws of Polity": 51:11–56:21; 60:1–66:17

5. The "Torah of the King": 57–59

Wilson and Wills supposed that these sources once circulated separately. The first to be combined were numbers 1 and 4. A later redactor added numbers 2 and 3, while number 5 may have been added either at the same time, or have been a part of number 4 prior to the later additions. The authors attempted to date neither the constituent documents nor the final redaction.

Wilson and Wills' study was an excellent first step in the source criticism of the TS, but it suffered from several problems. First, one of the major criteria on which the authors relied, the alternation in address between the second person singular and second person plural, is unreliable for source discrimination. Mayes has shown that it is of dubious value in the analysis of biblical texts.[149] Further, ancient Near Eastern texts also display the phenomenon

---

146. Yadin, "מגילת המקדש," p. 80.

147. Idem, מגילת המקדש (1977), 1:298.

148. A. Wilson and L. Wills, "Literary Sources of the Temple Scroll," *HTR* 75 (1982): 275–88. For a different sort of approach see P. R. Callaway, "Extending Divine Revelation: Micro-Compositional Strategies in the Temple Scroll," in *Temple Scroll Studies,* pp. 149–62.

149. A. D. H. Mayes, "Deuteronomy 4 and the Literary Criticism of Deuteronomy," *JBL* 100 (1981): 27–29. For a balanced statement on the use of stylistic criteria for source criticism, see J. Tigay, "The Stylistic

of changes in address,[150] yet for such texts there can be little question of an editorial or recombination process. This criterion has led Wilson and Wills astray at important junctures.[151] As a criterion for source criticism of the TS it should be discarded. Concomitantly, it is necessary to reassess those points in Wilson and Wills' analysis where it was of decisive importance.

Second, the authors never considered the implications of their own identification of a redactional hand in cols. 29:3–10 and 51:5–10. This identification should have led them to attempt to isolate additional redactional elements. Had they taken this next logical step, they might have solved several problems, prominent among them the character of their "Purity Source"[152] and the nature of col. 47.

Third, Wilson and Wills attempted to sketch a redactional history of the TS, but without availing themselves of the best witnesses to that process: the Rockefeller 43.366 fragments. An examination of these would undoubtedly have led them to modify some of their ideas.

Thus, in my view, the authors have taken some missteps in their attempt at source criticism of the TS. But they have also come to numerous important and correct conclusions. I propose to build on their work, learning from their problems, while attempting to apply a more refined technique.

The Provenance of the Temple Scroll

Turning now to views of the origin, date, and purpose of the scroll, it is expedient to depart from my earlier procedure. I review not only studies devoted specifically to these matters, but the entire spectrum of opinion as it has emerged from scholarly discussion of every sort.

As noted above, it was Yadin's opinion that the TS was sectarian.[153] (In the context of discussions on the TS, the term "sectarian" has meant "a product of the Qumran community.") The basis for his view was threefold: the laws it contains, its use of certain "sectarian" terminology, and presumed parallels with other DSS and Jubilees. Many scholars have

---

Criterion of Source Criticism in the Light of Ancient Near Eastern and Post-biblical Literature," in *Empirical Models for Biblical Criticism,* ed. J. Tigay (Philadelphia: University of Pennsylvania Press, 1985), pp. 149–73.

150. E.g., cf. Sefire I B 21–45; at least three 2mpl forms appear, although in this text the 2ms form predominates. The alternation follows no clear pattern. See J. A. Fitzmyer, *The Aramaic Inscriptions of Sefire.* Biblica et Orientalia no. 19 (Rome: Pontifical Biblical Institute, 1967), pp. 16–18.

151. E.g., they suggest on p. 277, in large part because of this faulty criterion, that cols. 33–39 may have originated in an independent source. On the grounds of content and form criticism, such a judgement appears extremely unlikely.

152. P. Callaway, "Source Criticism of the Temple Scroll: The Purity Laws," *RQ* 12 (1986): 213–22, has also found Wilson and Wills unsound in their discrimination of this source. See my detailed discussion in chapter 5.

153. For his last published statement on the matter, see Yadin, "The Temple Scroll—The Longest and Most Recently Discovered Dead Sea Scroll," *BAR* 10 (1984): 32–49.

followed Yadin in identifying the TS as sectarian.[154] Indeed, some have considered this question so settled that they reverse the direction of the arguments, and attempt to use the scroll to determine the identity of the Qumran sect.[155] But not all students of the scroll are convinced that it is a sectarian composition.[156]

Schiffman criticized Yadin's interpretation of the TS because he thought the Israeli scholar had improperly begun his analysis with the prior assumption that the scroll was a sectarian work. Schiffman countered Yadin by drawing attention to the absence in the scroll of many of the dialectal characteristics of the "sectarian" scrolls (e.g., the third-person pronominal forms היאה/הואה). On a lexical level, he argued, the "basic terms and expressions of Qumran literature" are completely absent.[157] Further, to Schiffman the underlying principles by which the TS derived its laws from the Hebrew Bible were different from those operative in other Qumran literature.[158] He concluded that the scroll emanated from circles ideologically midway between Qumran sectarianism and the Pharisaic tradition.[159]

154. As a partial list, see the following: A. Caquot, "Rouleau du Temple," p. 34; M. Delcor and F. García-Martínez, *Introduccion*, p. 202; Dimant, "Sectarian Literature," p. 530; T. Elgvin, "The Qumran Covenant Festival and the Temple Scroll," *JJS* 36 (1985): 103–6; Maier, "Kultfrömmigkeit," p. 34; W. McCready, "The Sectarian Status of Qumran: The Temple Scroll," *RQ* 11 (1982–84): 183–91; idem, "A Second Torah at Qumran?" *SR/SR* 14 (1985): 5; Mink, "The Use of Scripture in the Temple Scroll and the Status of the Scroll as Law," *SJOT* 1 (1987): 25; Schürer, *History*, 3:412–13 (written by Vermes); Smith, "Helios," p. 199*; Tov, "Orthography," pp. 31 and 56, and van der Woude, "Een Gedeelte," p. 387.

155. E.g., see W. Tyloch, "'Zwoj swiatynny' najwazniejszy rekopis z Qumran i czas jego powstania," [The Temple Scroll: The Most Important Manuscript from Qumran and the Period of its Composition] *SR* 19 (1984): 27–38; idem, "Le 'Rouleau du Temple' et les Esséniens," *RO* 41 (1980): 139–43; and idem, "L'importance du 'Rouleau de Temple' pour l'identification de la communaute de Qumran," in *Traditions in Contact and Change: Selected Proceedings of the XIVth Congress of the International Association for the History of Religions*, ed. P. Slater and D. Wiebe (Winnipeg: Wilfred Laurier University Press, 1983), pp. 285–93. Tyloch argued that the TS festival of new oil explains the curious passage in Josephus where that author comments on the Essene avoidance of oil (*BJ* 2.123). Tyloch understood the passage to indicate that the Essenes thought that oil was a source of ceremonial uncleanness. But his understanding of the relevant Greek word—upon which his entire argument depends—is questionable, as the term is apparently unattested in the required meaning. See H. G. Liddell and R. Scott, *A Greek-English Lexicon* (Oxford: Clarendon Press, 1968), s.v. κηλίς, and the comments by Rokeah, "The Temple Scroll, Philo, Josephus, and the Talmud," pp. 519–21.

156. In addition to those who have written detailed refutations of the "sectarian" origin of the TS, H. Burgmann has published a short note in which he argues that the scroll is a product not of the Qumran community, but of Sadducean Levites. See his "11QT: The Sadducean Torah," in *Temple Scroll Studies*, pp. 257–63.

157. L. Schiffman, "The Temple Scroll in Literary and Philological Perspective," in *Approaches to Ancient Judaism II*, ed. W.S. Green (Chico: Scholars Press, 1980), pp. 143–58. The quotation is from page 149.

158. Idem, *Sectarian Law in the Dead Sea Scrolls: Courts, Testimony and the Penal Code* (Chico: Scholars Press, 1983), pp. 13–14. See most recently his "The Law of the Temple Scroll and its Provenance," *FO* 25 (1989): 89–98.

159. Idem, "Literary Perspective," p. 154. See also his article, "Legislation Concerning Relations with Non-Jews in the Zadokite Fragments and in Tannaitic Literature," *RQ* 11 (1982–84): 383–84 and 389, and cf. his remarks in "The Sacrificial System," p. 233, "The book of Jubilees and the Temple Scroll constitute part of the world from which the Qumran sect emerged …" With this Finkel would evidently agree, "God's Presence," p. 41.

Stegemann also believed the TS to be nonsectarian in origin. He cited four reasons for his judgement that "... speziell mit der Qumrangemeinde hat dieses Werk nicht mehr zu tun ... die Qumrangemeinde hat es [nur] geschätzt."[160] First, he regarded the halakhot of the TS as "unqumranisch," and as conflicting with other halakhot of the community. Second, for him the feasts of the scroll lacked analogies in specifically Qumranic texts. Third, in contrast with the early Hasmonean period, the high priest and the king in the scroll are separate people. Since no hint of a polemic against the opposite situation appears—contrary to what Stegemann would have expected at the time of the Qumran community—the scroll must have a different origin. Finally, he pointed to the absence in the scroll of the community's self-designation יחד ("unity"). In its place the TS uses עם ("people") and עם הקהל ("people of the congregation").[161] Taking a cue from Yadin, Stegemann proposed that the Qumran community read the TS primarily to learn how to harmonize divergent halakhot.[162]

A third scholar who did not agree that the TS was a sectarian work was Levine. Like Schiffman and Stegemann, he was impressed by the absence of crucial "sectarian" lexical terms.[163] Another curious thing for Levine was the "official character" of the TS, as though it originated with an official body, not a sectarian, anti-establishment group of separatists. A final indicator, as noted earlier, was the calendar, which for him was not that of the Qumran community and Jubilees. Even if it were the same calendar, he contended, nothing would be proven, since that calendar was more widespread than scholars have realized. Levine grouped the TS with texts such as Jubilees, 1 Enoch, and the Psalms Scroll from Cave 11—texts which the Qumran sect preserved, but did not write.[164]

Yadin responded to his critics, singling out Levine in particular.[165] His defense hinged on the relationship of the TS to CD (which Yadin posited as sectarian). By showing that there are

160. Stegemann, "'Das Land'," p. 157. In "The Literary Composition of the Temple Scroll and its Status at Qumran," in *Temple Scroll Studies,* p. 128, Stegemann added two additional reasons: the lack of quotations from the TS in other texts from Qumran, and the different approach toward temple buildings taken by the scroll in contrast to "specifically Qumranic works."

161. See also Stegemann's other writings in which he discusses the origin of the TS: "Die Bedeutung," pp. 507 and 516 and "Some Aspects of Eschatology in Texts from the Qumran Community and in the Teachings of Jesus," in *Biblical Archaeology Today,* ed. R. Amiran (Jerusalem: Israel Exploration Society, 1985), p. 409. Most recently he has laid out his position in detail in "The Origins of the Temple Scroll," *Supplements to Vetus Testamentum XL (Congress Volume, Jerusalem 1986),* pp. 235–56, and has published a non-technical version in "Sixth Book."

162. Stegemann, "Origins," p. 255 n. 106.

163. B. Levine, "Aspects," passim. See also "Preliminary Reflections on the 'Temple Scroll'," foreword to *A History of the Mishnaic Law of Holy Things Part Six: The Mishnaic System of Sacrifice and Sanctuary,* by J. Neusner (Leiden: Brill, 1980), pp. xvii–xx.

164. Levine, "Aspects," p. 7. Also questioning the identification of the TS as a "sectarian" writing is M. Knibb, *The Qumran Community,* Cambridge Commentaries on Writings of the Jewish and Christian World 200 B.C. to A.D. 200 (New York: Cambridge University Press, 1987), p. 2.

165. Y. Yadin, "האם מגילת המקדש היא יצירה כתתית?" in *Thirty Years of Archaeology in Eretz Israel* (Jerusalem: Israel Exploration Society, 1981), pp. 152–71. An English translation was published, "Is the Temple Scroll a Sectarian Document?" in *Humanizing America's Iconic Book,* eds. G. M. Tucker and D. A. Knight (Chico: Scholar's Press, 1982), pp. 153–69.

close connections between the TS and CD, Yadin believed that he could demonstrate *ipso facto* the sectarian provenance of the TS. Unfortunately, in the course of this demonstration he overlooked literary-critical studies suggesting that the portions of CD with links to the TS are the oldest layers.[166] Relying on these oldest layers to link the two scrolls, Yadin simultaneously used the youngest portions of CD to show that it was sectarian. He compared these latest parts of CD to other "sectarian" scrolls, in which the same key terms and concepts appeared.

Obviously this procedure was unsound. Even granting the "sectarian" origin of the last named scrolls, there would be no automatic linkage between the group responsible for them and that responsible for the oldest layers of CD. With that linkage in doubt, Yadin's argument for the sectarian origin of the TS foundered and his attempt to rebut his critics fell short. The provenance of the TS is still an open question. What Yadin's reply effectively demonstrated was the need both for critical studies of the DSS and for recognition among scrolls scholars of the potential of such studies.[167]

The Date of the Temple Scroll

The spectrum of scholarly opinion on the date of the scroll has been extremely wide. The earliest date anyone has argued in detail has been Stegemann's fifth to third century dating.[168] Callaway agreed with the earlier range but extended the latest possible date down to 200 B.C.E.[169] Stegemann argued his case most fully in "The Origins of the Temple Scroll." He believed that the catalyst for the composition of the TS was Ezra's arrival in Jerusalem with a Persian-backed official form of the Pentateuch. Earlier forms having a somewhat different content were now shunted aside. Certain priests, however, did not believe that the "law of God" should so lightly be set aside, and certainly not by the command of the pagan Persian king. They gathered the now outlawed traditional expansions together with other materials to produce the TS. Needless to say, Stegemann's scenario is wildly speculative; falling back upon the very uncertain question of what law Ezra brought to Jerusalem as a partial explanation for the TS is a case of *obscurum per obscurius*. Further, he never satisfactorily explains the multifaceted relationship between CD and the TS, and his theory of "saving God's law" does not begin to account for the TS use of Deut, which was evidently a part of the new official law, but which the TS takes over largely unchanged. Callaway's view seems to derive solely from

---

166. J. Murphy-O'Connor, "The Essenes and their History," *RB* 81 (1974): 223–27.

167. Cf. the words of Murphy-O'Connor in "The Judaean Desert," in *Early Judaism and its Modern Interpreters,* eds. R. A. Kraft and G. W. E. Nickelsburg (Philadelphia: Fortress Press, 1986), p. 143:

> In the past, many problems seemed insoluble because the assumption was that the documents were literary unities. Now as the constituent elements (the sources) of documents are compared and contrasted new correlations should become apparent which will permit more precise descriptions of genres and a better appreciation of the social contexts which gave them birth.

168. H. Stegemann, "'Land'," pp. 156–57; "Die Bedeutung," p. 507, n. 37; "Eschatology," p. 409, and "Origins," *passim.* Stegemann's precise dating differs in his different articles; his most recent discussion, "Origins," can be taken as supporting a date as early as 450 B.C.E.

169. Callaway, "Canonization," p. 250.

the feeling that a work like the TS, taking liberties and feeling free to change as it does what later Judaism regarded as canonical scripture, could only have arisen before about 200. This seems an arbitrary judgement in view of how little is really known about the ebb and flow of ideas in Judaism in the centuries between Ezra and the Hasmoneans. Callaway's perspective is valuable in other regards, but it is not a satisfactory approach to dating the scroll.

Two scholars, Wacholder and Vermes, have proposed a date of about 200 B.C.E. Given its methodological and logical problems, detailed above, there is little to recommend Wacholder's line of approach or, consequently, his dating. Vermes based his opinion on the assumption that the TS must antedate CD, the War Scroll, and the Nahum Commentary, and on the probability that the TS had a history of development.[170] The first assumption in particular is debatable and, on the basis of these arguments alone, a very broad range of dating is possible. Before his position can be seriously entertained it will require a more detailed development.

Tyloch and Elgvin have each ventured a date of 150 B.C.E.[171] (As it happens, this study will argue for the same approximate date, but for very different reasons.) Tyloch felt that Yadin had not allowed enough time between the oldest copy of the TS—the Rockefeller 43.366 fragments—and the autograph. As this is his only difference with Yadin on the dating, his view is really just a subspecies of Yadin's, which I discuss below. Elgvin thought the scroll to be approximately contemporary with Jubilees, which he dated to ca. 150 B.C.E. In chapter 3, I discuss this problematic linkage of Jubilees and the TS.

By far the majority of scholars have accepted Yadin's dating of the TS to the reign of John Hyrcanus; the date usually quoted is 134 B.C.E.[172] Yadin settled on this date because he thought that the scroll originated early in that Hasmonean's reign (135/134–104).[173]

---

170. Schürer, *History,* 3:417 [written by Vermes].

171. W. Tyloch, "L'importance," p. 289, and more specifically "Zwój swiatynny," p. 6; most recently see "La provenance et la date du Rouleau du Temple," *FO* 25 (1989): 33–40; T. Elgvin, "Covenant Festival," p. 104.

172. Scholars accepting this date include M. Broshi, "Rouleau du Temple," p. 70; A. Caquot, "Rouleau du Temple," p. 446; M. Delcor, "Explication [II]," p. 260 and "Explication [III]," pp. 246–47; A. Finkel, "God's Presence," p. 43; B. Jongeling, "Tempelrol," p. 89; Levine, "Aspects," p. 21; F. Manns, "Nouveautes," p. 75; J. Milgrom, "The Temple Scroll," p. 119; H. Mink, "Præsentation," p. 103; J. Mueller, "Gospel Divorce Texts," p. 248; and A. S. van der Woude, "Tempelrol (I)," p. 180 and "Tempelrol (II)," p. 291.

173. Yadin believed that the TS reflected Hyrcanus' actions after his break with the Pharisees. He saw the rings of col. 34 as a symptom of this break. It should be noted, however, that Josephus puts Hyrcanus' break with the Pharisees not early but late in the Hasmonean's reign (see *Ant.* 13.288ff). Thus Yadin's date of 134 was, on his own evidence, erroneously early. See Rokeah, "The Temple Scroll, Philo, Josephus, and the Talmud," p. 517.

Another sizeable group of scholars has preferred to date the scroll to the reign of Hyrcanus' successor, Alexander Jannaeus (103–76),[174] or to the next in line, Alexandra (76–63).[175] Among this group, Hengel, Mendels, and Charlesworth presented a very detailed case for dating the scroll to Jannaeus' time, based on their analysis of the "King's Law" (TS 57–59). I consider their arguments in equal detail in chapter 4.

Finally, three students of the scroll have argued for a much later date—the reign of Herod the Great (37–4 B.C.E.). Of these, Soggin wrote before the publication of the *editio princeps*, and might wish to date the scroll differently in the light of the full publication.[176] The other two, Thiering and Eisenman, have written idiosyncratic treatments which, while offering brilliant insights, are largely unconvincing and require accepting a questionable scheme of development not only for the TS, but for the DSS as a whole.[177] Rather than attempt to refute them, which would occupy unwarranted space in the present context, I simply offer a different paradigm and let the choice fall to the reader.

As noted above, the largest group of scholars have agreed, either in detail or in broad outline, not only with Yadin's dating, but also with his reasons for his dating. This is surprising because Yadin's case was not particularly strong. He based his position on three arguments,[178] which are discussed below.

The first argument was linguistic. Because the TS uses a fair number of words heretofore known only from Tannaitic sources, Yadin concluded that the scroll should date to the period when Tannaitic Hebrew had begun to appear. He further argued that these data require a date near the end of the second century B.C.E. But two fallacies mar this argument. First, in a diglossic linguistic setting it is natural to have "Mishnaic" lexical items—the basis of Yadin's argument—evidenced well before the grammatical peculiarities of Tannaitic Hebrew.[179] Much

174. E. M. Laperrousaz, "Note à propos de la datation du Rouleau du Temple et, plus gènèralement, des manuscrits de la Mer Morte," *RQ* 10 (1981): 449 (Laperrousaz nuances his suggestion by concluding, after presenting evidence in favor of a date in the reign of Jannaeus, that the text should be dated "plus basse que l'époque de Jean Hyrcan." [p. 452]); (For further discussion of Laperrousaz' view see his "Does the Temple Scroll Date from the First or Second Century B.C.E.?," in *Temple Scroll Studies*, pp. 91–98); M. Hengel, J. H. Charlesworth, and D. Mendels, "The Polemical Character of 'On Kingship' in the Temple Scroll: An Attempt at Dating 11Q Temple," *JJS* 37 (1986): 28–38; see also J. H. Charlesworth, "The Date of Jubilees and of the Temple Scroll," in *SBL 1985 Seminar Papers*, ed. K. Richards (Atlanta: Scholars Press, 1985), pp. 201–2.

175. Thus Luria, "הערות," pp. 370–72, based on rabbinic sources on the "Zadokites."

176. J. Soggin, *I manuscritti*, p. 60. Soggin was impressed by the prepublication reports of the new temple and its architectural design, commenting that they were "un elemento in favore della datazione del rotolo prima della reconstruzione del Tempio fatta da Erode il grande ...." Presumably, since the full publication has shown that the temple of the TS is in no way like that of Herod, Soggin would argue differently today.

177. B. E. Thiering, *Redating the Teacher of Righteousness* (Sydney: Theological Explorations, 1979), p. 207 and "The Date of Composition of the Temple Scroll," in *Temple Scroll Studies*, pp. 99–120; and R. Eisenman, *James the Just*, pp. 87–94.

178. Yadin I, pp. 36 and 386–90.

179. This is the implication of E. Qimron's comments on 4QMMT in *The Hebrew of the Dead Sea Scrolls*, Harvard Semitic Studies no. 29 (Atlanta: Scholars Press, 1986), p. 117.

of the vocabulary of Tannaitic Hebrew must have been a part of the general resources of the spoken language in the postbiblical period, if indeed not beforehand.

Second, scholars simply do not know when, or at what rate of speed, Tannaitic Hebrew developed. There is no particular reason to suppose that the language did not exist, in some form at least, prior to the end of the second century B.C.E.[180] Documentary evidence on the question is exiguous. The arguments advanced early in this century by Segal, suggesting that Tannaitic Hebrew was a lineal descendent of the spoken (as opposed to the written) language of Judah in the biblical period,[181] still hold; one might therefore be inclined to see it beginning to emerge much earlier than Yadin allowed. Every manuscript discovery made since Segal's time, whether the DSS themselves or "uncorrected" Mishnah and Tosefta MSS, has supported his basic position.[182] It is possible that Yadin's linguistic dating is *approximately* correct, of course; but would that rule out a date of 150 for the scroll? Of 170? Of 200 B.C.E.? On the present evidence the answer is no. Perhaps the publication of the fragments of a scroll written in "proto-mishnaic" Hebrew, 4QMMT (מקצת מעשי תורה), will enable scholars to date the development of Tannaitic Hebrew more precisely.[183] For the present, an argument based on the linguistic phenomena of the TS can bear little weight. The scroll is undatable on this basis, except within the (uselessly broad) parameters of postbiblical Hebrew.

Yadin's second argument for dating the TS to the time of Hyrcanus rested upon the fragments known as Rockefeller 43.366. He identified these fragments as part of an early copy of the scroll. They are written in a so-called "Hasmonean" script that, according to the paleographical scheme of development to which Yadin adhered, would date the fragments to 125–75 B.C.E.

---

180. Cf. Kutscher's remark, concerning the linguistic situation which was brought to an end by the Bar-Kochba revolt: "It … was in Judea, the heart of the Jewish state of the Hasmoneans, that MH [Mishnaic Hebrew] had existed as the spoken language *for centuries.*" (emphasis mine) E. Y. Kutscher, *A History of the Hebrew Language,* ed. R. Kutscher. (Jerusalem: Magnes Press, 1982), p. 116.

181. See M. H. Segal, "Mishnaic Hebrew and Its Relation to Biblical Hebrew and Aramaic," *JQR* 20 (1907–08): 647–737, and idem, *A Grammar of Mishnaic Hebrew* (Oxford: Clarendon Press, 1927), pp. 11–12. For a critique and updating of Segal's position, see Kutscher, *History of the Hebrew Language,* pp. 115–47.

182. See E. Y. Kutscher, "לשון חז״ל," [The Language of the Sages] in *Eduard Yechezkiel Kutscher: Hebrew and Aramaic Studies,* eds. Z. Ben-Hayyim, A. Dotan, and G. Sarfatti (Jerusalem: Magnes Press, 1977), pp. 73–87. See also the shortened and revised German version, "Mischnisches Hebräisch," *RO* 28 (1964): 36–48.

183. For the fullest discussion of these fragments, see E. Qimron and J. Strugnell, "An Unpublished Halakhic Letter from Qumran," in *Biblical Archaeology Today,* ed. R. Amitai (Jerusalem: Israel Exploration Society, 1986), pp. 400–7, and Schiffman, "Systems of Jewish Law," pp. 245–50. Additional details can be gleaned by consulting E. Qimron and J. Strugnell, "An Unpublished Halakhic Letter from Qumran," *IMJ* 4 (1985): 9–12; E. Qimron, "The Holiness of the Holy Land in the Light of a New Document from Qumran," in *The Holy Land in History and Thought,* ed. M. Sharon (Leiden: Brill, 1988), pp. 9–13; J. T. Milik, "Le travail d'édition des manuscrits du Désert de Juda," in *Supplements to Vetus Testamentum vol. 4 (Strasbourg 1956)* (Leiden: Brill, 1957), pp. 24–26 (on the calendar fragments); idem, *DJDJ* III, pp. 221–27 [where he refers to the fragments in question as 4Qmišnique and 4QMišmarot]; E. Qimron, *The Hebrew of the Dead Sea Scrolls, passim;* and *The Jerusalem Post Magazine,* 14 June 1985, p. 6.

It should be noted first that many scholars of Hebrew MSS doubt the validity of such precise paleographical dating.[184] But this objection is scarcely the greatest problem with Yadin's argument; the greatest problem is simply that the fragments of 43.366 are not a copy of the present TS at all. Two of the three fragments in the grouping cannot be fitted into the text of the present scroll. As I attempt to show in chapter 2, these fragments are actually part of an early form of the TS. Thus they are of great usefulness in dating the scroll—but not in the way Yadin used them.

Yadin's third argument for dating the TS relied on the scroll's content. In particular, he found clues in the "King's Law" (cols. 57–59), and in col. 34, which mentions rings (טבעות) installed near the temple to aid in the slaughter of the sacrificial animals. Because his arguments for the use of the "King's Law" were not as well developed as those of Hengel and his coauthors, I do not consider his position on that portion of the scroll here, but in my discussion of Hengel's arguments in chapter 4. Here I consider only the dating based on the rings of col. 34.

Yadin drew attention to Talmudic sources which mention that John Hyrcanus installed rings, and concluded that the rings of the TS were the same ones. His approach was amazingly uncritical; the use of such sources for the dating of events before the destruction of the Second Temple is problematic at best. After all, they are as far removed from the Hasmonean period as is our own time from the Renaissance, and that in a time when record keeping was nothing like that of the present day. Yet Yadin manifested no skepticism about their use as historical sources.[185] Actually, even if—despite this chasm of time—one were to grant the theoretical possibility of using Talmudic sources to date Hasmonean events, in this case they would have to be ruled out.

For one thing Talmudic sources postdating the Tannaitic period are very confused about the person of John Hyrcanus. For example, they credit him with a reign of eighty years as high priest—nearly three times the reality.[186] On the basis of this confusion alone, it would be perilous to rely on Talmudic sources to date something to his reign. Yet a more profound problem with their use arises in the case of the rings.

The text which has provided Yadin with his argument about the rings is in the Babylonian Talmud, Sotah 48a. It comments on a much earlier Mishnah text, Maʿaser Sheni 5:15. The Mishnah text discusses various religious reforms which it says occurred during the time of John Hyrcanus. Among the reforms it lists is his abolition of "the Knockers" (הנופקין) and "the

---

184. For an incisive and, frankly, devastating critique of the methodology and reasoning which have often dominated the paleographic approach to dating the DSS, see R. Eisenman, *Maccabees, Zadokites, Christians and Qumran. A New Hypothesis of Qumran Origins,* Studia Post-Biblica no. 34 (Leiden: Brill, 1983), pp. 28–31 and 78–89. Eisenman develops further many of the arguments set forth by G. R. Driver in *The Judaean Scrolls* (Oxford: Basil Blackwood, 1965), pp. 410–20. Proponents of the common paleographical approach have still never satisfactorily answered these objections.

185. Cf. the words of Vermes in Schürer, *History,* 3:416, regarding the rings: "More skeptical students of rabbinic literature are less inclined to accept this argument as constituting solid evidence."

186. See J. Goldstein, *I Maccabees.* The Anchor Bible vol. 41 (New York: Doubleday & Co., 1976), pp. 67–69.

Awakeners" (המעוררין). The question with which the later Talmudic discussion wrestles is the meaning of these two terms. Who or what were the Knockers and the Awakeners? According to the text, the disputants decide that the Knockers were those who used to smite sacrificial animals between the horns. As this was a pagan practice, the sages were pleased by their abolition, and by their replacement with rings.

But did the Talmudic sages correctly identify the Knockers? Apparently not. Zeitlin has shown, based on internal discrepancies in the continuing discussion, that the scholars could not have known what the Knockers were.[187] Since the Talmudic text has incorrectly identified the Knockers, it follows that from a historical perspective its connection of them with the rings is worthless. So is the connection of these rings with John Hyrcanus.[188] Yadin's connection of the rings with Hyrcanus is, of course, only as reliable as the Talmudic identifications. The Talmudic sages were ignorant of the real function of the Knockers,[189] and had no idea when, or by whom, the rings were installed—so Yadin's argument cannot be sustained.

In fact none of Yadin's arguments can withstand scrutiny. Nor, in my view, can Stegemann's. No other scholars, except Hengel and his collaborators, have presented a full and detailed argument for a dating of the TS. Like its origin, the date of the scroll remains an open question.

The Purpose of the Temple Scroll

Consonant with their divergence on the other principal questions of the TS, scholars have offered widely divergent interpretations of the purpose for which it was written. As noted above for Yadin, the purpose was threefold. First, the redactor wanted to deal with duplicate and contradictory laws in the Torah, trying to resolve them by harmonization.[190] Second, he wished to provide laws which the Hebrew Bible mentions, but does not actually include, such as a Davidic temple plan (1 Chr 28) and a "Law of the King" (1 Sam 8).[191] In Yadin's view, however, the overriding concern of the TS was its third purpose: "We may not be straying far from the truth if we suppose that the real incentive to write the scroll stemmed from opposition to laws."[192] In other words the central concern of the scroll was to provide particular halakhot in the face of contemporary polemics.

---

187. S. Zeitlin, "Johanan the High Priest's Abrogations and Decrees," in *Studies and Essays in Honor of A. A. Newman,* eds. M. Ben-Horin, B. D. Weinryb, and S. Zeitlin (Leiden: Brill, 1962), pp. 577–79.

188. It should also be noted that rabbinic sources are not unanimous in assigning the installation of the rings to "the high priest Yohanan," a fact which Yadin does not mention. See R. Wilk, "יוחנן הורקנס הראשון ומגילת המקדש," [John Hyrcanus the First and the Temple Scroll] *Shnaton* 9 (1985): 226.

189. Zeitlin shows that both the Knockers and the Awakeners were probably cultic groups associated with the Hasmoneans at the time when they had no access to the temple in Jerusalem. When, later, this access was restored, the groups were no longer serving a useful function, and Hyrcanus abolished them.

190. Yadin, I, p. 74.

191. Ibid., pp. 82–83.

192. Ibid., p. 87.

Several scholars were in broad agreement with Yadin. Tyloch believed its purpose was to state the essential law of the Qumran community, in an imitation of Deut.[193] According to Finkel, the scroll "offers the basic interpretive differences with the Pharisees and the Sadducees for the newly formed theocratic state" under John Hyrcanus.[194] Van der Woude concurred; in his view the TS "... stamt en als beginselprogram van een religieuze beweging."[195] Falk, basing his view of the TS purpose on an examination of the "King's Law" (cols. 57–59), concluded that the author did not intend the TS as Torah or new revelation.[196] Rather, the scroll was a sort of "crib sheet," intended to aid halakhic study.

Wacholder felt that Yadin had underemphasized the scroll's claims. The TS was not intended as a mere harmonization of difficult texts; it was intended to supersede the old Torah, and to function as the new.[197] Smith agreed. The purpose of the TS was to supersede the Pentateuchal portions it parallels (Ex 25–Dt 34), and, with Jubilees, to form a new, two-part Torah.[198]

Stegemann took yet another stance. He held that the scroll essentially stood in the same relationship to Deut as that book did to the first four books of the Pentateuch. It was a reprise and supplement to the book of Deut.[199] As discussed, he went further to suggest that the TS comprises old traditional expansions to the Pentateuch, which Ezra excised when he promulgated the canonical Pentateuch. At that time, shortly after 458 B.C.E., "these former additions and expansions ... were collected and edited to form what we know as the Temple Scroll."[200] Thus it was not the author's intention to supplant the traditional Torah; he sought rather to complete it. Mink came to a similar conclusion, based on an examination of which biblical texts the TS used as the basis of its legislation.[201] For him the purpose of the TS was to define further the legislation in Deut, along Deuteronomic lines.

Maier noted that the scroll set out a program of concentric areas of holiness, radiating outward from the Holy of Holies. Within that framework, the author wanted to unify all relevant biblical traditions. Since the dominant concern of the scroll was really these areas of holiness, Maier urged that the scroll be called the "Holiness Scroll."[202]

---

193. Tyloch, "Zwój swiatynny," p. 38.

194. Finkel, "God's Presence," p. 45. Finkel's approach appears inconsistent. On p. 41, he identifies the TS as a "proto-Qumran" writing; yet on p. 45 he sees it as the central exposition of their position. It is unclear how these identifications can both be true.

195. van der Woude, "Tempelrol (II)," p. 292.

196. Z. Falk, "The Temple Scroll and the Codification of Jewish Law," *JLA* 2 (1979): 33–44, and "מגילת המקדש והמשנה הראשונה," [The Temple Scroll and the first Mishnah] *Sinai* 83 (1978): 30–41. The English article is a translation of the Hebrew one.

197. Wacholder, *The Dawn of Qumran, passim;* see also Kampen, "The Torah of Qumran?," p. 39.

198. Smith, "Helios in Palestine," pp. 206*–207*.

199. Stegemann, "'Das Land,'" p. 162.

200. Idem, "Sixth Book," p. 33.

201. Mink, "Use of Scripture," pp. 20–50.

202. Maier, *The Temple Scroll,* p. 6.

Thus scholars who have commented on the purpose of the TS are in profound disagreement. They cannot agree whether it was a mere halakhic aid or a form of divine revelation. They cannot agree whether it was to support or replace the Pentateuch. The question of the purpose of the TS still lacks an answer which commands assent.

The Present Study

The present study is an attempt to provide an answer to the purpose of the TS. As stated at the outset, it is hard to be confident about answering questions of origin, date, and purpose without first getting some feel for the literary composition of the TS. Ideally such a process would involve the discrimination and dating of each of its constituent sources before considering the date of the final redaction of the scroll. But the process just described is only an ideal; in fact it should be recognized that the task at hand requires recursive arguments. Any information about the scroll's final date, for example, suggests new possibilities for its purpose and helps date constituent sources.

My methodology relies upon various tried and tested techniques of critical inquiry—literary, form, and redaction criticism—but it is upon redaction criticism that I perhaps rely most heavily. This is a particularly promising approach because the TS is manifestly a redacted work. Furthermore, its redactor was no skilled surgeon, moving surely to join sources with precise and invisible sutures. He was a more careless sort, stitching unevenly and even leaving a sponge or two in the patient; and we may be thankful that he was such. Already scholars have acknowledged that cols. 29:3–10 and 51:5–10 are redactional compositions.[203] Study of these portions makes it possible to pick out the redactor's favorite phrases and typical vocabulary. One thus acquires a method wherewith to detect his hand. The recurrence of these favorite phrases may be taken to signal a redactional interpolation or reworking. Seeking egress from a dark cave one should follow the light, and it is redaction criticism which shines the most brightly here.

Perhaps a word is in order about the use here of "composition criticism," commonly regarded as a daughter of redaction criticism.[204] In the present context the term connotes the study of the different ways in which the authors of the constituent sources of the TS have used the Hebrew Bible. The technique considers the way they have selected and modified the biblical portions. The underlying assumption is that these processes reflect authorial intent—the author's stance toward both the Bible and his audience. This approach considers whence in the Hebrew Bible the material derived, the length of the portions used, and how the authors used

---

203. I noted Wilson and Wills on this point above. Callaway, "Exegetische Erwägungen," p. 95, comments, "Kolumne xxix,7–10 wird jedoch als eine redaktionnelle Interpolation verstanden." Regarding col. 51, Callaway accepts Wilson and Wills' assignment of 51:5–10 to a redactor in "The Translation of 11QT LI, 5b–10," *RQ* 11 (1982–84): 585. See also Finkel "God's Presence," p. 42, for the notion of applying redaction criticism to the TS.

204. See N. Perrin, *What is Redaction Criticism?* (Philadelphia: Fortress Press, 1969), pp. 65–67; S. Smalley, "Redaction Criticism," in *New Testament Interpretation: Essays in Principles and Methods* (Grand Rapids: Eerdmans, 1977), pp. 181–82.

the portions—e.g., did they quote verbatim, paraphrase, quote verbatim but in a rearranged order?[205] The differing use of the material, inasmuch as it potentially reflects somewhat different attitudes toward the biblical text and the presumed readers, is a promising criterion for source discrimination. On the whole scholars have neglected the ways in which Second Temple literature selected and arranged biblical portions;[206] thus the effort here is modestly innovative. The data of the composition-critical analysis, along with a methodological discussion, appears in the *Appendix*, to which the reader is constantly referred.

Finally, an added procedural basis for the present study is the examination of the 43.366 fragments, the analysis of which contributes to an understanding of the development of the TS.

In the chapters which follow I propose the delineation of four major sources in the TS: the Deuteronomy Source, the Temple Source, the Midrash to Deuteronomy, and the Festival Calendar. Added to these basic sources I argue that there are numerous laws of diverse origins, interpolated at particular junctures in the scroll. These elements of source criticism occupy approximately four and one-half chapters; in chapter 5 begins a gradual shift of attention from source criticism to the problem of the scroll's provenance. The investigation of provenance leads ineluctably to the person and time of the redactor, and the final redactional shape of the TS—the topics of chapter 6. Chapter 7 briefly summarizes and concludes this study of the Temple Scroll.

---

205. Scholars have devoted little time to these considerations. For a helpful if limited discussion of one of them, the rearranged verbatim quote, see P. C. Beentjes, "Inverted Quotations in the Bible: A Neglected Stylistic Pattern," *Biblica* 63 (1982): 506–23.

206. For the present see the brief treatments, only partially applicable to the problems presented by the TS, in B. Kittel, *The Hymns of Qumran,* SBL Dissertation Series no. 50 (Chico: Scholars Press, 1981), pp. 48–55 and E. Schuller, *Non-Canonical Psalms from Qumran: A Pseudepigraphic Collection* (Atlanta: Scholars Press, 1986), pp. 10–12.

2

THE DEUTERONOMY SOURCE

Introduction

A question which has puzzled scholars dealing with the TS is the way in which the scroll has attached extensive excerpts from Deut at the end. To some scholars this attachment looks like an afterthought, while others find in it an important clue to the purpose of the TS. Yet matters are actually even more complicated, since, as this chapter suggests, the redactor of the scroll did not use Deut. He preferred another collection of laws which I label the "Deuteronomy Source" (D). Here I draw out the evidence that the redactor of the TS indeed did use such a source, rather than making *ad hoc* extractions from Deut and parallel portions. The character and content of the proposed source, and its date, are of course problematic; an excursus therefore focuses on the 43.366 fragments, which promise to be helpful in turning the smoke into substance. The chapter concludes by discussing a possible date for this source of the TS.

Status as Separate Source

Several convergent lines of evidence point to the conclusion that, distinct from the biblical text, D was a separate source. The first such indicator is the uneven handling of the divine name throughout the text of D. Often the name "Yahweh" has been changed to the first-person, but there are a significant number of exceptions.[1] One would not expect total consistency in the work of an ancient editor, of course, but the degree of inconsistency here is difficult to explain

---

1. Yadin's explanation for the occasional retention of Yahweh is stylistic—the name had to be retained "because of a difficulty of style" (II, p. 248; cf. also II, pp. 3, 244, 275, etc.). This explanation will not suffice, as can be demonstrated with one example. According to Yadin's view, at 54:12 יהוה אלוהי אבותיכמה was one instance where Yahweh had to be retained. But this contention is belied by what the redactor did at the beginning of the very same line. There, where MT reads מנסה יהוה אלהיכם אתכם, the redactor produced מנשה אנוכי אתכם, simply leaving out אלהים for a more flowing text. If in this instance, therefore, the appearance of אלהיכם did not constrain the retention of Yahweh, why should the phrase at 54:12 do so? Could not the redactor simply have changed the entire phrase to אותי? Cf. also 55:13 and Deut 13:19; 55:16 and Deut 17:2. The explanation which Levine offers in "Aspects," p. 19, is that many of the phrases in which Yahweh was not changed were "bound" by liturgical usage and therefore could not be changed. In other cases, he argues, we are dealing with internal quotations. These explanations, while perhaps valid as far as they go, do not explain all the data—e.g., the retention of Yahweh at 39:8, which fits neither of these categories. Brin likewise fails to explain all the different unchanged divine names in "המקרא," pp. 210–12. The simplest explanation is probably the best. The redactor was just not concerned to be completely consistent in his handling of the divine name as it came to him in his different materials.

if one imagines the redactor carefully choosing each phrase as he composed his text. It is more reasonable to suppose that he took over and shaped an existing document.[2] In that case he might be expected to give the text a less thoughtful, consistent handling.[3] But apparently a predecessor *has* carefully weighed and shaped these portions of the TS. Since they comprise a rearrangement of biblical portions by topic, one cannot in any case say that the redactor simply took over biblical portions *per se.*

Another—perhaps the clearest—indication that D enjoyed a separate existence prior to incorporation in the TS is that it includes portions which contradict the redactor's ideology.[4] They remain in the text only because they do not do so explicitly, their implications apparently therefore having escaped his attention. Had the redactor been carefully pondering each phrase as he combed the biblical text, instead of taking over a preexisting source, it is hard to believe he would have overlooked even oblique contradictions of his views. Credulity is strained the more since his overall handling of the text makes it clear that he lacked neither nuance nor subtlety. The clearest examples of contradiction involve polygamy and divorce. As becomes clear in the sequel, the redactor opposed both as aberrations from God's original institution of marriage. The obvious explanation for the appearance in the scroll of portions which subtly contradict those views is that they were imbedded in a preexistent source.

One such portion is 54:4. In passing it mentions the divorced woman (גרושה), but explicitly it concerns vows. Presumably the redactor's interest in vows blinded him to the text's implicit sanction of divorce. Another example is Deut 21:15–17.[5] This portion speaks of two wives, the "beloved" and the "hated," although the real concern is equitable distribution of inheritance

---

2. For an overview of all the usages, see the *Appendix.*

3. It seems clear that the redactor made use of an earlier work in which "Yahweh" was consistently used, rather than finding the first person forms already present. Two phenomena support this interpretation. The more obvious is that in every passage which can be isolated as a redactional composition—such as 29:2–10 and 51:5b–10—God speaks in the first person without exception. Thus where the redactor was composing, he was careful always to avoid third person forms, which would blunt the claims he wished to make. The second reason for adopting this interpretation emerges from 53:8, where one encounters the strange ועשיתה הישר והטוב לפני אני יהוה אלהיכה. The portion corresponds to Deut 12:25, but the wording here differs from the known versions of the text. The pronoun אני—unattested in any version of Deut 12:25—is, of course, ungrammatical; the preposition לפני requires a suffix pronoun and is not used with independent pronouns. Thus this concatenation is inexplicable unless the text came to the redactor as לפני יהוה אלוהיכה. In this instance he could not follow his usual procedure and simply remove יהוה, because that would yield the undesirable phrase לפני אלוהיכה. The Hebrew reader's reflex upon encountering that phrase would be to read לְפָנַי, "before your God." It was important to forestall that likely misreading because, again, it would blunt the redactor's claim to personal discourse with God—a foremost concern of the scroll. Thus he simply inserted the pronoun. The result, while ungrammatical, powerfully emphasized to the reader that the scroll ultimately derived from God himself in the context of new revelation. Note that Yadin's translation, ordinarily almost excessively literal, departs at 53:8 and translates as though the text read בעיני "in my eyes" (II, p. 238). Maier, *Temple Scroll,* p. 47, Caquot, "Rouleau du Temple," p. 482, and García-Martínez, "Rollo del Templo," p. 229, are apparently unaware of the problem a comparison of the TS text and the biblical text poses at 53:8.

4. See the discussion of the redactor's shaping of the TS as a whole in chapter 6.

5. The corresponding lines in the scroll are unfortunately lost, but the size of the lacuna and the context virtually assure that they originally stood at 64:02–1. See Yadin, II, p. 287.

to their sons. The text implies polygamy; although it thereby contradicts the redactor's views, it remains in D. Another portion, 66:01 (lost but virtually certain in reconstruction),[6] contains a revealing phrase from Deut 22:19: לא יוכל לשלחה, "he shall not be able to send her away." This phrase sanctions divorce as a possibility in general, while prohibiting it in the specific case at hand. None of these examples explicitly contradicts the redactor's views. Contradictions arise only by inference. In contrast Deut 24:1–4, which legislates divorce laws *per se,* does blatantly contradict the redactor's ideas, and he excised it.

Thinking in terms of the canonical text of the Bible certain portions of D are additions, but they do not advance the clear polemics of the redactor. This situation seems to require that D had existed as a work separate from the Bible for some time prior to coming into the redactor's hand. Consequently, these portions comprise the third line of evidence for that view.

A premier example is found at 56:3b–4. It is an addition to Deut 17:10, and reads: ועל פי הדבר אשר יואמרו לכה מספר התורה ויגידו לכה באמת, "and according to the word which they shall say to you from the book of the law, and shall tell you in truth." This phrase is illustrative of the complexity of the relationship between D and the book of Deut. Every important element of the phrase is "Deuteronomic," yet none relates to the redactor's main concerns. Thus ספר התורה ("book of the law") is a Deuteronomic phrase (which also appears in the Chronistic History). Every time it is used in Deut it refers to Deut itself,[7] so naturally enough in D it comes to refer to D itself. Another term, באמת ("in truth"), led Yadin to write, "there is a plainly polemical element ... [which] conforms well with the doctrine of the sect."[8] He was apparently referring to the term's use in such texts as 1QS. Yet the term אמת in a moral sense is not uncommon in the Hebrew Bible, and באמת is particularly common with such a nuance. Its use in this sense is frequent in the Deuteronomic literature, and including the related book of Jeremiah it becomes even more common.[9] The mere fact that it happens to occur in 1QS, a sectarian work, does not mean that sectarians had a monopoly on its use. As to the other elements of 56:3b–4, they also have correspondents in Deut, often even in chapter 17.[10]

Another law in D which is not taken from the Bible as we know it, yet does not seem to promote the redactor's designs,[11] is 52:5b. Appearing in the natural context of laws dealing with animals unfit for sacrifice, this law prohibits the sacrifice of pregnant animals. Surrounding laws correspond to Lev 22:28 and Deut 22:6b, which prohibit the killing of

6. Ibid., p. 296.

7. Cf. Deut 28:61, 29:20, 30:10, and 31:26.

8. Yadin, II, p. 251.

9. Thirteen occurrences—cf. esp. 1 Kngs 2:4, 3:6, 2 Kngs 20:3, and Jer 32:41. For the relationship of Jer to Deut, see e.g., J. Bright, *Jeremiah,* 2nd. ed., Anchor Bible vol. 21 (Garden City: Doubleday & Co., 1965), pp. lxx–lxxi.

10. Thus for על פי הדבר, cf. Deut 17:10 (*bis*); for אשר יואמרו לך, cf. Deut 17:11; and for ויגידו לך, cf. Deut 17:10 and 17:11.

11. The redactor's major concerns emerge from a redactional analysis of the TS, carried out in chapter 6. See table 7 and the accompanying discussion, below. One must allow that the redactor did have a possible concern for the slaughter of pregnant animals, however, in light of this portion's similarities with a polemical law in 4QMMT.

with animals unfit for sacrifice, this law prohibits the sacrifice of pregnant animals. Surrounding laws correspond to Lev 22:28 and Deut 22:6b, which prohibit the killing of mother and live young in the same day. A third example, the phrase ("and you shall cover it with dust"), is added to 53:5 and is similar to Lev 17:13b, but it is not a verbatim quote; thus it does not accord with the compositional technique used in D. Like the others this phrase fails to promote the redactor's interests as they emerge from a redactional analysis.

A reasonable explanation for all these laws is that they arose as part of a topical collection of laws having Deut as its base, which acquired other material in the course of its separate development. D was apparently a law code independent of the biblical book of Deut. Stegemann has come to a similar conclusion in recognizing the independent character of this legal material in the TS.[12] This corpus, and not Deut directly, served as one source for the TS.

Character and Content

The data in the *Appendix* highlight the principal characteristics of the D source. It quotes Deut or passages related to Deut *in extenso,* but arranges them in an order different from the Bible. Where nonbiblical passages have been added, they are essentially "Deuteronomic,"[13] although sometimes the syntax deviates from Deut in a manner which seems calculated to recall important Levitical legislation. Combined with long stretches of verbatim quotes, D usually uses first-person pronouns and pronominal suffixes where the Bible has Yahweh. Textually, when it deviates from the MT the D source frequently accords with the LXX.

As they have these characteristics in common, I identify the following passages as comprising D: 2:1–15, 48:1–10a, 51:11–18, 52:1–12, 53:1–56:21, 60:12–63:14a, 64:1–6a, 64:13b–66:9b, and 66:10–12a. In this analysis the contents of D differ sharply from Wilson and Wills' roughly comparable "Laws of Polity" source, which embraces 51:11–56:21 and 60:1–66:17.[14] The basic reasons for this difference are: first, my contention that the redactor has interpolated the text of D with material drawn from other sources[15] (the reverse also occurs, as with 48:1–10a, which the redactor detached from D and positioned at an earlier point in the TS); second, a different analysis of the portion of the scroll they call the "Purity Laws" (for them, 48:1–51:10; for a full discussion, see chapter 5, below); and third, the results of the composition criticism of the scroll (see the *Appendix*).

For Wilson and Wills,[16] col. 2 is part of the "Temple and Courts" source. Yet the content has nothing to do with the temple, which is not even mentioned. On composition critical grounds, the portion actually belongs to the D source, for the following reasons:

12. H. Stegemann, "Sixth Book," p. 33.

13. Cf. 54:13, 56:5, and esp. 56:3b–4, discussed above. 51:16b–18 and 51:14b–15 are nonbiblical additions which are likewise not redactional.

14. Wilson and Wills, "Sources," pp. 281–82.

15. For one proof of this assertion, see the discussion of fragment 3 of the 43.366 group below.

16. Wilson and Wills, "Sources," pp. 275 and 278.

For Wilson and Wills,[17] col. 2 is part of the "Temple and Courts" source. Yet the content has nothing to do with the temple, which is not even mentioned. On composition critical grounds, the portion actually belongs to the D source, for the following reasons:

1. It quotes long portions of text verbatim.
2. It "Deuteronomizes" Exod 34 by adding material from Deut 7.[18]
3. Like D, it is inconsistent in dealing with the divine name, leaving it in the third person in line 11, but changing to the first-person in line 9.
4. It witnesses a text characterized by expansion relative to MT, and by frequent agreement with the LXX when there are textual variants.

The following list comprises the suggested redactional interpolations into D.[19] In addition to the reasons given here, their identification is supported by the analysis of the overarching redactional scheme of the scroll in chapter 6.

1. 51:19–21.

> You shall not do in your land as the nations do (לוא תעשו ... כאשר הגואים); for they sacrifice everywhere, and plant Asheroth, and erect pillars, and set up figured stones to bow down to them.

These lines contain a crucial phrase, לוא תעשו כאשר הגויים, which appears in 48:11. On the basis of composition criticism and form criticism that passage appears to be a redactional addition to the Temple Source.[20] Since 48:11–17 is a redactional composition, the present passage is also suspect. Further, on composition critical grounds it is distinct from D.

2. 52:13b–21.

> You shall not sacrifice a clean ox or sheep or goat in any of your towns within a distance of a three-day journey to my temple. Rather, you shall sacrifice it at my temple, to make it a burnt offering or a peace offering. You shall eat and rejoice before me in the place where I choose to establish my name (במקום אשר אבחר לשום שמי עליו). But any clean animal which has a defect you shall eat within your towns, at least four miles from my temple. You shall not slaughter it near my temple, for it is foul flesh. You shall not eat the flesh of any ox or sheep or goat in my city—which I sanctify in order to establish my name there—(אשר אנוכי מקדש לשום שמי בתוכה) which has not been slaughtered in my temple. They shall slaughter it there and throw its blood on the base of the altar of burnt offering; and they shall burn its fat ...

---

17. Wilson and Wills, "Sources," pp. 275 and 278.

18. For the significance of such "Deuteronomizing," see the discussion of 43.366 fragment 1 below.

19. I mean here those redactional interpolations for which the final redactor of the TS was responsible. That some earlier redactors may have added short portions to D as it was transmitted is probable *ex hypothesi*.

20. See chapter 3 for the form critical analysis which reveals 48:11–17 as redactional; see the *Appendix* for the composition critical data.

A combination of factors compels the conclusion that this passage is an interpolation into the D source. First, it is distinct from D on the basis of composition criticism, for it is not an extended biblical quotation. Second, it repeats a phrase which is redactional elsewhere, במקום אשר אבחר לשום שמי עליו.[21] Third, it has important terminological and phraseological connections with col. 47, which I shall argue in chapter 6 is a redactional composition. The terms include מקדשי ("my temple"),[22] פגול ("foul flesh")[23] and עירי ("my city").[24] The redactor's tendency to repeat favored phrases[25] shows in comparing 52:20 אשר לוא יבוא לתוך מקדשי ("which has not come into my temple") with 47:9 ואל עיר מקדשי לוא יבואו("and they shall not come into the city of my temple"). Finally, the two portions have general concerns in common. Col. 47 forbids the skins of animals slaughtered elsewhere to enter the temple city. 52:13–20 forbids the slaughter of animals anywhere but the temple city, unless they are too far away to be brought in. Priestly interests in purity (and perhaps profit) underlie both passages.

3. 63:14b–15a.

> And she shall not touch the "Purity" for seven years, nor shall she eat the peace offerings until seven years pass; afterwards, she may eat.

This is an addition to the "Beautiful Captive" law of Deut 21. Form critically it is identical to the laws of col. 45, and very similar to those of cols. 49–50. I discuss this portion more fully in chapter 5.

4. 66:9.

> And she is legally permitted him (והיא רויה לו מן החוק).

This phrase is unlike D because it is not an extended biblical quotation. Further, the redactional shaping of the TS shows that one of the redactor's major concerns was marriage laws. This short passage probably comes from his hand.

5. 66:12b–17.

> A man shall not marry his brother's wife, so as to uncover his brother's skirt, whether it be his father's son or his mother's son, for this is impurity. A man shall not marry his sister—the daughter of his father or his mother—for that is an abomination. A man shall not marry his father's sister nor his mother's sister because it is wickedness. A man shall not marry his brother's daughter nor his sister's daughter, for it is an abomination. A man shall not marry...

21. See chapter 6, table 7.
22. Cf. 52:14, 15, 17, 18, and 20 with 47:13, 16, and 18.
23. Cf. 52:18 and 47:14 and 18.
24. See 52:18 and 47:15, 18, the only occurrences in the entire scroll.
25. See chapter 6, table 7.

These extra-biblical marriage laws are composed on the basis of midrash[26] and modeled on Deut 23:1. They are distinct from the D source in their compositional method, and, like 66:9, tie in with the redactor's concern for proper marriages.

6. The redactor has inserted portions belonging to another source, which I call the "Midrash to Deuteronomy," in addition to or in place of sections of D. These passages are 57:1–59:21 (the so-called "King's Law"), 60:2–11, and 64:6b–13a. Since these portions are the subject of chapter 4, they require no further discussion here.

Textual Character

It is possible to assess the textual character of the D source because it quotes so extensively from biblical texts. An understanding of the textual nature of D is crucial for deciding questions such as dating and "sectarian polemics."[27] On the whole, the text of D is expansionistic relative to the text of MT. Most of the additions have clear text critical explanations, but some may be evidence of the character of D as a law code *per se,* separate from the biblical text. The same can be said for the much less frequent omissions. Not infrequently it is difficult to decide which is the better explanation. The purpose of the listing here is not to provide an exhaustive text critical comparison of D with all the relevant versions. The objective instead is to offer proof of the expansionistic character of D.[28] The following tables collect the additions and omissions in D vis-à-vis the MT. They also note where there is an agreement with the text of "the" LXX,[29] and occasionally include other text-critical comments.

As tables 1 and 2 show, the ratio of additions to omissions in D relative to the MT is greater than 2:1. On these grounds it would seem justifiable to call the text expansionistic. Also, the discrepancy in agreement with the LXX between the two tables is noteworthy. D's additions are found in the Greek text in nearly half of the 65 cases (a total of 27 times), while its omissions agree only 4 times in 31. Although further study might suggest an explanation, it would be premature to do more than simply note this discrepancy here. At least one instance, however—the omission of the long phrase from Deut 14:21 in 48:6—is likely to be an intentional alteration at the hand of the redactor. The phrase reads לגר אשר בשעריך תתננה ואכלה או, "to the sojourner who is in your gates you shall give it, and he shall eat it, or ..." The omission would be consistent with the redactor's treatment of all the Deut passages on the גר (sojourner or proselyte).[30]

26. See the *Appendix.*

27. Yadin regards a great many of the departures from the MT as polemical—see e.g., II, pp. 228–29. The evidence listed here questions that interpretation. As for the relevance of textual criticism for dating, see chapter 4.

28. For a more detailed consideration of some of the examples listed in Tables 1 and 2, see E. Tov, "מגילת המקדש וביקורת," pp. 104–8.

29. Since the purpose here is not an in-depth text criticism, I have relied on A. Rahlfs, *Septuaginta* (Stuttgart: Württembergische Bibelanstalt, 1935). Of course, I am not under the illusion that this edition is "the" LXX.

30. See chapter 6 for a discussion of the problem of the גר.

Table 1. Additions to the Text of the MT in D

	Col. of TS	*Addition*	*Verse of MT*	*Note*
1.	2:3	ואת הגרגשי	Exod 34:11	Restored; LXX
2.	2:7–8	ואת פסילי ... באש	Exod 34:13; Deut 7:25	Restored; LXX
3.	2:9	ממנו	Deut 7:25	—
4.	2:12	השמר	Exod 34:12	—
5.	48:5	יש	Lev 11:21	—
6.	48:5	ולעוף בכנפיו	Lev 11:21	—
7.	48:5	בעוף ובבהמה	Deut 14:21	—
8.	48:5	וכול ... תואכלו	Deut 14:21	—
9.	51:12	במשפט	Deut 16:19	—
10.	51:13	מטה משפט	Deut 16:19	—
11.	51:15	ובאתה	Deut 16:20	LXX
12.	51:18	להמיתו	Deut 18:22	Implied in MT
13.	52:3	לכה	Lev 26:1	—
14.	52:11	בכה	Deut 15:22	—
15.	53:3	כברכתי	Deut 12:21	—
16.	53:4	בכה	Deut 12:22	LXX
17.	53:6	את	Deut 12:23	—
18.	53:7	עד עולם	Deut 12:25	LXX
19.	53:7	הטוב	Deut 12:25	LXX
20.	53:8	אלוהיכה	Deut 12:25	LXX
21.	53:16	על נפשה	Num 30:4	—
22.	53:17	בשבועה	Num 30:4	—
23.	53:20	הנה יאנה	Num 30:6	LXX
24.	54:4	וכול	Num 30:10	—
25.	54:6	היום	Deut 13:1	LXX
26.	54:9	אליכה	Deut 13:3	—
27.	54:10	ונעבודה	Deut 13:3	LXX
28.	54:13	אבותיכמה	Deut 13:4	—
29.	54:19	בן אביכה או	Deut 13:7	LXX
30.	55:3	כול	Deut 13:13	LXX
31.	55:6	בישראל	Deut 13:15	—
32.	55:6	כול	Deut 13:16	LXX
33.	55:8	כול	Deut 13:16	—
34.	55:8	תכה	Deut 13:16	—
35.	55:14	והטוב	Deut 13:19	LXX
36.	55:18	עליו	Deut 17:4	—
37.	55:19	את הדבר הזה	Deut 17:4	—
38.	56:2	אשר ... את	Deut 17:9	Compare Deut 17:8
39.	56:5	לשכן שמי עליו	Deut 17:10	LXX
40.	56:5	ושמרתה	Deut 17:10	LXX
41.	56:8	לוא ישמע	Deut 17:12	—
42.	56:11	בישראל	Deut 17:13	—

Table 1. Additions to the Text of the MT in D (*cont.*)

Col. of TS	Addition	Verse of MT	Note
43. 56:16	למלחמה	Deut 17:16	—
44. 56:17	לו	Deut 17:16	LXX
45. 56:17	כסף וזהב	Deut 17:16	Compare Deut 17:17
46. 56:19	מאחרי	Deut 17:17	—
47. 60:11	לפני	Deut 18:5	LXX
48. 60:11	ולברך	Deut 18:5	LXX
49. 60:11	וכול	Deut 18:5	—
50. 61:12	עליו	Deut 19:21	LXX
51. 62:4	פן	Deut 20:8	LXX
52. 62:14	את (*bis*)	Deut 20:17	—
53. 62:15	הגרגשי	Deut 20:17	LXX
54. 63:3	לפני	Deut 21:5	—
55. 63:5	ראוש	Deut 21:6	LXX
56. 63:8	את	Deut 21:9	—
57. 63:8	אלוהיכה	Deut 21:9	LXX
58. 63:8	הטוב	Deut 21:9	LXX
59. 64:6	בני	Deut 21:21	—
60. 64:13	או את חמורו	Deut 21:21	—
61. 65:3	את	Deut 22:6	—
62. 65:11	הנה	Deut. 22:16	—
63. 65:12	לה	Deut 22:17	LXX
64. 65:14	ההוא	Deut 22:18	LXX
65. 66:4–5	במקום ... העיר	Deut 22:25	Implied in MT

The next problem to address is the date of the D source. It is impossible properly to consider this point, however, prior to introducing the data from the fragments of another copy of the TS (or better, of a copy of another form of the TS). Because questions involved with all three of the fragments (Rockefeller 43.366) are interrelated, I analyze them all at this juncture. Although it is primarily fragment 1 which may help in dating D, one cannot hope to understand it in isolation from the other fragments. Further, the discussion of all three fragments undergirds chapter 3.

Table 2. Omissions from the Text of the MT

Col. of TS	Omission	Verse of MT	Note
1. 2:8	עליהם	Deut 7:25	—
2. 48:3–4	את (*quater*)	Lev 11:22	—
3. 48:6	לגר ... או	Deut 14:21	—
4. 51:11	אשר ... לשפטיך	Deut 16:18	—
5. 53:4	כאשר צויתיך	Deut 12:21	—
6. 53:4	בכול אות נפשך	Deut 12:21	—
7. 53:9	אשר יהיו לך	Deut 12:26	—
8. 53:13	ועשית	Deut 23:24	—
9. 54:10	ועבדם	Deut 13:3	LXX
10. 54:14	ואת מצותיו תשמרו	Deut 13:5	—
11. 54:15	ההוא	Deut 13:6	—
12. 55:4	אחרים	Deut 13:13	—
13. 55:18	אשר לא צויתי	Deut 17:3	—
14. 55:21	אשר ... האשה	Deut 17:5	LXX
15. 56:6	התורה אשר יורוך	Deut 17:11	—
16. 56:21	משנה	Deut 17:18	—
17. 60:12	ובא	Deut 18:6	LXX
18. 60:14	בשם יהוה אלהיו	Deut 18:7	—
19. 61:6	בכול חטא	Deut 19:15	Some MSS LXX
20. 61:9	היטב	Deut 19:18	—
21. 61:11	הרע	Deut 19:20	—
22. 62:9	כל	Deut 20:13	—
23. 62:13	האלה	Deut 20:16	—
24. 63:2	בו	Deut 21:4	—
25. 63:2	בנחל	Deut 21:4	—
26. 65:10	העיר	Deut 22:15	—
27. 65:11	והנה	Deut 22:17	—
28. 66:5	האיש	Deut 22:25	—

Excursus—An Examination of Rockefeller 43.366

Introduction and *Status Quaestionis*

Among the fragments which Yadin published in the supplementary volume of plates to his edition of the TS are the Rockefeller 43.366 fragments. Judging from the plates, they are all in the same hand, and belong to a MS which, he informs us, comes from Cave 4.[31]   Yadin

---

31. One scholar is apparently dubious of the provenance of these fragments. A.S. van der Woude, in the course of a general description of the number of different copies of the TS, speaks of "drie verschillende manuscripten, die waarschijnlijk alle in grot XI van Qumran werden gevonden." The ensuing discussion makes it clear that the three MSS to which he refers are 11QTemple, 11QTSb, and the MS which the 43.366 fragments represent. Unfortunately he does not elaborate on why he doubts the connection of 43.366 to Cave 4. See "Een Gedeelte," p. 387.

claimed that these fragments represent a copy of the TS with a text identical to that of the TS,[32] and as discussed in chapter 1, he relied on an analysis of their paleography to date this copy of the TS between 125–75 B.C.E. Most scholars writing on the TS have followed Yadin on this point.[33] A few, however, have voiced dissent regarding either the identity of these fragments, or their usefulness for dating the TS.

The first of these dissenters was Levine. He doubted the validity of Yadin's attempt to use fragment 1 (40*:1) to fill lacunae in TS 11.[34] Since it portrays Yahweh speaking to Moses, contrary to the TS—where the name of Moses never appears—Levine suggested that the fragment "be detached from the group numbered Rockefeller 43.366 and given a different catalogue designation."[35]

Strugnell has also disagreed with Yadin's interpretation of the fragments. He proposed instead that they come from a "wild" Pentateuch with frequent nonbiblical additions, some from the TS. He conceded that the relationship could also be seen in reverse, with portions of the "wild" Pentateuch serving as source material for the TS. Stegemann agreed with his assessment.[36]

For Wacholder the question thus posed is settled. The Rockefeller fragments are "citations from the sectarian Torah superimposed on the traditional Pentateuch and are thus necessarily antedated by their Qumranic archetype."[37] Mink, nuancing his earlier position, agreed with Levine that fragment 1 does not belong to a copy of the TS. He was uncertain about fragment 2 (40*:2) as well.[38]

---

32. Yadin, I, p. 8; II, p. 172.

33. A representative sampling includes A. Caquot, "Le Rouleau du Temple de Qoumrân," *ETR* 53 (1978): 445; idem, "Le Rouleau du Temple," *MB* 13, p. 34; J. Charlesworth, "The Date of Jubilees and the Temple Scroll," in *SBL 1985 Seminar Papers*, ed. K. Richards (Atlanta: Scholars Press, 1985), p. 197; Dimant, "Qumran Sectarian Literature," p. 527; T. Elgvin, "Tempelrullen," p. 2; J. Fitzmyer, review of *The Temple Scroll*, by Y. Yadin, in *CBQ* 48 (1986): 548; Hengel, Charlesworth, and Mendels, "Polemical Character," p. 29; J. Milgrom, "The Temple Scroll," p. 106; H. Mink, "Præsentation," pp. 91–92; J. Mueller, "The Temple Scroll and the Gospel Divorce Texts," p. 248, note 10; Stegemann, "'Das Land'," p. 156 note 14; and van der Woude, "Een Gedeelte," p. 387.

34. Levine, "Aspects," pp. 5 and 6. In fact, although Levine does not note it, the fragment is more nearly parallel to TS 23.

35. Ibid., p. 6.

36. Strugnell's views appear in a letter which he wrote to Wacholder dated 28 April 1981. Wacholder published an excerpt in *The Dawn of Qumran*, pp. 205–6. Stegemann believes that the fragments belong to an "expanded Torah" text provisionally numbered 4Q364–365—thus "Origins," p. 237. Note the change from Stegemann's earlier view, note 33 above.

37. Wacholder, *The Dawn of Qumran*, p. 206. Wacholder does not dispute Yadin's use of the fragments to date the TS, only the date at which he thereby arrives. Since Yadin compares the script of the fragments with that of 1QIsa[a] and 4QDeut[a], and according to Cross the Deut fragment dates between 175–150 B.C.E., Wacholder challenges Yadin's late dating. He himself appeals to the earlier date as support for his argument that the autograph of the TS dates to about 200 B.C.E.

38. H. Mink, "Use of Scripture," pp. 23–24. For Mink's earlier position see note 33. For a position similar to Mink's, see van der Woude, "Tempelrol (I)," p. 188, note 11.

Vermes has also sharply questioned Yadin's use of the fragments to date the TS. He sided with Levine on fragment 1, and was dubious about the nature of fragment 2 as well. He tentatively suggested that the fragments may testify to an earlier form, or source, of the TS.[39]

Before assessing these views, an analysis of the three fragments of 43.366 is necessary. In the process of such an analysis the merits of the varying views about the nature of the relationship between the fragments and the TS becomes clear.

Fragment 1 (40*:1)

General Description and Transcription

Observation proves that this fragment belongs to the upper right-hand portion of its column. Yadin transcribes part of lines 3–8 in II, p. 44, and part of lines 9–12 in I, p. 123, but he nowhere transcribes or discusses the crucial lines 1–2. It has not been possible to preserve the proportions of the fragment, i.e., the interrelationship of words and lacunae from line to line. The photographs must be consulted for these details.

1. ‏[בסוכ]ות תשבו שבעת ימים כול אזרח בישראל ישב בסוכות ל[מען ידעו דורותיכם]
2. ‏[כי בסו]כות הושבתי את אבותיכם בהוציאי אותך מארץ מצר[ים] אני יהוה אלוה[יכם]
3. ‏וידבר מושה את מועדי יהוה אל בני ישראל
4. ‏וידבר יהוה אל מושה לאמור צו את בני ישראל לאמור בבואכמה אל הארץ אש[ר]
5. ‏[אנ]וכי נותן לכמה לנחלה וישבתם עליה לבטח תקריבו עצים לעולה ולכול מ[לאכת]
6. ‏[הב]ית אשר תבנו לי בארץ ... [...] תתנו על מזבח העולה את העול[ה וגם את העצים]
7. ‏[...] ... לפסחים ולשלמים [ו]ל ...... ולנדבות ולעולות ובר[א]ש[י החודשים ......
8. ‏[......... ל[.]ל[.........]ל ...]ול ... ות ולכול מלאכת הבית יקר[יבו עצים .... [
9. ‏[............ מ[ועד היצהר יקריבו את העצים שנים [עשר מטות בני ישראל]
10. ‏[.................. והי]ו המקריבים ביום הריש[ון] לוי [ויהודה וביום השני]
11. ‏[בנימין ובני יוסף וביום השלישי ראו]בן ושמעון [וביו]ם הר[ביעי יששכר וזבולון]
12. ‏[וביום החמישי גד ואשר וביום הששי דן ונפתלי]

Notes on the Readings and Restorations

The length of the lines in this fragment can be ascertained on the basis of lines 1, 2, and 4, which are respectively 67, 69, and 66 characters and spaces long. This calculation is essential for any attempt to restore the broken lines.

Lines 1–3. One may be confident of every reading in these lines, even where the letters cannot be read clearly, since this is a quotation of Lev 23:42–44.

Line 5. ‏עצים. Yadin does not read this word, but it is crucial for a proper understanding of the subsequent lines. The *ʿayin* and *mem* are clearly legible, while the remaining traces suggest the reading which the context demands.[40]

---

39. Vermes in Schürer, *History* 3:407 and note 3. E. Qimron, "Further New Readings," p. 33, also thinks that the fragments may be part of a source which lies behind the present form of the TS.

40. After I had decided on this reading, I discovered that E. Qimron had come to the same conclusion. See E. Qimron, "‏הערות," p. 140 and note 5. He says, "In our opinion, the ṣade was effaced. Therefore it was rewritten between the lines above the ṣade which is on the line."

[מ]לאכת. Yadin does not read the *mem,* but it is clear on the photograph. The restoration is almost certain, based on the context and comparison with line 8, which includes a phrase virtually identical to the one at the end of line 5. Restoring this word constrains the reading of הב[ית in place of Yadin's בב.[ית.

Line 6. תבנו. Yadin reads יבנו, but the photograph shows the thick left stroke of the *taw,* with the faint keraia rising above the top of the right stroke.

את העולה]. Yadin does not read these words. The ʿ*ayin* and *waw* of העולה are uncertain, while את is a definite reading. The restoration is based on the repetitive character of this text, but it is only a suggestion.

[וגם את העצים]. This is a tentative suggestion. The continuation requires this phrase or one of similar content and length (10–12 letters and spaces).

Line 7. ובר[א]ש[י] החודשים]. Yadin does not attempt a reading here. The *bet, resh,* and *shin* of the first word are clear, but the ʾ*aleph* has been completely eroded. The restoration seems certain given the context, and if this reading is correct, then החודשים follows.

Line 8. ול..ות. Yadin's reading is לבית, without the *waw.* I cannot read the *bet* on the photograph, although traces can be seen which do not seem to fit a *bet.* In fact, the traces might be those of two, or even three, letters. Apart from its paleographical difficulty, Yadin's reading בית does not make good sense in the context. I have no other definite suggestion, but one would expect some type of offering with a feminine plural. Could the reading be ולמנחות?

Line 9. [מ]ועד. Yadin reads [מו]עד, but the *waw* is legible on the photograph.

Line 10. והי[ו. This is Yadin's reading. I regard the *waw* as uncertain, based on the traces. A *dalet* or *resh* would also be compatible with the traces.

Line 11. [בנימין ובני יוסף]. Yadin restores אפרים ומנשה and leaves בנימין out. The basis for his decision is unclear, since the relevant portions of the TS have Benjamin involved in the second day's offerings.[41] Thus I restore בנימין. According to the remaining space in the line, Ephraim and Menasseh can then only be included as the sons of Joseph, an option which is suggested by the TS itself.[42]

Line 12. Line 12 is not preserved in the fragment, but can be partially (wholly?) restored using the content of the previous two lines, TS 24:12–16, and fragment 38*:1.

Translation[43]

> (1) You shall dwell in *booths* seven days. Every native Israelite shall dwell in booths, *in order that your generations may know* (2) that I made your fathers dwell *in booths* when I brought you out of the land of Egypt. I am Yahweh, your God. (3) So Moses declared Yahweh's appointed times to the sons of Israel. (4) And Yahweh spoke to Moses, saying, "Order the sons of Israel as follows: when you come to the land which (5) I am about to give to you as an

41. For the clearest evidence see TS 24:12.

42. Cf. e.g., TS 24:13.

43. Restored words are italicized.

inheritance, and you dwell securely therein, you shall contribute[44] wood for the burnt offering and for all the *work of* (6) *the house* which you shall build me in the land ... You shall place the burnt offering on the sacrificial altar, *and the wood as well*. ... (7) for Passover sacrifices and thank offerings and for ... and for free-will offerings and for burnt offerings. And on the first of *each month* ... (8) and for ... and for all the work of the house, they shall contribute *wood* ... (9) the feast of the oil. The twelve *tribes of the sons of Israel* shall contribute the wood ... (10) those contributing on the first day shall be Levi and *Judah; and on the second day*, (11) *Benjamin and the sons of Joseph; and on the third day*, Reuben and Simeon; and on the fourth day, *Issachar and Zebulon;* (12) *and on the fifth day, Gad and Asher; and on the sixth day, Dan and Naphtali ..."*

Notes on the Text of Lines 1–4a (= Lev 23:42–24:2a)

1. אזרח. The MT reads האזרח, as does the LXX. The Peshitta preserves a shorter, variant text which is of no help in determining the original reading.
   ישב. The MT and the Peshitta read ישבו. Because of Greek idiom, it is impossible to ascertain the reading behind the LXX.

2. אבותיכם. The MT reads בני ישראל, as do the LXX and the Peshitta.
   אותך. All three versions read אתם.

Discussion

The first three and a half lines of this text, and what presumably preceded them, serve to establish the basic character of fragment 1. Since lines 1–4a are a quotation of Lev 23:42–24:2a, it seems reasonable to suppose that the rest of Lev 23 probably preceded. With line 4b begins a section unknown from the Hebrew Bible, but in lines 4b–5, at least, Levitical elements persist. Thus in line 4b appears the form "בוא אל הארץ אשר ... נותן לכם +" + cultic command." This is primarily a Levitical form.[45] The phrase וישבתם על הארץ (עליה) לבטח, attested only in Lev 25:18 and 25:19, occurs in line 5. The lines which follow, 6–12, do not conform to any particular biblical model in quite the way the same way. Nevertheless, the character of at least the first half of fragment 1 may legitimately be described as Levitical.

The word אבותיכם ("your fathers") in line 2 is a textual variant which is attested nowhere else. Its presence here is significant, because the term is practically limited to Deut in the meaning which this context requires.[46] Since the book of Deut addresses a generation which did not experience the Exodus events, it calls that earlier generation "the fathers." Because in their present canonical setting Exod, Lev, and most of Num are concerned with that previous generation, the term אבותיכם does not occur in those books in the same sense. The use of the term here therefore constitutes a sort of "Deuteronomizing" of Lev 23:43.

This "Deuteronomizing" of an essentially Levitical passage finds expression in two additional elements. The first is the use of the first-person pronoun אנוכי in line 5. As is well known, this form of the pronoun is ubiquitous in Deut, but it does not occur in Lev at all. Lev

---

44. For this meaning of תקריבו, see J. Milgrom, "Further Studies," pp. 10–12.

45. E.g., Lev 23:10, 25:2. Elsewhere the form occurs once, at Deut 26:1.

46. I include in this statement the variant with a 2ms suffix.

uses only אני, which conversely almost never appears in Deut. When it does make a rare appearance in that book, it is limited to liturgical expressions, or older poetic layers.[47] Furthermore, אני never refers to God in Deut.

The second "Deuteronomizing" element is found in line 5. It is נחלה, conventionally translated "inheritance." As a term for the land which God gives (נתן) his people, within the Pentateuch it occurs only in Deut.[48] נחלה is used in the Pentateuch outside Deut, but in such cases it always refers to the inheritance of a single family or individual, not to the land of Canaan. It is true that in Num 34:2 one reads that all Canaan "falls to the lot of Israel as an inheritance," but here there is no verbal connection with God's giving. The connection of נחלה with נתן is a stock formula in Deut, while elsewhere in the Pentateuch it is unknown.

These considerations argue that fragment 1 presents the "Deuteronomizing" of a Levitical composition. It seems to be a modification of material from Lev to give it a Deuteronomic perspective.[49] To these considerations must be added the implication of the fact that the D source has been redacted. Because of that fact, one may reasonably suspect that not all of it found its way into the present TS. If so, what was the whole of the D source like?

Perhaps in some ways it was analogous to Tatian's *Diatessaron* or portions of the Samaritan Pentateuch. These express the desire to harmonize which a group may feel when it has more than one authoritative description of the same event, or more than one set of legal enactments applying to the same situation. The ready solution in such situations is, of course, to prepare a synoptic view. By this means, the users can resolve apparent discrepancies, and at the same time gather related material together in one place.

D may have been such a synopsis, taking Deut as its "base text." This would be a logical choice, since Deut contains the laws that were to apply once Israel was in the land. It would be necessary to include Lev 23, presenting as it does many festal and sacrificial details not found in Deut 16. Fragment 1, then, apparently contains the last lines of Lev 23 as modified for a Deuteronomic literary context.

The idea of Levitical works being "Deuteronomized," or of Deuteronomic works taking over needed details from Lev, is no mere abstraction. Works fitting that description are actually known from Second Temple times. For example, 1Q22, the "Words of Moses," is just such a composition.[50] Its editor describes it as a "description des fêtes, plus élaborée que dans les passages parallèles du Pentateuque; elle commence avec l'année sabbatique ... après quoi suit probablement le rituel du Yom hak-Kippurim."[51] 1Q22 is nothing other than a

---

47. Deut 12:30, 29:5, 32:21, 39, 49, and 52.

48. Deut 4:21, 15:4, 19:10, 20:16, 21:23, 24:4, 25:19 and 26:1. This last verse is particularly close to the general phraseology of lines 4–5.

49. As suggested above, this description, *mutatis mutandis*, also fits the non-Deut material of the D source, such as Exod 34 in col. 2. That portion is "Deuteronomized" through the addition of material from Deut 7. Another example is TS 48:1–5, which "Deuteronomizes" Lev 11 by adding portions from Deut 14.

50. The *editio princeps* is *DJD* I, pp. 91–97 and plates 18–19.

51. The editor is J. T. Milik. The quotation is from *DJD* I, p. 91.

"Deuteronomized" form of Lev 16 and 25. It is full of Deuteronomic usage. For example, among the DSS אנוכי ("I") occurs only in the TS, fragment 1 of 43.366, and 1Q22 2:4.[52]

I would suggest then that fragment 1 is a part of the original D source which the redactor rejected when he chose portions for the TS. He did not need it because he replaced the Deut 16 portion of the synopsis—which included the modification of Lev 23 contained in fragment 1—with the Festival Calendar source.[53]

Qimron has presented a possible challenge to this view. He argues that fragment 1 is rather part of the TS in its present form, fitting between the present cols. 28–29.[54] In support of this notion he makes the observation that there are fragments of letters on the back of col. 29 which apparently deal with offerings, and yet do not fit the text of col. 28 as restored. He reasons that since the top of col. 29 discusses various offerings for the new temple, as does fragment 1, the unplaced letters on the back of the column belong to the lost portions corresponding to that fragment.

But a little reflection shows why this idea cannot be correct. Although it is not impossible that the content of the column supposed to be missing might be related to fragment 1, the order of the discussion of offerings in the TS is entirely different from that of fragment 1. TS 23–25 contains the discussion of the ceremony for the wood offering, which is then *followed* by a very short list of offerings in 29:2–6. In other words, the TS in its present form first discusses the wood offering, then the general offerings—precisely the opposite of fragment 1. The fragment first discusses the general offerings—judging from the preserved portions of Lev—then considers the wood offering.

The fragmentary condition of the text precludes definitive proof of any suggestion for the relationship of fragment 1 to the present TS. Still, the most economical explanation of whatever facts we do have clearly is to be preferred. As a working hypothesis the suggestion offered here meets that criterion. It explains the fragment's combination of Deuteronomic elements with a Levitical structure. And it explains why fragment 1 was a part of a MS which included material which, as I shall show, is indubitably part of the TS—fragment 3—as well as material which does not fit the present form of the TS. In fine, it appears that 43.366 was a "proto-Temple Scroll," which included an earlier form of the D source. The earlier form was not identical with the form of D which appears in the TS, and may have been considerably longer.[55]

Fragment 2 (40*:2)

General Description

Line one is the first line of the column, with a wide top margin visible. Both the left and right margins are lost, and since no line is complete, it is impossible to locate the lines in a left-right matrix. Accordingly, in the transcription below, the position of the lines is arbitrary.

---

52. Qimron, *Grammar*, p. 57.

53. For the apparent reasons for this decision, see chapter 5 on the Festival Calendar source, and chapter 6 on the redactional scheme of the TS as a whole.

54. Qimron, "הערות," p. 140.

55. It is even possible that 1Q22 was a part of the earlier form of D.

Including reconstruction, the longest line is line 2, measuring 24 spaces and letters in length. It therefore lacks about 45 spaces and letters, but comparison with lines 4–5 shows that not more than about 35 could be in the direction of either margin. (This observation assumes that the lines of this fragment are about the length of those in fragment 1.)

Transcription[56]

[	[ועשי]תה את הבית אשר תבנה] .1
[	כו]ל [הי]סוד גורׂיע שלוש אמות] .2
[	ה.[את הקיר שבע א]מות .3
[	לנגב ארבע] עשרה ולימה עש[ר/רים ואחת .4
[	] .[.. ח ב] .5

Translation

> (1) And you shall *make* the house which you build ... (2) The *entire* foundation built with recesses(?)[57] to a depth of three cubits ... (3) the wall seven *cubits* ... (4) *southward* four*teen* (?) and westward twenty-*one* (?) ... (5) ... ḥ b ...

Notes on the Readings and Restorations

1. ועשי]תה] is virtually certain, based on the appearance of the form "עשיתה plus architectural element" nineteen times in the extant portions of the TS.[58]

2. The scribe apparently first wrote גורע, then indicated by dots that the *waw* was misplaced. He replaced it with a superlinear *waw* to form גרוע.

3. א]מות. The restoration is certain in the context.

4. Assuming agreement with feminine אמה, עשרה indicates a number between 11–19. עשרים could actually be עשר or any number between 20–29. The numbers here are only suggestions based on considerations of probability, as discussed below. I have restored לנגב because of the presence of לימה, and because in the TS directions always proceed clockwise, starting in the east.[59]

Discussion

The fragmentary remains of these five lines permit only limited analysis, but it is still possible to draw some significant conclusions. Fragment 2 clearly contains instructions to build some kind of structure. The structure has a recessed (?) foundation and one or more walls. The dimensions are given.

In the Bible, the term יסוד ("foundation") does not appear in the descriptions of Solomon's temple. But 1 Kngs 5:31 contains the cognate verb, and reads in part, "to found the house upon hewn stones." The biblical text makes no connection between this foundation and the

---

56. Yadin provides a partial transcription of lines 1–2 in II, p. 130.

57. גרוע is a Qal passive participle, unless we are to read גורע, in which case it is probably a qutl segholate noun. In either case, the word is not attested heretofore. It seems to be related to מגרעות of 1 Kngs 6:6, itself a *hapax legomenon*. The consensus on the word in Kngs is that it refers to a type of ledge or rebatement. See *BDB* s.v., and E. Qimron, "למלונה," p. 259.

58. See the full discussion of this form in chapter 3.

59. See TS 38:13–14, 39:12–13, etc.

recesses of 1 Kngs 6:6. Nor does any biblical text describe a wall (קיר) with a dimension of seven cubits, whether it involve height, length, thickness, or distance to another structure. It follows that, unless the author has intentionally altered the biblical account beyond recognition, the building in this text is not a structure found in the Bible.

The only places in the TS where the term יסוד appears involve the sacrificial altar.[60] These are almost certainly irrelevant to fragment 2. The root גרע also occurs in the TS, but with a meaning different from that in line 2 of the fragment.[61] At several places in the scroll there is a collocation of the dimension seven cubits with the word קיר. In TS 31:13, the height of the gates set within the walls of the House of the Laver is seven cubits. TS 36:5 stipulates a width of seven cubits for the wall of the inner court's gate. According to 40:9 the same measurement applies to the width of the outer court's wall. The gates of that court also protrude outward seven cubits, according to 41:12. Finally, it is possible to infer a dimension of seven cubits for the cells in the walls of the inner court.[62] Yet none of the elements in the TS is identical to, or perhaps even related to, the description in fragment 2. Is it then possible that the fragment could be "pigeonholed" into one of the lacunae in the TS—particularly in cols. 3–12, which consist of fragmentary architectural descriptions?

At first glance it would seem that this possibility could not be ruled out, given the extensive amount of text in these columns which has not survived, but that first impression is misleading. It is important to notice that fragment 2 represents a considerable amount of text in its own right. Since the lines in the fragment were presumably 65–75 characters and spaces long, five lines is equivalent to nearly 350 spaces. Even discounting the fifth line because of its extremely fragmentary condition still leaves 260–300 spaces. Distributed along the shorter lines of the TS, this is the equivalent of six or seven lines. If fragment 2 is to fit in one of the lacunae of the TS, then, that lacuna cannot be less than six or seven lines long. Furthermore, for the fit to be possible the introduction of fragment 2 cannot disrupt the logic of the overall movement of the TS text.

The logic of this movement is discernible in spite of the considerable gaps in cols. 3–12. The description begins in col. 3 with the command to build, and moves outward from the inner sanctum. By col. 12 the focus is on the altar of burnt offerings, immediately in front of the sanctuary. In the intermediate columns, the fragmentary remains primarily describe temple furnishings.

According to the criteria set forth above, no place can be found for fragment 2; it simply does not fit in cols. 3–12. Nor can a place be found for it in cols. 30–46, when the architectural plan resumes. It is perhaps possible that fragment 2 does describe one of the structures in these columns, but if so, it does not describe that structure in the same way that the present TS does. The result is the same. Fragment 2 contains a description which is not a part of the present redactional form of the TS.

---

60. TS 23:13, 34:8 and 52:21.

61. TS 54:7. Here the meaning is "scrape."

62. Cf. TS 38:15, 40:10 and Yadin, I, p. 245.

Is it possible to deduce anything more about the structure in fragment 2? Tentatively, one might apply form criticism using the עשיתה ("you shall make") passages in the TS. These passages reveal a tripartite pattern consisting of: (1) a command to build; (2) a location, and (3) building dimensions. If fragment 2 accords with this pattern, then lines 1–2 contain the command to build a house of some sort. Line 3 would indicate the location of the building, evidently distancing its wall seven cubits from the wall of a previously described structure. (The TS twice uses precisely this method for locating a structure.)[63] Then the fragment gives the measurements for the building, which continue into line 4 and perhaps beyond. Exactly what these measurements were must remain a mystery, but it is clear that the north-south dimension was between 11–19 cubits, and the east-west side measured either 10 cubits or something between 20–29 cubits. Based on the septimal system which underlies the TS measurements,[64] the most probable dimensions are 14 x 21. If this conclusion is correct, then the structure of fragment 2 has dimensions identical with those of the houses in the Aramaic New Jerusalem text.[65] As the sequel will show in chapter 3, such concord is not at all unlikely.

This form critical analysis of fragment 2 must of course remain tentative. Of more importance is the conclusion that the structure described in the fragment is not found in the present form of the TS, and that furthermore, it could not have fit into any of the lacunae in that text. Therefore, like the D source, the Temple Source of the TS was once somewhat longer; as with the D source, the redactor has omitted an unknown amount of it.

Fragment 3 (38*:5)

Since Yadin accurately transcribes the whole of fragment 3,[66] there is little point in transcribing the text here. With fragment 3, unlike the other two fragments, we are unquestionably dealing with a portion of the TS. Col. I aligns with TS 38:4–15, and col. II is a form of 41:5–42:3. Nevertheless, a text critical comparison between the text of the fragment and that of the scroll provides significant insight into the topic of chapter 3, the Temple Source.[67]

---

63. TS 30:6–7 and 33:9.

64. This system is a major subject of discussion in chapter 3.

65. For bibliographic details see chapter 3, note 21.

66. For col. I see II, pp. 160–61; for col. II see II, pp. 172–73.

67. With such lacunose texts, direct word-for-word comparison is often impossible. Accordingly, I have relied upon the following procedure. Beginning with a word which has survived in both texts, I count the number of spaces to the next word which has survived in both, and which is sufficiently distant from the first word to make the count meaningful. The second word is ordinarily in the subsequent line. Then I compare the counts for the two texts, drawing inferences as to whether the counts imply texts of equal length. If so, one can assume the two texts did not differ greatly. If not, then one of two explanations probably applies. It may be that one text was longer or shorter because of recensional differences or scribal processes. Or, it may be that the two texts varied in their use of intralinear blanks. Based on a study of the extant portions, the first explanation is generally preferable. For this method to work, it is necessary to know how long the lines were in both the fragment and the TS. The line lengths in the fragment can be ascertained using II:2–3, where the lines are nearly complete. These lines indicate an average length of about 70 spaces. For the TS the lines of cols. 38–40 average about 50 spaces in length, and col. 41 has lines averaging about 40 spaces.

Discussion

Because fragment 3 contains portions of two columns, and because the lines are observably at the bottom margin, it is a simple matter to determine how many lines of text stood between TS 38:15, where the equivalent column of the fragment ends, and TS 41:4, where the second column of the fragment begins. Thirty-five lines intervened between col. I:10 and col. II:1—a surprising result, because it means that each column of 43.366 totaled 46 lines. As the comparisons in table 3 show, 43.366 was therefore extraordinarily long. In fact, its columns would be the longest of any of the published DSS. And analogy with rabbinic and Masoretic traditions (although admittedly of uncertain application because of their much later date) raises questions about such a crowded MS.[68]

---

67. (*cont.*)   Column I

From TS 38:8 עליה to 38:9 ולימין = 43 spaces. Fragment lines 4–5 = 58 spaces. The fragment is longer by 15 spaces.

From 38:9 הזה to 38:10 יהיו = 50 spaces. Fragment lines 5–6 = 53 spaces. The texts are identical.

From 38:10 אוכלים to 38:10 העוף = 12 spaces. Fragment lines 6–7 = 10 spaces. The texts are identical.

From 38:13 לרוח to 38:13 לכול = 45 spaces. Fragment lines 8–9 = 60 spaces. Fragment longer by 15 spaces.

From 38:14 רוחותיה to 38:15 ובין = 87 spaces. Fragment lines 9–10 = 50 spaces. Fragment shorter by 37 spaces.

Visible textual variants: Fragment line 4 omits לתירוש, probably by scribal error; the fragment reads תו where the TS reads התאו.

Column II

From TS 41:5 ומשער to 41:6 ומשער = 44 spaces (with restoration). Fragment line 1 = 40 spaces. The texts are identical.

From 41:6 גד (restored) to 41:7 ושטים = 24 spaces. Fragment lines 1–2 = 12–14 spaces. The fragment is 10–12 spaces shorter.

From 41:16 ומצופים to 41:17 נשכות = 58 spaces. Fragment line 7 (with restoration) = 57 spaces. The texts are identical.

Visible Textual Variants: עצי ארז of fragment three line 11 does not appear in TS 42:2, nor can it be restored there. The phrase עד המשקוף of TS 42:2 is not found in the fragment, line 11.

Conclusion: For col. I there are fairly significant differences between the texts (about 15% variance), while for col. II only minor differences exist between the texts. On the whole, there can be no question that fragment 3 is indeed a form of the TS.

68. The text would have 3220 letters and spaces per column.

Table 3. Rockefeller 43.366 and Other Complete or Restorable[1] DSS MSS

Scroll	Lines/Col.	Average Spaces/Line[2]	Comments
1. 4QpNah	12	70	—
2. 3Q15	13 col. III 16 col. X	13–25	All columns between extremes
3. 4Q185	15	46	—
4. 4Q Wiles	17	63	—
5. 1QpHab	17	35	Length est.[3]
6. 4QpHos[a]	18	40	—
7. 4QFlor	19	68	—
8. 5QJNar	20	70	Length est.
9. 2QNJar	21	38	Length est.
10. 11QTemple	22 cols. I–XLVIII, LXI–LXVII; 28 cols. XLIX–LX	48	—
11. 1QS	26	45 col. I 85 col. IV	All columns between extremes
12. 4QpPs[a]	26 col. II	45 27 col. IV	—
13. 11QTS[b]	26	65	Recons.
14. 1QS[a]	29 col. I 45 col. II	60 col. I	No lines unbroken or fully legible
15. 4QTestim	30	43	—
16. 1QIsa[a]	31	50	—
17. 1QapGen	34–37	78	—
18. 1QIsa[b]	35	50	—
19. 1QH	40	60	—
20. 43.366	46	74	—

[1]By "restorable" I mean to include MSS whose data can be estimated within very narrow parameters, even if no certain conclusion is possible. [2]The average is a single figure based on complete lines without internal blanks. If, because of extreme variability, an average would not fairly represent the phenomena of a given scroll, I give a range. [3]See W. Brownlee, *The Midrash Pesher of Habakkuk* (Missoula: Scholars Press, 1979), p. 85.

SOURCES: In all cases it is necessary to consult the plates or photographs, as type distorts the relationships in question. According to the item numbers in the table, the sources are: for nos. 5, 11, and 16, J. Trever, *Scrolls from Qumran Cave I: The Great Isaiah Scroll, The Order of the Community, The Pesher to Habakkuk* (Jerusalem: The Albright Institute of Archaeological Research and The Shrine of the Book, 1972); for nos. 18 and 19, E. L. Sukenik, אוצר המגילות הגנוזות שבידי האוניברסיטה העברית (Jerusalem: Bialik Foundation and the Hebrew University, 1954); for no. 14 *DJD* I, plate 23; for nos. 9, 8, and 2 *DJD* II, plates 16, 40–41, and 47, respectively; for nos. 6, 1, 12, 7, 15, 4, and 3 *DJD* V, plates 10, 13, 15 and 17, 19, 21, 28 and 29–30, respectively; for no. 17 N. Avigad and Y. Yadin, *A Genesis Apocryphon: A Scroll from the Wilderness of Judaea* (Jerusalem: Magnes Press and Heikhal [*sic*] ha-Sepher, 1956); for nos 10, 14, and 20, Yadin III and Supplementary Plates.

The later groups had elaborate rules governing the production of biblical scrolls (a category which would probably include this text).[69] The halakhot which they developed were primarilyconcerned to regulate the amount of material in a column and on a sheet. Among other things, these halakhot spelled out the dimensions of columns, the breadth of lines (no more than three words of ten letters), and the length of spaces between letters, words, lines, and columns.[70] It was important that biblical scrolls not appear too crowded, since reader errors and misunderstanding could result:[71]

> Our masters have taught that one should use from three to eight columns per sheet. The use of too many columns makes the text look like a legal document, and the use of too few obscures the contents (because the lines are too long to be read easily).

It is especially interesting to read here of the confusion with a legal document which might arise from an overcrowded biblical text.

It would be folly to suppose that the rules which governed the production of 43.366 were necessarily the same as the rabbinic regulations. Nevertheless it is certain, based on studies of scribal techniques in the DSS, that rules of a similar sort were operative. Martin's examination of the major scrolls from Cave One came to the conclusion that these scrolls were "executed according to a certain observable plan ... the scribes worked within a definite framework of rules concerning column-division, line-length, word-spacing and paragraphing."[72]

The Qumran tefillin published by Yadin furnish additional evidence regarding the scribal regulations which were in force. These follow many of the later rabbinic halakhot for tefillin, including the lack of ruled lines, the avoidance of letters touching each other, and the requirement that letters and words not hang above the line. The capsules containing the tefillin

---

69. Yadin has argued from the outset that the TS claims to be a biblical book, and was regarded as such. His arguments are twofold: (1) the scroll has God speak in the first person singular, even where texts are borrowed from biblical portions wherein God is represented in the third person; and (2) the way the scroll handles the tetragrammaton, which is analogous to the usage in the DSS biblical scrolls. See, e.g., "The Temple Scroll," p. 136. His second argument is questionable, while the first does not apply to the 43.366 fragments. In spite of his uncertain reasoning, his conclusion seems right; in fragment 1 God is depicted speaking to Moses, revealing not only what is known from Leviticus, but new law as well. This depiction suggests that the fragments were making a pseudepigraphic claim. Of course, there is no way to be certain of the attitude the user community had toward the text of these fragments. For a helpful perspective, see J. Sanders, *Canon and Community: A Guide to Canonical Criticism* (Philadelphia: Fortress Press, 1984) and the literature which he cites.

70. I. Yeivin, *Introduction to the Tiberian Masorah,* trans. and ed. by E. J. Revell (Missoula: Scholars Press, 1980), pp. 7, 36–37, 43–44, and 136–37.

71. Ibid. p. 44. The quotation is from Menahot 30a. I have slightly modified Revell's translation so that it more accurately reflects the Talmudic text.

72. M. Martin, *The Scribal Characteristics of the Dead Sea Scrolls,* 2 vols. (Louvain: University of Louvain, 1958), 1: 202–3. See also 1: 99, 102–4, 108, and 143.

also agree with later tradition on important points, although there are significant differences as well.[73]

Thus, there were certainly regulations governing various facets of DSS scroll production. Many of the rabbinic halakhot on these matters were apparently already operative during the period in which the DSS were written and copied. It is therefore likely that when 43.366 was produced, there were rules aimed at avoiding an overcrowded text. This possibility encourages a reexamination of 43.366 fragment 3. Could it be that its columns actually contained less text than it seemed on a first examination?

Comparison with 1QIsa[a] underscores this question. Of all the scrolls in table 3, that scroll is the most readily comparable with 43.366. Like 43.366 (but unlike nearly all the other texts in that list), 1QIsa[a] is a biblical scroll. It is also akin to 43.366 in its script, commonly called "Hasmonean." In the light of these similarities, it is suggestive that the Isaiah scroll has only 31 lines per column.

Thus more than one line of analogy nurtures the suspicion that 43.366 did not have 46-line columns. One potential cause of inflation in the calculations which produced this number would be the presence of interpolations in the TS portions with which I compared fragment 3. The redactor of the TS might have interpolated material into the portions of the TS between cols. 38–42. Any such interpolations would, of course, skew calculations of the original columnar length. Based on differences from the surrounding text, several passages in cols. 38–42 are indeed likely candidates for identification as interpolations.

TS 39:5–11a, for example, is distinct from the rest of col. 39 in terms of subject matter, vocabulary, composition criticism, and the use of the divine name. Likewise 40:6–7 differs from its literary surroundings in terms of subject matter and compositional technique. Significantly, both texts are related to Deut 23:2–9, a portion which is (designedly) absent from the present form of the D source. As I show in the analysis of chapter 6, if the redactor excised Deut 23:2–9, he would have replaced the portion with other laws. These portions are the only candidates.

These considerations tend to confirm the suspicion that the redactor of the TS interpolated material from elsewhere into the Temple Source.[74] He inserted it where appropriate to his plan for the shaping of the new work. If correct, this conclusion would account for the differences in the material at the points noted, and require a reduction of the amount of text estimated for each column of 43.366.

Deleting 39:5–11a and 40:6–7 from the calculations removes the equivalent of six lines from the fragment, and the amount of text in each column is thereby reduced to 40 lines. The scroll's columns would still be the longest known (along with 1QH), but they would be more nearly analogous to the length of those in 1QIsa[a]. In addition, to judge from the exiguous remains, it is possible that TS 40:1–3 (and the missing lines 01–07?) was another interpolation.

---

73. Y. Yadin, *Tefillin from Qumran (XQ Phyl 1–4)* (Jerusalem: Israel Exploration Society, 1969), pp. 9–11 and 21.

74. For additional evidence that these portions are indeed interpolations into the Temple Source, see chapter 5.

If so, the text of 43.366 would have scribal characteristics nearly identical to those of the Isaiah scroll.

The Fragments of 43.366: Conclusions

This analysis of the fragments of 43.366 yields the following conclusions. Fragment 1 was probably a part of an original D source. The final redactor of the TS removed that portion in favor of the Festival Calendar source of TS 13–29, preferring the Calendar both to the "Deuteronomized" Lev 23 and to Deut 16, for reasons which are discussed in chapter 5.

Fragment 2 indicates that the Temple Source was originally more extensive than its present form in the TS. And fragment 3 proves that these fragments are indeed a form of the TS, a "proto-Temple Scroll." This earlier form combined the D source and the Temple Source. In addition, a close study of fragment 3 points to the presence of interpolations in the present TS, deriving from sources other than D and the Temple Source.

Thus, the fragments show that the redactor of the TS both deleted portions of the "proto-Temple Scroll," and added new materials garnered from other places. They also suggest that he was quite free in his approach. While he worked according to an ideology similar to that of his source texts (else why choose them?), his concept was also distinctly different. His cutting and splicing produced a work with a design and objectives different from those of its literary forebears.

It is now possible also to evaluate earlier ideas about 43.366. Quite apart from the question of paleographical dating, Yadin and his followers are certainly unjustified in relying upon these fragments to determine a *terminus ante quem* for the TS. The fragments cannot serve to date a work to which they do not actually belong.

On the other extreme, the suggestion of Levine and Mink, to remove at least fragment 1 from 43.366, appears arbitrary. Arguments in favor of keeping the fragments together are strong. First, they are apparently in the same hand.[75] Second, in terms of content, although they are not identical to the TS, they do present a work which is much more like it than unlike it. The analog of the TS is a strong argument for the *a priori* working assumption that the fragments represent a single literary work, and means that the burden of proof is on those who would separate the fragments. Third, fragment 2 is formally identical to the Temple Source as witnessed by the TS.

Contrary to Levine's assertion, the presence of the name of Moses in fragment 1 is no reason for removing it from the 43.366 group. The absence of the name from the TS is not a problem; in fact it is the whole point. The redactor of the TS has methodically removed the name from D, judging from the parallel biblical texts. Thus we may be sure that the name Moses was present in at least some of the sources which the redactor used. As a matter of fact, the name's appearance in fragment 1 is evidence of the direction of development. The

---

75. Actually, I have certain reservations about this point. Fragment 3 may be in a different hand. Yadin, however, never made that observation, and as he examined the original MS while I have had access only to photographs, I tentatively defer to his judgement. Even if the fragments are not in the same hand, that does not mean that they did not belong to the same work, as the TS and other multiscribal texts prove.

advantages which removing the name would afford to a redactor's revelatory claims are patent. But what would it profit him to insert an intermediary, even Moses? That would only serve to distance the TS one stage further from the mouth of God.

The position for which Wacholder argues (and which Strugnell agrees is possible), that the fragments derive from a "wild" Pentateuch on which someone has superimposed quotes from the TS, runs aground on fragment 1. It is possible to prove, by reconstructing the relevant portions of the TS, that lines 6–12 are not a quotation from the scroll.[76] Since economy of explanation dictates that some relationship exists between the TS and the fragments, and the TS is demonstrably not the source for lines 6–12 of the fragment, it follows that the direction of influence was the opposite: the text from which the fragment derives was a source for the TS.

In the light of the foregoing analysis, it becomes clear that those who have seen the fragments as evidence for earlier sources of the TS are correct. This analysis not only confirms that suggestion, but has gone farther, to explain how the fragments relate to the TS. In the process, it affords valuable insight into the problem of the final redaction of the scroll.

A Date for the Deuteronomy Source

Lines 6–12 of fragment 1 guide a determination of a *terminus post quem* for the D source. They speak of providing wood for various uses in the temple. The lines are written in LBH, thus pointing to the postexilic period as the time of composition.[77]

A narrower dating is possible on the reasonable conclusion that these lines take as their model Neh 10:33–35.[78] Verse 33 of Neh 10 describes the covenanters' decision to devote one-third shekel to the temple annually. Verse 34 lists the occasions and activities this annual gift would support. The list includes the Bread of the Presence, the daily offering, the sabbath offering, the new moon sacrifices, the festivals, holy days, and sin offerings. In short, it encompasses "all the work of the house (מלאכת בית) of God." In verse 35 one reads that the covenanters cast lots to determine who would bring the wood offering (קרבן העצים) to the temple, and when, "according to what is written in the Law" (ככתוב בתורה).

Commentators disagree on the implication of the reference to the law (tôrāh) of Moses here. Many argue that there is no such law of wood offering in the Pentateuch as we know it. Others reply that Neh relies on a midrashic application of Lev 6:5–6. The question of the referent of the word תורה in Neh 10:35 is bound up with the much more vexing problem of the nature of Ezra's law. Was it the present Pentateuch, or did it have a somewhat different

---

76. See my, "A New Manuscript Join." The join, and the restorations it suggests, prove that while there is a relationship between fragment 1 and TS 23, it is one of adaptation rather than quotation.

77. This judgment is based on the appearance in line 7 of פסחים ("passover offerings"), a plural not used in SBH, and the construction in line 4, לאמור בבואכמה. If the author had written in SBH one would have expected (with the orthographic and morphological peculiarities of the TS) לאמור והיה בבואכמה. See R. Polzin, *Late Biblical Hebrew: Toward a Historical Typology of Biblical Hebrew Prose,* Harvard Semitic Monographs no. 12 (Missoula: Scholars Press, 1976), pp. 42 and 46.

78. That is to say, on the assumption that the inspiration is essentially our present form of Neh, not some earlier form or sources.

content, including laws which have since been lost?[79] According to how that question is answered, Neh 10:35 is either midrashic application of earlier law or refers to an otherwise unknown law.

If the reference is to an unknown law, could it be that 43.366 has preserved it? Perhaps it is not impossible, but if so, the law has been modified in the fragment. The fragment commands the wood offering in the context of the temple service. Moses, of course, never spoke of the temple in the Pentateuch as we have it; he only gave instructions for the tabernacle. In fact the lack of Mosaic authority for the Solomonic temple concerned certain circles of Second Temple Jews, so much that they produced texts which provided it.[80] The text of 43.366 fragment 1 was probably inspired by such concerns. It appears very unlikely that it preserves a genuine preexilic law. Any such "Mosaic" law to which Neh 10:35 referred would surely mention neither the Temple, nor the festival of oil (line 9).

What is germane here is that in the present Pentateuch, there is no clear statement of a tribal obligation to provide wood. Fragment 1, lines 6–12, serves to provide this law in pseudepigraphic form. The general concerns and the specific vocabulary of the lines are the same as Neh 10:33–35. They speak of providing wood for מלאכת הבית, then list the occasions and activities which this gift will support.[81] This list, in lines 7-8, is clearly modeled after the list of Neh 10:34. Lines 9–12 legislate an idealized, twelve–tribe procedure for the wood offering. (Presumably, the background understanding would be that Nehemiah had modified Mosaic procedure for the changed circumstances of his own day. The fragment implicitly claims that the law of lines 9–12 was that which Nehemiah found in the Torah.)

Thus, fragment 1 depends on Neh 10, whose date in turn provides a *terminus post quem* for D. The date for the final form of Ezra-Nehemiah, whether it belongs to the work of the Chronicler or not, is, according to most commentators, about 300 B.C.E.[82]

The combination of the D source with the Temple Source, which already appears in the 43.366 fragments, provides the *terminus ad quem*. The earliest possible date for that combination therefore depends also on the date of the Temple Source, so I must anticipate the argument of the next chapter in saying that the Temple Source probably dates no later than 190 B.C.E. If this reasoning is correct, then a date for D should be sought somewhere between ca. 300–190 B.C.E. In all probability, then, D presents a third century law code which unknown redactors, shortly after the turn of the second century at the latest, combined with the Temple Source.[83] It is to this source that I now turn.

---

79. For recent surveys of scholarly opinion on the nature of Ezra's law, see U. Kellermann, "Erwägungen zum Esragesetz," *ZAW* 80 (1968):373–85, and C. Houtman, "Ezra and the Law: Observations on the Supposed Relation Between Ezra and the Pentateuch," *OS* 21 (1981): 91–115.

80. Cf. e.g., 2 Baruch 4:5 and 59:4.

81. For helpful comparative comments on the wood-offering, see M. Delcor, "Réflexions sur la fête de Xylophorie dans le Rouleau du Temple et les textes parallèles," *RQ* 12 (1985–87): 561–70.

82. See e.g., the most recent full scale commentary on the books by H. G. M. Williamson, *Ezra, Nehemiah*, Word Biblical Commentary no. 16 (Waco: Word Books, 1985), pp. xxxv–xxxvi.

83. It is possible, of course, that a form of D circulated even earlier than the date I am suggesting. But if so, it would not be the form attested by the 43.366 fragments.

3

THE TEMPLE SOURCE

Introduction

The "Temple Source" is that source of the TS which, baldly characterized, comprises its instructions for the building of a Cyclopean temple. Having first considered precisely which portions of the scroll to assign to this source, I take up the matter of the relationship between it and the Qumranic work known as the New Jerusalem text (NJ). If they are indeed related, as I am persuaded, then fresh light may be shed on the larger complex of traditions ancestral to the temple description. Such a backdrop may also help to bring into clearer focus the question of the independent circulation of the Temple Source. Here, too, I discuss the nature of another relationship, that between the TS and the book of Jubilees. Most scholars agree that the two have important linking elements, but no consensus has yet emerged to guide this agreement into more precise channels. The problem is more sharply defined in the context of the Temple Source than elsewhere in the scroll, for it is here, if anywhere, that evidence for literary filiation probably resides. It is therefore appropriate to investigate the existence and direction of such dependence in the present chapter. Furthermore, by defining the relationship between the Temple Source and Jubilees it may be possible to get a handle on at least the relative dating of the source.

The Character and Content of the Temple Source

Wilson and Wills assign to their "Temple and Courts" source TS 2:1–13:8 and 30:3–47:18.[1] This demarcation is, however, only very roughly correct, because of the effects of two factors which they neglected to consider. They apparently did not contemplate the possibility of either large-scale interpolation or of redactional composition (except for the meagre passages they assigned to that shadowy figure). Both possibilities have to be reckoned with. In fact, as I show in chapter 5, the Temple Source has frequently been interpolated with legal materials. Also, portions of their source are probably spurious—redactional compositions detectable with form criticism.

In order to establish the formal structures which the Temple Source uses, it is necessary to begin with portions which are sufficiently well preserved to permit meaningful analysis: those in columns 31 and following. Only later can one return to the opening columns of the scroll.

---

1. Wilson and Wills, "Literary Sources," pp. 277–78.

TS 31:5–7a is the first well-preserved text of the necessary length. It is divisible into four portions according to function:

1. And you shall make the circular stairway

ועשיתה את מסבה[2]

2. north of the sanctuary,

צפון להיכל

3. a square structure twenty cubits from corner to corner, for each of its four corners,

מרובע מפנה אל פנה עשרים באמה לעומת ארבע פנותיו

4. and seven cubits distant from the sanctuary wall to the northwest.

ורחוק מקיר ההיכל שבע אמות במערב צפונו

The form here consists of four elements:

1. Command to build a new structure, beginning with ועשיתה[3]
2. Specification of the structure's location
3. Dimensions of the structure
4. Additional specifications

Elsewhere one finds that when the text does not concern a new structure, but only a portion of one already partially described, element 2 is often absent. The text then skips from point 1 to point 3, as for example at 30:7b–10a.[4] But since this is not a meaningful distinction from a form critical perspective, it is convenient to call both the full form and the apocopated form "form 1."

At 31:12 another form appears. The text reads ושערים עשו לה מהמזרח ומהצפון ... ורוחב השערים, "and they shall make gates for it from the north and from the east ... and the width of the gates..." Here the instructions begin with a substantive, not the verb. As with form 1, the location and dimensions follow. In this form, which may be called "form 2," the verb is either an imperfect or imperative form of the verb עשה.

An analysis of the entire scroll shows that form 1 functions to introduce new structures, while form 2 serves for portions of structures already introduced. The following lists contain all the examples of both forms. As they show, form 1 is by far predominant.

---

2. Written without the definite article. This writing may, of course, be a scribal error; but is it possible that it may reflect a spoken Hebrew akin to that written in the Murabbaʿat letters? There occur phrases such as 43:5, שאני נתן ה כבלים. The last two words were evidently pronounced "ta-kevalim," with syncopation of the definite article. See *DJD* II, esp. items 42–46.

3. Rarely, as we shall see, does the command begin with a plural verb—cf. 33:8 in the list which follows below.

4. ועשיתה רוחב קירו ארבע אמות [ ] כהיכל ממקצוע אל מקצוע שתים עשר]ה באמה[. ועמוד בתוך באמצעו מרובע רוחבו ארבע אמות לכול רוחותיו "You shall make the thickness of its wall four cubits ... like the sanctuary, from corner to corner twelve cubits. And (there shall be) a pillar in it, located at its center, square in form, measuring four cubits in every direction."

Form 1

1. 30:3–4   And you shall make ... for the stairs of a circular stairway ... (ועשיתה ... למעלות מסבה)
2. 30:5–7a   And you shall make the circular stairway ... (ועשיתה את המסבה)
3. 30:7b–10   And you shall make ... its wall ... (ועשיתה ... קירו)
4. 31:10–12a   And you shall make a house for the basin ... (ועשיתה בית לכיור)
5. 32:8–12a   And you shall make in the wall of the house ... cabinets ... (ועשיתה בקיר הבית ... בתים)
6. 32:12b–15   And you shall make an aqueduct ... (ועשיתה תעלה)
7. 33:8–15(?)   And you (m.pl.) shall make a house ... (ועשיתמה בית)
8. 34:15–(?)   And you shall make chains ... (ועשיתה שלשלות)
9. 35:10–(?)   And you shall make a place ... (ועשיתה מקום ... עמודים)
10. 37:8–11   And you shall make ... a dining hall ... (ועשיתה ... בית מושבות)
11. 37:13–14(?)   And in the four corners ... you made [*sic*] ... stoves (ובארבעת מקצועות ... עשיתה⁵ ... לכירים)
12. 38:2–(?)   And you (m.pl.) shall make ... (uncertain ... ועשיתמה)
13. 38:12–15   And you shall make a second court ... (ועשיתה חצר שנית)
14. 40:5–9   And you shall make a third court ... (ועשיתה חצר שלישית)
15. 46:5–6   And you shall make a terrace ... (ועשיתה רובד)
16. 46:9   And you shall make a fosse ... (ועשיתה חיל)
17. 46:13–16   And you shall make a latrine for them ... (ועשיתה להמה מקום יד)
18. 46:16–(?)   And you shall make three places ... (ועשיתה שלושה מקומות)
19. 5:13–(?)   And you shall make a stoa ... (ועשית[ה] פרור)
20. 7:13–(?)   And you shall make a gold curtain ... (ועש[י]תה פרוכת זהב)
21. 8:6–(?)   And you shall make ... (ועשית[ה)
22. 10:9–(?)   And you (m.pl.) shall make above the gate ... (ועשי[תמה מעל השער)
23. 12:15–(?)   And you shall make ... (ועשיתה ע ...)

Form 2

1. 31:6–9   And in the upper story of this house you shall make a gate ... (ובעלית הבית הזה תעשה שער)
2. 31:12   And gates you (m.pl.) must make ... (ושערים עשו)
3. 42:4–5   And between gates you shall make eighteen compartments ... (ובין שער לשער [תעשה שמונה עשרה נשכה)
4. 42:7–9   And a staircase you shall make ... (ובית מעלות תעשה)
5. 42:10–11   And on the roof of the third you shall make pillars ... (ועל גג השלישית תעשה עמודים)
6. 46:7   Steps you shall make ... (מעלה תעשה)
7. 3:8   All its implements they shall make ... (כול כליו יעשו)
8. 12:11–12   You shall make all its rows ... ([...] ת[עשה כול שורותיו)
9. 12:13–(?)   You shall make for it ([...] תע[שה לו ...])
10. 13:2–(?)   You shall make ... (תעשה [ )

The regularity of these forms renders it very unlikely that 48:11–17 belonged originally to the Temple Source. Although those lines do bear a superficial resemblance to 46:16–18, they do not conform to either form 1 or form 2. Therefore I suspect that this portion is a redactional composition.[6]

5. This seems to be a "mixed form," with elements of forms 1 and 2. Note that, as it stands, the command or statement is in the wrong tense, since it is unconverted.

6. See chapters 5 and 6 for further discussion.

I assign the following passages of the TS to the Temple Source: 3:1–13:8;[7] 30:3–31:9a;[8] 31:10–34:12a;[9] 34:15–35:9a;[10] 35:10–39:5a;[11] 39:11b–40:5;[12] 40:7–43:12a;[13] 44:1–45:7a;[14] 46:1–11a;[15] and 46:13–47:2.[16] The use of periphrastic tenses characterizes this source as stylistically distinct from the other sources of the scroll.[17] Unlike the D source, for example, it consists almost entirely of free composition (see the *Appendix*). Important conceptual differences also mark the Temple Source off from the other portions of the TS.[18] In the present form of the TS it is impossible to know what divine referent, if any, may have originally appeared in this source. All the divine names now found in it appear either in interpolations from legal sources or in redactional compositions.[19] Also, note the discussion in chapter 2 concerning the evidence from 43.366 fragment 2 for a form of this source which was somewhat longer than what we have in the TS. The Temple Source as we have it is truncated.

The Temple Source and the New Jerusalem Text

"Now that the Temple Scroll has been published, it is clear that it contains no clues to the obscurities of the DNJ (Description of the New Jerusalem) for it is concerned with contingent, but not identical, subjects."[20] So concluded Licht in his recent study of the NJ. But it seems to me that important details may have escaped Licht's attention, and that the texts do sometimes describe the same subjects. In fact, each can aid the understanding of the other. I undertake

7. For col. 2, see chapter 2.

8. On 31:9b, see chapter 6, table 8.

9. On 34:12b–14, see chapter 5.

10. For 35:9b, see chapter 6, table 8.

11. As discussed in chapter 2, 39:5b–11a is almost certainly an interpolation. For further evidence and discussion, see chapter 5 and chapter 6, table 7.

12. On 40:6, see chapter 2 and chapter 6, table 7.

13. On 43:12b–17, see the discussion of the "second tithe," below, and chapter 6, table 7.

14. Substantial legal interpolations begin at this point; see chapter 5 for details.

15. For 46:11b–12, see chapter 6, table 7.

16. See chapter 6 for the identification of 47:3–18 as a redactional composition.

17. See Wilson and Wills, "Literary Sources," p. 285.

18. For example, the relative importance of the various tribes seems to be slightly different in the Festival Calendar source (columns 23–25) than in the Temple Source. The order of the tribes in the Festival of Wood is not the same as the order of importance in which their gates are arranged in the Temple Source. See Maier, *Temple Scroll*, p. 114 for a graphic comparison. Another conceptual difference attaches to the relationship of the יסוד המזבח to the עזרה in the Temple Source as compared with the Festival Calendar. Cf. 34:8 for the Temple Source, and 23:13–14 for the Calendar. For an interesting apparent discrepancy with the "King's Law," note that in the Temple Source the king is not included in the list of officials who celebrate the Feast of Tabernacles in the outer court. The explanation for this surprising omission seems to be that the author(s) of the Temple Source did not imagine a king.

19. See notes 5–13, above.

20. J. Licht, "An Ideal Town Plan from Qumran—The Description of the New Jerusalem," *IEJ* 29 (1979): 46.

here to show that the NJ reflects an ideological program fundamentally identical with that of the Temple Source. If this contention is correct, it has important implications for the purpose of the TS; it gives new insight into the redactor's ideology. The fact that the Temple Source is written in Hebrew, while the NJ is in Aramaic, may lead down other interesting if twisting pathways.

Description of the New Jerusalem Text

Qumran caves 1, 2, 4, 5, and 11 contained at least six exemplars of the NJ. Publication of those from caves 1, 2, and 5 is now complete, but only preliminary descriptions and partial publications of the other materials have appeared.[21] According to Milik, the work's beginning is preserved in col. I of a 4Q manuscript,[22] where an angel, equipped with a seven-cubit cane, leads the author-seer to the city wall and begins to measure it. As in the Temple Source, measurements begin at the northeastern corner and move clockwise.[23] At the end of that 4Q MS's first column is a line which immediately precedes the first line of 5Q15 i, at which point the seer enters the city. Thus it would appear that the vision moves from the outside in, as in Ezekiel 40–41, and unlike the Temple Source, which has the opposite direction of movement.[24]

21. Milik edited the fragments from cave 1 as 1Q32 in *DJD* I, pp. 134–35. Baillet published those from cave 2 in *DJD* III, pp. 84–89, as 2Q24. His preliminary publication of these fragments has a much more extensive discussion of various points of interpretation than the *editio princeps,* and therefore remains important. See M. Baillet, "Fragments araméens de Qumran 2: description de la Jérusalem nouvelle," *RB* 62 (1955): 222–45. J. Starcky has provided an overview of the contents of fragments from one 4Q MS, along with a photograph of col. II of the copy, in "Jérusalem et les manuscrits de la Mer Mort," *MB* 1 (1977): 38–40. Cf. the preliminary descriptions in P. Benoit, et al., "Le travail d'édition des fragments manuscrits de Qumrân," *RB* 63 (1956): 66 and idem, "Editing the Manuscript Fragments from Qumran," *BA* 19 (1956): 94. Milik has also utilized these 4Q fragments for his edition of the cave 5 fragments in *DJD* III, pp. 184–93. He provides different readings from the cave 4 MS, where it overlaps his materials. Cave 11 contained a complete scroll of the NJ, but it was petrified and it proved impossible to open it. 26 fragments were salvaged from a protuberance which was not petrified. Jongeling has published two in "Publication provisoire d'un fragment provenant de la grotte 11 de Qumran (11Q Jér Nouv ar)," *JSJ* 1 (1970): 58–64, and "Note additionelle," *JSJ* 1 (1970): 185–86. For his description of the petrified scroll and what he could glean from the unconnected fragments, see J. van der Ploeg, "Les manuscrits de la grotte 11 de Qumrân," *RQ* 12 (1985–87): 14. A second 4Q MS, apparently quite fragmentary, is a part of Strugnell's allotment—see Jongeling, "Note additionelle," p. 185. Of great importance for the study of the NJ fragments, particularly the cave 5 fragments, is J. Greenfield's review article, "The Small Caves of Qumran," *JAOS* 89 (1969): 130 and 132–35. Greenfield offers corrections to some of Milik's lexicographic suggestions. It is worth noting that J. Fitzmyer and D. Harrington have included most published fragments of the NJ in their handy collection, *A Manual of Palestinian Aramaic Texts (Second Century B.C.- Second Century A.D.),* Biblica et Orientalia 34 (Rome: Biblical Institute Press, 1978), pp. 46–64.

22. Milik, *DJD* III, p. 185.

23. Starcky, "Jérusalem," p. 39.

24. This is not a point of programmatic difference, but is attributable to the biblical texts which served as models for the two texts. The Temple Source takes as its model the description of the building of the tabernacle in Exod 25–40. The NJ follows the model of Ezekiel's vision in Ezek 40–48.

If, as seems reasonable, it is correct to assume that the direction of movement is essentially constant in the NJ, it is possible to arrange the larger fragments of the various known MSS in an order approximately as they would have occurred in the intact work. This arrangement must be tentative, of course, in view of the unpublished materials. Alongside the notation of order, I suggest below a possible relationship between the fragments and the spatial concepts of the Temple Source.

1. 4Q col. i—outside the Temple City
2. 4Q col. ii–iii/ 5Q15 i—second column of the text, within the Temple City (2Q24 i = 5Q15 i 01–2)
3. 4Q col. iv–v/ 5Q15 ii–iii—within the Temple City; (the reconstruction of 5Q15 ii is quite uncertain)
4. 1Q32 xiv–xvi (with the other 1Q fragments?)—in the inner court
5. 2Q24 iii—the table of incense, within the inner court
6. 2Q24 iv—the ritual of the shewbread, in the inner court (11QNJ 1–7 = 2Q24 iv 8–15)
7. 2Q24 v–viii—the altar and its sanctum; the dimensions of the inner court(?)

This listing implies a considerable lacuna between 5Q15 ii–iii and the fragments of numbers 4–7 in the list. Here presumably would have been found many details of the Temple City and a description of the outer portions of the temple complex, perhaps including the temple itself. Such a suggestion is not mere supposition; Jongeling states that many of the 11Q fragments apparently detail the measurements of the temple and the altar.[25]

The argument that the NJ and the Temple Source are programmatically related rests on several considerations. First, the two works reflect in their measurements an identical ideology of numbers. Second, they describe in several places similar, perhaps identical, structures and rituals. Third, the two have certain general phenomena in common. Each of these points is discussed in turn below.

Connections Between the Temple Source and the New Jerusalem Text

Ideology of Measurements

The easiest way to compare the numerical ideology of the Temple Source and the NJ is to list the major structures of each with their measurements. Accordingly I list them below in the order in which they occur in the texts, with their measurements in cubits. Asterisks denote those measurements divisible by seven, for reasons which will become clear below.

---

25. Jongeling, "Publication provisoire," p. 59.

The Temple Source

I. Temple and Inner Court

    A. Terrace around temple walls(?): 4 or 14* wide

    B. The vestibule: 20 x 10(?) x 60

        1. Vestibule gate(?): width 12 height 21*

    C. Holy of holies(?): 20 x 20

    D. Upper chamber of temple(?)

        1. Chamber itself(?): 28* x 28*

        2. Another structure: 4 thick

        3. Entablature(?): 10 high

        4. Gates(?): 21(?)* x 12

    E. Pillars

        1. Capitals(?): 10 (?) high

    F. Staircase tower north-west of temple: 20 x 20

        1. Distance from temple: 7*

        2. Wall: 40(?) x 4

        3. Interior measurement angle to angle: 12

        4. Central pillar: 4 x 4

        5. Bridge from tower to temple: 7* (implied)

    G. House of the laver: 21* x 21*

        1. Distance from altar: 50

        2. Walls: 20 x 3

        3. Gates: 7* x 4

        4. Another structure: 3 (high? wide?)

        5. Niches in walls: 1 deep; distance from ground 4

    H. House of sacrificial utensils: 21* x 21*

        1. Distance from house of laver: 7*

        2. Walls: 20 x 3

        3. Niches: 2 x 4

    I. Slaughterhouse: 12 pillars

    J. Dimensions of inner court

        1. Corner of court to corner of gate: 120

        2. Gate: 40 in every direction(?)

        3. Wall: 45 x 7*

    4. Side rooms, angle to angle: 26

    5. Gates: 28* x 14*

    6. Ceiling structure of gates: 14* high

II. Middle Court

    A. Distance of wall from wall of inner court: 100

    B. Walls

        1. Length: 480

        2. Height: 28*

        3. Thickness: 7*

    C. Distance between gates: 99

    D. Width of gates: 28*

III. Outer Court

    A. Distance of wall from wall of middle court: 560*

    B. Walls

        1. Length: 1600

        2. Height: 49*

        3. Thickness: 7*

    C. Gates

        1. Height and width: 70* x 50

        2. Distance between gates: 360

        3. Outward protrusion: 7*

        4. Inward protrusion: 36

        5. Entrance—height and width: 28* x 14*

    D. Rooms in outer wall: 14* x 20 x 14*

        1. Thickness of walls: 2

    E. Chambers in outer wall: 10 x 20 x 14*

        1. Thickness of walls: 2

        2. Width of entrance: 3

    F. Stoas width: 10

    G. Chambers between gates: 28* in number

    H. Booths with columns: 8 high

IV. Structures outside the Outer Court

    A. Terrace: 14* wide

        1. Steps: 12 in number

    B. Fosse: 100 wide

The New Jerusalem Text

I. The Insulae

    A. Measurements: 357* x 357*

    B. Open area: 21* wide

    C. Surrounding streets: 48* wide

    D. "Great" streets

        1. East-west: 2 streets: 70* wide; 1 street north of temple 126* wide

        2. North-south: 2 streets: 67 wide; middle street 92 wide

    E. Doors in small gates

        1. 80 in number

        2. 14* wide

    F. Doors on gates of precious stone: 7* wide

    G. Another structure (function lost)

        1. 12 in number

        2. Gates: 21* wide

        3. Doors of gates: 10.5 wide

        4. Stairway towers flanking gates: 35* x 35*

        5. Width of stairs: 5

II. Gate to an Insula[26]

    A. Width: 14*

    B. Vestibule

        1. Width: 14*

        2. Lintel: 1

        3. Interior measurements:[27] 13(?) x 10

    C. Inner gate

        1. Width: 4

        2. Height: 7*

        3. Entrance vestibule: 7* x 14* x 14*

    D. Gate to insula (interior of A and B)

        1. Width: 14*

        2. Vestibule

            a. Width: 14*

26. The interrelationship of these structures involved with the gate is difficult to visualize. I follow the solution of Licht, "Town Plan," pp. 54–58.

27. Milik, *DJD* III, p. 192, says that this reading is uncertain in the 4Q MS. Consequently, he has taken this measurement from Ezek 40:11. But the relationship of the NJ with Ezek is not sufficiently direct to warrant such borrowing. In light of the other measurements in the text, and the fact that the NJ freely changes the Ezekielian schema for its own ends, the length of 13 is particularly suspect.

       b. Lintel: 1

       c. Interior measurements:[28] 13 x 10

    E. Interior staircase: 14* x 14*

       1. Central pillar: 6 x 6

       2. Width of stairs: 4

III. The Houses

    A. Number

       1. In one direction to corner: 8

       2. From corner to other gate: 7*

    B. Dimensions: 14* x 21* x 14*

    C. Chambers attached to houses

       1. Height: 14*

       2. Gates in middle: 14* wide

       3. Interior of chambers (= "middle" of houses)

          a. Length: 4

          b. Height: 7*

    D. Houses for eating (?)

       1. Hall: 19 x 14*

       2. Couches

          a. Number: 22

          b. Windows above couches: number: 11; dimensions: 4(?) x 2

    E. Platforms: 12 x 19

    F. Another structure (function lost): 14* x 10

This listing makes it clear that the number seven was of "prime" importance in the plans of the Temple Source and the NJ. The numbers three and four, which add to seven and multiply to twelve (another significant number), are factors of most of the dimensions which are not divisible by seven. This commonality seems to be programmatic. It takes on additional significance in view of the fact that the vision of the new temple and city of Ezek 40–48 (a general inspiration for both texts) does not place much stress on the number seven. In the biblical description the programmatic number is 25.[29] That the same numerical system underlies both the Temple Source and the NJ argues for a close relationship between them.

---

28. See footnote 27.

29. W. Zimmerli, *Ezekiel* 2 vols. (Philadelphia: Fortress Press, 1979–83), 2:344, 358–59, 362, and 399. In Zimmerli's opinion, those parts of the temple description which follow the basic "guidance vision," and which do not fit a 25–50 scheme, are interpolations. For the vision of Ezekiel as a general inspiration for the Temple Source, see Yadin, I, pp. 190–92.

Description of Identical Structures and Rituals

The New Jerusalem Text and Temple Scroll 37:4

In at least three instances, the Temple Source and the NJ describe either identical structures or aspects of identical rituals peculiar to these two texts. The first of these involves 2Q24 viii. This fragment of the NJ text preserves portions of eight lines. Though they are lacunose, it is possible to gain a general impression of their contents. The seer has just been shown the altar of burnt offerings, "on which they shall continue making atonement" (line 5). Then the *angelus interpres* directs his attention elsewhere:

7. [ ] the courtyard. And he showed me another [ ] outside [ ]	] אוחרי בר מן [	עזרתא [ו]אחזינ[י] [ ] 7.
8. [ ] one hundred and ten / twenty[ ]	[מאה ועשר] [	] 8.

In the context, it is virtually certain that עזרתא should be restored in the lacuna before אוחרי, as Baillet has noted.[30] Thus the seer is looking from the עזרתא, "courtyard," of the altar and sees another outside (בר מן) of the one in which he stands. Line 8 is almost completely lost, but a number is legible—probably either 110 or 120 (מאה ועשר[ין]).[31] This number must be a measurement in connection with the other court or enclosure which the seer is being shown. It is not unlikely that this description is connected with the inner court of the Temple Source.

According to TS 37:4, an altar enclosure (עזרת המזבח) was a distinct element of the architecture of the inner court. It formed a tighter "holy area" around the altar; it probably also surrounded the entire sanctuary, laver, and inner stoa.[32] If these two text portions do indeed correlate, then the seer is looking out from what the Temple Source calls the altar enclosure to the corner of the inner court's wall. As the Temple Source describes it, this court measured 120 cubits from one corner of the courtyard to the corner of its gate.[33] The TS calls this court החצר הפנימית, but according to ordinary usage it would be עזרתא in Aramaic, just as 2Q24 has it.[34] Based on terminology and the identical measurement of 120 cubits, 2Q24 viii may well be describing the inner court of the Temple Source.

---

30. Baillet, *DJD* III, p. 89. Note that עזרתא is feminine and that אוחרי is the feminine form of the adjective אוחרן, "other, another."

31. Theoretically one could argue for a number between 121 and 129, but ordinarily then we would not expect the *waw* preceding the number "twenty."

32. TS 35:8–9 stipulates that this area—otherwise referred to only obliquely in the extant portions of the scroll—is to be sanctified and regarded as "holy of holies" forever. On the matter of an enclosure distinct from and within the inner court, see Yadin I, pp. 205–6; II, pp. 149–50.

33. TS 36:4, 12–13.

34. Although חצרא did exist in postbiblical Palestinian Aramaic, it was not used for the temple courts. Rather, it was applied to smaller courtyards, usually private property. See Jastrow, s. v. חצרא and עזרתא.

The New Jerusalem Text and Temple Scroll 38

Another possible correlation between the Temple Source and the NJ involves 2Q24 iv 7–16, 11QNJ 1–7, and several heretofore problematic passages in the Temple Source. The easiest way to compare these texts is to collate the two parallel NJ passages first. This process leads naturally to the relevant TS portions. I give first the texts as read by their respective editors.

11QNJ 1–7		2Q24 iv 7–16	
כועל יום שביעי קודם אל דכר]ן	.1]	סדרין על פתח]ורא	7.
לבראַ מן היכלא לימין מערב]ה [	.2]	תרי סדרי לח]מא	8.
ל]]ג לתמנין ארבעה כהנין ש]	.3]	לחמא ויסבון לחמ]א	9.
מן כול שבעת פלוגת פתורי]א [	.3a]	מערבה ויתפלג]ון	10.
בה]ון וארבעת עשר כה]נין	.4]	וחזית עד די פל]יגה לחמא	11.
תרתי לחמ]א די הות לבונתא [עליהין	.5]	רושמתא כ] [ע]	12.
י]היבת לכהנא [רבא	.6]	שביא די בהון וארבעת עשר כה]נין	13.
ל ... פנבד] [	.7]	כהניא תרתי לחמא די הו]ת	14.
		הוית עד חדא מן תרתי לחמא יהיבת [ל]כ]הנא רבא	15.
		עמה ואחריתא] י]היבת לתנינה די קאם פנבד	16.

On the basis of triangulation between overlapping portions of Starcky's 4Q MS, 5Q15 and 2Q24 fragment i, it is possible to ascertain that 2Q24 was a MS with columns of 25–27 lines and 55–60 characters and spaces per line.[35] Because 2Q24 iv and 11QNJ overlap, one can also determine that the 11Q MS had lines of 60–65 spaces and characters. Collation yields the combined text which follows. 2Q24 is taken as the base text, inserting portions of 11QNJ with due regard for spacing and line-length. Several words are also restored according to the context.

סדרין על פתורא] דכיא קדם אל	7.	[
תרי סדרי לח]מא 12–15 spaces כו]ל יום שביעי קודם אל דכר]נא וינטלון[36]	8.	
לחמא ויסבון לחמ]א 12–17 spaces וינפקון] לברא מן היכלא לימין	9.	
מערבה ויתפלג]ון Vacat?	10.	[
וחזית עד די פל]י.[ג37].] לתמנין וארבעה כהנין ש] 16–21 spaces [	11.	

35. It is necessary to assume that the MS was reasonably consistent in these matters of presentation, but this is reasonable in light of table 3 in chapter 2. I plan to publish elsewhere in more detail on the method of triangulation involved with the reasoning here.

36. In this dialect of Aramaic there was apparently intermittent dissimilation of gemination by nasalization in פ"ן verbs. The Genesis Apocryphon attests forms both with and without assimilated nun. See J. Fitzmyer, *The Genesis Apocryphon of Qumran Cave I: A Commentary* (Rome: Biblical Institute Press, 1971), p. 212. It seems on the basis of what has been published that the dialect of the NJ fragments is essentially that of the Genesis Apocryphon, but until the publication of the 4Q MSS it is impossible to be certain of the degree of identity.

37. The ל and the ג are certain readings; the פ is probable. The form remains problematic because there is room for more than one letter in the lacuna.

.12 ריש ביתא[^38] מן כול שבעה פלוגת פתורי[א   22–27 spaces]

.13 שביא די בהון וארבעת עשר כה[נין   25–30 spaces]

.14 כהניא   תרתי לחמא די הות לבונתא [עליהין   15–18 spaces   וחזה]

.15 הוית עד חדא מן תרתי לחמא יהיבת [ל]כ[הנא רבא   14–19 spaces]

.16 עמה   ואחריתא [י]היבת לתנינה די קאם פנבד]   [

Translation

(7) pure rows upon the table before God ... (8) two rows of bread[   ] every seventh day as a memorial before God. And they shall take up (9) the bread and carry the bread[   ] and they will exit the sanctuary to the south (10) -west, and they will divide it. [   ] (11) And I watched until it was divided among eighty-four priests s[   ] (12) a priestly head from each of the seven divisions[^39] of the tables [   ] (13) the elders who were among them, and fourteen priests [   ] (14) the priests. The two (loaves) of bread[^40] upon which was frankincense [And I was] (15) watching until one of the two loaves of bread was given to the hi[gh priest   ] (16) with him. And another was given to his assistant who was standing apart (?) ...

It might seem from line 7 that the text concerns the Bread of the Presence, which consisted of two loaves. But line 4 implies more than two loaves, and the amount of leaven mentioned in 2Q24 iv, eight seah, would more than suffice for twelve loaves.

Noting these things, Baillet suggested that his text (2Q24) dealt with a meal combining the two loaves of Pentecost with the twelve of the the shewbread.[^41] Baumgarten, however, has rightly called this combination implausible. He argues instead that the text refers only to the removal of the old shewbread, with the simultaneous placement of two rows of new bread. The loaves of Pentecost are not in view. Since rabbinic sources clearly state that the incoming and outgoing courses of priests would divide the old bread among them, Baumgarten argues

---

38. Baillet's reading of רושמתא, "mark," makes no sense in the context restored by this collation. In fact, his reading is materially uncertain as well. My suggestion is equally possible based on the traces, and makes sense in the context. For בית meaning "priestly division" see e.g., Taʿanit 2:6. Note also that the term אב ראש בית is that which Tannaitic texts use to mean the "director of the daily course."

39. This portion of line 3 is very difficult. The sense seems to require that one construe פלוגה, "(priestly) division," as masculine, since it apparently agrees with שבעת. Jastrow lists the noun as feminine only. This difficulty has led Jongeling, "Publication provisoire," pp. 60 and 62, to translate שבעת by "se rassasia." Jongeling was not working with a collated text, and one might argue that his suggestion was plausible for 11QNJ alone, although even that seems difficult to me. With the collation, however, his translation certainly makes no sense. This is probably a case of *constructio ad sensum*.

40. Since the noun לחמא is nearly always masculine, this is probably an elliptic expression with the noun גריצתא, "bread, cake," suppressed. This expression would then be equivalent to the Tannaitic Hebrew expression for the shewbread, שתי הלחם, with ככרות falling out by ellipsis. See GKC §134n. Although much less likely in my view, it is not beyond the pale that לחמא itself was construed here as feminine. See S. Gevirtz, "Asher in the Blessing of Jacob," *VT* 37 (1987): 161–63.

41. Baillet, "Fragments araméens," pp. 233–34.

[^38]:
[^39]:
[^40]:
[^41]:

that the text refers to this division.[42] This suggestion makes good sense. Further, several puzzling Temple Source passages apparently related to the collated NJ description become much clearer if he is correct.

In this connection, lines 9–10 of the collation are important. Jongeling struggled with the phrase in line 2 of that text, לימין מערב]. Although he never arrived at a clear understanding of it, he did suggest, "one might think of a place located to the southwest of the sanctuary."[43] With the addition of the *heh locale* supplied by the collation with 2Q24, this option is unquestionably correct.

Armed with this understanding one can turn to TS 38. Although this column is poorly preserved, enough remains to determine that it discusses the places in the inner court where the priests are to eat their portions. They are to eat different types of offerings in different parts of the court. Our concern focuses on lines 6–9:[44]

6. [אוכלים אצל שער המערב
7. [ ] ל כול עץ אשר יבוא ל [ ]
8. [ ] מנחת הקורבנים הבאה]עליה לבונה ול [
9. [ולימ]ין ה]שער הזה [

According to line 6, the text is listing the offerings the priests will eat near the western gate of the court. By line 8 the topic has apparently shifted to another type of offering, that to which frankincense is added. Evidently the priests are to eat this offering, also, near the western gate. Then, in line 9, the description rotates south of that gate, i.e., to the southwest of the sanctuary. What would the priests eat at that location? Taking col. 38 as a whole, it stipulates that offerings of similar types should be enjoyed in the same general area.[45] Since the shewbread involved frankincense, it follows that in the Temple Source schema the priests would eat the bread in the same vicinity as other offerings involving the spice. In other words, line 38:9 probably commanded the consumption of the shewbread "to the south" of the western gate.

This location is precisely that which the collated NJ text indicates for the division—and presumably the consumption—of the bread. The NJ text dovetails perfectly with the Temple Source. The same ideology of "location-consumption" which is explicit in the Temple Source is implicit in the the NJ text.

---

42. J. Baumgarten, review of מגילת המקדש, p. 585.

43. Jongeling, "Publication provisoire," p. 61.

44. Rockefeller 43.366 38*:5 line 4 suggests the restoration מנחת הקורבנים הבאה before עליה in line 8. Yadin, II, pp. 160 and 162, read היאה, but the photograph supports the reading adopted here. It was suggested first by Qimron in "New Readings," p. 165. He has had access to an additional infrared photograph of the column, which he says confirms the *beth* of הבאה. For other new readings and suggested restorations, which I think might be improved by comparison with the NJ text, see Qimron, "Further New Readings," pp. 33–34.

45. According to 38:4, the text groups all the first fruits together, apparently because the priests should eat them in one location. TS 38:10 indicates that all bird offerings are to be eaten in one location—probably at the southern gate.

The New Jerusalem Text and Temple Scroll 45

The collated NJ text raises another question involving the changing of the priestly courses. And again a correspondence between the Temple Source and the Aramaic text apparently exists. The question concerns the relationship between the eighty-four priests in NJ 11, and the fourteen priests which line 13 mentions. Since 2Q24 iv 15–16 clearly indicates the presence of the high priest and his assistant (תנינה), it seems probable that the fourteen priests included these two men and twelve others.

Seeking the identity of these twelve men, Baillet suggested that the NJ text may reflect the same concept as 1QM ii 1–2.[46] That text reads:[47]

‎1. ... ואת ראשי הכוהנים יסרוכו אחר כוהן הראש ומשנהו ראשים שנים עשר להיות משרתים
‎2. בתמיד לפני אל וראשי המשמרות ששה ועשרים במשמרוחם ישרתו ...

"And they will arrange the heads of the priests behind the high priest and his assistant. Twelve heads are to serve continually before God, while the heads of the twenty-six priestly divisions will serve (only) with their divisions." According to the most thorough textual analysis to date, these lines of the War Scroll belong to the text's oldest redactional layer.[48] They probably date to a period during and immediately after the Maccabean wars. Line 1 mentions twelve "heads" of the priests, who were to serve in the temple "continually" (בתמיד) according to line 2. In contrast, the "heads of the courses" were to serve "in their courses," i.e., to rotate in and out of service. Thus, like the high priest and his assistant, the twelve heads were permanently in place in the temple, and did not rotate. It is a reasonable conclusion, then, that the fourteen priests of NJ 5 are the fourteen priests who were permanently stationed in the temple. The text treats them as a group because of this commonality. It follows that the eighty-four priests of line 11 include these fourteen and seventy others.[49] This number results from subtraction, but the original text of NJ may have mentioned them explicitly.[50]

Considering that the collated NJ text describes activities involved with the changing of the priestly courses, it is only logical that the seventy priests represent either a course or, more probably, part of a course. The sheer size of the temple complex of the Temple Source, and concomitantly the magnitude of the city which the NJ describes, makes it hard to believe that seventy priests would represent an entire priestly course. A Tannaitic source informs us that it was the custom for the priestly courses to divide up into smaller groups, one for each day of

---

46. Baillet, *DJD* III, p. 87.

47. E. L. Sukenik, אוצר המגילות הגנוזות , plate 17, lines 1–2.

48. P. R. Davies, *1QM, the War Scroll from Qumran* (Rome: Biblical Institute Press, 1977), pp. 58–67 and 123. Davies believes that col. 2 is part of a pre-Qumran composition which the "Qumran sect" subjected to a redaction some two centuries later.

49. The reason for the NJ describing the priests in groups of 14 and 70 may be its septimal ideology.

50. Note the end of line 11 in the collated text, ‎שׁ. Quite possibly, as Jongeling suggested, we should restore this as ‎שׁ בעין. See "Publication provisoire," p. 62.

the week.[51] Probably the seventy priests make up one of these smaller groups, and therefore comprise one-seventh of a course.[52]

TS 45:1–4 can be reconstructed using a fragment (40*:5) from another copy of the TS. As reconstructed, it illuminates the connection between the number seventy and the rotation of the courses. TS 45:1–4 as preserved reads as follows:

[		ומש]	1.
[		שבעים]	2.
[	ה]שני יהיה בא לשמאול]	וכאשר י]	3.
א[	יצא הרישון מימ]י[ן ולוא [יהי]ו מתערבים אלה באלה ובכליה]מה		4.

Clearly lines 3–4 concern the changing of the courses, a topic which continues for several lines afterward. But what of lines 1–2? Yadin understood them as a summary of the allocation of chambers in the outer court, a subject which begins at 44:3.[53] But the identification of 40*:5, which Yadin left unidentified, as a parallel to this portion makes Yadin's view untenable. The fragment reads as follows:

באים [	]	1.
פטכה]	]	2.
יה בא]	]	3.
אלה]	]	4.

The MS to which this fragment belongs, 11TS[b],[54] had lines of sixty to seventy spaces and letters. Since בא and אלה can be read in corresponding places of lines 3 and 4 of the fragment, the next step is to investigate where, in the preserved portions of the TS,[55] these two terms occur in this order, separated by a distance of sixty to seventy spaces. Because a lacuna precedes אלה, one must also consider the possibility that an inseparable preposition or copulative was attached to it; therefore, it is also necessary to investigate באלה, ואלה and the like. The result of such an investigation is that there is only one place in the TS where all the criteria are met: 45:3–4. The יה[of line 3 in the fragment should therefore be restored to read יה]יה. We thus obtain יהיה בא, a phrase which is also preserved in TS 45:3. This unidentified fragment indisputably parallels TS 45:1–4.

---

51. See tTaʿanit 2:2.

52. Four hundred and ninety priests would make up a complete course. A calculation based on this figure, and assuming 24 (or 26) courses, results in a total of 11,760–12,740 priests. This figure is comparable to the figure of 7,600 priests for the Herodian temple which J. Jeremias estimates in *Jerusalem in the Time of Jesus* (Philadelphia: Fortress Press, 1969), pp. 147 and 198–205.

53. Yadin, I, pp. 267–68; II, p. 190.

54. See van der Ploeg, "Les manuscrits," p. 9, and idem, "Une halakha inédite de Qumran," pp. 107–14.

55. It is possible that these two words occurred in a portion of the scroll now destroyed, but the likelihood of their being in the required order and at the required distance from each other is negligible. A study of the lacunae, with a view to determining their probable contents, supports this assertion.

The next step is to combine the text of the fragment with that of TS 45. Keeping in mind that the two MSS had different line-lengths (which are known), it is a simple matter to calculate the relative distances between preserved words. The result is a fuller text which reads as follows (line-lengths follow the fragment):

```
באים [ ca. 15 spaces    ומש] [ ca. 40 spaces                              ] 1.
פטכה] ca. 20 spaces             שבעים [ ca. 30 spaces                      ] 2.
שני יהיה בא] ca. 20 spaces        כאשר י] [ ca. 25 spaces                   ] 3.
לשמאול [ ca. 10 spaces ] יצא הרישון מימין ולוא יהיו מתערבים אלה באלה        4.
```

The appearances of באים in line 1 and of מש]פטכה (?) after שבעים in line 2 make Yadin's restorations impossible. The fact is that all four of these lines, not merely the latter two, deal with the changing of the priestly courses. Consequently, just as in the NJ, the term "seventy" is here associated with the courses. Just as in TS 38, so here too in TS 45 the text correlates with the NJ regarding the courses.

I suggest the following restoration of TS 45:1–4, basing it on the repetitive style evident throughout the Temple Source and on 45:5–7:

```
ומש]מרות יהיו יוצאים ו]באים [          ]                                  1.
כול שבועה ליום השמיני ומספרמה יהיה] שבעים לכול יום ויום כמש]פטכה         2.
כאשר י]בואו המשמרות כן יצאו ה]שני יהיה בא [          ]                    3.
לשמאול [          ובבואו] יצא הרישון מימין ולוא יהיו מתערבים אלה באלה      4.
```

Translation

> (1) [   ] and priestly divisions shall exit and enter (2) every week, on the eighth day. They shall number seventy for every day, according to your law. (3) As the divisions enter, so shall they exit. The second shall enter (4) at the left, and as it enters, the first shall exit to the right. They shall not intermingle.[56]

56. Based on the apparent connection between the Temple Source and NJ as they conceive of the shewbread and the changing courses, it may be possible to clarify a third problematic portion in the TS. TS 8:8–14 clearly deals with the shewbread, but most of the text has been destroyed. The text refers to the "two rows" and the frankincense. Then follow the broken lines 13–14:

עו]לם לדורתם וה] יה ה]ל]ח]ם הזה

או[יבואו א]   [   ]

Yadin suggests in his commentary (II, p. 33) that line 14 may have attempted to go beyond Lev 24:9 to specify exactly where and when to eat the bread. Given the extremely fragmentary remains of the text, his explanation certainly cannot be disproved. Yet, in the light of our analysis of TS 45 and its relationship with NJ, it is intriguing to find the verb יבואו in line 14. It is this same verb, of course, which describes the movement of the incoming priestly course in TS 45. According to NJ, it was at that time that the priests would divide the old bread. It therefore seems that, in preference to Yadin's explanation, one ought to see here a stipulation that the old bread belongs to the priestly courses at the time of their exchange. I therefore tentatively suggest the following restoration of 8:14, basing the wording on TS 45:3–6. According to the photographs which Yadin provides, and a study of the TS MS as a whole, the lacuna at

The New Jerusalem Text and the Named Gates of the Temple Scroll

Thus far in this investigation of the relationship between the Temple Source and NJ, I have pointed out striking examples of agreement on ritual and structures. With a common ideology of numbers, the two texts seem to have identical concepts of the arrangement of the inner court, and also agree on details involving the shewbread and its consumption by the priests. A third example of agreement regarding structures is perhaps the most telling yet. It involves the gates.

In the plan of the Temple Source, each court is surrounded by a wall pierced by gates at specified intervals. For the inner court, there are only four gates, one at each point of the compass. In contrast, for the middle court and the outer court, there are twelve gates. These gates, unlike those of the inner court(?), have names.[57] The names are those of the twelve sons of Jacob. The twelve gates are arranged with those named for Judah and Levi at the two most important locations, on the eastern wall. Because the gates are laid out beginning with the northeast corner and proceeding clockwise, the last gate, named for Asher, is on the north wall at the east corner, on a diagonal from the first gate, named for Simeon. Although the Bible contains numerous lists of the twelve tribes and the twelve sons of Jacob, none is in the order of these gates. Ezekiel's visionary description of a new Jerusalem includes named gates, but the names are not in the order of the Temple Source.

Since the order of gates in the Temple Source bears only an obtuse relationship to that of Ezekiel's gates, and is found nowhere else in Second Temple Jewish literature, it is very significant that the 4Q MS of the NJ contains twelve named gates in exactly the same order (see figure 1).[58] True, in the surviving portions of the NJ these gates are not part of the temple complex; they are the gates of the city wall. But there can be little doubt that the lost NJ portions which described the temple courts would have used the same names for the gates of those walls. In the concept of the Temple Source, the temple is surrounded by concentric

---

the beginning of line 14 is about 35 spaces long. I venture שולחנות because 11QNJ 3a indicates a multiplicity of tables for the bread, as in Chron. יביאו begins the stipulations for the bread's removal—cf. NJ 2 ויסבון לחמא. Presumably the lines following, now lost, briefly detailed the process of dividing the bread.

14. [לכוהני המשמרות ליום השמיני כאשר] יבואו א[ל השולחנות יבי]או

(14)   "for the priests of the divisions on the eighth day. When they come to the

tables, they shall bring..."

57. The portions of the Temple Source which gave the names of the four gates to the inner court are lost. Yadin thinks that they were simply called by the four points of the compass (II, pp. 203–4), while other scholars have suggested that they were named according to the quadripartite division of the Levites: the sons of Aaron, Merari, Kohath and Gershon. 2Q24 iii 2, however, which apparently belongs in the inner court in the Temple Source's schema, may mention a Sapphire Gate. The text is broken, but reads (with the editor's restoration) תרע ספי[ר א]ל. Cf. Is 54:11. In light of the other commonalities between the NJ and the Temple Source, this named gate may be suggestive.

58. According to Starcky's description, col. i describes the gate of Simeon at the northeast, then proceeds clockwise through Levi, Judah, Joseph, Benjamin, Reuben, Issachar, Zebulon and Gad. Col. ii includes the northern wall with the gates of Dan, Naphtali, and Asher. A distance of either 25 or 35 rês separates the gates from one another and the corners of the wall. See Starcky, "Jérusalem," p. 39.

"squares" of holiness. Each court, with its wall, represents one square. Apparently, the city wall of the NJ would form a fourth holiness "barrier."

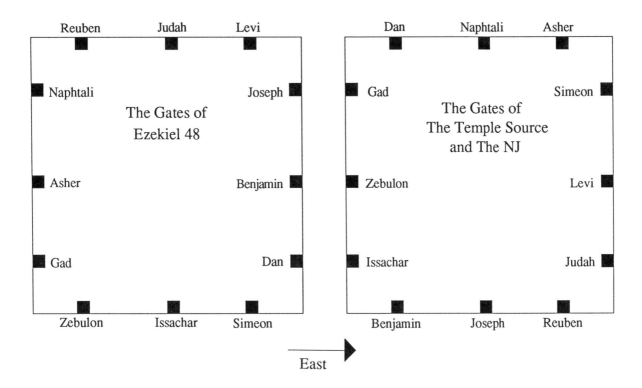

Figure 1. A Comparison Between the Gates of the Temple Source and the Gates of Ezekiel 48.

In addition to the points of contact I have noted, Yadin has pointed out additional important links between the NJ and the TS.[59]

General Phenomena in Common Between the Two Texts

A very suggestive connection between the Temple Source and the NJ is in the way they give their measurements. Naturally, when such texts give architectural instructions, they must make use of the words "length" and "width." In biblical instructions of this sort these terms are used according to a regular pattern in which אֹרֶךְ almost always precedes רֹחַב.[60] This

59. Yadin was not concerned to argue for a relationship between the TS and the NJ, but he has mentioned parallels. 1Q32 xiv–xvi is extremely fragmentary, but it includes the words "wheel(s)" and "pillars." Yadin noted that the collocation of the terms is reminiscent of TS 35 and the slaughterhouse of the inner court. See Yadin, I, p. 235. Second, he noticed that the stairhouses near the gates of the outer court in the TS are similar to a structure in the gate description of the NJ (II, p. 178). Related to this point, he emphasized that the staircase tower of TS 30–31 has the same exterior dimensions as the staircase tower of 5Q15 ii 2–5 (I, pp. 216–17; II, pp. 132–33). Last, it may be noteworthy that the houses and their gates in 5Q15 ii 6–9 have the same dimensions as the House of the Laver and its gates according to TS 31 (I, p. 220; II, p. 136).

60. The only exceptions are Ezek 45:6, 48:8, and Zech 2:6.

pattern holds true for Ezekiel, the general model for our texts.[61] Thus it is significant and, presumably, meaningful, that in the Temple Source, the order of the biblical pattern is without exception reversed—width, then length.[62] The NJ is about midway between the Bible and the Temple Source in this regard. Of its nine preserved occurrences, all in the 5Q fragments, five follow the width-length pattern[63] and four follow the biblical length-width ordering.[64]

Although it is unclear why this patterning shift occurred, it does seems clear that it characterized the programmatic architectural scheme from which the Temple Source and the NJ derive. It may be that the redactor regularized the Temple Source description; more likely, the Temple Source had already regularized the data. Such a regularization would have smoothed out the inconsistency which the NJ exhibits in its patterning, carrying the tendency to give the width first to its logical conclusion. It is unlikely that the difference from the biblical patterning reflects linguistic undercurrents. This conclusion is borne out by the Mishnah. Of twenty-one instances in the Mishnah where ארך and רחב appear together in measurements, the order is always that of the Bible.[65] Thus evidence both preceding and following the period of our texts indicates that their pattern is anomalous. Accordingly the patterned use of these two terms is further evidence for a relationship between the NJ and the Temple Source.

Another point at which the two texts are noticeably similar is the great number of pillars in both architectural designs. It is true that multiple-pillared buildings were not uncommon in the Hellenistic period. Certainly the fact that both designs make such great use of them may reflect no more than a common cultural heritage. Yet their use of pillars may also be seen as a conscious or unconscious openness to Greek culture. One should be wary of the simplistic assumption that conservative Jewish circles, such as undoubtedly produced these two texts, were adamantly opposed to any and all "Hellenizing" ways. Significant evidence to the contrary is not hard to find.[66] It may be that the use of so many pillars is a programmatic intention which the texts share.

A third general phenomenon uniting these two texts is peculiar linguistic usage. Both prefer the term מרובע (or its Aramaic equivalent, מְרַבַּע), meaning "square," over the biblical equivalent

---

61. Cf. e.g., Ezek 40:30, 36, 42, and 47.

62. TS 4:11–13 (uncertain textually), 5:9–10, 31:7–8, 11–12, 12–13, 33:12, 36:5–6, 36:8–9, 38:14–15, 40:9–10, 12–13, 41:14–15, 42:02–03, and 42:05–2.

63. 5Q15 i 12, i 19–ii 1, ii 3, ii 4, and ii 15.

64. 5Q15 i 17, ii 7–8, ii 10–11, and ii 13. The first example, however, is textually doubtful—see footnote 27 above.

65. See Ch. Kassowsky, אוצר לשון המשנה [Concordance of the Language of the Mishnah] (Jerusalem: Massadah, 1956), s.v. ארך and variants.

66. As one example, cf. the Ionian world map which, instead of a Babylonian concept, served as the basis for the map of Jubilees. One might have expected to find Babylonian influence on a conservative writer such as the author of Jubilees, but instead we find him "Hellenized" (or, at least, knowledgeable about Greek geographical literature). See P. Alexander, "Notes on the 'Imago Mundi' of the Book of Jubilees," in *Essays in Honour of Yigael Yadin,* ed. G. Vermes and J. Neusner (Totowa, New Jersey: Allanheld, Osmun & Co. [for the Oxford Centre for Postgraduate Studies], 1983), pp. 197–214.

רבוע.[67] And both also use an unusual phrase for "enclosed windows" in certain structures.[68] Neither term nor phrase appears in the Bible except for Ezek.[69] Obviously not much weight can be put on this peculiar usage, for it might have arisen from the common model or contemporary spoken language. Nevertheless, because both texts depart from Ezekiel's terminology so often, it is at least a little suspicious when both choose not to depart.

Summary of Evidence for the Relationship of the Two Texts

The following arguments support the conclusion that the Temple Source and the NJ text advance the same programmatic position—if from different perspectives and deriving from different biblical models—and that they are therefore related. A comparison of their measurements shows that the number seven and its multiples figure programmatically in both texts. In both texts the numbers three, four, and twelve also prove significant. This scheme is sharply distinct from the programmatic use of numbers in Ezek, where the number twenty-five and its multiples are the focus.

The evidence presented here also shows that the Temple Source and the NJ describe similar or identical structures and rituals. It can be shown, admittedly with varying degrees of certainty, that both describe portions of the inner court, perhaps including the slaughterhouse. Both texts include descriptions of very similar staircase towers, with some measurements identical. Both describe aspects of the procedures for changing priestly courses. They agree that the old shewbread is divided among the priests at that time, and agree on where it is to be eaten. Concerning structural communalities, the fact that the texts agree on the order and names of the twelve gates is virtually decisive proof of their interrelatedness all by itself.

Finally, attention is drawn to general phenomena which appear to link these two texts. It is suggestive that the Temple Source and the NJ both break the biblical and Mishnaic pattern for giving length and width. The numerous pillared structures in both plans, and the common use of certain peculiar terms, are likewise suggestive. Taking all the evidence together, the conclusion that the Temple Source and the NJ derive from the same traditions and priestly circles seems inescapable. This conclusion raises a new question: is it possible to determine which text is earlier?

The Question of Priority

For several reasons the priority of the NJ text seems clear.[70] First there is the gigantic size of the temple complex which the Temple Source commands. Although certain details of the plan are foggy, the outer wall of the third court was apparently to be 1,700 cubits long, thus

---

67. See E. Qimron, "למילונה," p. 251.

68. Cf. 5Q15 ii 11 כוין אטימן and TS 33:11 חלונים פנימה אטומים.

69. For the latter phrase see Ezek 40:16, 41:26, and 41:16. A similar phrase occurs in 1 Kngs 6:4. For the former term see Ezek 45:2 and 40:47. Cf. the similar usage of 1 Kngs 7:31.

70. Although I am speaking here in terms of texts, I am not oblivious to the possibility that the traditions and the texts are not necessarily of identical date. In terms of economy of explanation, however, there is no clear evidence that I should be speaking in terms of traditions; what we have are *texts*.

totaling 6,800 cubits around the perimeter.[71] To put this size in perspective, the complex would equal in size the entire Hasmonean city of Jerusalem (although it would require apocalyptic adjustments to the landscape, notably on the western and eastern sides, to build it on the site at all).[72] Why would the author command the building of a temple which is obviously far too large for its intended location?[73]

Of course in general such problems are hardly stumbling blocks for eschatological texts such as the TS, but there is more to it than that, as becomes clear when one studies the NJ text. The city of that text is much larger than any ancient city, and all but the largest modern metropolises. It measures 140 stadia on the east and west, and 100 stadia on the north and south. These measurements result in a total perimeter of nearly 100,000 cubits, or 18.67 miles x 13.33 miles.[74]

Furthermore, it is certain that there was a proportionately huge temple complex in the city of the NJ.[75] According to the 5Q fragments, the city of the NJ was divided into exactly 3,500

71. I follow Maier, *The Temple Scroll,* figure 3. See also his explanation on pp. 63–64.

72. As noted by e.g., L. Schiffman, "Exclusion from the Sanctuary," p. 317.

73. Note the comments of M. Broshi, "The Gigantic Dimensions of the Visionary Temple in the Temple Scroll," *BAR* 13 (1987): 37, "To build the complex described in the Temple Scroll would require solving serious topographical problems. Creating a level space on which to build this gigantic project would require as much work as the building project itself. Leveling the ground would require filling in the Kidron Valley (to raise it about 250 feet) on the east and quarrying rock on the west. This would have meant removal of millions of tons of rock and soil, all by human muscle."

74. Why did the author of the NJ choose this figure for the size? As Milik, *DJD* III, p. 185, points out, the total perimeter of the tᵉrumah or "holy portion" in Ezek is 100,000 cubits, 25,000 to a side. The author apparently took over this measurement, but transformed the square of the biblical text into a rectangle. Why? Milik's explanation is "il etait plus à l'aise dans ses calculs ulterieurs"(*DJD* III, p. 185). But in fact the resulting calculations are not easier, and do not result in round numbers, thus belying Milik's thesis. The actual reason for the change is the ideology of the number seven. With the change, the author was able to retain the biblical mandate for total area and simultaneously make the longer sides divisible by seven (140 ris). Further, by this maneuver the smaller measurements, which depend on the larger, also become factors of seven. The author has accomplished another transformation as well. He has taken Ezekiel's תרומה and made it into his קריתא. In the book of Ezek, the city is separate from the "holy portion." In the NJ, the two are identical. It is as if the author of the NJ wanted to improve on the biblical concept.

75. Scholars disagree about the exact placement of the temple in relation to the city, basically because in Ezek the temple is separated from the city. Thus Milik, *DJD* III, p. 185, sees the temple within the city, on the southern edge of a putative northern quadrant. His entire quadrangular schema depends on the assumption that the author of the NJ has simply taken over the Ezekielian scheme. Based on the extant portions of the text, this is a very questionable assumption. Licht, "Ideal City," p. 48, sees the temple located to the south of the city, outside its confines, just as in Ezek. This is not the place to take up the argument in detail, but I would suspect on the basis of the now palpable relationship with the Temple Source that the temple of the NJ was in the city—either in its center, or north of that point (the latter on the basis of the proportions between the biblical tabernacle and its court). The few data on the question in the extant published text are consistent with either idea. See especially 5Q15 i 3–5, which locates the temple to the south of the "middle" (literally, "third" תליתיא) road. The temple in the Temple Source is at the center of an ever-broadening series of concentric areas of holiness. If the temple complex relates to the NJ plan, then the logic of the Temple Source plan may dictate that in the NJ the temple was also at the center. The problem with simply saying that such was certainly the case is, of course, the fact that the NJ text has

insulae.[76] The size of four of these blocks is 1,680 x 1,680 cubits, almost exactly identical with the 1,700 x 1,700 cubits for the outer wall of the TS temple complex. The difference is easily within the "tolerance" of the NJ text, which often rounds numbers off. It is also possible that some structure, whose description has not survived in the NJ fragments, would make up the difference of twenty cubits.

The Temple Source almost certainly took its temple from the NJ traditions. Within those traditions, the huge size of its temple complex is quite at home, with a size congruent with the mammoth dimensions of every other element of the city plan. It is only when introduced into the new literary setting of the TS that the size is startling and hard to explain.

Besides the difficulty or impossibility of building such a temple on the site of Jerusalem, other aspects of the present TS setting clash with the size of the temple. For example, 46:13–16 requires adherents to build a "place of the hand" (latrine) for the city. It is to be erected to the northwest, at a distance of 3,000 cubits from habitation, invisible to the city's inhabitants. A distance of a mere 3,000 cubits is certainly disproportionately short in the context of such an enormous temple, but it becomes ludicrous in a city nearly twenty miles long. Hence the requirement can only have been added after the shift of the temple from its' original setting in the city of the NJ.

Another example of this lack of proportion occurs in col. 52, where the redactor introduces a law requiring all people at a distance of three days from the temple to have their clean animals slaughtered in Jerusalem as sacrifices, rather than slaughtering the beasts in their own cities. Now in the second century B.C.E. (traveling with a beast for sacrifice and in a caravan for safety), a pilgrim might travel fifteen to twenty miles on an average day.[77] Thus, in three days, he could perhaps cover forty-five to sixty miles. But this distance is only about two to three times the length of the city! In the same column, it is forbidden to slaughter clean but imperfect animals within a zone four miles in every direction from the city. Again, these distances are Lilliputian in the context of the NJ city.

Such distances make little sense in an eschatological city of the magnitude of the NJ, but they make very good sense in real life, in the context of the second century B.C.E. In the Temple Source, and more broadly in the TS, one perceives the beginning of a process of compromise between the ideal of the NJ text and the reality of halakhic requirements based on a

---

changed the biblical city precisely *from* a square into a rectangle. Clearly the matter is complex and will require further study, if indeed it is soluble at all on the basis of the few data at hand.

76. The figure is not actually given, but we can figure it out on the basis of what is. Adding the measurements of the insulae, the "free" areas around each insula, and the roads surrounding each, one arrives at a "block" of 420 x 420 cubits (357 + 42 + 21). Dividing this into the lengths of the sides gives exactly 70 insulae along each long axis and 50 along each short axis. Thus there are a total of 3,500 insulae. Note, incidentally, that these numbers are factors of seven.

77. In the Roman period, when roads were much better than in the presumed time of the TS's composition, it was a three-day journey from Galilee to Jerusalem. See S. Safrai, "The Temple," in *The Jewish People in the First Century. Compendia Rerum Iudaicarum ad Novum Testamentum, Section One, Volume 2* ed. S. Safrai and M. Stern (Philadelphia: Fortress Press, 1976), p. 901. On the slow pace of caravan travel in the period, see Jeremias, *Jerusalem,* p. 60.

somewhat different concept of the eschatological era. The redactor of the TS was probably willing to make such compromises because he really intended to build his temple.[78]

Thus, the Temple Source and the NJ text come from the same priestly or scribal circles. The NJ text (or at least its traditions) is earlier, and the source for the temple complex of the Temple Source.[79] Yet the two texts are written in different languages—the Temple Source in Hebrew, the NJ in Aramaic—a fact which may have interesting implications for the circulation of their common ideology. In order to explore these implications a brief survey of the linguistic situation in Palestine in the period concerned may be helpful.

The Implications of the Language of the New Jerusalem Text

After the return from the Babylonian exile, the people settled in a small area extending from Bethel in the north to Beth Zur in the south, and westward about as far as a line drawn from Emmaus to Azekah.[80] During the exile, Aramaic, the lingua franca of the Near East generally, had become the language of many of the repatriates, and presumably of a percentage of those who had been left behind in the land. Many in both groups were largely ignorant of Hebrew. Consequently, for the entire period of the Second Temple the Jews of Palestine as a group were bilingual and, later, multilingual. The question of how much Hebrew was actually spoken, where, and by whom is complicated,[81] but a measured consideration would indicate that the Jews of Yehud in the Persian period knew Hebrew as both a literary and a spoken language.[82]

---

78. Cf. the remarks of J. Maier in "Die Hofanlagen im Tempel-Entwurf des Ezechiel," p. 57:

> Nun ist freilich die erhebliche Differenz zwischen Idealentwürfen und den durch die topgraphischen und kostenmässigen Bedingungen bestimmten Realisierungen immer mitzubedenken. Schon ein oberflächlicher Blick auf die herodianische Tempelanlage zeigt, dass sie der Tendenz nach durchaus vergleichbare Ziele verfolgte, diese aber trotz riesigen bautechnischen Aufwands nur begrenzt erreichen konnte.

79. Although he has not defended the idea in print, apparently J. Strugnell also believes that the NJ measurements were the basis for those of the TS. Wacholder indicates that Strugnell has communicated this opinion to him privately. See Wacholder, *The Dawn of Qumran*, p. 96 and note 394. Wacholder himself holds the opposite view, but his reasoning is unconvincing. See ibid., pp. 95–96.

80. For details, see e.g., M. Avi-Yonah, *The Holy Land From the Persian to the Arab Conquest (536 B.C.– A.D. 640). A Historical Geography*, revised ed. (Grand Rapids: Baker Book House, 1966), pp. 11–31.

81. For a succinct listing of much of the evidence for the use of Aramaic in this period, see K. Beyer, *Die Aramäischen Texte vom Toten Meer* (Göttingen: Vandenhoeck & Ruprecht, 1984), pp. 55–58. Beyer's conclusion is overstated. He believes Hebrew was only a literary and not a spoken language after ca. 400 B.C.E. On the contrary, Hebrew was probably spoken until one or two generations after the Bar Kochba revolt (and even longer in certain pockets of the population), but the totality of the evidence does favor the idea that Aramaic was better known among Palestinian Jews outside of Judah in this period. For another interpretation of some of the materials Beyer considers, see J. Fitzmyer, "The Languages of Palestine in the First Century A.D.," *CBQ* 32 (1970): 501–31.

82. See J. Naveh and J. Greenfield, "Hebrew and Aramaic in the Persian Period," in *The Cambridge History of Judaism, Volume 1: Introduction; The Persian Period*, eds. W. D. Davies and L. Finkelstein (Cambridge: Cambridge University Press, 1984), p. 119.

But if the geographical boundaries are extended outside Yehud and the survey continued down to the Hasmonean period, the situation was somewhat changed. By this time large numbers of Jews lived in the coastal regions, in Galilee, and in the Transjordanian region of Peraea. They probably did not speak Hebrew to any large extent, relying on Aramaic and, increasingly, Greek for their daily lives.[83] Within Judah itself, a wide variety of evidence indicates that the dominant spoken language of Jerusalem and the cultural centers was Aramaic. For example, one might cite the linguistic peculiarities reflected by the Hebrew of 1QIsa[a].[84] In addition, there was a continuous influx of Aramaic speakers to Judah in the form of Jewish pilgrims who would come for one of the great festivals of the cultic year and decide to remain. Other Jewish speakers of Aramaic were brought to Judah during the early Hasmonean period to protect them from their anti-Hasmonean neighbors.[85] Thus by the period ca. 200 B.C.E. to 150 B.C.E., substantial numbers of Jews, within and particularly without Judah, communicated primarily in Aramaic, and understood it much better than they did Hebrew.

These considerations suggest an explanation for the fact that the NJ text was written in Aramaic, even if its ideology[86] were originally worked out in Hebrew-speaking priestly circles.[87] Within the priestly classes of Jerusalem, and by and large in Judah, one could

---

83. Cf. the judgement of E. Y. Kutscher, "לשונן של האגרות העבריות והארמיות של בר כוסבה ובני דורו," *Leshonenu* 26 (1962): 22,

> We may suppose that the language of the scholars [Hebrew] was never spoken except in that small area of the land where the returnees settled in the time of Zerubbabel and Ezra, that is to say, in the region of Judah. But [in] the Galilee, which was only conquered by the Hasmonean dynasty in the first century B.C.E., and whose inhabitants were not all Jewish (it is doubtful that even the majority were) ... the language of its inhabitants was certainly not Hebrew, but rather Aramaic ....(translation mine)

84. Idem, *The Language and Linguistic Background of the Isaiah Scroll* (Leiden: E. J. Brill, 1974), pp. 12–13.

85. In 165 or 164, according to 1 Macc 5:23, Simon and Judah went out to Galilee and the Transjordan, leading the besieged Jews of those regions to Judah. Cf. Josephus, *Ant.* 12.332–349.

86. Probably at the back of the traditions of the NJ (and Temple Source) ideology lay the conviction that the temple of that period was inferior and, in fact, impure. A tradition of hostility to the temple at Jerusalem went all the way back to the fifth century B.C.E. For works of the Second Temple period which evidence antipathy to the temple, cf. e.g., Jubilees 1:10; 1 Enoch 93:8; Testament of Levi 9:9, 14:7–8; Assumption of Moses 2:8–9; and Psalms of Solomon 1:8, 2:2–3, 8:11–12. In connection with opposition to the temple see R. G. Hamerton-Kelly, "The Temple and the Origins of Jewish Apocalyptic," *VT* 20 (1970): 1–15.

87. At least one copy of the NJ text in Hebrew is known. The sort of material which the NJ text contains would probably take Hebrew as its appropriate language of composition. Thus it is conceivable that the Hebrew text(s) of the NJ indicate an earlier stage of the traditions than the Aramaic fragments. According to Starcky, "Jérusalem," p. 39, a Hebrew MS from cave 4 describes a temple precincts surrounded by a wall, pierced by the usual twelve named gates. The rampart forms a square which Starcky describes as 650 m on a side. Resolved into cubits of the ordinary size, it would be approximately 1400 cubits on a side. This measurement is not identical with any of the three walls of the TS, which suggests that the TS and the NJ derive from a larger body of related literature. Undoubtedly various outworkings of the basic numerical and concentric ideology of those texts existed. J. T. Milik, with the collaboration of Matthew Black, in *The Books of Enoch: Aramaic Fragments of Qumrân Cave 4* (Oxford: Clarendon Press, 1976), p. 59, mentions a tiny fragment from cave 4, to be called 4Q232, which "seems to provide us with a specimen of the Hebrew version of the Aramaic work edited under the title 'Description of the New Jerusalem.'" It is uncertain whether the text Milik refers to is the same one to which Starcky makes reference. Thus it is still unclear whether we have one or two Hebrew MSS related to the NJ.

disseminate ideological materials in Hebrew and confidently expect that they would be comprehensible to most readers. Outside of Judah, however, in the coastal regions, Galilee, and the Transjordan—not to mention the eastern Diaspora[88]—Hebrew materials would not be well understood. To communicate with such groups, and to insure the broadest readership in Judah itself, Aramaic would be the language of choice.[89]

Therefore, the fact that the NJ is in Aramaic probably reflects a conscious decision. The supporters of the ideology which gave rise to the texts under discussion were not content to limit the knowledge of their ideas to Hebrew speakers in Judah. The choice of Aramaic was a bid for broader support for their program. Were the group at all successful in their intentions, the programmatic architectural ideas encoded in the NJ and the Temple Source became fairly well known. If my inferences about the priority of the NJ to the Temple Source are correct, the NJ probably antedates the Hasmonean period.[90] It may well be a third century text, or at least reflect third century ideas.

88. See the remarks of C. Rabin, "Hebrew and Aramaic in the First Century," in *The Jewish People in the First Century. Compendia Rerum Iudaicarum ad Novum Testamentum, Section One, Volume 2*, ed. S. Safrai and M. Stern (Philadelphia: Fortress Press, 1976), p. 1029.

89. It might be thought that the documentary discoveries in the Judaean desert from the time of the Bar Kochba revolt (132–135 C.E.) raise questions about this assertion. These documents include materials in Hebrew, Aramaic, and Greek. (For the letters and contracts from the Wadi Murabbaʿat, see P. Benoit, J. T. Milik, and R. de Vaux, *DJD* II, especially nos. 22–46; for the materials from Naḥal Ḥever and Naḥal Ṣeʾelim, which are still unpublished except for preliminary reports, see Y. Yadin, "Expedition D," *IEJ* 11 [1961]: 36–52, B. Lifshitz, "The Greek Documents from Naḥal Ṣeʾelim and Naḥal Mishmar," *IEJ* 11 [1961]: 53–62, Y. Yadin, "Expedition D—The Cave of the Letters," *IEJ* 12 [1962]: 227–57, and B. Lifshitz, "Papyrus grecs du désert de Juda," *Aegyptus* 42 [1962]: 240–56. Further details about some of the texts are found in Y. Yadin's non-technical work, *Bar Kokhba* [London: Weidenfeld and Nicolson, 1971], esp. pp. 124–39 and 172–83.) In fact these documents do not contest my assertion, for the following reasons:

    1. The Bar Kochba revolt was largely confined to Judaea; it apparently did not spread to Galilee, except for a few minor incidents. Thus, the evidence of these texts is not applicable to the question of language outside of Judaea. See B. Isaac and A. Oppenheimer, "The Revolt of Bar Kochba: Ideology and Modern Scholarship," *JJS* 36 (1985): 53–54.

    2. Even within Judaea, at least one text seems to show that Hebrew was not as well known as Greek, at least as a written language. In a papyrus written in Greek, sent from one of Bar Kochba's outposts, the following sentence is found: "This is written in Greek because we did not desire to write it in Hebrew." (Lifshitz, "Papyrus grecs," p. 241. More recently, a better reading for the Greek word which Lifshitz restored as "desire" has been suggested. Rather than reading [ὁρ]μὰν, an anomalous Doric accusative, G. Howard and J. Shelton, "The Bar-Kokhba Letters and Palestinian Greek," *IEJ* 23 (1973): 100–1, have proposed [Ἑρ]μᾶν, "Hermes." With this reading, the translation would be, "This is written in Greek because Hermes could not be found to write it in Hebrew." If this reading is correct, it implies that even within the circle of the leader of the revolt, only Hermes was competent to write letters in Hebrew. Others, however, had no difficulty producing a document in Greek.) The author is evidently apologizing for writing in Greek, rather than in Hebrew, and explains that the approaching holiday constrained his action. Perhaps it would be correct to infer that the use of Hebrew was preferable for nationalistic reasons, but that only a minority of scribes could produce documents in it. For discussions of the implications of the choice of Greek for the letter, see Yadin, *Bar Kochba*, pp. 130–32, and M. Mor, "The Bar-Kochba Revolt and Non-Jewish Participants," *JJS* 36 (1985): 200–7.

90. A possible objection is that E. Y. Kutscher's study of the Aramaic of the Genesis Apocryphon (which is written in the same type of Aramaic as the NJ) dates the text much later. Kutscher concludes that the language of the Genesis Apocryphon is in transition from Imperial Aramaic to Middle Aramaic (by which he means the dialects of the Christian era). He eventually dates the text to the period of the first century B.C.- first century C.E., but he is rightly very tentative, saying "... the determination of the time of

The Temple Source and Jubilees

General Relationship

As I have remarked more than once already, the relationship between the TS and the book of Jubilees is one of the crucial issues in the study of the TS. Some scholars have taken the

---

origin is much more difficult ... since the material between the two periods [Imperial Aramaic and Middle Aramaic] from Palestine and elsewhere is very scanty, we know very little concerning the transition period." (E. Y. Kutscher, "The Language of the Genesis Apocryphon," *ScH* 4 [1957]: 1–35. The quotation is from p. 15.) In fact, all that Kutscher really demonstrates is that the language of the text is transitional between Imperial Aramaic and the dialects of the Christian era. His analysis does not rule out a date in the second century B.C.E. More recently, K. Beyer has examined the language of all the Aramaic materials of the DSS, the Murabbaʿat texts, and certain portions of the Mishnah and Tosefta to isolate what he calls "Hasmonean Aramaic." He views it as distinct from Imperial Aramaic in several ways, such as the morphology of deistic pronouns, the preference for ד instead of די, and the use of the accusative particle ית. He connects its emergence with the achievement of Judaean independence in 142 B.C.E. and the simultaneous emergence in Judaea of nationalistic feeling for their language. (See Beyer, *Aramäischen Texte*, pp. 34–35.) Beyer thus recognizes the tentative character of Kutscher's conclusion, and he is not hesitant to date the emergence of Qumran Aramaic to a century earlier than did the Israeli scholar. But his conclusions are open to fundamental criticisms. First, the date of 142 B.C.E. is in itself arbitrary, and does not accord with what history shows usually happens with national languages and nationalistic movements. (To call the Maccabean Revolt an outbreak of nationalism may seem anachronistic, since the term nationalism has a technical meaning whose elements have only come to the fore in the last two centuries or so. I am aware of the danger of anachronism here, but would argue that if any ancient movement could accurately be called "nationalistic," it was the upheaval in Judea against foreign domination in the period 175 B.C.E. to 135 C.E. See the comments of F. Millar, "Empire, Community and Culture in the Roman Near East: Greeks, Syrians, Jews and Arabs," *JJS* 38 [1987]: 147, "The ... great Jewish revolts ... were religious and nationalistic movements of a strikingly modern kind: they were also almost unique instances of state formation." For the connection between the Maccabean Revolt and the First Revolt of 66–70 C.E., and the general concept of an ancient Jewish nationalism, see W. Farmer, *Maccabees, Zealots and Josephus: An Inquiry into Jewish Nationalism in the Greco-Roman Period* [New York: Columbia University Press, 1956].) Commonly, the nationalistic use of a language is not tied to the actual achievement of nationalistic goals, but to a point near the movement's inception. Cf. e.g., K. Symmons-Symonolewicz, *Nationalistic Movements: A Comparative View* (Meadville: Maplewood Press, 1970), pp. 31–39. Note especially his remarks on pp. 35–36, "*As soon as* an ethnic group makes a claim to nationhood, that is to a definite historical and territorial individuality, it has to begin working to sustain this claim" (emphasis mine). Language is a principal means for sustaining the movement's claim. Rather than a date of 142 B.C.E., then, one would expect nationalistic linguistic feelings to emerge about 170 B.C.E., with the beginning of the Hasmonean movement, or even earlier in response to advancing Hellenization. Second, it is hard to believe that nationalistic feelings would attach to an Aramaic dialect, rather than to the more natural choice, Hebrew. (According to 2 Macc., at the beginning of the Hasmonean resistance, and even earlier, at the beginning of Antiochus' persecutions, it was noteworthy to hear people speak "in the language of their fathers." See 2 Macc. 7:8, 7:21, etc. These statements refer most naturally to the nationalistic revival of Hebrew, rather than to the use of a non-standard dialect of Aramaic.) In fact I do not believe that Beyer is correct to state that the NJ was written in a new dialect of Aramaic, nor is Kutscher's methodology the right one. I prefer the paradigm of J. C. Greenfield, "Standard Literary Aramaic," in *Actes du Premier Congrès International de Linguistique Sémitique et Chamito-Sémitique. Paris 16–19 juillet 1969*, eds. A. Caquot and D. Cohen (The Hague: Mouton, 1974), pp. 280–89, and J. Greenfield, "Aramaic and its Dialects," in *Jewish Languages: Themes and Variations*, ed. H. Paper (New York: n.p., 1978), pp. 34–36. He argues for the existence of a "Standard Literary Aramaic," which functioned as the written dialect for speakers of widely different Aramaic dialects. I would suggest that the deviations of NJ Aramaic from Imperial Aramaic are therefore not clues pointing to the existence of a "Hasmonean Aramaic," but the intrusion of the scribal copyists' spoken dialects into this literary language. Linguistic analysis is thus useless for dating the NJ, since the possible dates of its composition all fall within the period in which Standard Literary Aramaic was used.

position that the TS and Jubilees are two halves of one whole; that together, they constitute a two-volume "second Torah."[91] This idea originates in a certain superficial similarity between the two, and the fact that taken as a unit they may be thought to embrace roughly the entire Pentateuch.

But the idea that these two works originally made up a single book is untenable if the differences between them are balanced against their admitted similarities. I list several of the principle differences below, though the list could easily be twice as long.

1. The literary character of the two compositions

The TS is a composite work. The component documents fit together roughly, with ragged edges, and the text seems to end very abruptly. Jubilees, most scholars agree, is a much more unitary composition with a well-crafted beginning and end.[92]

2. The nature of the apparent pseudepigraphic fiction in each

The TS eliminates the name of Moses wherever it is found in the biblical portions cited. Thus the scroll's redactor sought to portray the contents as recording unmediated speech between himself and God (although, as is perhaps appropriate, God does all the talking). Jubilees retains the figure of Moses, and between him and God stands an intermediary, the Angel of the Presence. It is this figure who actually communicates to Moses nearly all of the book's contents. This is a radical difference in outlook between the two books.

3. The apparent purposes of the two books, as evidenced by redactional emphases

The TS is a new "law of the land" for Israel, as it were a kind of second chance. If they will obey its laws and build its temple, they will be assured continued dwelling in the land. God promises them his continued presence. Jubilees, on the other hand, retells the story of Gen and the first twelve chapters of Exod in order to make several points which scarcely have anything in common with the message of the TS. One concern is to divide the entire period

---

91. Among these scholars are M. Smith, "Helios in Palestine," pp. 206*–7*, B. Z. Wacholder, "The Relationship between 11Q Torah (The Temple Scroll) and the Book of Jubilees: One Single or Two Independent Compositions," in *SBL 1985 Seminar Papers,* ed. K. Richards (Atlanta: Scholars Press, 1985), pp. 205–16 and J. L. Wentling, "Unraveling the Relationship Between 11QT, the Eschatological Temple, and the Qumran Community," *RQ* 14 (1989), pp. 61–74. Wacholder's argument signals a change from his earlier position in *The Dawn of Qumran,* pp. 41–62. There he argued that the TS was a source for the book of Jubilees, whose author "goes on to cite at length numerous portions of the scroll ... . " (p. 61). Wacholder offered no examples of such citations, and, to judge from his shift of position, even he did not find his suggestion very persuasive.

92. For a brief discussion of the major questions involved in the study of Jubilees, see the introduction to the most recent English translation by O. S. Wintermute. This is found in *The Old Testament Pseudepigrapha,* 2 vols, ed. J. Charlesworth (Garden City: Doubleday and Company, 1983–85), 2:35–142. With regard to beginning and end, one point should suffice. The projected total of fifty jubilees is nearly completed at the point in time that the author ceases his narration. Thus 50:13, "the account of the division of the days is complete." It is almost inconceivable, then, that another 66 columns would follow in the form of the TS.

from the creation to the entry into Canaan into fifty jubilee periods. Jubilees dates each major biblical event and birth according to its jubilee period. Thus the word and concept "jubilee" (יובל) is fundamental to the purpose of Jubilees, but neither even occurs in the TS. Jubilees is also anxious to put a good face on questionable Patriarchal deeds, while simultaneously seeking to demonstrate that they kept the Law in conformity with the interpretations held by Jubilees' author. In the course of this demonstration Jubilees emphasizes certain legal and moral concerns about which the TS is completely silent.[93] Finally, the book seeks to add haggadic information to the Patriarchal stories, while haggada—indeed, narrative— is alien to the TS.

4. The order of material in the two works

Viewed superficially, the TS seems to jump around in the Pentateuch from book to book, quoting or referring now to Exod, then to Deut, and again to Lev.[94] Its method of organization is very different from that of Jubilees, which proceeds directly through Gen-Exod 12 *seriatim*.

5. The Hebrew style of the two works

The TS, and in particular the Temple Source, manifests LBH syntax, and is remarkable for its preference for the periphrastic use of היה with a participle. This feature occurs only occasionally in the Hebrew Bible, chiefly in the later books. Its attestation in the DSS is not limited to the TS, but it is far more frequent there than anywhere else in the corpus.[95] The style of Jubilees is in sharp contrast to that of the TS, insofar as published Hebrew fragments are indicative.[96] These fragments appear to show that the book was written in a style closely

---

93. E.g., keeping the sabbath, fleeing fornication, and avoiding all public nudity.

94. Some scholars have thought that the order is roughly that of the Pentateuch, with excursus only for the purposes of harmonization of problematic passages, or to group like materials together. See e.g., Yadin I, p. 74; Wacholder, as cited in Kampen, "The Torah of Qumran?," p. 42; and Schiffman, "Literary and Philological Perspective," p. 153. This analysis cannot stand scrutiny, as I hope to show in Chapter 6.

95. Qimron, *Grammar*, p. 70. Almost all the examples within the TS are found in the Temple Source.

96. Hebrew fragments of Jubilees are known from caves 1, 2, 3, 4, and 11. In the light of these finds most scholars now agree that Hebrew was the original language of its composition. The publications are as follows:

Cave 1 = 1Q17 and 1Q18, published by J. T. Milik in *DJD* I, pp. 82–83 and 83–84, respectively.

Cave 2 = 2Q19 and 2Q20, published by M. Baillet in *DJD* III, pp. 77–78 and 78–79.

Cave 3 = 3Q5, which Baillet edited in *DJD* III under the title "Une prophétie apocryphe," pp. 96–98. Two scholars independently realized that the fragments were part of Jubilees 23, and published corrections to Baillet's work. See R. Deichgräber, "Fragmente einer Jubiläen-Handschrift aus Höhle 3 von Qumran," *RQ* 5 (1964–66): 415–22, and A. Rofe, "קטעים מכתב יד נוסף של ס היובלים במערה 3 של קומראן," *Tarbiz* 34 (1965): 333–36.

Cave 4 = 4Q221, published by J. T. Milik in "Fragment d'une source du psautier (4Q Ps 89)," *RB* 73 (1966): 104. Most recently M. Kister, "Newly-Identified Fragments of the Book of Jubilees: Jub. 23:21–23, 30–31," *RQ* 12 (1985–87): 529–36, has suggested that portions of 4Q176 belong to a Hebrew MS of Jubilees.

approximating to SBH, with regular consecution of tenses, for example, and no signs of periphrastic tenses.

For all these reasons and more the two books are not two halves of a single work—not literarily and not conceptually. Nevertheless, a relationship of some sort is evident in many ideas and particulars. The fullest study of a single topic comparing the two books is Schiffman's analysis of sacrificial laws for festivals.[97] He shows that regarding sacrificial stipulations there is both agreement and disagreement. He concludes—and I concur—that the explanation which best fits the evidence is that the two works emanated from similar circles. But they should not be credited to the same group, at least not in the same stage of its development.

The only portion of the TS which apparently complicates this explanation of the interrelationship between the two texts is TS 43: 2–17, particularly 43:4b–12a, a portion found in the Temple Source.[98] When compared with Jubilees 32:10–15, the two texts have an obvious similarity, extending even to apparent verbal identity.[99] It would seem that here, at least, there is a literary relationship between the two texts. Consequently, several scholars have argued that the TS borrowed from Jubilees, thereby granting Jubilees temporal precedence—an argument which, if valid, would potentially aid greatly in dating the Temple Source and the TS.[100] Unfortunately for the scholar anxious to date the TS, the other two possibilities cannot so easily be shunted aside. It is theoretically possible that Jubilees borrowed from the TS, and also that both relied upon an unknown earlier work. Because of the implications which this

---

Cave 11 = 11QJubilees. A. S. van der Woude published a portion in "Fragment des Buches Jubiläen aus Qumran XI (11Q Jub)," in *Tradition und Glaube: Das frühe Christentum in seiner Umwelt. Festgabe für Karl Georg Kuhn zum 65. Geburtstag,* ed. G. Jeremias et al. (Göttingen: Vandenhoeck und Ruprecht, 1971), pp. 140–46. See also J. T. Milik, "À propos de 11Q Jub.," *Biblica* 54 (1973): 77–78.

Since the fragments thus far published are not very extensive, I put no great emphasis on the argument from style.

97. L. Schiffman, "Sacrificial System." VanderKam does not go along with all of Schiffman's particular points, but he comes to the same general conclusion: the texts are related because they "belong to the same legal and exegetical tradition." (VanderKam, "The Temple Scroll and the Book of Jubilees," passim; the quotation is from p. 232.) In the terms of the present study, what Schiffman is essentially comparing is the Festival Calendar source (see chapter 4) and Jubilees.

98. For the possibility that at least a portion of this passage is a legal interpolation or even a redactional composition, see chapter 6.

99. M. Delcor, "Explication [III]," p. 247, seems unaware of these passages when he says, "Rien n'indique donc une interdépendance littéraire entre les deux écrits."

100. This is the conclusion of Schiffman, "Sacrificial System," p. 227; J. Charlesworth, "The Date of Jubilees and the Temple Scroll," in *SBL 1985 Seminar Papers,* ed. K. Richards (Atlanta: Scholars Press, 1985), p. 203; and Yadin. Yadin never directly addresses the question of priority in the *editio princeps* of the TS, or in the English translation, but his view is implicit in statements he makes in *Hidden Law,* p. 232. J. Baumgarten, "The Calendar of the Book of Jubilees and the Temple Scroll," p. 77, has briefly discussed the question of priority, but without reaching a conclusion. Uncertainty is also the position of J. Cook, review of *The Dawn of Qumran: The Sectarian Torah and the Teacher of Righteousness,* by B. Z. Wacholder, in *BO* 41 (1984): 709–10.

apparent literary relationship has for the dating of the Temple Source, it is necessary to investigate the question in some detail. As something of a consensus exists that Jubilees probably dates between 168 B.C.E. and 152 B.C.E., a definite literary relationship between the two works—in either direction—would point to a comparable date for the Temple Source, and obviously require a later one for the TS itself.[101]

Comparison of TS 43:4b–12a with Jubilees 32:11b–13

A meaningful comparison of these two portions requires at least a glance at their broader literary context, for which the following translations (Jubilees from Ethiopic and the TS from Hebrew) furnish a convenient starting point.[102]

Jubilees 32:10–15

> (10) And therefore it is decreed in the heavenly tablets as a law to tithe the tithe again in order to eat it before the Lord from year to year in the place where it is determined that his name shall dwell. And there is no limit of days to this law forever. (11) This ordinance is written to observe it year after year to eat the second tithe before the Lord in the place where it is determined. And there is not to be (anything) left over from it from this year to the year which is to come. (12) For in its year the grain will be eaten until the days of the harvest of the grain of the year, and the wine (will be drunk) until the days of the wine, and the olive (will be used) until the day of its season. (13) And everything which is left over from it and which grows old will be unclean. Let it be burned in the fire because it has become impure. (14) And thus they shall eat it together in the sanctuary and they shall not let it become old. (15) And the whole tithe of oxen and sheep is holy to the Lord and it will belong to the priests who will eat it before him year after year because it is so ordered and engraved on the heavenly tablets concerning the tithe.

101. The date of Jubilees is a difficult question, which I cannot investigate in detail here. For a succinct description of the various views and their supporters, see Charlesworth, "Date of Jubilees," pp. 193–97. I find the most convincing dating to be 169–167, as argued by J. Goldstein, "The Date of the Book of Jubilees," *PAAJR* 50 (1983): 63–86. For a view which dates the book slightly later, to about 152, see J. VanderKam, *Textual and Historical Studies in the Book of Jubilees.* Harvard Semitic Monographs no. 14 (Missoula: Scholars Press, 1977), pp. 214–88. Since the discovery of the DSS, most scholars would date the book somewhere in the period bracketed by these two options. A complicating factor, which not many scholars seem to have considered recently, is that the book of Jubilees itself evolved in reaching its present form. Thus the passages used to date the book as a whole really do not suffice for that purpose unless it can be shown that no other passages were ever added later.

102. The translation of Jubilees is by Wintermute (see note 92 above). This is a very literal translation based on the text of R. H. Charles, *The Ethiopic Version of the Hebrew Book of Jubilees* (Oxford: Clarendon Press, 1895). I have preferred Wintermute's translation over C. Rabin's revision of Charles' own translation, in *The Apocryphal Old Testament,* ed. H. F. D. Sparks (Oxford: Clarendon Press, 1984), pp. 10–139, precisely because its literalness facilitates verbal comparison between the two texts. The translation of the TS, which is mine, is purposely very literal for the same reason.

TS 43:2–17 (lines 2–4 are partially lost)

> (2) ... on the sabbath days and on the days of ... (3) ... and on the days of the first fruits of grain, of wine and oil[103] (4) ... the wood. On these days it shall be eaten, and they shall not leave (5) a portion of it from one year to the year following. Rather, they shall eat it thus: (6) from the festival of first fruits for the grain of wheat they shall eat the wheat (7) until the second year, until the day of the festival of the first fruits; and the wine, from the day (8) of the feast of the new wine, until the second year, until the day of the feast of (9) the new wine; and the oil, from the day of its feast until the second year, (10) until the feast of the day of offering new oil on the altar. And everything which (11) remains from their feasts is holy—it shall be burned in the fire, it shall not be eaten again, (12) for it is holy. Now as for those dwelling at a distance of three days from the temple, (13) let them bring as much as they are able to bring. If they are unable (14) to carry it, they may sell it for money and bring the money, and purchase with it grain (15) and wine and oil and cattle and sheep. They shall eat it on feast days—they are not (16) to eat of it on working days in uncleanness[104] for it is holy. (17) It shall be eaten, therefore, on holy days, and not on work days.

Although the Temple Source does not use the phrase "second tithe" in the portion which has survived, various clues point to its presence in the lost lines preceding line 3. These clues consist of the unexpressed subject of יאכל in line 4, the partitive ממנו in line 5, and the suffixed direct object marker at the end of the same line. As the phrase is explicit in Jubilees 32:11, the subject of both texts is the second tithe.

In order accurately to assess those lines which exhibit verbal correspondences, it may be helpful to ask whether the two texts agree or disagree in general. Some important areas of agreement are immediately evident. Both the Temple Source and Jubilees stipulate that the tithe be eaten in the sanctuary, although the TS is more restrictive, specifying (by means of the context of this portion of the scroll) that the consumption must be in the third court. In striking contrast to the much later rabbinic practice, the texts further agree that the second tithe is an annual requirement.[105] They agree also that the tithe may be consumed only in the year in which it is offered. No portion is to be left for the subsequent year.

On the other hand, the texts differ on the vital matter of how to regulate the year. The TS regulates the annual cut-off by festivals, while Jubilees uses harvest times for that purpose.[106]

---

103. I follow Yadin's restoration at II, p. 182 for the end of line 3.

104. The context requires such a translation of לאונמה. Cf. Deut 26:14 on the second tithe, where the term און parallels ממא. Cf. also Hosea 9:4, and see the discussion in J. Baumgarten, "Tithes," pp. 11–12. For a related perspective on the relationship of און to working days, see J. Milgrom, "Further Studies in the Temple Scroll," pp. 193–94.

105. For a succinct description of the rabbinic system, and a comparison of it with the position of Jubilees, see L. Finkelstein, "The Book of Jubilees and the Rabbinic Halakha," *HTR* 16 (1923): 52.

106. Yadin understood the text of Jubilees to refer to the same feasts as the TS (I, p. 115). The problem with his view is that, as Schiffman has shown, Jubilees is unaware of any feasts for new wine or new oil; see

Other important differences in the law of the second tithe are also evident. The TS prescribes the consumption of the tithe only on holy or feast days. Jubilees does not even mention this matter, although it would seem to be a vital concern since, according to the TS, ignorance of this law would result in eating the tithe in uncleanness. The TS considers the question of whether it is permissible to sell the tithe. Again, Jubilees does not mention the matter, although it was something which the later Tannaim debated heatedly. It is hard to believe the question would not have evoked equally heated debates in some circles of Second Temple Judaism.[107]

When the texts discuss who is to eat the second tithe a truly fundamental disagreement surfaces. In the TS the layman is to eat the entire tithe, as the scroll interprets Deut 14:23 straightforwardly. But Jubilees apparently allows the layman to eat only the agricultural tithes. The first-born animals, as "tithes" of the livestock, are licit only for priests.[108] This distinction arises from a bifurcation of Deut 14:23, in which Jubilees understands Deut 14:23a to apply to the layman and 14:23b to apply to priests. The hermeneutic behind this bifurcation constitutes a major exegetical disagreement between the TS and Jubilees.

Jubilees has superimposed Lev 27:32 as a sort of "grid" to guide its exegesis of Deut 14:23. The division of Deut 14:23 is an attempt to harmonize these two verses. In other words, the author of Jubilees understood Lev 27:30–32 to apply to the second tithe, while the redactor of the TS evidently did not. Presumably he would have said that those verses apply instead to the "first" or "Levitical" tithe.[109] This disagreement between the TS and Jubilees arises from an exegetical crux which has always plagued interpreters. Does Lev 27:30–32 relate to the first or to the second tithe? Jubilees has sided with the option usually endorsed in rabbinic texts, while the TS interpretation is the one preferred by most modern exegetes.[110] This disagreement between the two texts is very significant.

Schiffman, "Sacrificial System," p. 227. It follows, then, that the Jubilees reference to the grain harvest is just what it seems, and does not imply the feast of first fruits which accompanied the harvest.

107. Baumgarten, "Tithes," p. 13. Baumgarten concludes that the majority opinion among the Tannaim was that the second tithe could not be sold.

108. Finkelstein, "Jubilees and Halakha," pp. 52–53, has a different understanding of the law in Jubilees. He believes that all the tithes, not merely the livestock, were to be eaten by the priests. His view cannot be ruled out, although it depends heavily on his interpretation of an ambiguous phrase in Jubilees 32:9, "and it was sanctified to him." Finkelstein's interpretation requires that "him" refer to Levi, which is problematic since both "the Lord" and "Jacob" are closer noun referents for the pronoun and would make good sense. His explanation also fails to give full weight to Jubilees 32:15, "the *whole* tithe of oxen and sheep." The Ethiopic word *kʷellu* (= Hebrew כול) may hint at polemics about whether, by analogy with the agricultural tithe, the layman was to eat at least some of the flesh of the first-born. The author of Jubilees replies in the negative: the priests were to eat *all* of the flesh. In its favor, Finkelstein's interpretation does result in a situation wherein the law of the second tithe in Jubilees is analogous with its law for the "fruits of the fourth year." A similar symmetry is known from rabbinic texts, which may commend Finkelstein's view. Whether my understanding or Finkelstein's is correct is of secondary importance in any case. Either way, the law of Jubilees differs from that of the TS.

109. This section of Lev apparently underlies a portion of the Midrash to Deuteronomy, and is found at TS 60:2–3. It is applied there to the Levitical tithe. Cf. E. Qimron, "הערות לנוסח," p. 141 for the possible reading of מעשר in TS 60:2.

110. On the exegetical understanding of Lev 27:30–32, see Baumgarten, "Tithes," p.6.

Based on this brief comparison it can be said that, regarding the laws of the second tithe, Jubilees and the TS sometimes agree and sometimes disagree. This is not a surprising result, given earlier studies of the interrelationship between the legal materials of these two texts. All the same, the conclusion is important, and should help to guide any examination of those portions of the laws which may have a literary relationship. Within the parameters now set down, the preferred explanation of such a relationship must be that both texts relied on an earlier work, because that is the hypothesis which best accounts for a situation in which two texts agree in important ways while also disagreeing radically. In the nature of things it is impossible to rule out that one or the other text used the other only where it agreed with it. But if such were the case, one would expect at least some hint of a polemic against the other text where it seemed faulty to the writer of the first text. On the strength of this reasoning it will require virtually an air-tight case for verbal dependence to overturn the *prima facie* conclusion pointing to an earlier common source.

The passages which apparently have verbal connections are TS 43:4b–12a and Jubilees 32:11b–13. For the clearest possible comparison of the two portions it is necessary to retrovert the Ethiopic text of Jubilees into the Hebrew in which it was originally composed.[111] Ordinarily retroversion is a perilous venture whose very tentative results hardly justify the dangers. In this case, however, the usual problems are somewhat ameliorated. VanderKam has shown that even though Jubilees was first translated from Hebrew into Greek,[112] and only then into Ethiopic, that text still very accurately reflects the Hebrew (where the DSS fragments make comparison possible).[113]

Since Jubilees 32:11b–13 consists of five separate stipulations, I indicate those here and refer to them henceforth as Jubilees A-E.

Jubilees 32:11b (A)
Ethiopic text: wa-ʾalbo la-ʾatrefo ʾemmennēhu ʾemze ʿāmat la-ʿāmat la-za-yemaṣṣeʾ
Suggested Hebrew text: ולוא יניחו ממנו מהשנה הזאת לשנה הבאה[114]

---

111. I have used the Ethiopic text of Charles. No significant textual variants occur in these lines.

112. The Greek Jubilees has survived only as fragments quoted by later Greek authors. Most recently, A. M. Denis has collected these fragments in *Fragmenta Pseudepigraphorum Quae Supersunt Graeca* (Leiden: E. J. Brill, 1970), pp. 70–102. Unfortunately our passage has not survived.

113. VanderKam, *Textual and Historical Studies,* pp. 18–95. After a detailed comparison of all published DSS fragments of Jubilees with the collation of the four texts (A-D) which Charles published in his *Ethiopic Version,* VanderKam concludes on p. 95, "The text of Jub. which the Ethiopic manuscripts provide is very accurate and reliable. It reproduces the Hebrew text … literally and precisely in nearly all cases."

114. For יניחו, יותירו is also possible. The Ethiopic root here is *tarfa-tarafa,* which in Jubilees E below renders יתר.

Jubilees 32:12a (B)

Ethiopic text: ʾesma ba-ʿāmatihu yetballaʿ zarʾ ʾeska ʾama mawāʿela ḥarifa zarʾa ʿāmat

Suggested Hebrew text: כי בשנתו יהיו אוכלים את הדגן עד יום קציר דגן השנה[115]

Jubilees 32:12b (C)

Ethiopic text: wa-wayn ʾeska ʾama mawāʿela wayn

Suggested Hebrew text: והיין עד יום התירוש[116]

Jubilees 32:12c (D)

Ethiopic text: wa-zayt ʾeska ʾama mawāʿela gizēhu

Suggested Hebrew text: והיצהר עד יום מועדו

Jubilees 32:13 (E)

Ethiopic text: wa-kʷellu za-yetarref ʾemennēhu wa-za-yeballi yekun saʾuba ba-ʾessāt
         yaʾay ʾesma kona rekusa

Suggested Hebrew text: וכול אשר נותר ממנו ואשר ישן[117] יהיה טמא באש ישרף כי טמא הוא

Now it is possible to compare Hebrew with Hebrew, and so, one hopes, to arrive at a more accurate estimate of the verbal overlap between the texts:

Jubilees A   ולוא יניחו ממנו משנה הזאת לשנה הבאה

TS 43:4b–5a   ולוא יניחו ממנו שנה לשנה אחרת

115. At two points one cannot be certain of the Hebrew equivalent of the Ethiopic in Jubilees B, because more than one possibility exists. The Ethiopic *yetballaʿ* can be a reflex of two different Hebrew passive constructions. I have chosen יהיו אוכלים, frankly because this is the phrase found at TS 43:5. In view of the clear verbal equivalents between the texts it seems reasonable to assume that this is another. But יֵאָכֵל (Niphal 3ms imperfect) is better style for SBH, which, as noted above, is the type of language found in Jubilees generally. Perhaps any difference could be attributable to different *Vorlagen,* since if the two texts did rely on a third, earlier text, it may have come down in different textual forms. The second point in the Ethiopic text involves *mawāʿela,* the plural of *maʿalt,* "day." Ambiguity arises because the plural can also mean "period, era." Consequently the term here could represent an original Hebrew ימי, the construct plural "days"—as Wintermute translates the term. It could also translate the singular יום, which can mean simply "time, period" in Biblical Hebrew—cf. *BDB* s.v., and note Gen 35:3, Jer 18:17, Proverbs 24:10, etc. I have chosen the second option because it results in a textual ambiguity which helps explain the present form of the texts in the TS and Jubilees, as I discuss below.

116. Although the Ethiopic text has only one word for wine, I suggest that the Hebrew original had both יין and תירוש, as does the Temple Source. The probable explanation for only a single word in the Ethiopic text is that the Greek intermediary translated both Hebrew terms with a single Greek equivalent, *οἶνος.* The Ethiopic translator thus saw only one word and rendered it *wayn* both times. This suggestion is reasonable in light of usage in the LXX. The Greek renders both תירוש and יין with *οἶνος* (the former 35 times in 39 occurrences, and the latter 144 out of 146 times). See E. Santos, *An Expanded Hebrew Index for the Hatch-Redpath Concordance to the Septuagint* (Jerusalem: Dugith, n.d.), s.v. תירוש and יין.

117. It seems likely that the original Hebrew of Jubilees here read ישן rather than בלה, since the former term is particularly associated with grain which is no longer usable. Cf. Lev 25:22 (*bis*), etc.

Jubilees B   כי בשנתו יהיו אוכלים את הדגן עד יום קציר דגן השנה
TS 43:6–7a   מחג הבכורים לדגן החטים יהיו אוכלים את הדגן עד השנה השנית עד יום חג הבכורים

Jubilees C   והיין עד יום התירוש
TS 43:7b–9a   והיין מיום מועד התירוש עד השנה השנית עד יום מועד התירוש

Jubilees D   והיצהר עד יום מועדו
TS 43:9b–10a   והיצהר מיום מועדו עד השנה השנית למועד יום הקרב שמן חדש על המזבח

Jubilees E   וכול אשר נותר ממנו ואשר ישן יהיה טמא באש ישרף כי טמא הוא
TS 43:10b–12a   וכול אשר נותר ממועדיהמה יקדש באש ישרף לוא יאכל עוד כי קדש

A close reading of these lines does reveal substantial verbal identity, but it is balanced by equally substantial differences in phrasing and concept. For example, although Jubilees B has a kernel of words in common with the TS, its additions tie the grain to harvest time rather than to feasts, as in the TS. Jubilees C and D are substantially shorter than the equivalent TS portions. One might assume that the author of the Temple Source knew the text of Jubilees here and simply expanded it for increased specificity. Perhaps; but such an explanation would hardly suffice for Jubilees E and the TS.

Jubilees calls the remnant of the tithe טמא, while the TS calls it קדש. These terms are polar opposites; this is a truly basic conceptual difference. Furthermore, the TS makes no mention of the remnant becoming "old." Perhaps the TS simply changed the Jubilees terms for legal reasons, but then what explains the lack of any polemic against the other text's view? Further, the difficulties with such an explanation become more pronounced in light of how much longer the TS text is at Jubilees B and C. Why would the author of the Temple Source have added so much rather redundant material in that case—on the given theory thus evincing a very full reaction against the Jubilees text—and then have said nothing about the much more profound differences with Jubilees in the case of E?

If it is difficult to suppose that the TS knew Jubilees, the opposite is even more difficult. If Jubilees knew the Temple Source, surely there would be some response to the TS linkage of the tithe to the yearly feasts. As noted above, there is no evidence in the book of Jubilees that the author even knew of the feasts of new wine and new oil. But even if Jubilees simply rejected these feasts and therefore did not mention them,[118] Jubilees B remains unexplained. Jubilees clearly refers elsewhere to the feast of the first fruits for grain,[119] but, significantly, does not mention it here. Jubilees unquestionably knew this feast, but nevertheless the text of Jubilees B confines its discussion to the harvest.

---

118. Such a contention seems impossible to defend when faced with Jubilees 7:36, which mentions offerings for the first of the wine and the oil, but without any festivals. These offerings are set in the context of the "fruit of the fourth year." The concept of these tithes is fundamentally different from that of the TS.

119. Cf. Jubilees 15:1–2, 16:13, 22:1–6.

The two texts really share only a common kernel of words in each of the various stipulations. Even where the two texts agree on a given stipulation, frequently the word order differs. Retroversion only supplies additional evidence for the *prima facie* notion: both texts look back to a third source. It is even possible to reconstruct the contents and purpose of that earlier work—tentatively, of course.

The reconstruction of this putative ancestor is possible based on what is common to both Jubilees and the Temple Source, and, where they diverge, on the assumption of ambiguous terminology which could give rise to both interpretations. Perhaps this reconstruction will make the superiority of the common source explanation self-evident. I suggest that the common source read approximately as follows. (Lines correspond to the stipulations of Jubilees and the Temple Source.)

A. לוא יניחו ממנו משנה לשנה

B. כי בשנתו יהיו אוכלים את הדגן עד השנה השנית

C. והיין עד יום מועד התירוש

D. והיצהר עד יום מועדו

E. וכול אשר נותר באש ישרף

Translation

> (1) They shall not leave any of it from year to year. (2) Rather, they shall eat the grain in its year until the second year, (3) and the wine until *ywm mwʿd* of the must, (4) and the oil until *ywm mwʿdw*. (5) And everything which remains shall be burned with fire.

I have left the crucial ambiguities untranslated, because precisely these terms resulted in the divergent interpretations of the Temple Source and Jubilees. If this reconstruction is essentially correct, the putative source was clearly an attempt to understand and apply the difficult phrase in Deut 14:22, שנה שנה. The practical difficulty of this phrase led to similar attempts at explanation very early in the textual history of the Hebrew Bible.[120] The source applies the exegesis of this phrase to each of the agricultural elements in Deut 14:23, in the order in which they occur.

Essentially, different interpretations of מועד in lines C-D shaped Jubilees 32:11b–13 and TS 43:4b–12a. As I noted above, יום is also ambiguous in this context, and its ambiguity reinforces that of מועד. מועד can mean "appointed time," i.e., for harvest, as well as "appointed festival."[121] יום can mean both "day" and "time." The author of Jubilees apparently understood

---

120. Thus the Peshitta reads *šnʾ bšnʾ*, a reading with which some MSS of the MT agree. Cf. also Deut 15:10, possibly the basis for these early attempts at explication.

121. For the meaning "appointed time," see Hosea 2:11, Ps 1:3, etc.; for the meaning "appointed festival," see Ezek 46:11, Num 10:10, and commonly.

line C of the common source as "until the time of the harvest of the (grapes for) must," i.e., the time when the must was prepared in order to make wine. On this basis he inferred that the references throughout the text must be to the harvest time. Accordingly he inserted the word "harvest" in Jubilees, simultaneously guaranteeing the proper interpretation of the text and obviating the need to repeat the term in each succeeding line.

The author of the Temple Source read line C as "until the day of the appointed festival for new wine." Consequently he deduced that the period in line B must be from one festival to another. This reading defined for him the limits of the "second year." Perhaps he also knew some form of the Deuteronomy Source, which describes a festival of new wine.[122]

Both authors incorporated the document into their works, adding phrases or changing the wording slightly to reinforce their interpretations.[123] Jubilees and the Temple Source expanded line E with opposed explanations, reflecting the fact that divergent cultic notions motivated their prohibition on consumption of the remnant beyond its year.[124] That the Temple Source and Jubilees both drew on an earlier (third-century?) source seems to be the best way to account not only for what each says, but also for what each does not say. Neither text actually quotes the other; probably their composers did not know the other text, at least not in the form in which we know them. It remains to suggest what implications this understanding has for the date of the Temple Source.

The Date of the Temple Source

Based on this study of the relationship between the Temple Source and Jubilees, the only conclusion possible is negative—though even that is, in a sense, positive. Since Jubilees is not ancestral to the Temple Source, it is of no help in dating that source. Even at the point of their closest intersection the relationship of Jubilees to the TS is not as direct as scholars have believed.

What, then, can be said about the date of the Temple Source? I show that the NJ, or its traditions, was a source for the Temple Source, a source probably antedating the Hasmonean period. Unfortunately, this fact, helpful as it may be in other ways, affords no precise dating for the Temple Source.

An important factor complicating dating is our ignorance of how rapidly such works might be adopted and elevated to authoritative status. The time involved would presumably be a logarithm dependent on many variables: the size and coherence of the community involved, for example, and the person of the author. In terms of production and adoption by a large Jewish community of an authoritative (canonical, semi-canonical?) document, a generation may seem

---

122. Rockefeller 43.366 40*:1 line 9. See also our conclusions below.

123. The rather extreme length and repetitive phrasing of lines 3 and 4 of the TS suggest that here the final redactor made further additions, perhaps adding to each line the words following השנה.

124. The danger of interpreting the DSS legal material as monolithic is underlined when one considers that the law of Jubilees is a natural complement to the law of Ḥadash in 4QHalakha[a], while that of the TS is not. Cf. J. Baumgarten, "4QHalakha[a] 5, the Law of Hadash, and the Pentecontad Calendar," *JJS* 27 (1976): 36–46, esp. p. 45.

too short. But one might point to Sibylline Oracles Book 3 as proof to the contrary. That book apparently reflects the adoption of Daniel in Egypt already by 145 B.C.E., only about twenty years after Daniel reached final form.[125] And one might imagine that a work by an acknowledged prophet, for example, would be instantly authoritative to those who recognized the author's stature. But of course the Temple Source not only had achieved some sort of authoritative status, as indicated by its choice for the TS, but also required modification *twice* in the face of new circumstances in the user community. First it was modified—or, perhaps better, amplified—by being combined with the Deuteronomy Source, as shown by the 43.366 fragments. Then it was again reworked to produce the TS itself. Would a span of forty years between original composition and radical modification allow enough time for such a course of events? It is simply impossible to say. Nevertheless, the only way to date the Temple Source more "precisely" than merely to say that it postdates the development of its shared ideology with the NJ is to make some such estimate, and then backdate from the presumed date of its "final" form, the TS. And, of course, the variables demand considerable diffidence about the result—it may not be a more "precise" date.

Still, the foot must come down somewhere. Since I argue below for a date of approximately 150 B.C.E. for the final redaction of the TS, the Temple Source must antedate that year. Its dependence on the NJ requires that it postdate that work (or—again a complication—its traditions). It therefore can be dated as far back as the third century, although ca. 190 B.C.E. is more conservative and thus, presumably more secure. The work originated somewhere in those years; factoring in the 43.366 fragments, I am inclined to date the source earlier rather than later.

Somewhere between the early third century or so and about 190 B.C.E., at any event, an unknown priest or scribe took up the Deuteronomy Source, which mentioned a "house" that the people of Israel were to build the Lord upon entering the land (43.366 fragment 1). He was moved to add the architectural specifications for that temple, relying upon the authoritative traditions of the NJ. Based on the choice of Aramaic as the language of the NJ fragments, one may probably conclude that the work's ideology was known outside the author's immediate circles, perhaps even in the Babylonian diaspora. The resulting literary work is, as I argue, partially extant in the 43.366 fragments. This proto-Temple Scroll circulated for an unknown length of time. The period of its circulation depends, as already stated, on many sociological variables which are not well understood. At some decisive, perhaps eschatologically pregnant, moment a new figure of great authority took it up, cut it down, added legal and calendrical materials, and produced the TS.

125. Not all scholars would agree with such an assessment, but see A. Lacocque, *The Book of Daniel* (Atlanta: John Knox Press, 1979), p. 7. The second earliest possible reference to Daniel seems to be 1 Macc 1:54, which dates 30–60 years after Daniel's completion.

4

THE MIDRASH TO DEUTERONOMY SOURCE

Introduction

The third major source which emerges in these researches I (somewhat hesitantly) entitle the "Midrash[1] to Deuteronomy Source" (MD). This chapter first focuses on the reasons for suspecting the source's existence, on a delineation of its contents, and, very briefly, on an attempt to characterize its original purposes. Then, as a consensus seems to emerge which relies upon portions of this source to date the TS, the remainder is devoted to a consideration of this quest.

The Identification of Midrash to Deuteronomy as a Source

The following portions of the TS apparently derive from a common source distinct from the other portions of the scroll: 57:1–59:21 (the so-called תורת המלך or "King's Law;" henceforth TM); 60:2–11; and 64:6b–13a. The reasons for assigning these portions to a hypothetical common source are four in number:

1. The portions have in common a compositional method which occurs nowhere else in the TS.

2. The portions are interrelated; those which are later in the order of the book of Deut rely upon the exegesis which the earlier portions establish.

3. These portions share some unusual vocabulary which is virtually unattested elsewhere.

4. These portions clash with the Deuteronomy Source, in which they are now found, on important legal or ideological matters.

---

1. I am aware of the difficulties this term raises, but for the present there seems to be no better alternative. I follow R. Bloch's classic definition of midrash as "an edifying and explanatory genre closely tied to Scripture, in which the role of amplification is real but secondary and always remains subordinate to the primary religious end, which is to show the full import of the work of God, the Word of God." See R. Bloch, "Midrash," trans. M. H. Callaway, in *Approaches to Ancient Judaism: Theory and Practice,* ed. W. S. Green, Brown Judaic Studies no. 1 (Missoula: Scholars Press, 1978), p. 29.

These four arguments are perhaps not equally important or equally well evidenced, but, taken as a whole, they are persuasive that MD constitutes a separate source.

To demonstrate that these portions do have a common method of composition, it is necessary to analyze several selections from MD with regard to their use of the biblical text. It is not essential to consider each and every portion of the proposed source, as such an exhaustive examination would quickly become redundant and tiresome. Along with the three representative examples I include for detailed discussion, the *Appendix* will suffice, I believe, to prove that the methods used in the selections were in fact used throughout MD, but nowhere else.

Compositional Method[2]

TS 57:1–5a: Session, Conscription, and Appointment

וזאת התורה] אשר יכתבו לו מלפני] הכוהנים [	.1
ביום אשר ימליכו א[ת המלך ³כראוש] בני ישראל מבן	.2
עשרים שנה ועד בן ששים שנה לדגליהמה ופקד	.3
בראשיהמה שרי אלפים ושרי מאיות ושרי חמשים	.4
ושרי עשרות בכול עריהמה	.5a

Biblical sources (in the order in which the scroll refers to them):[4]

והיה כשבתו על כסא ממלכתו ... וכתבו לו ... התורה הזאת	Deut 17:18
זה יהיה משפט המלך אשר ימלך עליכם את בניכם יקח ושם לו במרכבתו	1 Sam 8:11
הזכר מבן עשרים שנה ועד בן ששים שנה	Lev 27:3
וחנו ... איש על דגלו לצבאותם	Num 1:52
ויפקד דוד את העם אשר אתו וישם עליהם שרי אלפים ושרי מאות	1 Sam 18:1
ואקח את ראשי שבטיכם ... אתן אתם ראשים עליכם שרי אלפים ושרי	Deut 1:15
מאות ושרי חמשים ושרי עשרות	

This portion of TM takes as its starting point the biblical "law of the king," in Deut 17:18. There the author found reference to a "law" (תורה), which he evidently understood to refer to legislation specifically directed to the king—and not, as modern exegetes would understand, to the book of Deut. The word תורה here reminded the author of 1 Sam 8:11, which to his mind provided additional details relevant for the "law" (משפט) of the king. Operating from a peculiar (but, given his presuppositions about the nature of the biblical revelation, legitimate) understanding of that text, the author concluded that scripture required the king to form from the sons of the Israelites an army. Thus he understood even historical portions of the biblical

---

2. To facilitate the reader's involvement in the discussion, the text of the TS portion under consideration is reproduced, and, following that, the biblical portions which I believe served as the basis for MD.

3. Yadin's suggested restoration of אותו את before ראוש (II, p. 255) results in a very unbiblical syntax. One would expect instead of את either no particle, ב, or כ. The photograph shows that the lacuna is about ten spaces and letters long. Thus a restoration evidently requires not merely the *nota accusativi* with suffix, but that plus a noun. The logical noun would, of course, be מלך.

4. Cf. also Exod 18:21, Num 1:3, 1 Sam 8:12, and 1 Sam 22:7.

text as normative, once properly interpreted. Accordingly, for him 1 Sam 8:12 specified that the king was to appoint at the head of the army commanders of thousands and commanders of hundreds. Recalling that Moses had also appointed such commanders, Deut 1:15 provided the author with additional necessary details; he found there mentioned commanders of fifties and of tens. The author was also aware that the same elements were to be found in 1 Sam 18:1, where David—the paradigmatic once and future king—mustered (פקד) the troops and appointed commanders. The crucial verb פקד led in turn to passages in Num, set during the wilderness travels of the Israelites. Num 1:3 contained the verb and, just a few verses later, at 1:52, the text revealed that the muster was according to units (דגל).

Taking additional clues from the biblical texts, the author had also to be concerned with the age specifications for the troops. From the passage in Num 1:3 he could glean only the lower limit, but, by associating verbal elements common to both portions (מבן עשרים), the author linked it with Lev 27:3. There he found the essential upper limit.

The reasoning process involved in the composition of this portion, while perhaps not conforming with modern canons of exegesis, is not hard to understand. It was a common method of reasoning in the study of ancient texts in antiquity, with analogs in many contemporary and later interpretive writings, such as Philo and the Tannaitic midrashim.[5] Basically, the author has relied upon two different types of analogy for his hermeneutical approach. He has triangulated texts which mention "the king," a known historical king (David), or a leader analogous to the king (Moses). And he has used verbal analogy, i.e., association, tracing a given word from portion to portion to incarnate the bones of his new construct. For reasons which will become clear shortly when discussing dating, it is important to observe that, based on these methods, everything the author has said is clearly derived from the Bible. So far as can be determined, he has not imported ideas from elsewhere, nor does the text raise any such suspicions. It is likewise important to notice that the author has begun his midrashic process with Deut 17 and 1 Sam 8. As these are the biblical portions which mention a "law of the king," it was reasonable for the author to make them the cornerstone of his new law.

TS 57:5b–11a: The Body Guard

וברר לו מהמה אלף אלף	.5b
מן המטה להיות עמו שנים עשר אלף איש מלחמה	.6
אשר לוא יעזבוהו לבדו ויתפש ביד הגואים וכול	.7
הברורים אשר יבור יהיו אנשי אמת יראי אלוהים	.8
שונאי בצע וגבורי חיל למלחמה והיו עמו תמיד	.9
יומם ולילה אשר יהיו שומרים אותו מכול דבר חט	.10
ומן גוי נכר אשר לוא יתפש בידמה	.11a

5. For a helpful consideration of hermeneutical methodology including the Targumim, the Tannaitic midrashim, Philo, and the DSS, see G. Brooke, *Exegesis at Qumran: 4QFlorilegium in its Jewish Context.* Journal for the Study of the Old Testament Supplement Series no. 29 (Sheffield: *JSOT* Press, 1985), pp. 1–79.

Biblical sources[6]

ואת בחוריכם הטובים ... יקח	1 Sam 8:16
ויאמר אחיתפל אל אבשלם אבחרה נא שנים עשר אלף איש	2 Sam 17:1
אלף למטה אלף למטה לכל מטות ישראל	Num 31:4
שנים עשר אלף חלוצי צבא	Num 31:5
ויאסף שלמה ... שנים עשר אלף ... עם המלך	1 Kngs 10:26
ואתה תחזה מכל העם אנשי חיל יראי אלהים אנשי אמת שנאי בצע	Exod 18:21
ויבחר משה אנשי חיל	Exod 18:25
הנה מטתו של שלמה ששים גברים סביב לה מגברי ישראל כלם אחזי חרב	Cant 3:7–8
מלמדי מלחמה איש חרבו על ירכו מפחד בלילות	
והקפתם על המלך סביב איש וכליו בידו והבא אל השדרות יומת יהיו	2 Kngs 11:8
את המלך בצאתו ובבאו	

For the author, the connection between the conscription of an army and the selection of a bodyguard began in 1 Sam 8. After the stipulation that the king should select the sons of the Israelites for his army, 8:16 gave the author details of a more demanding selection process. The king was to take "your choice ones" (understanding בחור with the author as from בחר, "to choose"). The author preferred the synonym ברר in his wording, perhaps because of the other overtones of the term, "clean, pure." His choice of wording may have been further conditioned by the fact that the two words sounded alike in contemporary spoken Hebrew.[7] Perhaps, like many Hebrew writers, he had an ear for paronomasia and double entendre. Next, two additional passages, 2 Sam 17:1 and 1 Kngs 10:26, provided supplemental evidence for royal selection procedures. The first of these, confirming the author's procedures by the appearance of the key term בחר, made it clear that the number of men to be chosen was 12,000. 1 Kngs 10 agreed with this number and also clearly stated the function of this entourage: to be "with the king."

But whence, precisely, were the 12,000 to come? Num 31:4 provided the answer: one thousand were to come from each of the twelve tribes. (Note the idealistic situation the adoption of this number implies; the author envisions the twelve tribes regathered from among the nations.) Since in that passage, Moses was the leader making the choice, the author naturally thought of another passage which describes a Mosaic selection process, Exod 18:25. Further, this passage had a very significant verbal connection to those the author had already used, the term בחר. Exod 18:25 described the chosen men as אנשי חיל. The author recognized

---

6. Cf. also 2 Sam 11, 2 Sam 12:1–2, 1 Sam 15:8, 1 Kngs 20:13–21, 1 Sam 24:1–7, 1 Sam 26:6–12, 2 Kngs 14:1–4 (regarding Deut 17:20), Jer 34:3, 38:23, Ezek 21:28 (English 21:23), 21:29 (English 21:24), and Ps 10:2. Many of these texts concern kings being captured or sinning while alone.

7. In the language of the scrolls there is abundant evidence that the gutturals had weakened to the point that, at least in many environments, they sounded alike. *Resh* had undergone a similar weakening, particularly in the environment of the gutturals. In certain environments, all these letters may have been virtually silent. For example, often *resh* was not written at the end of a word, just like ʾaleph. See Qimron, *Grammar*, pp. 26–27.

in this phrase a shortened form of the description of these men in Exod 18:21, and preferred that longer description for its greater specificity.[8]

But he still needed additional information on the meaning of the phrase "with the king." He found some in Cant 3:8, which is connected by verbal association to the Exodus passage; it mentioned that the guard it describes was with Solomon at night—and thus, as the author inferred, "day and night." Reinforcement for his inference came from the description of Joram's bodyguard in 2 Kngs 11, where that king's guard was with him "in his going out and in his coming in." Thus these passages supplied many of the particulars concerning the choice and character of the bodyguard—and yet there remains another aspect of the author's midrash of which they give no hint.

It is the full function of this bodyguard which particularly draws attention to an important literary characteristic of MD. To be precise, the function is twofold: to prevent the king from falling into enemy hands, and to keep him from being "seized" by a sinful act or attitude.[9] This second assignment exemplifies the idealistic aspect of MD—it is hardly descriptive of real life in the here and now.[10] The text is emphatic, "they shall not leave him alone" (57:7), and "they will be with him always, day and night" (57:9–10). Indeed, the emphasis in the description of the bodyguard is as much on keeping the king from being alone as it is on guarding him from enemy capture. It seems clear that the author feared that the king, if left alone, might commit sinful acts which could have dire consequences for the entire nation, a notion which, of course, he got from the Bible.

It is likely that he had in mind various episodes in the history of Israel in which kings sinned, and believed that an attentive guard could have prevented such actions. One thinks naturally of the most famous such instance in the Bible—the events surrounding David and Bathsheba.[11] It will be recalled that on that one occasion, contrary to his custom, David did not go out with the army to campaign. Instead he sent Joab to lead the army to besiege Rabbat

---

8. For the phrase גבורי חיל למלחמה instead of the MT phrase אנשי חיל, see Y. Thorion, "Zur Bedeutung von גבורי חיל למלחמה in 11QT LVII, 9." Thorion shows that in LBH חיל was ambiguous, meaning both "strength, power" and "wealth," and that the author of MD added the qualifier to resolve the ambiguity.

9. The phrase in 57:11, אשר לוא יתפש בידמה, refers both to enemies and to דבר חם, as noted by Yadin, II, p. 257. For the use of תפש in connection with sin, cf. Ezek 21:28–29 and Ps 10:2.

10. Thorion would appear to be misled on this point in "Zur Bedeutung von חמא in 11QT." Since he reasons that 12,000 men could not possibly have as their job preventing the king from sinning, he seeks another meaning for חמא. He finds that on rare occasions in the Bible, the term means not "sin," but the consequences of sin, i.e., "misfortune." He therefore suggests that the meaning of the TS "they will guard him from all manner of חם" is that the men were to guard the king from "dangers" (Gefahren). Yet Thorion has apparently not noticed that in each passage in the Bible where the meaning of חמא might be "misfortune," the text carries the overtone that the misfortune is divine retribution for a sinful act. The misfortune comes directly from God—it is thus no mere "danger." Further, it is incredible to suppose that the author of TM would have wanted to prevent such retribution from falling on the king, or that he believed it possible. The incongruity of such a supposition with TM as a whole allows no other understanding of חמא than its usual sense of "sin."

11. In anticipation of the discussion in chapter 5, cf. CD 5:5, מלבד דם אוריה ויעלו מעשי דויד. Not surprisingly the events surrounding Bathsheba bothered those who saw in David an ideal king and expected another in his mold.

Ammon. Further, 2 Sam 11:1 specifies that David sent not only Joab, but also "his servants" (עבדיו). Given that this term elsewhere signifies the foreign corps of mercenaries who served as David's bodyguard, the author of MD may well have understood the text to say that the king's guard left him alone.[12] The seduction of Bathsheba and the arrangements for Uriah's death followed. *Post hoc, ergo propter hoc.* When, later, Nathan confronted the king with his action, David admitted, "I have sinned against Yahweh" (חמאתי—cf. 57:10 חמ דבר[*sic*]).

The author of MD would also have been familiar with various biblical episodes in which enemies might have seized or killed an unprotected king. For example, on more than one occasion David came upon Saul when that ruler was alone, and easily could have harmed him.[13] The author doubtless realized that a less scrupulous foe probably would have left Saul dead.

The story of Amaziah furnished another example of a lone king being captured (תפש). According to 2 Kngs 14:1–4, Jehoash of Israel captured this king of Judah and, read in a certain way, the author could understand the text as meaning that Amaziah was alone at the time this event occurred. "And Judah was smitten ... so each man fled to his tent. *Then* Jehoash ... captured Amaziah." An intriguing aspect of this episode is its verbal connection with Deut 17:20 and TM 57:14, both of which warn against the king "lifting up his heart." Jehoash accused Amaziah of "lifting up his heart," but the Judahite refused to listen and instead foolishly engaged the northern king in battle, resulting in his own capture.

Through this analysis of the "Bodyguard"[14] portion of TM it is possible to reach several conclusions. First, as before, the basic technique which the author has used is analogy, both verbal and conceptual. And, as noted, the text is not mundane or simply descriptive, as it mixes together "real" and "ideal" (perhaps even unreal) elements.[15] Third, the author has turned frequently to the historical books, and other non-Torah passages, to find the information he sought. Apart from the passages assigned to the MD source, a similar use of non-Torah portions occurs nowhere else in the TS. Possibly this is a conceptual distinction differentiating MD from the other sources of the TS.

---

12. E.g., 2 Sam 20:6 and 1 Kngs 1:33.

13. 1 Sam 24:1–7; 1 Sam 26:6–12. Notice in the second episode that Saul's men were all asleep, and cf. the phrase in TM יומם ולילה.

14. Regarding the royal bodyguard, M. Weinfeld, "The Royal Guard According to the Temple Scroll," *RB* 87 (1980): 394–96, has drawn attention to some interesting parallels in a description of the Egyptian royal guard written by Diodorus Siculus. The selection process is somewhat similar, as are the physical and moral functions of the guards. Yet the points of contact are quite general, sufficiently so that one might easily see here parallel, independent developments. When Weinfeld urges that more is evident I agree with M. Delcor, "Explication [I]," p. 230, "on a relevé ici et là des parallèles forcés entre les deux écrits." It is also important to realize that Diodorus has relied on Hecataeus of Abdera, whose *floruit* was under Ptolemy I, ca. 300 B.C.E. Thus, even if the parallels involved were less general, one could not without qualification take this description as evidence for a late Hasmonean date for TM, as does Weinfeld. The words of Maier, *The Temple Scroll*, p. 123, are relevant: "In all cases we could be dealing with material that was already available in the third century." For Hecataeus, see *The Oxford Classical Dictionary,* 2nd ed. 1970, s.v. "Hecataeus (2)."

15. I attempt an explanation of this character in chapter 6.

Turning to TS 64:6b–13a, once again the same techniques are in use, and the same willingness to use non-Torah texts to compose new law is manifest. This portion is a midrash of Deut 21:22–23, and explicates a form of that text which, except for one reading, did not vary significantly from the MT.

TS 64:6b–13a

כי	6b.
יהיה איש רכיל בעמו ומשלים את עמו לגוי נכר ועושה רעה בעמו	7.
ותליתמה אותו על העץ וימת על פי שנים עדים ועל פי שלושה עדים	8.
יומת והמה יתלו אותו העץ כי יהיה באיש חטא משפט מות ויברח אל	9.
תוך הגואים ויקלל את עמו ואת בני ישראל ותליתמה גם אותו על העץ	10.
וימות ולוא תלין נבלתמה על העץ כי קבור תקוברמה ביום ההוא כי	11.
מקוללי אלוהים ואנשים תלוי העץ ולוא תטמא את האדמה אשר אנוכי	12.
נותן לכה נחלה	13a.

Biblical sources

לא תלך רכיל בעמיך (עמך LXX)	Lev 19:16
כלם סרי סוררים הלכי רכיל[16]	Jer 6:28
כי ידעתי את אשר תעשה לבני ישראל רעה	2 Kngs 8:12
ותליתם אתו על עץ והומת (versional-cf. Peshitta)	Deut 21:22b
על פי שנים עדים או שלשה עדים יומת המת לא יומת על פי עד אחד	Deut 17:6
יד העדים תהיה בו בראשנה להמיתו	Deut 17:7
וכי יהיה באיש חטא משפט מות	Deut 21:22a
אלהים לא תקלל ונשיא בעמך לא תאר	Exod 22:27
ויאמרו הכהנים ... לאמר משפט מות לאיש הזה כי נבא אל העיר הזאת	Jer 26:11
ויאמרו השרים ... אין לאיש הזה משפט מות כי בשם יהוה אלהינו דבר	Jer 26:16

The author of MD faced problems of definition with two phrases as he set about explicating Deut 21:22–23: משפט מות and קללת אלהים. He knew that the first phrase must connote some serious crime, since the biblical text required that the guilty party be executed. Yet, owing to the phrase's rarity,[17] he needed to fall back upon his usual exegetical techniques in order to explicate exactly what it meant. One thing he did know from the start was that there must be an equivalence between this phrase and קללת אלהים, since in both cases the convicted person was to be "hung on a tree." Therefore, by determining the meaning of one phrase he might hope to elucidate the other.

Investigating משפט מות, he perhaps came first to Deut 19:6; this portion proved no great help, since it did not define the crime. But by the same process of verbal association he also contemplated Jer 26:11 and 26:16, and these portions were presumably much more

---

16. This passage may be a kind of literary "binder" in the TS. It includes elements connecting it to the topic of crucifixion, specifically רכיל (cf. Lev 19:16 and the discussion below), and elements connecting it to the prior topic, the rebellious youth (סורר).

17. Altogether, this phrase, or similar ones, occur only five times in the Hebrew Bible. משפט מות appears at Deut 19:6, Deut 21:22, Jer 26:11, and Jer 26:16. The similar חטא מות occurs only at Deut 22:26.

enlightening. Jeremiah declares, "I will make this city a curse to all the peoples of the earth." The author may have understood the prophet to mean more or less, "I will curse it before them," in which case the response of the priests would be most instructive: "This man is guilty of a death sentence (משפט מות) because he has prophesied against this city." Although the sentence of death was not carried out in this particular instance, the author of MD could nevertheless draw the logical inference that cursing Israel was a crime potentially invoking the משפט מות. Perhaps the appearance here also of the other key word the author was investigating—קללה—convinced his exegetical sensibilities that he was indeed on the right track.

Investigating the other phrase, קללת אלהים, he would have arrived at conclusions similar to those discovered in tracking משפט מות, but with additional details. Verbal association led him to Exod 22:27—which it seems he read in a way contrary to the later Masoretic accentuation[18]—and this verse in turn led him to Lev 19:16. Thus was forged a verbal chain joining Deut 21:23, Exod 22:27, and Lev 19:16, which can be represented in the form of a simple schematic:

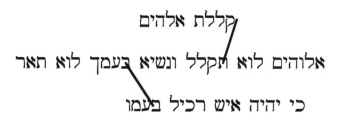

Figure 2. An Exegetical Chain

This verbal chain allowed the author to draw valuable conclusions. Not only was it confirmed that cursing his people was a crime worthy of crucifixion, but now he also knew that to curse God was to incur that same penalty. And by analogy with Exod 22:27b[19] he realized that the difficult portion in Lev 19 amounted to further evidence for the crime of cursing Israel, so he wove it, also, into his midrash.

Verbal association with וימת accounts for most of the remainder of that midrash. Because of the defective orthography, it is uncertain whether the author understood the reading as a simple Qal with explicative *waw,* or as a Hophal imperfect.[20] But since he also turned to Deut 17:6–7,

---

18. With the Masoretic accentuation, the verse reads, "You shall not curse God, nor shall you curse a prince among your people." By dividing the verse differently, the author of MD understood, "You shall not curse God, nor a prince; you shall not curse your people." With this division there are three rather than two elements to the command not to curse. The last he evidently associated with Lev 19:16.

19. The singular noun of Exod 22:27b is found in the LXX., while the reading of the MT is the plural.

20. Both readings are attested in the non-Hebrew textual tradition. The LXX majority reading agrees with the Qal; the Peshitta, with the Hophal.

which involves cases of putting people to death,[21] it seems probable that he read the Hophal. Based on verbal and conceptual analogies, the author concluded that the laws which these passages give must also apply to cases of משפט מות. He now knew that this phrase referred precisely to קללת עמו and קללת אלהים (אנשים).

Through this analysis of 64:6b–13a it becomes clear that the methods used in the TM were relied upon here as well. Also like TM, this portion turns to non-Torah passages for some of its legal interpretation. It is further noteworthy that all three portions examined are formally identical, i.e., they quote the biblical passages being interpreted as part of the midrash, weaving other materials together with them.[22] This interpretive technique is a formal characteristic of other portions of MD as well; compare TS 57:14 with Deut 17:20, TS 59:21 with Deut 17:20, and TS 60:10b–11a with Deut 18:5. From the perspective of composition criticism, these portions clearly are a matched set, alike both exegetically and formally.

Other Reasons to Regard Midrash to Deuteronomy as a Distinct Source

In addition to composition critical commonalities, several additional arguments suggest that one should recognize in MD a distinct source for the TS. For example, both TS 57:11 and TS 64:7 include the phrase גוי נכר—a very rare phrase virtually unknown elsewhere. Neither the Hebrew Bible nor the DSS (with one exception) use it at all.[23] Of course it would be unwise to put great weight on a single phrase such as this, but it is a pointer, however small, in the direction of my view of MD.

A stronger argument is the fact that some portions of MD are evidently dependent for their exegesis on others. For example, the topic in TS 58:11b–15a is the division of booty taken in battle by the king and his army. The system whereby the troops divide the booty with the king, priests, and Levites is peculiar: the king is to take a tenth of the total, the priests 1/1000, and the Levites 1/500. Based on Num 31:27–30, Gen 14:20, and Deut 17:17 (see the *Appendix*), the method of reasoning is identical with that of the portions discussed above. This portion then informs TS 60:3b–5, where the topic is the sacrificial portions which belong to the priests; these lines group "tithes" of the hunt together with booty, as both are "unearned." The stipulations in 60:3b–5 undeniably presuppose 58:11–15, especially 58:13. TS 60:7–8, where the concern is Levitical portions, likewise depends on 58:11–15 (and that portion's midrashic exegesis of Num 31:30) for its stipulation of Levitical rights to the booty. These portions are all interrelated.

Finally, as I argue in chapter 2, the redactor had interpolated the Deuteronomy Source with portions which represented his own negative attitudes toward polygamy and divorce. I point out in that discussion that these portions conflict with their present literary setting. Therefore, it seems logical to conclude that they have an independent origin. Now, the passages in question are found in TS 57, a part of TM; thus, as several scholars have already suggested, TM has an

---

21. Note the causatives, יומת in 17:6 and להמיתו in 17:7.

22. Cf. G. Brin, "המקרא," p. 201.

23. CD 14:15.

origin independent of its present setting.[24] Given the compositional techniques and other commonalities which align it with both 60:2–11 and 64:6b–13a, it is an economical and reasonable hypothesis to assign all three portions of the TS to one and the same independent source.

Curiosity then prompts the question whether anything more can be deduced about this putative common source. I call the source "Midrash to Deuteronomy" because the redactor has inserted excerpts from it in lieu of, or in addition to, passages of the Deuteronomy Source. The source thus appears to have been related specifically to Deut, but this appearance may be an illusion created by the redactor's choice of excerpts. It is by no means certain, therefore, whether mine is an accurate characterization. One might arrive at a different characterization by considering the portions of Deut upon which it commented.

TM supplements Deut 17:14–20, which concerns the king; 60:2–11 replaces Deut 18:1–5, which discusses priests and Levites; 64:6b–13a replaces Deut 21:22–23,[25] the topic of which is crucifixion as the penalty for unspecified crimes. In the context of the temple state of the restoration period, these portions have in common definite political overtones. It is therefore entirely possible that MD was not really a commentary on Deut, but more a political treatise formulated by means of interpolative scriptural exegesis.[26]

The Use of *Torat Hammelekh* to Date the Temple Scroll

A substantial number of scholars have thought that the expansions to Deut 17:14–20 which constitute TM contain clues to dating the TS as a whole. Yadin was the first exponent of this view, noting,[27]

> The main themes discussed in the additional Statutes of the King hint at the date of their composition ... All of this would indicate that the Scroll was composed in the Hasmonean period, at the close of the second century B.C.E. or the beginning of the first century.

---

24. Recognized already by Wilson and Wills, "Literary Sources," pp. 287–88, although on different grounds.

25. Cf. the comments by M. Bernstein, "Midrash Halakhah at Qumran? 11Q Temple 64:6–13 and Deuteronomy 21:22–23," *Gesher* 7 (1979): 157,

> We suggest that 64:6–13 be considered an interpolation into TS, but not one inserted without any prior connection. It is our contention that an "original" version of TS contained a passage which paraphrased Deut. 21:22–23 more closely, after the fashion of the recasting of the biblical material in the surrounding portions.

26. Such a work would be an appropriate Jewish response to the political "how-to" treatises which were common in the Hellenistic world. If this idea is in fact correct, it would have implications at the level of exegesis of the scroll. For example, עמו in 64:7 would probably mean "army" in a political text such as MD may have been. In its present literary context, there is no particular reason to suspect this meaning.

27. Yadin I, pp. 345–46. Yadin specified later in the discussion that the principal themes which serve as clues are the king's bodyguard (I, p. 348), the section on the king's wives (I, pp. 353–54), and the type of battles found in TS 58 (I, p. 359).

Since Yadin wrote these lines, various scholars have adopted his basic approach. The most important contributors to this growing consensus include Mendels, van der Woude, and Delcor.[28] The joint effort of Hengel, Charlesworth, and Mendels represents the fullest development of Yadin's approach so far published.[29]

This approach calls for a response. Is it indeed possible to date the scroll by means of clues hidden in TM? And if so, does such an investigation pinpoint the Hasmonean era in general, and specifically the time of Alexander Jannaeus (103–76 B.C.E.), as claimed?

Since Hengel, Charlesworth, and Mendels have drawn on earlier work to produce the most complete and, presumably therefore, most persuasive case for dating the TS on the basis of TM, it seems best to focus on their arguments. In this way I can in effect respond also to less assiduous advocates of the same approach. Since their discussion is detailed, it requires a comparably detailed evaluation. Thus I consider each of the seven major points they have raised, beginning with what seem to me the strongest (i.e., the least subjective) arguments, and proceeding to the weakest.

The Argument from Textual Variants

According to the three coauthors, the textual variants from the MT in col. 56 (where the scroll quotes Deut 17) constitute responses to actual historical problems raised by the reign of Alexander Jannaeus.[30] The added phrase למלחמה reflects the conviction of the author of TM that Jannaeus was insufficiently cautious in his policy toward Egypt.[31] The variant יכתבו for the MT's וכתב means that instead of the king copying out a scroll of Deut himself, the author

---

28. D. Mendels, "'On Kingship' in the Temple Scroll and the Ideological *Vorlage* of the Seven Banquets in the 'Letter of Aristeas to Philocrates,'" *Aegyptus* 59 (1979): 130. He concludes, "the treatise 'on kingship' in the Temple Scroll presents, we believe, an antithetic model to the kingship then existing in Judea, whose imitation of Hellenistic kingship was becoming more obvious." A. S. van der Woude, "Een Gedeelte," p. 390, opines that TM "als polemiek tegen het optreden van de hasmoneese konigen van de tweede eeuw v. Chr. worden uitgelegd." This apparently is a change from his earlier view, expressed in "De Tempelrol van Qumran (II)," p. 286. At that time he suggested, "vele bepalingen bevat die moeilijk als polemisch van kerakter kunnen worden beschouwd, althans niet in verband met de Hasmoneeën." M. Delcor, "Le statut du roi d'apres le Rouleau du Temple," *Henoch* 3 (1981): 47–68, derives a Hasmonean date from the discussion of the king's bodyguard, the interdiction of marriage to foreign women, and the description of the king's qualities as judge.

29. M. Hengel, J. Charlesworth, and D. Mendels, "Polemical Character." The authors state their thesis on p. 31: "our document [the TS] presents ... an antithesis to some *real* Jewish king ... none other than Alexander Jannaeus."

30. Although the authors do allow on p. 32 that it is possible that these textual variants may merely reflect a different version of Deut, they give this possibility no serious attention in their subsequent analysis. Their strongest arguments assume that in fact the author of TM made the changes deliberately.

31. Ibid., pp. 31 and 35–36. Z. Falk, in "מגילת המקדש," pp. 31–32 (= idem, "The Temple Scroll and the Codification", pp. 34–35), makes a similar argument for the significance of the textual variants in col. 56.

wanted the priests to do it for him. This change signifies an attempt by the priests to circumscribe the king's power, and to make him dependent on them in legal matters.[32]

Before taking up the specific points the authors have raised, it might be well to consider briefly the methodology implicit in their suggestions. Their entire argument really rests on the prior assumption that the author of TM had before him a *Vorlage* identical to the MT. Then, where the text of col. 56 varies from that of Deut 17, the variants are seen as deliberate alterations. This is not only a dubious, but a puzzling *a priori* in the light of the well–attested textual fluidity of the Hebrew Bible in this period. More specifically, their approach does not reckon with the evidence of the TS itself, even in the very column under discussion. As is shown in chapter 2, the text of the Deuteronomy Source is expansionistic relative to the MT.[33] It need hardly be emphasized that it is methodologically unsound to ignore the general text critical character of a text when making specific text critical arguments about portions of that text.

In fact, the textual variants upon which these authors base this their strongest argument are almost certainly not deliberate alterations by the author. Rather, they are to be explained by the ordinary canons of textual criticism, and are also attested outside the TS. Thus, the variant יכתבו appears in Targum Pseudo-Jonathan.[34] There one finds ויכתבון לה סביא, "and the elders shall write for him ..." The insertion of "elders" is clear evidence that the targumic compilers knew a plural verb in their Hebrew textual tradition, and in good targumic fashion added this word to make the subject of the verb explicit. The textual tradition of the LXX is also uncertain about who was to write the scroll of the Law mentioned in Deut 17.[35] In view of the targumic text, in particular, no historical argument should be based on יכתבו.

A much more intriguing textual addition is למלחמה, added to the text corresponding to Deut 17:16. The MT's interdiction of a return to Egypt has often perplexed commentators. According to Hengel and his collaborators, this addition simultaneously resolved the question of the Bible's meaning and criticized Jannaeus' military policies. Unfortunately, in their fascination with this variant, the authors appear to have overlooked a second variant, וכסף וזהב. This variant occurs in the same verse and, in my view, is the key to the likely explanation of the phrase למלחמה. The text of the scroll is apparently the result of a two-step scribal process, both steps of which are common and well known to textual critics. A text nearly identical to the

32. Hengel, Charlesworth, and Mendels, "Polemical Character," p. 32. The recent approach along similar lines by L. Schiffman, "The King, His Guard, and the Royal Council in the Temple Scroll," *PAAJR* 54 (1987): 237–60, does not advance the discussion beyond that of Hengel and his coauthors.

33. See chapter 2, table 1.

34. E. G. Clarke, *Targum Pseudo-Jonathan of the Pentateuch: Text and Concordance* (Hoboken, New Jersey: Ktav, 1984), ad loc.

35. A. Brooke and N. McLean, ed., *The Old Testament in Greek According to the Text of Codex Vaticanus, Supplemented From Other Uncial Manuscripts, with a Critical Apparatus Containing the Variants of the Chief Ancient Authorities for the Text of the Septuagint. Vol. 1: The Octateuch, Part III. Numbers and Deuteronomy* (Cambridge: Cambridge University Press, 1911), ad loc. Vaticanus reads γράφει, but some witnesses have γράφεις or γράφῃς (= כתבה).

MT lies behind the scribal process. The following diagram illustrates what happened in the course of transmission (the underlined words are the textual variants):

רק לא ירבה לו סוסים ולא ישיב את העם מצרימה למען הרבות סוס	*Vorlage*
רק לא ירבה לו סוסים ולא ישיב את העם מרצימה למען הרבות סוס <u>וכסף וזהב</u>	Step One
רק לא ירבה לו סוסים ולא ישיב את העם מרצימה <u>למלחמה</u> למען הרבות סוס וכסף וזהב	Step Two

At some point anterior to the text's incorporation into the TS, mechanical scribal error introduced the phrase underlined in step one into the text. This addition occurred by the well–known phenomenon of "expansion by anticipation."[36] In this type of error, the scribe, anticipating the next sentence or paragraph, inadvertently inserts a phrase at a point earlier in the text than it belongs. In the MT, the phrase וכסף וזהב appears in Deut 17:17, i.e., immediately after the verse in which this addition appears here. Significantly, expansion by anticipation is relatively common in the text of Deut as it appears in the TS.[37]

Subsequent to this expansion, the nuance of the text is subtly different. Instead of merely multiplying horses, the text now prohibits the king from increasing his hoards of gold and silver as well. While the first phrase could easily suggest peaceful trade (among other possible interpretations), the addition of the precious metals to the horses results in a list of items which typically constitute plunder in the Hebrew Bible.[38] In addition, the word עם which is used here has a well–attested secondary meaning of "army."[39] To the scribe, familiar as he was with the Hebrew Bible, the implicit meaning of the sentence in step one was that the king was forbidden to return to Egypt for a war of plunder. It was then a small and natural step to make this implicit meaning explicit—he added למלחמה. Textual critics know such additions as "expansion by explicitation," and it is a relatively common form of textual corruption in the Hebrew Bible.[40] Like expansion by anticipation, it also occurs elsewhere in the TS.[41]

By this two-step process the text of the TS emerges, lacking all polemical significance or historical implication. The canons of textual criticism favor this suggestion over that of Hengel and his collaborators; where a mechanical textual explanation can be found, it is *ipso facto* preferable to suggested intentional alteration, simply because mechanical scribal processes were constantly operative, whereas intentional alterations were quite rare. The presumption is always

36. For an excellent brief discussion and examples from the Hebrew Bible, see P. Kyle McCarter, *Textual Criticism: Recovering the Text of the Hebrew Bible* (Philadelphia: Fortress Press, 1986), pp. 28–29.

37. Cf. TS 53:7 with 55:14; 55:1 with 56:11; 55:3, 6, and 8 with Deut 17:10 and 17:11. I could easily multiply examples. See chapter 2, table 1.

38. Among many examples, cf. Jos 6:24, 1 Kngs 16:18, and, with the explicit mention of Egypt in the context, Dan 11:8.

39. For biblical attestation, see BDB s.v. For this meaning in the DSS, see Brownlee, *Habakkuk*, pp. 75–76. For a discussion of עם meaning "army," see R. M. Good, *The Sheep of His Pasture. A Study of the Hebrew Noun ʿAm(m) and its Semitic Cognates.* Harvard Semitic Monographs no. 29 (Chico: Scholars Press, 1983), p. 60.

40. McCarter, *Criticism,* pp. 34–35.

41. E.g., 51:18, where the text makes the explicit addition להמיתו.

against any suggestion of intentional change, leaving a heavy burden of proof with Hengel and his collaborators.

Additionally, there is textual proof to fortify the view that textual processes best explain the variants. Psalms of Solomon 17:33 reflects an underlying Hebrew text very close to that of TS 56:16, a fact which is doubly significant because the text of this Psalm follows its biblical *Vorlagen* very closely.[42] In 17:33b one reads, οὐδὲ πληθυνεῖ αὐτῷ χρυσίον οὐδὲ ἀργύριον εἰς πόλεμον. A possible Hebrew *Vorlage* for the text would be ולא ירבה לו זהב וכסף למלחמה. This Psalm thus furnishes powerful evidence that both וכסף (ו)זהב and למלחמה appeared in a circulating form of Deut somewhat different from the MT. And it was this version of Deut 17 which both the TS and the Psalms of Solomon used. To my mind, proper text critical methodology and actual textual evidence combine to render the text critical arguments of Hengel and his coauthors virtually indefensible.

The Argument from Defensive Warfare

The second argument our authors advance for dating TM, and thereby at least the final form of the TS, depends upon the type of wars which they believe the scroll describes in col. 58. They contend that the column's laws for defensive wars manifest concern for the defense of Judea in Jannaeus' time. They do not believe that the three or four scenarios for defensive wars which the text apparently sets forth would have been necessary in the reign of Jannaeus' predecessor, John Hyrcanus.[43]

In making this argument the authors evidently accept Yadin's understanding of col. 58: the column provides directions for two types of warfare, offensive and defensive. According to this understanding, TS 58:15b begins the discussion of offensive warfare, while the scenarios in the earlier part of the column are for defensive wars.[44]

Yet several considerations make this interpretation of col. 58, and therefore any argument based on it, problematic. First and foremost, it is questionable that 58:15b–17 really concerns offensive warfare, in contradistinction to the rest of the column. That the text does not intend to distinguish between two types of warfare only becomes apparent in the light of the biblical texts which it exegetes.

TS 58:15b–17

ואם יצא למלחמה על	.15b
אויביו ויצא עמו חמישית העם אנשי המלחמה כול גבורי	.16
החיל ונשמרו מכול דבר חטא ומכול ערוות ומכול עוון ואשמה	.17

42. D. Rosen and A. Salvesen, "A Note on the Qumran Temple Scroll 56:15–18 and Ps of Solomon 17:33," *JJS* 38 (1987): 99–101. These authors have also noted the apparent connection between the text of the TS and that upon which the author(s) of this Ps relied.

43. Hengel, Charlesworth, and Mendels, "Polemical Character," pp. 34–35.

44. See Yadin, I, pp. 358–60, and II, pp. 259, 263–4. Most recently, L. H. Schiffman, "The Laws of War in the Temple Scroll," *RQ* 13 (1988): 299–311, has taken this same position.

Biblical sources

כי תצא מחנה על איביך ונשמרת מכל דבר רע   Deut 23:10

ולא יראה בך ערות דבר   Deut 23:14

Comparison of TS 15b–17 with Deut 23:10 shows that the scroll certainly has this biblical portion in mind, and evidently intends to provide an exegesis of it. The underlined portions of the biblical text appear in expanded form in the text of the TS. The author of TM essentially quotes the protasis, כי איביך, in 15b-17a. Then the apodosis of the biblical text follows, with embellishments of the biblical terms רע and ערות (the latter coming from Deut 23:14). The only word in Deut 23:10 which is unaccounted for in the scroll is מחנה. This is not by coincidence. On the contrary, the author of TM was more interested in that word than in any which he actually quoted; he intended to define precisely that term. To that end, he added חמישית ... החיל. In other words, the question troubling the author here was, When does a military force become the biblical "camp?" The question was significant because at the point that the force became a "camp," certain biblical purity laws would need to be observed.[45] The author concluded (on the basis of the sort of triangulation between biblical portions discussed above) that if the king were accompanied by one-fifth of the army, those laws should take effect. Thus he specifically excluded certain military situations involving fewer troops, such as retaliation for raids, which he described in 58:3–6a. Whether a force would become a "camp" was a function of its size and the length of time which it was likely to spend in the field.

Yadin's translation makes plain that he did not perceive the nuance of the relationship between the biblical text and the scroll here:[46]

> And if he will go out to battle against his enemies, [*then*] one-fifth of the people shall go out with him, the warriors, all the mighty men of valour, and they shall keep themselves from all unclean things ... (emphasis mine)

Yadin thus understood the *waw* of ויצא as the *waw* of apodosis, a perfectly legitimate understanding if one had nothing to consider but the text of the TS alone. In view of the relationship the text has with Deut, however, it is unlikely to be the correct interpretation. To conform with the pattern of the biblical text, it is the *waw* of ונשמרו which should be understood as the *waw* of apodosis. The *waw* of ויצא merely introduces a sub-conditional of the protasis, and should be translated as an ordinary copulative. The following translation results:

> And, if he goes out to war against his enemies and one-fifth of the army accompanies him, the men of war, all the mighty men of valor, *then* they shall guard themselves from all uncleanness ... (italics for emphasis)

45. For example, the laws on nocturnal emission, the use of a latrine outside the camp, and the application of purification procedures after battle (cf. Deut 23 and Num 31).

46. Yadin, II, pp. 263–64. Among the other translations of the scroll, Maier (*The Temple Scroll,* pp. 50–51) and Caquot ("Rouleau du Temple," p. 492) follow Yadin. Garcìa-Martìnez, "Rollo del Templo," p. 284, appears to agree with my line of interpretation, but he does not discuss the point.

Seeing the text as framed by the biblical portion transforms it from Yadin's offensive war scenario into a general rule for all warfare, provided certain numbers of troops are involved. Within the immediate context, this view has the additional advantage vis-à-vis Yadin's of providing an exegetical rationale for the mention of one-fifth of the army: the author was defining מחנה.[47]

The broader context of TM also encourages this interpretation of 58:15b–17. Column 58:18–21 requires that the king consult—through the high priest—the Urim and Thummim. These will provide God's directions for the conduct of the war. On Yadin's understanding the king would seek the oracle only in the case of offensive warfare, a limitation which is not easily reconciled with the emphasis which the whole of TM places on the king's relationship with God. For example, TM 57:01–07 comprised a slightly expanded version of Deut 17:19–20,[48] a biblical portion which demands the king's obedience to God. And it will be recalled that one purpose of the bodyguard was to prevent the king from sinning against God. And his advisory council was to include priestly and Levitical elements, in part to insure against the king's "lifting up his heart," so losing sight of a proper relationship with God. And the whole of col. 59 emphasizes that the fate of the nation and the king's own person and line hinges on his obedience. Examples could be multiplied, but these few suffice to make the point: TM puts great emphasis on the king seeking God constantly. It therefore is very difficult to suppose that the author of TM meant to say that in a potentially catastrophic situation such as warfare, the king need seek God only when he was on the offensive. No, understanding both 58:15b–17 and 58:18–21 as dealing with warfare in general provides a much more plausible explanation of the matter.

Two arguments external to the text itself further undermine the suggested distinction between offensive and defensive warfare. The first is the weight of the biblical paradigms for warfare which the author of TM has relied upon for every detail of his midrash (see the *Appendix*). When these biblical texts mention a king seeking the Urim and Thummim, they make no distinction between offensive and defensive situations. If, however, one were to apply such a distinction artificially (as perhaps a Second Temple exegete might do), it turns out that in each case they describe not offensive, but defensive warfare.[49]

A second external argument against distinguishing between the two types of warfare here is that roughly contemporary texts seem to be oblivious to such a distinction. For example, in 1 Macc 3:46–60, Judas Maccabee was involved in what later Judaism would call a defensive

---

47. On Yadin's assumptions, there is no apparent reason for the stipulation that one-fifth of the army accompany the king in an offensive war. Yadin virtually admits as much in I, pp. 358–59.

48. According to Yadin's analysis, restoring the top of column 57 according to the MT of Deut 17:19–20 indicates that the text of the TS was one to two lines longer than the MT.

49. Thus, Saul in 1 Sam 14:18–19, a defensive war against the Philistines; 1 Sam 14:41–42 (full text only in LXX) is in the same context. With David, 1 Chr 14:10 is a defensive war against the Philistines, as is 1 Chr 14:14, 1 Sam 23:2, and 1 Sam 23:4. 1 Sam 30:7–8 involves a defensive war against the Amalekites. In 1 Sam 23:9, David uses the ephod in a matter which does not concern warfare.

"war of duty."[50] It is thus significant that he applied to this war the rules of exemption from warfare found in Deut 20, which later Judaism understood to apply only to offensive warfare.[51] Evidently he was unaware of any distinction between the two types of war. 1QM, the War Scroll, is similarly unaware of such a distinction.[52] These texts suggest that the rabbinic distinction between types of warfare, which in fact structures Yadin's entire approach, was not yet an issue when TM was composed.

Thus both intra- and extra-textual considerations make the proposed distinction between offensive and defensive warfare in TS 58 dubious. If this distinction were nonexistent in the mind of its author, then certainly he cannot have been mandating defensive war stratagems out of concern for Jannaeus' inadequate preparations. Accordingly, no palpable connection exists between this aspect of TM and the historical realities of Jannaeus' time.

The Argument from Absence of the King's Sacerdotal Function

The third argument that Hengel, Charlesworth, and Mendels proffer is that a cardinal element of the king's function is missing in TM: his priestly or religious function. They say that its absence results from opposition to the unity of the high priesthood and monarchy in the person of Jannaeus.[53] But, like their earlier argument from textual criticism, a methodological problem hamstrings this contention. Before asking historical questions of any literary text— which are not, after all, first-order historical sources—it is essential to subject it first to a thorough analysis, so as to establish what sort of questions the text can properly be expected to answer. Unfortunately our authors (and others using the technique of dating the TS by TM) have attempted such literary analysis only in desultory fashion.[54] If they had carried it out thoroughly and systematically, they would doubtless have found the reason for the absence of the king's sacerdotal function—it is not a reaction to historical circumstances, but results from the method by which the author composed TM. This point can be made graphically by means of table 4.

---

50. See J. Goldstein, *I Maccabees*, p. 263. Cf. the comments of R. de Vaux, *Ancient Israel, volume I: Social Institutions* (New York: McGraw-Hill, 1965), p. 265, concerning Judas and the Urim and Thummim.

51. E.g., mSotah 8:2–7, mSanhedrin 2:4, and tSotah 7:24.

52. See Y. Yadin, *The Scroll of the War of the Sons of Light Against the Sons of Darkness* (Oxford: Oxford University Press, 1962), pp. 65–70. It is interesting to note that in this early work, Yadin was much more reticent about applying rabbinic typology of warfare to texts centuries older than he was when analyzing the TS.

53. Hengel, Charlesworth, and Mendels, "Polemical Character," pp. 32 and 37.

54. Delcor, "Statut du roi," p. 65, notes, "Pour réaliser son dessein, d'une part il rassemble les données éparses dans l'A.T ... d'autre part il apporte das modifications substantielles aux données bibliques ..." He fails to consider the all important matter of how the author accomplished the second part. Hengel, Charlesworth, and Mendels, "Polemical Character," p. 30, say, "Our author certainly had two different foci before his eyes when writing this chapter: the biblical משפט המלך on the one hand, and the practical customs (*praxis*) emerging from the Hebrew Bible relating to kingship on the other." This statement is precisely correct; thus the fact that the authors have not considered its practical consequences in the matter at hand is surprising. They say nothing more about the literary character of TM.

Table 4. The Structure of TM

	Topics	Reference in TM	Reference in Biblical "King's Law"
1.	Accession, Conscription, Appointment	57:1–5a	Deut 17:18 "When he sits upon the throne of his kingdom" 1 Sam 8:11 "… he shall take your sons and place them in his chariot…" 1 Sam 8:12 "… and to set up for himself captains of thousands …"
2.	The King's Bodyguard	57:5b–11	1 Sam 8:16 "And … your chosen ones (=בחורים) he shall take."
3.	The Royal Council	57:11b–15	Deut 17:20 "… that his heart might not be lifted up above his brethren …"
4.	The Queen	57:15b–19	Deut 17:17 "… and he shall not multiply wives for himself …" 1 Sam 8:13 "… and he shall take your daughters"(i.e., not daughters of nations)
5.	The King as Judge	57:19b–21	1 Sam 8:5 "And now, give us a king to judge us like all the nations." 1 Sam 8:14 "… and he shall take your best fields and vineyards and olives."
6.	The King in War	58:1–21	1 Sam 8:20 "… our king, and he shall go out before us and fight our wars."
	a. Battle strategies	58:1–11a	1 Sam 30:24–25 "… like the portion of those going down to war, so shall be the portion of those guarding the supplies … and he made it a statute and law …"
	b. Booty division	58:11b–15a	Deut 17:17 "gold and silver he shall not increase for himself overmuch." 1 Sam 30:24–25 (as above) 1 Sam 8:10 "and your seeded fields and vine-yards he shall tithe."
	c. Seeking God	58:15b–21	Deut 17:19 "in order that he may learn to fear Yahweh."
7.	The King and Curses or Blessings	59:2–21	Deut 17:20 "in order that he might increase the length of his reign, he and his sons."

This table, together with the *Appendix* (see for greater detail on the relationships between the TS and the biblical portions), discloses the compositional plan which guided the author of

TM. He relied upon Deut 17:17–20 and 1 Sam 8:5–20 for the basic framework. These texts provided him with a skeleton, and he fleshed it out by the usual methods. In every subject discussed he stayed within the guidelines set forth by the biblical "King's Law" passages, never straying. It is thus manifest why there is no mention of the king's sacerdotal function in TM: the framework passages do not mention it. Since they do not, neither does TM; it is as simple as that. The explanation is entirely literary,[55] with no element of polemical reaction to the contemporary political scene.[56] Thus the third argument these authors have devised proves to be a chimera.

Remaining Arguments

According to the fourth argument of Hengel and his coauthors, the description of the king's bodyguard in col. 57 is another reason to date the text to the time of Jannaeus. They regard the description as "an obvious criticism of the *philoi* or *hetairoi* of Jannaeus and his foreign mercenaries." They further suggest that the stipulation that the bodyguard not leave the king, thus preventing his capture by foreign nations, reflects a Nabatean ambush on Jannaeus from which he narrowly escaped with his life.[57]

I show above that the description of the king's bodyguard is compounded of biblical phrases. The idea that the king should have a bodyguard is found already in the biblical text. The author of TM adds nothing substantive to the biblical portions; he merely gathers them together topically. Essentially biblical commentary, nothing of what is said need be a reaction to historical events. Furthermore, as noted above, elements of the description are otherworldly. One does not get the feeling in reading them that they have been informed by hard-nosed political realities. The description more likely represents the fruit of a theological or theoretical inquiry into the biblical stipulations bearing on the king.

Again, Hengel and his fellow scholars claim that since TM mentions a מלך, it must postdate Aristobulus I, the first Hasmonean to claim the crown, while especially noting that the title also belonged to Aristobulus' successor, Jannaeus.[58] This argument is one which could not stand independently of the other arguments our authors make. The mere mention of a "king" in a

---

55. M. Sweeney, "Midrashic Perspective in the Torat Ham-Melek of the Temple Scroll," *HS* 28 (1987): 51–66, also criticizes Hengel and his collaborators for giving scant attention to the literary character of TM. In general, his views on the nature of the text are compatible with those argued here, but in my view his otherwise excellent study suffers from two deficiencies. First, he argues that cols. 57–59 are a midrash of Deut 17:14–20 only; he does not reckon with the influence of 1 Sam 8 and passages about kings from the historical books. Second, he tries to interpret the variants of col. 56 without recourse to textual criticism. Like Hengel and his collaborators, he sees all the variants as intentional alterations by the author of the TS. Because of these problems, I do not find his study comprehensively explanatory.

56. The subjective character of the collaborator's argument is underlined by the fact that even without full-scale literary analysis, several scholars have come to a conclusion diametrically opposed to them on this point. Both Stegemann and Maier have remarked on the lack of polemic against a unification of the offices of king and high priest as evidence of a pre-Hasmonean dating for at least this portion of the scroll. See J. Maier, *The Temple Scroll*, p. 123, and H. Stegemann, "'Das Land'," p. 157.

57. Hengel, Charlesworth, and Mendels, "Polemical Character," p. 33. The quotation is on the same page.

58. Ibid, pp. 32 and 35.

discussion of a biblical topic is meaningless for dating in and of itself. Since their foundational arguments are unconvincing, this superstructural argument cannot stand.[59]

For their sixth argument our authors maintain that the stipulation in TM that the king must be monogamous is a criticism of Jannaeus' many concubines.[60] This argument, also, cannot stand as an independent point in favor of dating the text to the time of Jannaeus. And, once again, these stipulations regarding the queen in TM represent comparatively straightforward exegesis. They mirror a traditional understanding of Lev 18:18. The author evidently understood the first portion of that verse to mean, "You shall not marry two Israelite women." In a recent study, A. Tosato, examining Lev 18:18 from the perspectives of philology, literary analysis, and history, argues convincingly that the understanding held by the author of TM is in fact the original sense of the biblical law. In contrast to those who see here a reference to the Hasmonean period, he concludes:[61]

> ... the date of appearance of the anti-polygamy and anti-divorce law should be backdated by two or three centuries (to the fifth-fourth centuries B.C.). It should be attributed to the official Jewish world, not to the secessionist one.

Finally, Hengel and his coauthors see as significant the fact that the TM system for division of the booty from war is, though biblical, reinterpreted. They state that it results from antipathy to the manner of Hellenistic rulers, who lived on booty and used it to create plutocracies with their friends.[62] Their concession that the system is biblical zeroes in on a fundamental problem at the very heart of their methodology. If what the scroll records is taken from the Bible, then how can anyone know whether it reflects some aspect of contemporary society as well? No one would want to deny that it is possible that some statements in TM have such a double meaning. But what tool or technique could serve to discern such situations? Perhaps it is frustrating, but the only safe position is a minimalist one. If any portion of the scroll is derived from the text of

---

59. Incidentally, the authors do not seem to have considered the fact that in postbiblical Hebrew, the term מלך need not refer to a king. It can refer to various types of leader. For example, nothing precludes the equation of the term with the Greek ἐθνάρχης. Various Jewish leaders under the Ptolemies and Seleucids prior to the Hasmonean period held this title. In light of the relationship between TM and Deut 17, it is ironic for their argument that the LXX translates מלך throughout that chapter by ἄρχων, "ruler," and never by βασιλεῦς, "king." For the translators of the LXX, even in this chapter—the biblical *locus classicus* on the king—another translation of the term מלך was possible and, indeed, preferable. The reason why the translators preferred ἄρχων over βασιλεῦς in Deut probably has to do with politics. The Egyptian Jews were always vulnerable to criticism of their loyalty to the Ptolemies, and they wanted to avoid an unpatriotic translation. This is the attractive suggestion of E. Bickermann, "The Septuagint as a Translation," in *Studies in Jewish and Christian History,* 3 vols. (Leiden: Brill, 1976), 1:194 and note 70. Of course, my point is unaffected by this explanation, since all I am saying is that the semantic field of מלך at this time was broad enough to permit its application to subroyal functionaries.

60. Hengel, Charlesworth, and Mendels, "Polemical Character," pp. 33–34.

61. A. Tosato, "The Law of Lev 18:18: A Reexamination," *CBQ* 46 (1984): 199–214. The text quoted appears on p. 214.

62. Hengel, Charlesworth, and Mendels, "Polemical Character," p. 36.

scripture by an identifiable hermeneutical process, it is hopelessly subjective to search for a concrete historical event lurking behind the curtain just offstage. And since, as I show above and in the *Appendix*, all that TM says does have a hermeneutical or textual explanation, nothing remains which Hengel and his collaborators can embrace as evidence for dating the TS. TM contains nothing but the most general clues to the time of its composition. Certainly it affords no secure basis by which to date the scroll to the reign of Alexander Jannaeus.

The Use of Temple Scroll 64:6b–13a to Date the Scroll

In addition to TM, scholars have singled out TS 64:6b–13a as providing data useful for dating the scroll. Their arguments constellate a scholarly consensus which can be reduced to two basic points:

1. The author of the TS has deliberately changed and supplemented the text of Deut at this point to provide explicit Pentateuchal justification for the death penalty by crucifixion. According to this understanding, the author is writing in the immediate wake of actual historical events to produce a *post factum* apologetic. Proponents base this idea on two considerations. First, in their view the author has reversed the order of the verbs "hang" and "die" in Deut 21:22–23, in order to make the text explicitly support the exegetical position he held.[63] Second, they argue that since the author has not engaged in "serious exegesis," he could have no biblical basis for what he says. Therefore, what he says must be "eisegesis" of contemporary events into the biblical text.[64]

2. The TS is sectarian, hence this portion of the text is also sectarian. It represents nothing more than the minority view of a small and fanatical offshoot of Second Temple Judaism.[65] Further, the TS text is related to a portion of the sectarian 4QPesher Nahum. Since that text describes events in the reign of Alexander Jannaeus, so must this portion of the TS. The crucifixion of 800 Pharisees by Jannaeus in 88 B.C.E. thereby provides the *terminus ad quem* for the TS.[66]

---

63. Thus M. Bernstein, "Midrash Halakhah," p. 150; O. Betz, "מותו של חוני," p. 91; J. Fitzmyer, "Crucifixion in Ancient Palestine, Qumran Literature, and the New Testament," *CBQ* 40 (1978): 505; D. Halperin, "Crucifixion, the Nahum Pesher, and the Rabbinic Penalty of Strangulation," *JJS* 32 (1981): 43; M. Wilcox, "'Upon the Tree'," p. 89; van der Woude, "De Tempelrol (II)," p. 287 ("De waw vóór talita wordt explicatief opgevat."); and Yadin, I, p. 375 and II, p. 289.

64. M. Berstein, "Midrash Halakhah," pp. 155 and 159. The phrase "serious exegesis" is his.

65. So A. Dupont-Sommer, "Observations nouvelles," p. 715; Bernstein, "Midrash Halakhah," p. 149; D. Flusser, review of מגילת המקדש, p. 273; van der Woude, "De Tempelrol (II)," pp. 287–88; and Yadin, I, p. 378.

66. Bernstein, "Midrash Halakhah," pp. 156–58 (although Bernstein is tentative on this point); Betz, "מותו של חוני," p. 91; Fitzmyer, "Crucifixion," pp. 504 and 507; Hengel, Charlesworth, and Mendels, "Polemical Character," p. 37; Yadin, I, pp. 373–74 and idem, "Pesher Nahum," p. 9.

The Textual Argument

At two points, 64:8 and 64:10,[67] the TS reverses the word order of the MT, with תליתמה preceding וימות (on the verbal form of the latter, see below). This reversal has the effect of making hanging or crucifixion the explicit cause of death. But was this inversion really an exegetical device of the author? Significant evidence suggests that instead the author found the inversion already present in the source he was using. This evidence consists of the following:

1. The Peshitta. The text here reads, "If a man is guilty of a sin whose penalty is death, let him be lifted up on a tree and so put to death."[68]

2. Medieval texts of the LXX. Two Greek texts, *Parsinus graecus* 3 and *Vaticanus graecus* 1238, have long been known to attest the inverted word order. An Ethiopic text related to their tradition also shares this reading.[69] The Greek texts were part of medieval Italian collections and date to about 1100 and 1200 C.E., respectively. Rosso, who recently studied these texts, concludes in favor of the antiquity of the variant word order they contain.[70]

3. Philo Judaeus. A passage in *De specialibus legibus* indicates that he understood Deut 21:22–23 to refer to hanging a still-living person on a tree. In discussing this portion of the Mosaic legislation, Philo says:[71]

---

67. D. Schwartz, "(64, 12 מקוללי אלהים ואנשים (מגילת המקדש," *Leshonenu* 47 (1982): 19, believes that although the author has inverted the order of the verbs twice, in a third instance, at 64:9, he retained the order of the MT. If true, this retention would support the view that the author had before him a *Vorlage* identical to the MT. But Schwartz has misread the text. The instance of "retention" at 64:9 is actually two separate statements. True, the two verbs occur in contiguity, but one sentence, based on Deut 17:6, ends after וימות. The term יתלי is the first word of the next stipulation, which is based on Deut 17:7. Thus, each time the author refers to Deut 21:22 the verbs are inverted.

68. wʾn ḥyb gbrʾ ḥlp ḥthʾ dynʾ dmwtʾ wnzdqp ʿl qisʾ wntqtl. The translation is mine.

69. *Parsinus graecus* 3 and the Ethiopic text were cited in the early part of this century by Brooke and McClean in *The Old Testament in Greek,* ad loc. It is unfortunate that J. Wevers has not discussed these manuscripts, nor Vaticanus graecus 1238, in his excellent text critical work, *Text History of the Greek Deuteronomy,* Abhandlungen der Akademie der Wissenschaften in Göttingen, Philologisch-Historische Klasse: Folge 3, no. 106 (Göttingen: Vandenhoeck & Ruprecht, 1978). Really complete study of the textual affinities these texts may have with other MSS of the LXX thus remains a desideratum.

70. L. Rosso, "Deuteronomio 21, 22," esp. p 236:

> Escluso che si tratti di una coincidenza fortuita o dell' intervento di una mano "cristiana" che volesse adattare il testo veterotestamentario alla procedura dell' esecuzione di Gesù seguita dai Romani...dai date esposti si puo concludere che il Rotolo del Tempio LXIV, 9–11 fornisce la prova dell' antichità della variante contenuta nei MSS citati...

71. *De specialibus legibus* 3.151–152. The translation is that of F. H. Colson in the Loeb Classical Library edition of Philo, vol. 7. The Greek text reads:

> ἐπεὶ δὲ τοῦτ' οὐκ ἐνδέχεται τιμωρίαν ἄλλην προσδιατάττεται κελεύων τοὺς ἀνελόντας ἀνασκολπίζεσθαι. καὶ τοῦτο προστάξας ἀνατρέχει πάλιν ἐπὶ τὴν

But since this was impossible he ordered another penalty as an addition, and ordered the manslayers to be crucified. Yet after giving this injunction he hastened to revert to his natural humanity and shews mercy to those whose deeds were merciless when he says, 'Let not the sun go down upon the crucified but let them be buried in the earth before sundown.'

Clearly Philo describes men who are not yet dead when they are suspended. The mercy he mentions would consist of breaking bones and other expedients aimed at insuring a rapid death for the criminal. Of course, simply because Philo interpreted Deut 21:22–23 in this way does not prove that he knew of a text identical to that of the TS *Vorlage*. It only means that he was familiar with an understanding of the text of Deut which, in contrast to later rabbinic opinion, held that the hanging or crucifixion occurred before death, not after. Nevertheless, the variant would lead directly to his position, and since it is present in more than one textual tradition— including that of the LXX, Philo's Bible—it is entirely plausible to suggest that he knew of it.

With regard to the relationship between the Peshitta and the above-mentioned MSS of the LXX, there is another point which should not be overlooked. The reading of the last part of Deut 21:22 in the Peshitta, ntqtl, shows that the translator probably had before him a text identical to the MT, והומת. Both texts have passive verbal forms. The reading of the LXX, however, is ἀποθάνῃ, reflecting a Hebrew original וימות (Qal with simple *waw*).[72] Thus the texts of the Peshitta and the LXX MSS do not reflect an entirely identical tradition for this verse; their value as independent witnesses for an early textual variant in Deut 21:22 rises accordingly.

The evidence that the inversion was already in the *Vorlage* of the TS author's source is strong. It occurs in MSS of both the LXX and the Peshitta. In general, and in the specific instance of this verse, these witnesses represent different textual traditions vis-à-vis the MT. Further, Philo Judaeus may well have known this variant. Added to the fact that in the textual transmission of biblical texts presumption opposes intentional changes, this evidence is sufficient to cast grave doubt on the textual argument.

The "Sectarian Texts" Argument

According to the second argument emerging from the consensus, both the TS and 4QPesher Nahum are products of the same sectarian group at more or less the same period in its history.[73] They refer to the very same historical event in the reign of Alexander Jannaeus,

---

αὐτοῦ φιλανθρωπίαν πρὸς τοὺς ἀνήμερα εἰργασμένους καὶ φησι· μὴ ἐπιδυέτω ὁ ἥλιος ἀνεσκολοπισμένοις, αλλ' ἐπικρυπτέσθωσιν γῇ πρὸ δύσεως καθαιρεθέντες.

72. This conclusion is probable in light of the revisions by Aquila and Theodotion. Both these versions read θανατωθῇ, the equivalent of the MT והומת. Presumably, they were trying to bring the Greek text into line with the Hebrew version which they knew.

73. By this statement I mean that the material in 4QpNah which describes the events in question is approximately contemporary with the TS material, by implication of the consensus argument. I believe many scholars would argue that the pesher contains later material as well.

his crucifixion of 800 Pharisee opponents. Now, I believe that I have satisfactorily demonstrated in the first portion of this chapter that the text of MD is entirely biblical interpretation. If so, the TS cannot be "describing" any historical event at all, and certainly not in a way which present critical tools can discern. But perhaps not everyone will agree that this portion of the TS, belonging originally to MD, is merely midrashic biblical interpretation. Suppose for the sake of argument that one could somehow determine that the text did reflect a real event. And suppose that in fact it is referring to a particular incident or policy of crucifixion. Do such concessions lead ineluctably or even probably to the consensus conclusion? In other words, what are the probabilities that both the pesher and the TS could be reacting to the same incident? Because the answer depends largely on how rare or remarkable crucifixions were in Palestine in the pre-Roman period, a brief résumé of the evidence on that matter is in order.

Even before Rome conquered the East, crucifixion was extremely widespread as a mode of execution. Sources such as Esth 7:9–10, Ezra 6:11,[74] and Herodotus[75] suggest that it originated among the Persians. This mode of punishment was familiar in the Greek-speaking world by the fourth century B.C.E. at the latest. It is apparently attested by Ptolemaic papyri,[76] and during the course of the fourth and third centuries Alexander the Great, the Diadochoi, the Ptolemies, and the Seleucids all employed it.[77] Among the Seleucids, it is perhaps particularly noteworthy that Antiochus III crucified certain individuals, considering the excellent relations which the Jewish temple state enjoyed with that monarch.

Substantial evidence supports the notion that crucifixion was a penalty for state crimes in the period of the Maccabean revolt, and later under the early Hasmoneans. According to Josephus, *Antiquities* 12.256, Antiochus IV Epiphanes imposed the penalty on Jewish loyalists who refused to apostatize in 168/167 B.C.E.:[78]

> Indeed, they were whipped, their bodies were mutilated, and while still alive and breathing, they were crucified, while their wives and the sons whom they had circumcised in spite of the king's wishes were strangled, the children being made to hang from the necks of their crucified parents.

74. The exact meaning of this verse is still unclear. The relevant portion of the Aramaic reads: כל אנש די יהשנא פתגמה זנה יתנסח אע מן ביתה וזקיף יתמחא עלהי. The crucial terms are the verbs מחא and זקיף. Some have seen in מחא a reference to impalement, but the verb does not easily support such an understanding. זקיף may already mean "crucified" here as it can in later Aramaic; the problem is precisely that such usage is not attested outside of this text for several hundred years. See Williamson, *Ezra, Nehemiah*, p. 72.

75. E.g., *Hdt.* 1.128.2, of Cyprus. For further details from the classical sources see M. Hengel, *Crucifixion*, trans. J. Bowden (Philadelphia: Fortress Press, 1977), pp. 22–39.

76. Ibid., p. 71.

77. Ibid., pp. 73–75.

78. The translation is that of R. Marcus in the Loeb Classical Library. The Greek text reads:

καὶ γὰρ μαστιγούμενοι καὶ τὰ σώματα λυμαινόμενοι ζῶντες ἔτι καὶ ἐμπνέοντες ἀνεσταυροῦντο, τὰς δὲ γυναῖκες καὶ τοὺς παῖδας αὐτῶν, οὓς περιέτεμνον παρὰ τὴν τοῦ βασιλέως προαίρεσιν, ἀπῆγχον, ἐκ τῶν τραχήλων αὐτοὺς τῶν ἀνεσταυρωμένων γονέων ἀπαρτῶντες.

During his reign the high priest Alcimus once executed a large number of Hasidaeans who came over to him from Judas Maccabee. Judging by the arrangement of the material in 1 Macc, this event took place in 162/161. Although it is not absolutely certain, numerous scholars believe that these executions were effected by crucifixion.[79] *Testament of Moses* 8:1 refers to the same or roughly contemporary crucifixions.[80]

Not too many years after the successful Maccabean revolt, the book of Esth was translated into Greek in Jerusalem.[81] This version unquestionably understood Haman's execution as a crucifixion, rendering the ambiguous Hebrew תלה by the Greek σταυρόω.[82] Presumably the Jewish translator interpreted the biblical events in the light of contemporary usage of תלה. Finally, the targum of Ruth lists among four approved methods for inflicting the death penalty "hanging on a tree." Scholars believe the targum represents the legal position of a time before the Tannaim; it may also antedate the Christian era.[83] If so it would provide further evidence relevant to this discussion.

This brief historical review supports the conclusion that crucifixion was employed by the Jews by the early second century B.C.E. at the latest. Indeed, thinking paradigmatically, in a later period the Jews borrowed important elements of capital punishment from the surrounding nations; it is therefore perhaps the more likely that they borrowed crucifixion from the Ptolemies in the third century.[84] Since the penalty was an option for at least the next several

---

79. Goldstein, *I Maccabees*, p. 9; M. Hengel, *Rabbinische Legende und frühpharisäische Geschichte* (Heidelberg: Carl Winter Universitätsverlag, 1984), p. 34 n. 63; and E. Stauffer, *Jerusalem und Rom in Zeitalter Jesu Christi* (Munich: Francke Verlag, 1957), p. 124. Maccabees does not specify the method of execution, although the language allows one to understand crucifixion. It is later rabbinic texts which definitely indicate that Alcimus used this method. See Stauffer, *Jerusalem und Rom,* p. 161, n. 11, for the specific texts and discussion.

80. This text, also known as *The Assumption of Moses,* is notoriously hard to date. According to a theory which J. Licht has proposed in "Taxo, or the Apocalyptic Doctrine of Vengeance," *JJS* 12 (1961): 95–103, and which J. J. Collins has modified ("The Date and Provenance of the Testament of Moses," in *Studies on the Testament of Moses,* ed. G. W. E. Nickelsburg [Cambridge, MA: Society of Biblical Literature, 1973], pp. 15–32; and idem, "Some Remaining Traditio-Historical Problems in the Testament of Moses," in ibid., pp. 38–43), the document consists of two successive redactional layers. The earlier layer dates from the Maccabean period, and includes chapter 8. With Collins' modifications, the theory appears convincing.

81. The colophon at 11:1 of the LXX provides the date for the translation, Ἔτους τετάρτου βασιλεύοντος Πτολεμαίου καὶ Κλεοπάτρας. The two major options for dating this reference are to 114 B.C.E. and Ptolemy VIII, with C. A. Moore, *Daniel, Esther and Jeremiah: The Additions* (Garden City: Doubleday & Company, 1977), p. 250, or to 77 B.C.E. and Ptolemy XII. E. J. Bickerman argues for the latter position in "The Colophon of the Greek Book of Esther," *JBL* 63 (1944): 339–62.

82. Cf. e.g., Esth 7:9.

83. For text, introduction and commentary see E. Levine, *The Aramaic Version of Ruth,* Analecta Biblica 58 (Rome: Biblical Institute Press, 1973). On pp. 60–62 Levine argues that the basic elements of the text may be pre-Christian. D. R. G. Beattie concurs that the targum must be pre-rabbinic; see "The Targum of Ruth—18 Years On," *Hermathena* 138 (1985): 57–61, and "The Targum of Ruth—A Sectarian Composition?," *JJS* 36 (1985): 222–29.

84. Cf. the remarks of Hengel, *Rabbinische Legende,* p. 34:

centuries—a very volatile period during which there were many political criminals who would be likely candidates for crucifixion—why suppose that both the TS and 4QpNah are concerned with the same events? The probability is not especially great. Therefore, even if the TS were describing events—which cannot be demonstrated—the likelihood that both texts are dealing with the same events seems remote.[85]

This second argument recurring in the writings of the nascent consensus thus makes its appeal to improbabilities. Of course, *ab initio* it also begs one of the major questions in TS research—whether the TS is in fact "sectarian." If it is not, then this argument is invalid. It is a form of circular reasoning anchored in a certain view of the DSS materials, according to which they are essentially a homogeneous collection.[86] This view is simplistic, however, as seems increasingly to be recognized. And, historically speaking, there is nothing particularly "sectarian" in the position which either text takes on crucifixion.[87] In the Hasmonean period both the Pharisees[88] and the Sadducees[89] evidently practiced this method of execution. In no sense was the practice itself "sectarian." It belonged to the repertoire of the major political factions.[90]

"Aus alledem darf man schliessen, dass auch die Juden, die ja auch später in ihren Kapitalrecht die Bräuche ihrer Umwelt zumindest zum Teil ubernähmen ... schwere politische Vergehen in der hellenistisch-vorrömischen Zeit mit der Kreuzigung ahndeten."

85. A philological argument which might be arrayed against the consensus position has appeared in the literature. According to this approach, the two texts cannot be referring to the same situation because the TS uses the term תלה, while the pesher uses the phrase תלה חי. The first term without further qualification is supposed to mean "hang," while the two-word phrase would signify "crucify." This is the argument of J. Baumgarten in "Does TLH in the Temple Scroll Refer to Crucifixion?," *JBL* 91 (1972): 472–81 and idem, "Hanging and Treason in Qumran and Roman Law," *EI* 16 (1982): 7*–16*, and of F. García-Martínez, "4QpNah y la Crucifixión. Nueva hipótesis de reconstrucción de 4Q169 3–4 i, 4–8," *EB* 38 (1979–80): 226–27. Unfortunately this argument, although tending to support my position, is persuasive neither philologically nor historically.

86. Further complicating the suggestion that the two texts contain a small group's reaction to the same events is that the two texts may have different opinions on the use of crucifixion. The TS clearly prescribes it in certain cases, while it is possible to understand the pesher as opposed to its use.

87. Some scholars have argued that the pesher regards the use of crucifixion as a cruel abomination. But there is otherwise no hint in the evidence regarding crucifixion which has survived that any segment of the Jewish population opposed it as excessively cruel *at this time*. Scholars who argue that the Jews had such feelings about the method in the Hasmonean period are perhaps too much under the influence of Josephus, who opposed it for its cruelty (cf. *Ant.* 13.380–83). But Josephus, after all, wrote more than two centuries after the period in question. In that time much had changed; Josephus viewed the Hasmonean events of which he wrote through the prism of Roman cruelty and contemporary Jewish horror at the practice. Crucifixion had become much more common in the years leading up to, and during, the First Revolt.

88. Ibid. Cf. *BJ* 1.97, 1.113, and *Ant.* 13.410.

89. Hengel, *Crucifixion,* pp. 84–85, and *Rabbinische Legende,* passim.

90. As an aside, the identification of the TS and 4QpNah as products of the same group may involve some members of the consensus position in an inconsistency (e.g., Hengel, Charlesworth, and Mendels, "Polemical Character," p. 37.) These scholars urge that TM and TS 64:6b–13a are reactions to the activities and policies of Alexander Jannaeus. As discussed above, they see TM as extremely critical of that monarch. The inconsistency arises in the light of what pNah implies about the agent of the crucifixion it describes. It calls the king כפיר חרון (4QpNah 3–4 i 5. The *editio princeps* is J. Allegro, *DJD* V, pp. 37–

The arguments in favor of using TS 64:6b–13a to date the scroll have been weighed and found wanting. As with TM, its midrash is constructed entirely from biblical elements; it is impossible to distinguish supposed historical references. Nor can one safely ground an argument on the reversal of verbs in the text vis-à-vis the MT, since that variant is attested in other manuscript traditions. It is hard to believe that it originated with the TS and moved thence to the Greek MS tradition, for example. Finally, historical facts by no means compel the consensus conclusions about the relationship between the TS text and 4QpNah. Even supposing that somehow the TS is writing a *post factum* apologetic, probability casts grave doubt on the view that both texts concern the same historical event.

Conclusions

In this chapter I advance literary and composition critical reasons for the view that TS 57:1–59:21, 60:2–11, and 64:6b–13a derive from a single source, MD. I also show that scholarly attempts to derive a date for the TS from portions of MD fall short of conviction. In fact, given the nature of the relationship between MD and the biblical text, for all practical purposes this source is undatable, except that it necessarily antedates the final form of the scroll. One must seek other avenues of approach if there is to be any hope of dating the final redaction of the scroll. I lay the foundation for one such strategy in Chapter 5, while taking up the Festival Calendar Source and the laws of the TS.

42.) Now, in 4QpHos[b], כפיר חרון is the praiseworthy instrument of God (4QpHos[b] 2 2, as compared with 5–6 3 and 7–9 1–2.) If, as seems probable, the same circle composed both pesharim, then pNah regards Jannaeus very favorably, while, according to these adherents of the consensus, the TS anathematizes him. Given the ideological character of the discourse, it is hard to believe that one group would be simultaneously positive and negative about this king.

5

THE FESTIVAL CALENDAR AND THE LAWS

Introduction

The "laws" of the TS (defined below) fairly cry out for redaction and form critical analysis, which are the main topics of this chapter. The results of this analysis are also included with crucial facts which now come to the fore concerning both the redaction and the redactor of the TS. Prior to a discussion of the details of those facts, however, and a review of the background of some the "laws," it is necessary to consider the source known here as the "Festival Calendar." I therefore first briefly discuss the content and character of this source, thence moving to a consideration of its redactional purpose and date. A brief discussion of this source will suffice since its delineation is straightforward and noncontroversial, unlike the other sources of the scroll.

The Festival Calendar

Content and Character

Wilson and Wills specify the content of their "Festal Calendar" as 13:9–30:2, with 29:2–30:2 forming a redactional conclusion.[1] I concur with their analysis, save for the minor adjustment that the source should begin at 13:8 rather than 13:9.[2] The use of the tetragrammaton to refer to God characterizes this document. It draws upon a variety of compositional techniques, but is especially notable for its many examples of "verbatim rearranged" quotations (see the *Appendix*). This technique sets it apart from the other sources of the TS. From the standpoint of verbal usage, the source is clearly distinct from the Temple Source within which it is presently imbedded. For example, it virtually never displays the periphrastic use of the participle, so common in the Temple Source.[3] Because the Festival Calendar source has a clear beginning and end, unity of concept, and purposeful progression, it is likely that it once circulated separately.

---

1. Wilson and Wills, "Literary Sources," pp. 275 and 279–80.

2. See Yadin, II, p. 52.

3. Wilson and Wills, "Literary Sources," p. 285. They suggest that the only two attested uses of the periphrastic tenses in the Calendar source may be redactional. Based on the ubiquity of this verbal usage in col. 47, a redactional composition, I believe they may well be right.

Table 5. A Comparison of Festival Calendars

TS 13–29	Num 28–29	Lev 23	Deut 16	TS 11:9–13[1]
The Tamid 13:8–16	The Tamid 28:3–8	–	–	–
Sabbath Offering 13:17–14:?	Sabbath Offering 28:9–10	Sabbath 23:3	–	Sabbath 9b[2]
New Moon 14:?–14:8	New Moon 28:11–16	–	–	New Moon 9b
First Month of New Year 14:9–15:?	–	–	–	Lacuna 10a
Milluʾim 15:13–17:5	–	–	–	–
Pesaḥ 17:6–9	Pesaḥ 28:16	Pesaḥ 23:5	Pesaḥ 16:1–5	–
Unleavened Bread 17:10–16	Unleavened Bread 28:17–25	Unleavened Bread 23:6–8	–	Unleavened Bread 10b
Lacuna? 18:?–18:?	–	–	–	–
Omer/First Fruits Barley 18:?–18:10	Omer 23:10–14	–	Omer 10b	Lacuna 11a
Weeks 18:10–19:9	Weeks 28:26–31	Weeks 23:15–22	Weeks 16:9–12	Weeks 11b
First Fruits Wine 19:11–21:10	–	–	–	Lacuna 12a
First Fruits Oil 21:12–23:02	–	–	–	Oil 12b
Wood Festival 23:03–25:2	–	–	–	Wood 12b–13a
New Year Seventh Month 25:2–25:10	New Year Seventh Month 29:1–6	New Year Seventh Month 23:24–25	–	Lacuna 13a
Day of Atonement 25:10–27:10	Atonement 29:7–11	Atonement 23:27–32	–	Lacuna 13a
Tabernacles 27:10–29:2	Tabernacles 29:12–34	Tabernacles 23:34–36, 39–43	Tabernacles 16:13–17	Tabernacles 13b
Eighth Day Assembly[3] 29:2	Assembly 29:35–39	Assembly 23:36	–	Assembly 13b

[1]This is not a festal calendar in the strict sense, but a list of occasions on which the priests will use the altar. I include it because it may have influenced the redactor's positioning of the Festival Calendar.

[2]Whether this is indeed the first item in the list is not absolutely certain because of the preceding lacuna.

[3]This festival is located here if Yadin's restorations of 29:09–29:2 are correct.

Redactional Purpose

Why did the redactor position the Festival Calendar in the middle of the Temple Source? Indeed, why is it a part of the TS at all? Scholars have not addressed these important questions in any detail; table 5 may help suggest some answers.

It appears that col. 11 may have influenced the positioning of the Calendar. Since this column was a part of the proto-Temple Scroll, the redactor presumably found it as we do, immediately prior to the altar description[4] of col. 12. It seems the redactor wanted to balance col. 11 with his Festival Calendar, to "bracket" the altar description in col. 12. It is also probable, based on the lacunae in col. 11 and the possibilities for reconstruction,[5] that he wanted to add at least one festal occasion to the list of col. 11—the Festival of Millu'im, which does not appear to have been in col. 11's list. Thus the redactor wished to balance, and to a degree correct, the contents of col. 11. (Another reason for its placement, indeed probably the best explanation, concerns the redactional shape of the TS as a whole, and is discussed in chapter 6.)

The proposal that the redactor wished to add additional festivals gains support from a study of col. 43. This column, part of the Temple Source, provides a list of occasions for the consumption of the second tithe, as noted earlier in connection with Jubilees. According to 43:15 and 17, the only days on which it would be permissible to eat the tithe were "holy" or festival days. TS 43:1–3 comprised a list of those occasions, presumably all-inclusive. In terms of table 5, this list should correspond to the items in the TS cols. 13–29, excepting the occasions of the Tamid, Unleavened Bread, the Day of Atonement, and perhaps the eighth day Assembly. Apart from those occasions, any item in cols. 13–29 which is not in 43:1–3 constitutes an addition which the redactor wished to effect by means of the Festival Calendar. Unfortunately, comparison of the two lists of occasions is hampered by the substantial lacunae which interrupt the legible text of col. 43:1–3. Hence, although it is undeniable that all the occasions in the Festal Calendar do not now appear in those lines, Yadin has maintained that all the missing festivals were once there, filling the lacunae.[6]

But Yadin's contention is impossible. The list of missing occasions totals twelve items, while the first lacuna, at 43:2, is about 15 spaces long. The phrase ראשי החודשים should fit there, based on a comparison with TS 11:9, and it entirely fills the lacuna. This probable restoration would leave only the second lacuna, in 43:3a, to absorb all eleven additional occasions—and this lacuna is only 10–12 spaces long. It would be impossible for all the remaining festal occasions to fit here. Therefore, one can conclude that col. 43 never comprised all the occasions found in TS 13–29. The column provides convincing evidence that the

---

4. Little remains of the column, but enough can be made out to agree with Yadin that the altar is the subject of col. 12. See Yadin, II, p. 43. J. Baumgarten, in his review of the *editio princeps* of the TS (*JBL* 97 [1978]:528), holds that two altars are in view here. This suggestion is also possible, but for our purposes the number of altars involved does not matter.

5. See Yadin, II, p. 46.

6. Yadin, II, p. 182: "the other festivals [of the calendar in cols. 13–29] were ... mentioned there."

redactor inserted the Festival Calendar in order to expand the festal lists he found in the proto-Temple Source.

The most likely candidates for identification as added festivals are the New Year of the first month, the Festival of Millu'im, and the First Fruits of Barley. This inference is based on the absence of these occasions in the list in col. 43 (also, they are only conjectured for col. 11). They are unique to the Festival Calendar source, appearing in no other source of the Second Temple period.

The proto-Temple Scroll, as represented by the 43.366 fragments, indicates another possible reason for the inclusion of the Festival Calendar. Fragment 1 appears to show that the festal calendar in the proto-Temple Scroll was modeled on Lev 23; indeed, it may essentially have *been* Lev 23. Table 5 shows that the Festival Calendar source, in contrast, corresponds more to Num 28–29. The difference between the two biblical sources is principally inclusiveness and detail. Num 28–29 includes three more sacrificial occasions, the Tamid, the New Moon, and the Omer. Perhaps more important, Num has many more details for the sacrificial procedures, all of which the Festival Calendar adopts (see the *Appendix*). It is a reasonable inference that the redactor replaced the "Deuteronomized" Lev 23 he found in the proto-TS with the Festival Calendar because he wanted those details. In so doing, he was again seeking to correct or embellish the earlier form of the scroll.

Two additional reasons for the inclusion of the Festival Calendar document may be noted in passing. (I do no more than point them out here, since their mention necessitates anticipating the discussion later in this chapter; that discussion does, I believe, justify these suggestions.) First, the redactor wanted to specify details of the sacrificial offerings for given occasions. This was a part of the process of providing exact rules for offerings,[7] rules which his community believed it possessed in contradistinction to Judaism generally. Elements of these rules were extrabiblical. Second, he wanted to buttress his community's claim that its calendar was the one which God had originally given to Israel. In their view many in Israel had subsequently forgotten this fact.[8] Once the claim of the TS's author to immediate revelation was accepted, the scroll's calendar would, of course, constitute an incontestable divine imprimatur for the community's position.

Date

We possess few data by which to date the Festival Calendar. Two pieces of evidence may perhaps be taken to indicate that it postdates, and relies upon, the Temple Source (or its traditions). First, it includes more sacred occasions than the Temple Source, while having in

---

7. Cf. CD 6:20, ‎להרים את הקדשים כפירושיהם‎.

8. Cf. CD 6:18–19. The knowledge and observance of the correct rules for the sabbath, the ‎מועדות‎ (*sic*) "festivals", and the ‎יום התענית‎ "Day of Atonement," were basic to the covenant underlying the CD community. Among these rules was the calendrical basis for determining when the occasions would fall. Cf. the words of P. R. Davies, *The Damascus Covenant: An Interpretation of the "Damascus Document,"* (Sheffield: *JSOT* Press, 1983), p. 86: "Whether or not the solar calendar originated as a theological doctrine in the Babylonian exile, both CD and Jubilees regard it as being once upon a time known and subsequently forgotten or lost." He refers to CD 3:14–15 and Jubilees 6.

common with it several peculiar festivals. Given that festal lists generally tend to lengthen with the passage of time, one can tentatively infer the relative lateness of the Festival Calendar with respect to the Temple Source. Second, at 17:8–9 and 19:5 there are reference to the "courts" and "inner court" of the temple. These references may hint at a knowledge of the Temple Source. It is also possible, however, that they are redactional adjustments made to accommodate the Calendar to its present literary setting. Further, it is equally possible to see here no reference to the concentric square courts of the Temple Document. The document may mean to describe the courts of the *quondam* temple, presumably a form of the temple of Zerubbabel. It is prudent to fall back and state only the obvious: the date of the Festival Calendar must be earlier than the present form of the TS.

The Laws

Character and Content

In the first chapter I note that Wilson and Wills discern a "Purity Collection" at TS 48–51:10, and that this suggestion is problematic. Callaway has already drawn attention to some of the problems with their analysis.[9] On grounds of content, he shows that cols. 45–47 are much more like 48–51 than they are like the "Temple and Courts" document in which Wilson and Wills locate them. Therefore, he says, to assign the two groups of columns to different sources runs against the grain of the evidence. Thus far I agree; but Callaway then draws the curious conclusion that no "Purity Collection" should be isolated at all. It is apparently his opinion that the "Temple and Courts" document should include 48–51:10 as well as 45–47. Yet this suggestion is difficult to accept because the differences between the Temple Source and cols. 48–51 are manifold. The complexities here are greater than either Wilson and Wills or Callaway have apparently recognized.

With the exception of cols. 29:2–10 and 51:5b–10, the hand of the redactor is nowhere more evident than it is in the environment of the laws (for now, roughly cols. 45–51). The import of this fact for the discrimination of a "Purity Source" is considerable. In order to explain why this is so, I briefly anticipate the discussion of chapter 6 here.

Among scholars working on the literary criticism of the TS, there is a consensus that 29:2–10 and 51:5b–10 are redactional "seams," composed by the redactor as a bridge between major sources. Yet scholars have thus far not taken this finding to its logical conclusion. By an analysis of the known redactional compositions, one can isolate certain phrases, which I call "redactional phrases." When they appear elsewhere, particularly where there is "free composition," it is probable that here, too, the redactor has been especially active.[10] An

---

9. P. Callaway, "Source Criticism," pp. 213–22.

10. One cannot be absolutely certain, of course, that the presence of these phrases means that the redactor has inserted them. It is possible that their appearance in the source at hand attracted him to the source in the first place. Nevertheless, one suspects that in fact the redactor has added the phrases, because when removed, the resultant text is unbroken and flowing.

interesting pattern emerges when one considers selected redactional phrases found in 29:2–10 in terms of where they or their variants appear in the TS:[11]

1. אשר אשכין שמי עליו (29:3–4, 8–9)—45:12, 47:10–11, 52:19–20.
2. כתורת המשפט הזה (29:4)—50:6–7, 7, 17.
3. לעולם ועד (29:8)—35:9, 45:14, 46:3–4.
4. אקדשה את מקדשי בכבודי (29:8)—30:1 (?), 47:4, 52:19–20.
5. אני שוכן בתוכם (29:8)—45:13–14, 14; 46:4, 12; 47:3, 18; 51:7–8.

As this listing shows, these five redactional phrases alone occur seventeen times between cols. 45–52, while elsewhere in the scroll they are seldom encountered. It seems the redactor has taken a much more active role in the composition of these columns than he has generally in the scroll. The portions he was working with were evidently short, and required frequent bridging to fit their new literary context.

A further indication of the nature of these laws is their content. For example, col. 45:7–18 comprises a list of six short laws. On form critical grounds, these laws belong together, as is demonstrated below. On the other hand, col. 52:13–20 differs substantially from the laws of col. 45, both form critically and stylistically. Its content is also distinctly different. It does not seem likely that these two portions derived from the same source.

In chapter 2, I argue from form criticism that 48:1–10 belonged to the D source; yet most of D now appears in 51:11–66:17. The redactor has extracted 48:1–10 and interpolated it into an earlier part of the TS. If, then, on at least this one occasion, there is strong evidence for interpolation as a technique in the composition of the final form of the scroll, why not look for the same process elsewhere? Taking this approach together with the evidence for intermittently heavy redactional activity, in cols. 45–52 in particular, a conclusion rather different from that of earlier scholars emerges: the so-called "Purity Collection" is no single source at all. Instead, the laws comprise a heterogeneous grouping which the redactor culled from various sources. Occasionally he interpolated these extracts into the Temple Source and D, but in large measure he concentrated them between these two sources. I believe that this hypothesis succeeds in explaining a great deal of the form critical and literary critical data of the scroll.

In my view the following portions of the TS are legal interpolations into the major sources of the TS, and in listing them, I briefly describe the basis for their isolation:

1. 34:12b–14. These lines quote Lev 1:5b and 1:9b verbatim. Thus, on composition critical grounds they are distinct from the Temple Source in which they are now imbedded.[12] Further, they differ from their surroundings in terms of verbal usage. In 34:5–11, periphrastic tensing (participle plus imperfect of היה) occurs fifteen times. In lines 12b–14, in contrast, a sudden shift is evident; the periphrastic is completely absent, while the perfect consecutive (rare in the Temple Source) shows up in והקטירו. A third reason for suggesting that these lines are an

---

11. For a full listing of all redactional phrases and their locations in the TS, see chapter 6, table 8.

12. As the *Appendix* indicates, the Temple Source was composed almost entirely by "free composition." Verbatim quotations of the biblical text are therefore suspect.

interpolation is the appearance in line 14 of יהוה; this divine name does not occur elsewhere in the Temple Source.

2. 39:5–11a. Reasons are advanced in chapter 2 for suspecting that these lines are an interpolation.[13] In brief, they stand out from the Temple Source in terms of content, composition criticism (these lines quote portions of Exod 30:12–16 verbatim—see the *Appendix*), and use of the tetragrammaton.

3. 40:6. Detailed reasons are also given in chapter 2 for seeing this line as a legal interpolation. Both this portion and 39:5–11a concern entry into the sanctuary or congregation *qua* sanctuary.[14] It is not surprising, then, that both would be interpolations. The redactor had the same reason for inserting them both.[15]

4. 43:12–19. Beginning with והיושבים, the redactor has apparently supplemented the law of the second tithe which he found in the Temple Source. The major reason for identifying these lines as an addition is the crucial phrase דרך שלושת ימים, which also appears in 52:13b–21. The latter lines are certainly an interpolation (see below). It is also noteworthy that the law of 43:12–19 can stand on its own; it does not rely on the context for its coherence. In its present context its purpose is probably to elaborate on the lines at the beginning of col. 43, now mostly lost.

5. 45:7b–18. On grounds of content and form criticism, the conclusion may be drawn that these lines are an interpolation in the Temple Source. One cannot simply conclude that a new "legal source" begins here, however, because 46:1–18 is undoubtedly to be assigned to the Temple Source. It is true that the redactor has introduced several of his favorite phrases into col. 46, but its content, form critical character, and style (periphrastic tense usage) argue decisively against divorcing it from the Temple Source.

6. 47:3–18. This portion is no mere interpolation, but a redactional composition (see ch. 6).

7. 48:11–17 and 49:1–51:5a. I do not differ with Wilson and Wills in seeing these passages as distinct from the Temple Source and D. They do not require extensive discussion, since their content and formal character is so evidently different from the latter two sources. As noted in chapter 3, 48:11–17 is probably a redactional composition.[16]

8. 52:13b–21. In these lines are found three laws on sacrifice inserted into D. With regard to composition criticism, they are unlike D, since they do not quote extensive passages from Deut or parallel passages. As briefly stated in chapter 2, they share an impressive amount of peculiar

---

13. See p. 57 above.

14. For a discussion of these passages, and a comparison of their legal perspective with that of rabbinic sources, see L. Schiffman, "Exclusion from the Sanctuary and the City of the Sanctuary in the Temple Scroll."

15. See chapter 6, table 7.

16. See p. 63 above.

vocabulary with col. 47, a redactional composition.[17] In addition, redactional phrases appear in lines 16 and 19. Line 21 is probably a redactional addition in light of 23:13–14.

9. 63:14–15. This passage is an addition to the law of the "Beautiful Captive" of Deut 21:10–13. It clearly breaks with D. It is not a quote from Deut, nor easily explicable as part of a synoptic law code. Furthermore, the passage is formally identical with the laws of 45:7b–18, as table 6 below demonstrates. The phrase לוא תגע לכה בטהרה is very significant, as it links the *Sitz im Leben* of this passage to the laws of col. 49.

10. 66:12b–17. According to composition criticism, these lines are redactional additions. Unlike D, in which they are imbedded, the method used to formulate these laws was "midrash" (see the *Appendix*). Deut 23:1 was the formal model, but the content derives from Lev 18 and 20. Thus the laws did not arise from the straightforward combination of verses, as sometimes happens in D (e.g., 48:1–7).

Considering the categories of legal material here, one finds laws about exclusion from the sanctuary, sacrificial practice, purity, and marriage. The next question to investigate is whether or not it is possible to learn something more about the *Sitz im Leben* in which they functioned.

Sitz im Leben of the Laws

The purity laws of the TS are amenable to form criticism, and in this way one may potentially gain valuable insight into their *Sitz im Leben*. Table 6 is an exercise in the form criticism of these laws, which begin at 45:7b. (Because of its different origin, I do not include col. 47.) The table reveals a striking and perhaps surprising fact: the laws of these columns are incomplete. Now, some of this incompleteness can reasonably be attributed to the redactional shaping of the laws. For example, the man who has had a flux (45:15–17a) is tacitly prohibited entry into the temple city, a prohibition which is implied by the positioning of this law immediately after the law for the blind (45:12b–14), where entry is explicitly forbidden. Perhaps it would be more accurate to call this type of unstated entry a laconism, rather than incompleteness. But can one say the same about the unstated purification procedure for the man who is unclean because he has touched a dead body (45:17b)? Or can one attribute to laconic expression the fact that there is no stated purification procedure for the leper (45:17c–18)? Perhaps one might assume that in these cases the biblical text was thought to contain the needed details. Yet this assumption is dangerous, as Milgrom has shown. Certain aspects of the laws here not only vary from the biblical requirements, but actually violate the scriptural system for dealing with impurities.[18] In addition, taking just one example, table 6 shows that not all seven-day procedures were identical; therefore it is illicit to assume that the redactor omitted those which are unstated simply because they were tautologous. It must further be supposed that for the leper elaborate procedures existed. In addition to these unstated purification

---

17. See pp. 38–39 above.

18. See J. Milgrom, "The Qumran Cult: Its Exegetical Principles," pp. 171–72.

procedures, beginning with col. 50 (or, to look at it another way, 49:5) there occurs a whole series of unstated "prohibitions." What is one to make of the incompleteness of these laws?

For one thing, the form of these laws implies a detailed discussion lying behind them.[19] In only a few cases do the laws here appear in their full form. Perhaps 49:5–21 illustrates something of what the missing fuller discussions would look like. More importantly, this defective character is a guiding light for the scholar investigating the background of the TS because, as given, many of these laws could not be applied. Starting from the reasonable supposition that they were intended to be applied (even if perhaps only idealistically, like some of the Mishnah), it follows that since the redactor did not give the full form of the laws, he must have assumed that the reader either knew or could find the full form. Consequently, these laws would not be *de novo* for their intended audience. This fact clearly requires that the *Sitz im Leben* of the laws was a group united and educated in their view of these matters.

The phrase in 49:21, לגעת בכול טהרתמה, "to touch any of their 'purity,'" provides additional evidence for the communal origin of these laws. It is clear from the context that טהרה carries its technical sense, "secular food prepared according to levitical rules originally pertaining to sacred food."[20] This meaning attaches to none of the thirteen attestations of the word in the Hebrew Bible;[21] the meaning of the term here arose in a particular postbiblical sociological environment.

Within the corpus of the published DSS, טהרה in the sense it bears here occurs only in 1QS, CD, and 4Q513.[22] It is obviously "sectarian" *a natura,* although not necessarily in the sense that that word has been used in TS studies. טהרה also appears in the developed sense in the law of the "Beautiful Captive" (63:14–15). With this fact the trail doubles back to table 6.

19. Thus this situation is analogous to that of CD and 1QS with regard to legal materials. After a complete study of CD's laws on judges and court composition, Schiffman notes, "The documents before us do not represent the earliest phase of ... thought and law. Rather, the materials as they are preserved are the result of an evolutionary process which took place before and during their composition and redaction." See L. Schiffman, *Sectarian Law in the Dead Sea Scrolls: Courts, Testimony, and the Penal Code* (Chico: Scholars Press, 1983), p. 40. Later he notes that both CD and 1QS "have been observed to quote from an otherwise unknown but common source containing legal maxims of some kind." (p. 214). See also T. Zahavy, "The Sabbath Code of Damascus Document X, 14–XI, 18: Form Analytical and Redaction Critical Observations," *RQ* 10 (1979–81): 588–91, who argues that the laws of CD 10:14–11:18 are composite.

20. See Jastrow, s.v. In rabbinic texts טהרה can mean not only food (though it especially refers to that), but also other items susceptible to ritual uncleanness, such as vessels and garments. For a further discussion of the term, see Ch. Rabin, *Qumran Studies* (Oxford: Clarendon Press, 1957), pp. 7–8.

21. Lev 12:4, 5, 45; 13:7, 35; 14:2, 23, 32; 15:13; Num 6:9; Ezek 44:26; 1 Chr 23:28, and 2 Chr 30:19.

22. 1QS 5:13; 6:16, 22, 25; 7:3, 16, 19, 25; 8:17, 24; CD 9:21, 23; 4Q513 (Baillet, *DJD* VII, pp. 287–95 and plates 52–53) fragment 2, col. ii, 1; fragment 10, col. ii, 6. See also 4Q514 and note 74 below.

Table 6. Form Critical Analysis of the Purity Laws

TS Reference	Situation	Prohibition	Period	Purification	Permission
45:7b–10	איש כי יהיה לו מקרה לילה	לוא יבוא אל כול המקדש	שלושת ימים	וכבס בגדיו ורחץ ביום הראישון ... שלישי	אחר יבוא אל המקדש ...
45:11–12a	איש כי ישכב עם אשתו שכבת זרע	לוא יבוא אל כול עיר המקדש	שלושת ימים	Unstated	Unstated
45:12b–14	כול איש עור	לוא יבואו לה	כול ימיהמה	Inapplicable	Inapplicable
45:15–17a	כול איש ... יטהר מזובו	Unstated	שבעת ימים	ויכבס ביום השביעי בגדיו ורחץ את כול בשרו במים חיים	אחר יבוא אל עיר המקדש
45:17b	וכול טמא לנפש	לוא יבואו לה	עד אשר יטהר	Unstated	Unstated
45:17c–18	וכול צרוע ומנוגע	לוא יבואו לה	עד אשר יטהרו	Unstated	כאשר יטהרו והקריב את [ ]
49:5–21	אדם כי ימות בעריכמה — 49:5–10 explicate situations	לוא תגע בטהרה — Implied by 49:21	שבעת ימים	יטהר הבית וכול אשר בו — 49:14–21 discuss different procedures	ויטהרו לערב
50:4–7	וכול איש אשר יגע בעצם אדם מת — 50:4–6 give equivalent	Unstated	Unstated	וטהר כחוק המשפט הזה	Unstated
50:8–9	וכול האדם אשר יגע בו	Unstated	לערב	יכבס בגדיו ורחץ	וטהר לערב
50:10–19	ואשה כי תהיה מלאה וימות ילדה במעיה	Unstated	שבעת ימים	Unstated	Unstated
50:12–13	כול הנוגע בו (בבית האשה)	Unstated	עד הערב	Unstated	Unstated
50:13–15	אם ... לתוך הבית יבוא	Unstated	שבעת ימים	וכבס בגדיו ורחץ ביום הראישון וביום השלישי יזה ויכבס ... וביום השביעי ...	ובאה השמש וטהר
50:16–19	וכול הכלים ... וכול כלי חרש	Unstated	Unstated	ישברו (כלי חרש)	Unstated
63:14–15	וראיתה בשביה אשה ... ולקחתה — In biblical text	לוא תגע לכה בטהרה וזבח שלמים לוא תואכל	שבע שנים	Inapplicable	אחר תואכל

As noted above, a series of purity situations lacking stated prohibitions begins in col. 50. Since these laws now follow col. 49, which intends to regulate who touches the "pure food," it is reasonable to conclude that these laws also have that concern. If so, then many of the purity laws of the TS originally did not pertain to entry into the temple. Instead, their concern was a "sectarian" dietary regulation. It therefore is necessary to explain the redactional concept behind their inclusion in the scroll, an explanation of which is considered below.

In concluding the *Sitz im Leben* of the laws was a community to which the redactor probably belonged. That the laws arose in a community follows from the incomplete way in which the laws are given and the use of the term טהרה.[23] That the redactor was a member of the community is a logical inference from the simple fact that he chose to adopt these laws which belonged to a certain community, when presumably he could have chosen others instead. He must have believed these laws were correct; it is hard to divorce that belief from the adoption of the perspective which produced them. But is it possible to go farther, and to identify the community specifically? I suggest that it is.

CD and the Laws of the Temple Scroll

Comparison of TS 45:11–12 with CD 12:1–2, and TS 66:15b–17a with CD 5:7–8, reveals similarities that can hardly be coincidental:

TS 45:11–12. ואיש כי ישכב עם אשתו שכבת זרע לוא יבוא אל כול עיר המקדש שלושת ימים

CD 12:1–2. אל ישכב איש עם אשה בעיר המקדש לטמא עיר המקדש בנדתם

TS 66:15b–17a. לוא יקח איש את בת אחיהו או בת אחותו כי תועבה היא

CD 5:7–8. ולוקחים איש את בת אחיהו ואת בת אחותו

Translation

TS 45:11–12: And a man who sleeps with his wife and has a seminal emission shall not enter any part of the temple city for three days.

CD 12:1–2: A man shall not sleep with his wife in the temple city so as to render the temple city unclean with their impurity.

23. It is possible that in 49:8–9 we find additional evidence for this conclusion. This portion can be read as establishing an opposition:

1.   כלי חרש יטמאו וכול אשר בהמה לכול איש טהור יטמא

2.   והפתוחים יטמאו לכול אדם מישראל

Viz., "(Every) earthen vessel, and all its contents, shall be unclean for every 'clean man'; while open vessels shall be unclean for every 'man of Israel.'" The phrases איש טהור and אדם מישראל can be understood as technical terms denoting two classes of people. The "clean man" is bound to observe a higher standard. For him, all earthen vessels in the house of a dead person are unclean, along with their contents. In contrast, for the "man of Israel," only the open vessels in that environment are unclean. This law could have arisen only in a group which distinguished levels of purity. Undoubtedly, they strove to maintain the higher standard; they would all be "clean men." But the portion is admittedly ambiguous; it may mean no more than that the "clean man" is any Israelite in a state of purity at the time he encounters the clay vessels. The term "man of Israel" would then simply be a synonym for "clean man."

> TS 66:15b–17a: A man shall not marry his brother's daughter nor his sister's daughter, for such is an abomination.

> CD 5:7–8: And they each marry his brother's daughter and his sister's daughter.

It is essential to consider which text presupposes the other, but in this discussion, the mere fact of the similarities strongly suggests that the community of the redactor is the community of CD. The suggestion is fortified by the fact that these laws are unattested elsewhere.

Because the community of the laws is evidently that of CD, a detour is appropriate at this juncture into a consideration of the most recent critical work on that scroll. The better one understands that scroll, the better one will presumably understand the *Sitz im Leben* of the TS laws. Further, a detailed consideration at this point, including details whose relevance is perhaps not yet obvious, provides the necessary groundwork for the discussion in chapter 6.

Recently, two scholars have dominated the study of CD. Although their analyses have built on earlier scholarly work, they have superseded that work so completely that for the present it suffices to concentrate on them alone. These scholars are Murphy-O'Connor and Davies. A short synopsis of each approach affords the easiest comparison between their conclusions.

According to Murphy-O'Connor, the "Admonition" of CD (cols. 1–8, 19–20) comprises four basic source documents:[24]

1. A Missionary Document designed to win converts to the community's position—2:14–6:1.
2. A "Memorandum" intended to stimulate members of the community to more faithful adherence to the group's laws—6:11b–8:3.
3. A document criticizing the ruling class of Judah—8:3–19.
4. A document composed after the death of the Teacher of Righteousness, whose purpose was to combat defections from the group. The *Grundschrift* is 19:33b–20:1b, 20:8b–13, and 20:17b–22b.

A redactor has combined these sources, adding to them the following portions:

1. 1:1–2:13—An addition which, unlike the rest of the Admonition, criticizes a particular group, not all Israel. It is an attack on "those who departed from the way" (1:13a). This document may be contemporary with document 4 above.
2. 6:2–11a—A "Well Midrash" on Num 21:18, from the period subsequent to the Missionary Document.

In addition, Murphy-O'Connor distinguishes numerous interpolations. He categorizes them according to their ideology. Some intend to reinforce the original Admonition (e.g., 3:15b–16a). Others evidence a shift wherein the community's opposition, which in the original

---

24. J. Murphy-O'Connor, "An Essene Missionary Document? CD II, 14–VI, 1," *RB* 77 (1970): 201–29; "A Literary Analysis of Damascus Document VI, 2–VIII, 3," *RB* 78 (1971): 210–32; "The Critique of the Princes of Judah," *RB* 79 (1972): 200–16; and "A Literary Analysis of Damascus Document XIX, 33–XX, 34," *RB* 79 (1972): 544–64.

Admonition was all Israel, is now a single individual (e.g., 4:19; 8:13). A third, smaller group of interpolations reveals no inner unity (e.g., 1:13b–c).

Davies presents his ideas in *The Damascus Covenant: An Interpretation of the "Damascus Document."* Like Murphy-O'Connor, he isolates four basic documents;[25] two of these he regards as secondary. In his analysis, he recognizes smaller, constituent sources, but argues that the unity of the four basic documents is such that it renders finer analysis barren. For Davies, the major sources are:

1. A historical document, describing the community's origins, nature, and purpose—1:1–4:12a.
2. A legal document, demonstrating that those outside the community do not have the true Law, while the community does; to this demonstration a brief résumé is attached—4:12b–7:9. 1 and 2 comprise the original Admonition.
3. A secondary expansion of the original Admonition, consisting of warnings and a midrashic critique of the "princes of Judah"—7:9–8:19.
4. A supplement to the original Admonition, made by a new group having a Teacher; Davies regards them as the "Qumran settlers"—19:33–20:34.

Like Murphy-O'Connor, Davies identifies numerous interpolations, notably each and every reference to the Teacher of Righteousness outside document 4. Thus, for him there were three recensions of the Admonition. The original consisted of 1:1–7:9. At a later point, someone expanded it with the addition of extended warnings to those who failed to respond to the Admonition's urgings toward repentance. Later still, the "Qumran settlers" took up the document (now comprising 1:1–8:19), and reworked it, adding 19:33–20:34. By "Qumran settlers," Davies means the יחד ("Unity") of 1QS and some of the pesharim. His proof for the agents of this last recension is that only in the final addition do lexical and "historical" connections between 1QS and CD occur.[26]

Perhaps the greatest virtue in Davies' formulation is his demonstration that—contrary to the assumptions of most previous scholars—CD describes a community which, while somehow related, is not identical to the community of 1QS and the pesharim. Further, he ties the "Laws" (CD 9–16) to this earlier community by proving that the legal résumé in 4:12–7:9 depends on them. Thus the Laws found in the Damascus Covenant are the laws of the earlier community.

Davies' ideas have generally met with a warm response.[27] In certain details, Murphy-O'Connor's analysis probably constitutes a better explanation of the data, but their approaches

---

25. Davies, *Damascus Covenant,* pp. 52–53.

26. Essentially, this idea is not much different from Murphy-O'Connor's proposal that a compiler brought together his four basic documents, since in his scheme the compiler was a member of the יחד.

27. The most substantial reviews are J. J. Collins, *JBL* 104 (1985): 530–33; F. García-Martínez, *JSJ* 14 (1983): 189–94; M. Horgan, *CBQ* 48 (1986): 301–303; A. R. C. Leaney, *JTS* 36 (1985): 195–98; E. Qimron, *JQR* 77 (1986): 84–87; and R. White, *JJS* 36 (1985): 113–15. Only Collins and Qimron express reservations about Davies' approach, but their objections are not persuasive. For a detailed consideration of both Murphy-O'Connor's and Davies' approaches, see P. R. Callaway, *The History of the Qumran*

are compatible, and a synthesis seems to be emerging.[28] In the present context the most important point on which they agree is that Davies has found the community of CD, and with them, some of their laws.[29]

But the "Laws" portion of CD (cols. 9–16) is not inclusive of all of the group's ordinances. Even with the unpublished cave 4 materials, CD almost certainly never included more than a selection of the group's legal materials.[30] It may also be significant that, in contrast to 1QS, for example, the laws of CD reflect a community surrounded by gentiles, or at least in constant contact with them.[31]

Given, then, that the laws which appear in CD are only a portion of those which that community possessed, it is natural to wonder whether the laws of the TS represent a further selection.[32] The suggestion is made above that the redactor was a member of the CD community, and I show that a few of the laws of both texts agree or coincide. Can one be certain, however, of the correct order of priority—in other words, that the laws of the TS did not *become* the laws of that community, but already *were* such? No doubt my assertion does require explicit defense, since scholars in general have, if anything, assumed the opposite stance.[33] And certainty on the order is important, since it is the fulcrum for one's view of the purpose and provenance of the TS (see discussion in chapter 6).

One argument in favor of my view has already been noted: the logic of the *Sitz im Leben*. Since the laws are incomplete, the reader must have been able to find more information somewhere. Logically, that source would be the legal resources of the group concerned, some of which are now found in CD 9–16. This argument is perhaps particularly strong because it arises from the data of the TS itself, rather than from external considerations. And it is important enough to bear repeating: as some of the laws of the TS now stand, they could not be applied.

The presence of considerable redactional activity in cols. 45–52 is a second argument in favor of the prior existence of the laws of the TS. This activity suggests that the redactor was

---

Community: An Investigation. Journal for the Study of the Pseudepigrapha Supplement Series no. 3 (Sheffield: Sheffield Academic Press, 1988), pp. 91–99.

28. See Murphy-O'Connor, "The Damascus Document Revisited," *RB* 92 (1985): 223–46, and P. R. Davies, *Behind the Essenes. History and Ideology in the Dead Sea Scrolls,* Brown Judaic Studies no. 94 (Atlanta: Scholars Press, 1987), pp. 33–49.

29. Murphy-O'Connor recognizes the significance of this advance in "Damascus Document Revisited," p. 241.

30. Davies, *Damascus Covenant,* pp. 107, 125, 132, and 210 n. 68.

31. S. Iwry, "Was there a Migration to Damascus? The Problem of שבי ישראל," *EI* 9 (1969): 80–88, esp. p. 85.

32. From a linguistic perspective, the laws of the TS may strike the reader as an older form of Hebrew than that found in CD 9–16. Closer analysis suggests, however, that the two forms of the language differ principally in that the redactor of the TS has been more concerned to write a "biblical" Hebrew than the author(s) of CD 9–16. From time to time, a later lexical item will intrude in the TS, in spite of the redactor's best efforts—cf. e.g., מלאה at 50:10, and Yadin's commentary *ad loc.* A detailed study of the language of CD 9–16 remains a desideratum.

33. E.g., Yadin, II, p. 300; Wacholder, *The Dawn of Qumran,* pp. 33–98 and 101–35.

patching together portions from pre-existent codes, and bridging the patches. Further, the frequency of the bridging implies diverse sources.

Third, comparison of texts in the TS and CD encourages this position. The correspondence between TS 66:15b–17 and CD 5:7–11, especially 5:7–8 is attested above. The two texts at these points are so similar that literary influence in one direction or the other seems undeniable—an observation several scholars have already made, but, in my view, not correctly explained. Wacholder, for example, asserts that the Damascus Document quotes the TS.[34] He argues that CD does not attribute the quotation because the audience the author addressed was hostile, and therefore not amenable to "sectarian" sources such as the TS.

But several considerations prove, to my mind, that Wacholder has got the relationship between the two scrolls the wrong way round. For one thing, there is the midrashic character of the passage in the TS. The reasoning process which has generated the laws of marriage here is really quite subtle. Indeed, the subtleties are such that the modern reader may puzzle over them for some time, even though he knows that the author has somehow "wedded" Lev 18 and 20 to Deut 23:1. The TS provides no clue to the reasoning process; yet CD furnishes the reason explicitly. Thus both scrolls are, as it were, incomplete halves, and one cannot simply assume the priority of the TS, as does Wacholder. Its command is just as dependent on the reasoning of CD as that scroll's wording might be thought to be on the TS.[35] The situation is undoubtedly susceptible to several interpretations, but perhaps the best is that both scrolls refer to an antecedent collection of the community's laws. The TS, in accordance with its claims to be on a par with the biblical revelation to Moses, dresses the law up in "biblical" language, while CD simply paraphrases.[36] It is true that the law is not found among the published portions of the Laws of CD, but the unpublished 4Q fragments evidently include additional marriage laws; perhaps this law will turn up among them.[37] Its presence there is not, of course, vital to my position, since as indicated above CD never included more than a selection of its community's laws.

A second problem with Wacholder's view—and, since they are opposites, a factor favoring mine—involves audience analysis. The terminology used in the scroll belies his statement that the audience CD addresses is hostile. The scroll calls its audience יודעי צדק ("those who know righteousness," 1:1), באי ברית ("those who are entering the covenant," 2:2), and בנים ("sons," 2:14). These appellations are not the sort which a group will use for hostile outsiders; they describe people who are viewed favorably. Beyond these terms of address, however, the data of CD are ambivalent. They indicate that the audience is, in sociological parlance, "in," but

---

34. Wacholder, *The Dawn of Qumran*, p. 126.

35. Both CD and the TS use the verb לקח to refer to marriage, although the verb does not appear in Lev 18:13, which lies behind TS 66:15b–17a.

36. The laws of CD regularly use אל with the jussive to frame negative commands. The TS uses לוא, the stronger apodictic negative, modeling Dt 23:1.

37. J. T. Milik, *Ten Years of Discovery in the Wilderness of Judaea*, trans. J. Strugnell, Studies in Biblical Theology no. 26 (London: SCM Press, 1959), p. 152. Milik describes the contents of the 4Q fragments fully on pp. 151–52.

apparently not securely so.[38] Perhaps this ambivalence can be attributed to the fact that CD is catechetical, rather than, as Wacholder would hold, apologetic.[39]

If the text is directed toward catechumeni, what better occasion to introduce the TS? It would represent a new book for them to recognize as authoritative. And CD does refer to such "extra-biblical" sources when appropriate. In addition to Jubilees at 16:3–4, it cites a legal work or midrash by one Levi ben Jacob at 4:16–17.[40] The text evidently had no hesitation about appealing to extra-biblical sources when addressing the prospective members of the group. Wacholder's explanation for the lack of attributed quotations from the TS is therefore unacceptable; the audience in fact was not hostile, and CD was quite willing to make appeal to "sectarian" texts. Certainly Jubilees, for example, is as "sectarian" as is the TS.

Thus, if the present form of the TS already existed, CD presumably would have attributed any quotation drawn from that work. Further, the manner of the quotation in CD makes it hard to believe the reference is to the TS. When the Damascus Document quotes authoritative sources such as the Bible, it never furnishes an explanation for the command. The command simply stands as ultimate authority, requiring no explanation. Given the nature of the TS—it claims to come from the very mouth of God—why does CD explain the reason for a TS law— if such it is? Probably it is *not* such. The likely explanation for the way CD handles the law is that it was unknown to the audience, and did not rest on ultimate authority. In other words, the Admonition is simply introducing to its catechumeni a traditional law of the community, which it drew from one of the group's legal texts. The TS did not yet exist.

Thus these problems with Wacholder's arguments amount to further evidence for the view I suggest: comparison between TS 66:15b–17a and CD 5:7–11 indicates their derivation from an antecedent source. The laws of the TS are not *de novo,* but are incomplete selections from existing community legislation.

A closer look at TS 45:11, as compared with CD 12:1–2, constitutes the fourth and final argument for the prior existence of the TS laws. The texts read (for a translation, see above):

אל ישכב איש עם אשה בעיר המקדש לטמא את עיר המקדש בנדתם   CD 12:1–2
ואיש כי ישכב עם אשתו שכבת זרע לוא יבואו אל כול עיר המקדש שלושת ימים   TS 45:11

Viewing these two laws[41] side by side, it seems obvious that the law of the TS is   but a further refinement of a basic principle laid down by CD: intercourse within the temple city is

---

38. Murphy-O'Connor, review of *The Damascus Covenant: An Interpretation of the "Damascus Document,"* by P. R. Davies, in *RB* 92 (1985): 275.

39. Davies, *The Damascus Covenant,* p. 77.

40. The reference may be to a form of the Testament of Levi, but because of the differences between the text attributed to Levi in CD and the relevant portion of the Testaments of the Twelve Patriarchs, this explanation has not been universally accepted. For an ingenious new explanation arising from an assumed Aramaic original, see J. Greenfield, "The Words of Levi son [*sic*] of Jacob in Damascus Document IV, 15–19," *RQ* 13 (1988): 319–22.

41. The phrase used by both, עיר המקדש, favors the idea that they are related, since it does not occur elsewhere.

forbidden.[42] Given that principle, the next step for adherents would be to consider the question of intercourse outside the city. When can those rendered impure by such intercourse enter the sacred confines? TS 45 supplies that law—but it makes no sense without presupposing the law of CD 12. The TS does not explicitly deal with the higher order problem. (To say that it implies the law of CD 12 ignores the essential nature of legal texts: they must be specific to be effective.[43]) The two texts are a paired set of purity laws concerning intercourse, in which the priority belongs to CD's law.[44]

Perhaps one might challenge this assertion of priority by arguing that the law began as one for pilgrims (TS), and was later extended to all the inhabitants of the city or עיר המקדש (CD).[45] The problem with this view is that it cannot explain why the TS law came to be applied to pilgrims in the first place. The basis for the laws is the concept that the city of the temple—considered the dwelling of God on earth—was to be equated with the camp of the wilderness wanderings; the rules which applied there, when God dwelt in the tabernacle in the midst of Israel, were to apply in the temple city. The TS law in question, for example, is a "midrashic" combination of portions concerned with that period, Lev 15:18 and Exod 19:11 (see the *Appendix*). The latter verse, and its immediate context, requires a three-day period of preparation and abstinence from intercourse before experiencing the presence of God on Sinai.

42. Now that the discovery of the TS makes it possible to compare these two texts, one must question the point which Ginzberg made early in this century (L. Ginzberg, *An Unknown Jewish Sect,* 2nd ed. rev. and updated, New York: Jewish Theological Seminary of America, 1970, p. 76) that the law of CD 12:1–2 applied only to pilgrims. This view has its modern adherents. Cf. Ch. Rabin, *The Zadokite Documents,* 2nd rev. ed. (Oxford: Clarendon Press, 1958), p. 59, and P. R. Davies, "The Ideology of the Temple in the Damascus Document," in *Essays in Honour of Yigael Yadin,* eds. G. Vermes and J. Neusner (Totowa, New Jersey: Allenheld, Osmun & Company, 1983), p. 293. The laws here do have an idealized quality, but that fact can be explained in a number of ways, and does not mean their application is limited to pilgrims. They were also to apply to the inhabitants of the city.

43. For example, the TS law does not deal with the question of the inhabitants of Jerusalem. These might appeal to the letter of the law in order to deny its spirit, and claim exemption on grounds of practicality. Were they supposed to exit the city in order to have intercourse? The apparent absurdity of that situation would be a powerful force for the circumvention of the spirit of TS 45:11; the point of attack would probably be the word יבואו.

44. It is possible, of course, that both the TS and CD refer to an earlier legal collection which contained both purity laws, but economy of explanation mitigates against this suggestion at present.

45. One must allow for the possibility that in CD, the phrase עיר המקדש refers not to all Jerusalem, but only to the temple mount. The Hebrew is ambiguous as it stands. In the TS, whatever the meaning of the phrase in the original laws, the phrase seems, by the redactor's treatment, to mean Jerusalem. Cf. 46:10, referring to the fosse "which will separate the holy temple from the city," where עיר seems clearly to refer to the city, not just to the temple mount. Col. 47 by its redactional position in the scroll is concerned with matters outside the temple mount, outside the third court. The opposition set up by 47:15 is particularly instructive. Here the scroll distinguishes between עירי, "my (i.e., God's) city," and עריכמה, "your cities," i.e., the other cities of the land. Unless one wishes to argue that the term עיר has two different meanings in the same phrase, and that the author nevertheless did not bother to resolve the ambiguity, we must conclude that the TS uses עיר המקדש to mean Jerusalem. Analogy with the explicit statement of 4QMMT supports this understanding. That text contains the assertion "Jerusalem is the holy camp, the 'place' which He chose from all the tribes of Israel" ירושלים היא מחנה הקדש היא המקום שבחר בו מכל שבטי ישראל). See E. Qimron, "The Holiness of the Holy Land," p. 12.

Thus the logic of the laws depends on the equation "Jerusalem (or, the temple mount) = the camp." It is not clear how such "camp holiness" could first have been applied to pilgrims, as "visitors to the camp," only later to be extended to inhabitants of the temple city. Given the nature of the "camp," all Israelites, both pilgrims and inhabitants, would have to maintain its purity. The logic of the biblical basis for the laws requires that the law of CD be established before that of the TS.

It is possible that physical evidence confirms this understanding of the two laws as a paired set. Among the fragments of CD from cave 6[46] is one bearing some lines which do not appear in the medieval MSS from the Cairo Genizah (the only "complete" copies thus far published). This fragment is known as 6QD 5, and, according to its editor, it belongs in the context of CD 12.[47] The first three lines, with the restorations which the editor proposes, are as follows:

1. [...] .. [...
2. אש[ר ישכב עם]
3. אל ישכב עם [זכר משכבי [אשה

Consulting the photograph, the *resh* in line 2 אש[ר could easily be a *yod*. Its traces are much like the form of the *yod* in ישכב immediately following, for example. Nothing therefore prevents restoring כ[י, although that restoration is not crucial for the point being made. In the light of the evident subject of discussion in the fragment, I propose the following restoration of line 2:[48]

2. איש כ[י ישכב עם [אשתו שכבת זרע אל יבוא אל כול עיר המקדש שלושת ימים]

The sense is appropriate, and the length of the line is consonant with the rest of 6QD. If this restoration is correct, it would mean there is documentary evidence of the relationship between TS 45:11 and CD 12. It is not unlikely that CD 12:1–2 occupied the lacuna in line 1. Incidentally, this restoration would also strongly suggest that the TS law quoted a form of CD itself, rather than some other legal source the community possessed.[49]

On the basis of all these considerations, then, the best understanding of the "laws" of the TS is clearly that they derive from various earlier legal compilations. Their present defective statement supports this view. So does the evident redactional activity, which seeks to facilitate their incorporation into a new literary setting. And comparison between textual portions of CD and the TS also affirms this conclusion.

---

46. Edited by M. Baillet, *DJD* III, pp. 128–31 and plate 26.

47. Ibid., p. 131.

48. The line lengths of 6QD vary, but fragments 1–3 consist of lines about the length of the one I propose.

49. In this connection it is important to notice that the line which immediately precedes the TS law being discussed, TS 45:10, bears such a strong verbal resemblance to the last phrase of CD 12:1–2 that it appears the redactor had that very portion in mind. CD 12:1–2 ends "to render the temple city unclean with their impurity" (לטמא את עיר המקדש בנדתם). TS 45:10 reads "and they shall not enter my city in their impure uncleanness, so as to render it impure" (ולוא יבואו בנדת טמאתמה אל מקדשי וטמאו).

The source for the laws of the TS was the legal heritage of the CD community. The redactor, a member of that community, excerpted portions from as yet unidentified sources and placed them strategically within the body of the TS, following an overarching redactional design which I consider in chapter 6. The next concern here must be whether it is possible to identify some of the unknown sources whence the redactor sought out his material. It would be hopelessly unrealistic to expect to identify a source for each TS law, but it may be possible to suggest sources for some of them. Any success in this venture should serve to confirm the view of the laws I am advocating.

The Sources of the Laws

In attempting to identify potential sources for the laws of the TS, what one is really doing, of course, is attempting to identify portions of the legal "library" of the CD community. In this process it will not do simply to pick and choose among the DSS. Drawing on earlier work, Davies has already shown that the community of CD was not the community of 1QS or the pesharim. Furthermore, nearly all scholars would agree that among the DSS are some texts which the "sect" did not write, but merely read. Stegemann, for example, has estimated that no more than twenty per cent of the texts are of Qumranic origin.[50] Golb has pointed to the complete lack among the DSS of any autographs, except for the Copper Scroll, a fact which virtually requires an origin for the caches somewhere other than the site of Qumran—most probably Jerusalem.[51] On either view it is flawed methodology simply to assume a necessary relationship between any two given scrolls among the DSS; any links must be established on the basis of literary study. On the other hand, the mere fact that the scrolls were found together justifies the assumption that in some way they may be related, even though the organizing principle is still unproven. Their origin may be tied to readers or writers, or, of course, to both or neither. It seems most probable that some at least represent private or communal collections from Jerusalem. In any case the reasonable assumption that they are somehow of similar provenance somewhat alleviates the burden of proof for demonstrating literary connections.

It is certain that at least one portion of the legal materials of the CD community was preserved among the DSS—the Laws of CD itself.[52] It is therefore a defensible working hypothesis that other portions of that community's legal literature were also preserved among the scrolls found in the caves. The following criteria are adopted here in searching for these additional sources. The texts must be legal texts, or at least contain legal material. They should reflect the same *Sitz im Leben* as the Laws of CD; i.e., they must reflect an agricultural

---

50. H. Stegemann, "The Literary Composition of the Temple Scroll," p. 131.

51. N. Golb, "Les manuscrits de la Mer Morte: une nouvelle approche du problème de leur origine," *AESC* 5 (1985): 1133–49; idem, "Who Hid the Dead Sea Scrolls?," *BA* 48 (1985): 68–82; and, for a less technical version, see idem, "Who Wrote the Dead Sea Scrolls?," *The Sciences* 27 (1987): 40–49. The earliest form of Golb's position is his "The Problem of Origin and Identification of the Dead Sea Scrolls," *PAPS* 124 (1980): 1–24.

52. Published portions come from caves 5 and 6, while cave 4 preserved extensive fragments, according to preliminary reports.

community which is in regular contact with both gentiles and the temple.[53] Finally, it must be possible to establish terminological or ideological links between a given text and CD or the TS. Where one or more of the above elements cannot be demonstrated—which unfortunately is often the case, especially with materials only partially published—the suggestion must be the more tentative. Indeed, all suggestions must remain tentative, even if all these criteria are met, since so much of the DSS material remains unpublished. What follows should be understood as one possible line of approach, since it is still unclear to what degree synthesis of different scrolls should be attempted.

Temple Scroll 39:5–11a

This passage is a law about exclusion from the sanctuary, which includes a provision for payment of the half-shekel tax to the temple. The most remarkable thing about this interpolation into the Temple Source is that it mandates a onetime payment of the tax, in contrast with the annual tax of the rabbinic materials and Josephus.[54] As Liver has shown, the scroll's understanding is the plain meaning of the biblical text, but the only other postbiblical source which agrees with the TS position is the text known as 4Q Ordinances (4Q159).[55]

It seems very difficult to reconcile the implied *Sitz im Leben* of 4Q159 with an ascetic community living at the remote site of Qumran. The laws include provisions for sacrifices (1 ii 14), indicating a group in contact with the temple. Legislation mandates access for the poor to the harvest (1 ii 3–5), and enjoins slavery to gentiles (2–4 1–3a). The scroll has many points of contact with the Laws of CD.[56] These factors initially led Weinert to conclude that the text came from a life-setting similar to that of CD; but he was rather perplexed by the presence of the text at Qumran, which, he thought, would have had little need for such legislation.[57] When, later, he came upon Murphy-O'Connor's work suggesting a Babylonian origin for the CD community, he embraced it as the only reasonable explanation for the phenomena of the text. His later study of 4Q159 concluded, "4Q159 corresponds in time and character to the

---

53. Murphy-O'Connor has consistently tried to prove that the laws of CD indicate only a minimal involvement with the temple. Cf., e.g., "Damascus Document Revisited," pp. 234–38. In the light of the purity laws of the TS, however, which imply regular commerce, not merely occasional pilgrimages, his argument requires a reassessment.

54. For an excellent historical perspective on the questions involved with this tax, see J. Liver, "The Half-Shekel Offering in Biblical and Post-Biblical Literature," *HTR* 56 (1963): 173–98.

55. *Editio princeps* by J. Allegro in *DJDJ* V, pp. 6–9 and plate 2. Allegro published one column of the text earlier, including a more extensive discussion than in the *editio princeps,* in "An Unpublished Fragment of Essene Halakhah (4Q Ordinances)," *JSS* 6 (1961): 71–73. The most important aids to the study of the text are J. Strugnell, "Notes en marge du volume V des 'Discoveries in the Judaean Desert of Jordan,'" *RQ* 7 (1970): 165 and 175–79; F. Weinert, "4Q 159: Legislation for an Essene Community Outside of Qumran?," *JSJ* 5 (1974): 179–207; idem, "A Note on 4Q159 and a New Theory of Essene Origins," *RQ* 9 (1977–78): 223–30; and J. Fitzmyer, "A Bibliographical Aid to the Study of the Qumran Cave IV Texts 158–186," *CBQ* 31 (1969): 59–60.

56. Weinert, "A Note," pp. 225–26 and 228 n. 29.

57. Weinert, "Legislation," p. 207.

legislation identified by Murphy-O'Connor as the 'former ordinances.'"[58] (This is Murphy-O'Connor's term for the legislation of CD 9–16.) Although Weinert may have been a bit overenthusiastic about Murphy-O'Connor's work as the decisive hermeneutical key to 4Q159—after all, the laws of the Mishnah, certainly deriving from Palestine, manifest many of the same characteristics which he finds so puzzling in this text—4Q159 does meet the criteria set out above, and thus is a potential source for the laws of the TS.

Is it possible that the TS mandate for a onetime payment of the half-shekel came originally from 4Q159, or legal source(s) behind that text? The relevant lines in the TS read:[59]

TS 39:7b–8 עד יום אשר ישלים חוק [ונתן כופר] נפשו ליהוה מחצית השקל חוק עולם

4Q159 1 ii 6 reads, in part, as follows:

... כסף הערכים אשר נתנו איש כפר נפשו מחצית [השקל

This line is in remarkably close verbal agreement with the TS; the last half consists of exactly that combination of Exod 30:12b and 30:13b found in the the scroll. For the lacuna which follows השקל, Weinert turns to the biblical texts in suggesting a restoration of [בשקל הקודש תרומה לאל].[60] This is basically a good suggestion, but what prevents restoring ליהוה instead of לאל?[61] Weinert admits that the only reason he has restored אל is the comparative rarity of the tetragrammaton in other DSS legal texts.[62] This is a strange argument, and hardly persuasive, given that he has already recognized the many disparities between 4Q159 and other DSS.

Restoring ליהוה results in a text even more nearly identical to the TS than before. If the law of 4Q159 were indeed the source for the TS law, it would furnish an explanation for the otherwise difficult appearance in TS 39:8 of יהוה. This name for God, as with all other divine referents, is absent from the portions of the TS which belonged originally to the Temple Source. The probable explanation for its appearance here is now manifest: it was used in the legal source from which the redactor took his excerpt. As often, he has not bothered to reconcile his handling of the divine name here with that generally found elsewhere in the scroll.[63]

I suggest, then, that 4Q159 preserves some of the legal heritage of the CD community. The redactor of the TS chose the particular law in question either from that source or from an antecedent legal text. In the process, he may have modified the wording slightly, although it is difficult to test that possibility because of the lacunose preservation of the texts.

58. Weinert, "A Note," p. 230.

59. I have adopted Yadin's attractive suggestion for the lacuna, which he bases on Exod 30:12. See Yadin, II, p. 166. Note that per the *Appendix*, this line of the TS can be analysed as "Exod 30:12b verbatim + Exod 30:13b verbatim."

60. Weinert, "Legislation," pp. 182 and 192.

61. Strugnell suggests ליהוה in "Notes en marge," p. 177.

62. Weinert, "Legislation," p. 192.

63. See the discussion of the divine name in chapter 2.

Temple Scroll 45:12–13, 17c–18

Although their actual sources still elude detection, it may be possible to shed light on two laws from TS 45. Column 45:17c–18 is a law forbidding lepers to enter the temple city unless they have been purified. The redactor abridged this law by omitting the purification procedure. Consequently it is instructive to observe that 4QD^a (also known as 4Q226) includes portions of it.[64] The procedure is a lengthy development of Lev 13. According to Milik, the text is known from three cave 4 exemplars of CD. Presumably, the redactor of the TS excised or shortened the purification procedure because of its length, knowing that the community for whom he intended his text could find the necessary information elsewhere.[65]

Another fragment from the 4Q fragments of the Damascus Covenant, this one still unpublished, aids the understanding of TS 45:12–13, which prohibits all blind people from ever entering the city of the sanctuary. Several lines of the 4Q fragment, known as 4QD^b, seem to provide the basis for the TS legislation:[66]

> Fools, madmen ... simpletons and imbeciles ... the blind (lit., those who, being weak of eye, cannot see), the maimed ... the lame, the deaf, and minors, none of these may enter into the midst of the community.

This portion apparently corresponds to a lacuna in the Cairo MS of CD, 15:15–17. The fragment makes explicit something which could in any case be inferred by a comparison of CD and the TS: in certain instances, the redactor of the TS has taken laws which originally prohibited entry into his community (קהל), and transformed them into laws prohibiting entry into the temple or temple city.[67] I consider this redactional adaptation more fully below.

Temple Scroll 45:17b

4Q512 contains a series of purification rites, accompanied by prayers.[68] Because the text is so fragmentary, one cannot be at all confident about deducing its *Sitz im Leben;* still, there are a

---

64. J. T. Milik, "Fragment d'une source du psautier (4Q Ps 89)," *RB* 73 (1966): 105 and plate 3. Although most of this article is concerned with other matters, Milik provides a photograph and transcription for one fragment of this copy of CD. On page 103 of this article, Milik notes some points of overlap between 4QD^a and the Cairo Genizah MS of CD, which seem to prove that this is indeed a copy of CD, and not of some other literary work.

65. Actually, it appears that the TS did include an abstract of the purification procedure for lepers. A fragment from the second exemplar of the TS, 11QTS^b, seems to preserve a portion of the procedure. Yadin published the fragment in his volume of supplementary plates, but was unable to determine where it fit in the scroll. The fragment is 40*:4. Parts of six lines are legible, including parts of the words עליו, בגדים, במים, and עד. It seems clear that this text describes a procedure based on Lev 13–14, and it can only fit at TS 49:01–07.

66. Milik, *Ten Years*, p. 114.

67. Cf. the formal identity of the phrase in CD 12:6, ואחר יבוא אל הקהל, with the "permission" clauses in the TS laws in table 6.

68. *Editio princeps* by M. Baillet, *DJD* VII, pp. 262–68, with plates 36, 38, 40, 42, 44, 46, and 48.

number of clues. Fragment 7–9 xi 3 preserves a reading בע]רי מושב[והם, "in the cities of their habitation." This phrase indicates that the people using the text lived in various places throughout the land, and is comparable to CD 12:19, מושב ערי ישראל, "habitation of the cities of Israel." Fragment 56–8 3 reads א]ל המקדש וירד, "to the temple, and he shall go down," implying use of the temple. Fragment 40–41 3–4 reads ותבדל לנו בין הממא לטהור, "and you separate for us the clean from the unclean." This phrase is strikingly reminiscent of CD 7:4 and TS 51:8–9 (part of a redactional seam). Insofar as there is evidence, this text reflects a community in an environment consonant with that of the CD community. Further, the last phrase represents an ideological or terminological link with both CD and the TS.

4Q512 includes a fragment of particular interest, because, as table 6 shows, TS 45:17b makes no explicit provision for purification for the טמא נפש (person impure by reason of contact with a corpse). Fragments 1–6 of 4Q512, which constitute col. xii, preserve portions of a lengthy and detailed description of the purification procedure for this type of impurity.

Fragment 11 of 4Q512 concerns purification from a flux, paralleling TS 45:15–17a. Although the latter portion of the TS purity laws is complete, fragment 11 confirms its procedure in that the two are identical. It thus seems that 4Q512 provides concrete evidence for the suggestion that the CD community had legal resources which could fill the gaps of the TS laws.[69]

Temple Scroll 49:12

According to TS 49:12, oil can convey impurity. The same legal concept underlies CD 12:16; it was evidently a principle of the system of purities to which the CD community adhered. This observation leads to 4Q513[70], which may well be a second exemplar of 4Q159.[71] 4Q513 preserves a considerable amount of text which has not survived in the latter copy. This additional material furnishes significant additional evidence for the connections noted earlier between the *Sitz im Leben* and ideas of 4Q159 and those of CD.[72] It also provides, unfortunately in a broken context, a discussion of impurity transmitted by oil.[73]

---

69. It is possible that 4Q512 42–44 ii 2 has another link with the TS. The line includes the phrase ואחר יבוא [...]. Considering the biblical parallels which the editor cites (e.g., Lev 14:8, Num 19:7), the logic of the text requires a restoration for the lacuna of אל המקדש or אל עיר המקדש. The resulting phrase is then identical with the "permission" clauses of several of the TS laws, as table 6 shows.

70. Baillet, *DJD* VII, pp. 287–95 and plates 62–63. For a helpful discussion of several of the most extensive and important fragments of this scroll, see J. Baumgarten, "Halakhic Polemics in New Fragments from Qumran Cave 4," in *Biblical Archaeology Today,* ed. J. Amitai (Jerusalem: Israel Exploration Society, 1985), pp. 390–99.

71. Baillet shows on p. 287 that 4Q513 fr. 1 = 4Q159 ii 12–15, and that 4Q513 fr. 17 probably = 4Q159 ii 6.

72. E.g., 4Q513 fr. 3–4 ii 3 manifests a concern for sabbath sacrifices, comparable with CD 11:17–18; the great emphasis which CD puts on זנות (with the developed meaning "unlawful marriage; incest") finds a resonance in 513 fr. 2 ii 2.

73. 4Q513 fr. 12–13.

Temple Scroll 52:16b–19

TS 52:16b–19 is a law which proscribes the consumption of a ritually clean but imperfect animal within a distance of four miles from the temple. A portion of this law reads רחוק ממקדש סביב שלושים רס. This line is virtually identical to one which Milik excerpted from an unpublished scroll:[74]

[　　　אל ימ]קדש שלושים רס　　אל ימ]　　 [

Milik briefly described the scroll to which this line belongs in his 1957 book, *Dix ans de découvertes dans le désert de Juda.*[75] Unfortunately, when the book was enlarged and translated into English two years later, Milik did not expand on the original description.[76] What can be derived from his descriptions is as follows:

1. The text is written in a "Herodian" hand.

2. One fragment contains prescriptions on sabbath observances identical to CD 10:14ff., but in a different order.

3. Another fragment picks up the ending of the sabbath ordinances and follows it with an abbreviated version of the laws known from 1QS 8:1–10, the "Council of Fifteen Men."

4. A third fragment, which Milik compares to Lev 12:2 and Jubilees 3:8–14, preserves laws on purification after childbirth.

5. Two additional fragments include a penal code similar to that in 1QS 6:24ff. and CD 14:18ff. The penalties here are only half as severe as those of the published texts.

6. The document apparently ends with a quote of Is 54:1–3.

This text resembles nothing so much as an ἐκλογή—a collection of extracts from various sources such as were common in classical antiquity. This ἐκλογή evidently derived from various legal collections. To judge from points 2 and 5 above, among these was the Laws of CD, or an antecedent source. One might suppose that the portion so similar to the TS was a quotation of the TS itself, but this supposition would probably be wrong. Yadin, who has seen the fragment to which Milik made reference, indicates that it is written in the third person.[77] The TS, of course, phrases the law in the first person, as it regularly does. Most likely the redactor of the TS found this law in a previously existing law code, written in the third person

---

74. J. T. Milik, *DJD* III, p. 188.

75. Milik, *Dix ans de découvertes dans le désert de Juda* (Paris: Éditions du cerf, 1957), p. 111.

76. See idem, *Ten Years,* pp. 37 and 96.

77. Yadin, I, p. 318. The photograph is known by its Rockefeller Museum designation as PAM 42.408. Yadin asserted that a definite blank separates רס from אל, which begins a new law.

as is usual in such codes. This code was a part of the legal "library" of the CD community. The redactor made the necessary changes to bring it into line with the new literary context he gave it, including the switch to first person. The unpublished scroll does not quote the TS, but goes back to that earlier legal source.

Touching the Purity and Entry into the Temple

4Q514 may be yet another exemplar of Ordinances.[78] Fragment 1 of this work comprises an eleven-line discussion of the man impure by reason of a flux. The question it considers is, when during the purification procedure can the man resume contact with the "purity?" In other words, does the man have to fast for the entire seven days, and if not, when can he eat?[79] TS 45:15–17a mandates the same basic purification procedure as this text, but is not concerned with the question of the man's eating pure food. Rather, it considers his admissibility into the temple confines.

TS 49:21, however, and the laws of col. 50, do concern the question of contact with the purity. I noted above the curious fact, made manifest in table 6, that these purity laws of the TS appear at first to have nothing to do with the temple, and thus seem out of place in the scroll. In 4Q514 one discovers the logic behind the redactor's inclusion of them in the TS.[80] After its description of a purification procedure identical to that of TS 45:15–17a, one reads in line 6: ואחר יאכלו את לחמם, "and afterward they may eat their bread." This permission clause is, of course, formally identical to that of the TS, אחר יבוא אל עיר המקדש, "afterward he may enter the city of the sanctuary." Thus these texts agree apart from the different objectives of their permission clauses. This comparison permits the conclusion that the community held to the equation, "permission to touch the purity = permission to enter the temple confines." The redactor has included laws about the purity in the TS because of this analogy; anyone who was permitted to touch the purity was *ipso facto* permitted in the temple confines as well. Of course, the reverse would also be true. One could not enter the temple or its city in a condition of impurity vis à vis the purity.

The Redactor and the Laws: Conclusion

In this chapter, I argue that the redactor was a member of the CD community. He drew on the legal heritage of that community as he reworked the proto-Temple Scroll, interpolating certain laws according to his master plan for a new literary work.

78. *Editio princeps* by M. Baillet, *DJD* VII, pp. 295–98 and plate 74. After identifying the scroll as another exemplar, he admits, "L'interprétation n'est certes pas de plus faciles et il n'y a pas de recoupement matériel avec 4Q159 et 513; mais il faillait bien adopter un classement commode." (p. 296).

79. Line 6 specifies that the man may only resume eating and drinking כמשפט הטהרה.

80. Actually, the solution is also present in the TS itself, but not explicitly. TS 45:17b (on the man impure because of contact with a corpse) disallows his entry into the temple, while omitting the purification procedure. TS 49:21 permits those who have been in the house of a dead person to touch the purity only after a seven-day purification procedure. One could infer that the same procedure applied to the טמא נפש by the placement of that law after the law for the זב, and by this inference arrive at the equation derived from 4Q514. See table 6.

Among the DSS, one cannot safely mine any and all texts in a quest for the sources of the TS laws. The search must be confined to those texts which demonstrably reflect both the ideas and *Sitz im Leben* of CD, and thus may preserve part of the legal "library" of the redactor's community. I have identified 4Q159, 4Q512, 4Q513, 4Q514, and some unpublished 4Q fragments as legitimate possible sources.

Can one be certain of the direction of possible influence between the TS and these legal texts? How do we know that the TS used these sources or their forebears, rather than the reverse? In fact certainty is impossible, but there is a line of reasoning which tends to point in the direction I have taken. I only state it here briefly, as chapter 6 provides many more details. The TS was an eschatological law, which derived its laws in part by a process of sifting the laws of this present era, the "wicked era." Not all the laws which were appropriate for the wicked era would function in the eschaton. The opposite was also true. As the TS was in a legal sense *sui generis,* it would not always be appropriate to follow its laws in this present wicked era. Therefore, other legal sources which were to operate in the wicked era could not simply take over the laws of the TS. Consequently, when the laws of other sources and those of the TS coincide, it seems more probable that the direction of borrowing was from the other sources to the TS; the particular laws in question had been judged suitable for the eschaton.

Although the texts I cite may not in every case be the immediate source for the particular laws of the TS, by using them I am able to fill or explain gaps which the redactor left as he incorporated the laws he chose into their new setting. The fact that I am able to do so reinforces my contention that the redactor was not writing new law. Nor does there exist a single "Purity Source," as some scholars have argued.

Thinking about the way the redactor reshaped his laws while—or merely by the act of—introducing them into their present context, one realizes an interesting point. The laws of the TS are in themselves particularistic, "contractile," and germinally sectarian. The contrast between this characterization and that of the other sources of the scroll helps in understanding what the redactor was seeking to do.

Taking laws which originally concerned entry into a community, he made them apply to entry into the temple. Taking laws which originally concerned how a community ate its food in levitical purity, he made them, also, apply to entry into the temple or temple city. By his incorporation of these particularistic laws into a new Law addressed to all Israel, he sought to apply them to everyone in the nation. He would have all Israel live by the laws of his community. Judging from the redactional shaping of the TS, he even believed that God would have it so.

It would seem there is little point to the question of the date of the laws. In some cases they may date back into the exilic period, as their community believed. The community's claim is not inherently improbable. The laws are virtually impossible to date, as there is almost no basis for comparison in the few texts which have been preserved from the period 300–150 B.C.E. What is most important is that they were in effect in the community at the time of the redactor; for the present purposes perhaps that is enough.

6

THE REDACTOR AND A DATE FOR
THE TEMPLE SCROLL

Introduction

This chapter focuses on the final form of the TS and on its redactor, his motives and identity. Unavoidably, given the recursive nature of this investigation, certain important previous arguments are incomplete; the discussion here seeks to round those earlier points out. First, I attempt to discern the basis for the redactional shape of the scroll as a whole. Why did the redactor arrange its elements as he did, and what is its conceptual relationship to the Hebrew Bible? The answers to these questions, combined with certain earlier conclusions, help to clarify the intended purpose of the TS. Then, analyzing redactional elements in the scroll, I seek to delineate those portions of the scroll which the redactor either wrote himself or substantially reworked. Based on these portions, the redactional purpose of the TS, and the fact that the redactor was a member of the CD community, I make bold to unmask that shadowy figure. That leads naturally and finally to a proposed date for the TS as we know it.

The Redactional Shape of the Temple Scroll

Baldly stated, the redactor intended the TS as an eschatological law for the land. I propose to support this assertion by an examination of its major elements in turn: first, I show that the redactor intended it as a law for the land; then, that he intended it as a law for the eschaton. But before considering either of those points, it is essential first to determine whether the TS is sufficiently complete to permit a meaningful redactional analysis.

The Completeness of the Temple Scroll

A significant contingent of scholars has assumed that, because the beginning and end of the TS seem to be broken away, large portions of the scroll are missing.[1] If such were the case, it

---

1. For the beginning, cf. Yadin, I, p. 5. In his discussion of the outermost fragment of the scroll, Yadin recorded, "The fragment had originally been preceded by at least one other column." Mink, "Use of Scripture," p. 35, states, "We may be sure that Col. 1 once existed." For the ending, cf. Stegemann, "'Das Land'," p. 158: "Der Schlussteil der Tempelrolle, vermutlich eine modifizierende Rezeption von Dtn 23–26, fehlt leider." See also Wacholder, "11Q Torah and the Book of Jubilees," pp. 215–16.

would gravely—if not fatally—impair any attempt at determining the redactional shape of the scroll, since it is precisely at the beginning and end of a literary work that one expects to find an explanation of its purpose—if one is to be found at all. In fact, however, with the exception of a few lines, the beginning of the scroll appears to have survived, and the end has certainly been preserved.

Regarding the missing beginning, Wacholder has made a good case that no "col. 1" actually ever existed.[2] He thinks that the scroll lacks a mere seven lines, probably from the top of col. 2. His argument is based on the sheets which were sewn together to create the scroll's writing surface. Apparently, no sheet could hold more than four columns, since, of the complete sheets which survive, seven contain three columns, and ten contain four. To assume that a col. 1 is missing requires that the first sheet contain five columns, more than any surviving sheet; since the scribal preparation of the physical aspects of the scroll appears very consistent, it probably did not.

Although convincing, at two points Wacholder's argument requires slight adjustment. First, although it is true that seven lines are missing from col. 2—if it had the same number of lines as other columns in its sheet—it is unlikely that all of the missing lines were at the beginning of the column. Given the need for a transition from the topic of col. 2 to that of col. 3, several of the missing lines should probably be located at the bottom of the column. Therefore, we do not know how many are missing from the top. Considering the redactional relationship of the scroll to Deut 12–26 (to be discussed below), it is possible that no more than two lines are missing from the beginning of the scroll.

These lines presumably comprised a modified form of Deut 12:1, which would have read approximately as follows: "These are the laws and statutes which you shall be careful to do in the land which I hereby give to you as an inheritance all the days which you shall live upon the land." In Hebrew,[3] this modified form of Deut 12:1 is eighty-eight characters long, precisely equivalent to two lines the length of those remaining in col. 2. It is unlikely that more of Deut 12 would have followed, because the surviving portion of the column, beginning with Exod 34:10, says essentially what Deut 12:2–4 does. Thus it is possible that only the first two lines of the TS are missing.

But there is another possibility which Wacholder apparently overlooks: an entire sheet could be missing from the beginning of the scroll. His argument makes it unlikely that a "col. 1" ever preceded the present col. 2 *on the same sheet*—but how to be sure that an entire sheet, with three or four columns, is not missing? The only argument against such a possibility is the difficulty of imagining what that much more text could say by way of introduction to the content of the TS. The present col. 2—whether with the beginning I have suggested or with a similar redactional introduction—makes an excellent beginning, given the scroll's redactional shape and revelational claims. But such an argument is far from conclusive; one must concede that it is possible that more than one column is missing. It seems much more probable, however, that no more than a few lines are lacking at the beginning of the TS.

---

2. B. Z. Wacholder, "11Q Torah and the Book of Jubilees," p. 215.

3. ‏אלה החקים והמשפטים אשר תשמרון לעשות בארץ אשר נתתי לך לרשתה כל הימים אשר אתם חיים על האדמה‎

That several columns are missing from the end of the TS is flatly contradicted by the physical evidence. That evidence indicates that the scribe intended to complete the scroll in the first several lines of col. 67, or, if possible, even earlier. As he drew close to the end, the scribe began to crowd more words and lines into each column. In col. 66, for example, he added three more lines than usual. By this expediency he hoped to avoid writing anything on the final sheet.[4] When that did not prove possible, he continued onto the top of col. 67, but for no more than six lines.[5] Following a practice known from other DSS, including 11QPs[a],[6] 1QpHab[7] and 11QpaleoLev,[8] he left the rest of the final sheet blank. And there is no reason to believe that the scribe cut away surplus parchment at the end.[9] All the evidence is consistent with the notion that from the very beginning, the scribe's intent was to end in col. 66 or 67.

Therefore, it is likely that both the beginning and the end of the TS are almost entirely preserved. A few lines are lacking, presumably a significant few; their presence undoubtedly would make an improved analysis of the scroll possible. Yet, since whole columns are unlikely to be missing, one may hope to arrive at a reasonably accurate conception of the redactional plan of the TS. Almost all the clues the redactor ever provided are present, including the most significant 29:3–10.

The Temple Scroll as a Law for the Land

Column 29 and the Redactional Purpose of the Scroll

Analysis of two bodies of evidence proves, to my mind at least, that the redactor intended the TS to serve as a law for the land. The first body of evidence consists of certain portions of the scroll which he himself wrote. Presumably, it is here that he will have said most clearly what he wanted to convey about the scroll's purpose. The second body of evidence is the Deuteronomy Source, which can be subjected to redaction criticism by means of comparison with the parallel portions of the Hebrew Bible. I begin here with the first approach. Of those portions of the scroll which he wrote himself, none more clearly shows how the redactor intended the TS to function than TS 29:3–10. The text reads:[10]

---

4. Yadin, II, p. 295.

5. Ibid., p. 300.

6. J. A. Sanders, *DJDJ* IV: *The Psalms Scroll of Qumran Cave 11 (11QPs^a)* (Oxford: Clarendon Press, 1965), plate 17.

7. Brownlee, *Habakkuk*, p. 215.

8. D. N. Freedman and K. A. Mathews, *The Paleo-Hebrew Leviticus Scroll (11QpaleoLev)*, with contributions by R. S. Hanson (Winona Lake: Eisenbrauns, 1985), p. 5 and plate 20.

9. Yadin, II, p. 301.

10. I follow Yadin's readings with the exception of הבריה in line 9, where he reads הברכה. There I prefer the reading suggested by Qimron, "מן העבודה," p. 142. For a more detailed analysis of this portion see M. O. Wise, "The Covenant of the Temple Scroll XXIX, 3–10," *RQ* 14 (1989): 49–60.

3. ‎[לעלותיכמה ולנסכיכמה] [בבית אשר א[שכין]
4. ‎שמי עליו] [עולות [דבר יום] ביומו כתורת המשפט הזה
5. ‎תמיד מאת בני ישראל לבד מנדבותמה לכול אשר יקריבו
6. ‎לכול נסכיהמה ולכול מתנוחמה אשר יביאו לי לרצון לה[מה]
7. ‎ורציתים והיו לי לעם ואנוכי אהיה להם לעולם [ו]שכנתי
8. ‎אתמה לעולם ועד ואקדשה [את מ]קדשי בכבודי אשר אשכין
9. ‎עליו את כבודי עד יום הבריה אשר אברא אני את מקדשי
10. ‎להכינו לי כול הימים כברית אשר כרתי עם יעקוב בבית אל

Translation

> (3) For your burnt offerings and your libations ... in the house upon which I will cause (4) my name to d[well] ... burnt offerings, [each item] on its day, according to the law of this ordinance (5) forever from the sons of Israel, apart from their free-will offerings, for everything which they will sacrifice, (6) for all their libations and all their gifts which they will bring to me to obtain my acceptance of th[em]. (7) Then I shall accept them, and they shall be my people, and I shall be theirs forever. [And] I will dwell (8) with them forever and ever. And I will sanctify [my t]emple with my glory. For I shall cause my glory to dwell (9) upon it until the Day of Creation, when I myself shall create my temple, (10) to establish it for me forever, according to the covenant which I made with Jacob at Bethel ...

I believe that the key to an understanding of this passage is the phrase in 29:10, "according to the covenant which I made with Jacob at Bethel" (כברית אשר כרתי עם יעקוב בבית אל). It clearly says that in some way the things the redactor is saying here are connected to Jacob, and to his covenant with God. The natural questions are, What exactly is intended by the term "covenant?" And, how does the TS fulfill or relate to this covenant? The wording of this portion of the scroll connects to three biblical passages: Gen 28:13–29, Gen 35:1–15, and Lev 26:42. The first two passages describe those occasions on which Jacob experienced a theophany at Bethel, while the third passage is the only one in the Hebrew Bible which contains both the name Jacob and the term ברית, "covenant."

Although the term "covenant" is absent from Gen 28:13–29 and 35:1–15, it is obvious that the redactor thought of those passages as embodying a one. Therefore, one should analyze them in terms of the elements which made up the covenant the chapters describe. The following is a breakdown of the terms in Gen 28:

God's promises	*Jacob's promises*
1. I will give this land to you and your seed (v 13)	1. Yahweh will be my God (v 21)
2. Your seed will multiply and spread (v 14)	2. This stone will become the house of god (v 22)
3. All the families of the earth will be blessed by you and your seed (v 14)	3. I will tithe all you give me (v 22)
4. I am with you (v 15)	
Condition of Promises: "If you do what I say to you." (v 15)	Condition of Promises: God must protect and provide (vv 21–22)

It is important to notice that the names of Abraham and Isaac are connected in 28:13 to this covenant with Jacob.

Gen 35 contains no promise by Jacob to God, but God repeats to Jacob several of those found in chapter 28. He commands Jacob to build him a place of worship (an altar—v 1),[11] and Jacob instructs his family to put away their foreign gods (vv 2–4).[12] Most significant is verse 35:12, "The land which I gave to Abraham and Isaac, I will give to you, and I will give the land to your descendents after you." In this verse there is again found the connection of Abraham and Isaac to the covenant with Jacob, and, notably, that connection is in the context of a promise to give the land to Jacob and his descendents. The land is central to the covenant in both chapters of Genesis.

The only text in the Bible which juxtaposes the name of Jacob with the term "covenant" is Lev 26:42. One should appreciate the importance of this fact as a clue to the redactor's meaning. As he possessed a remarkably intimate knowledge of the Bible, until demonstrated otherwise the presumption must be that he was thinking specifically of Lev 26:42 when he wrote TS 29:3–10.

It would be a mistake to suppose, however, that the redactor was thinking of this verse in isolation from the rest of Lev 26. An analysis of the chapter reveals the recurrence of certain terms which weighed heavily in the redactor's thought, judging by the redactional phrases in table 8. For example, the term מקדש ("temple") appears in 26:2 and 31. This term (and its equivalent, בית) is found five times in TS 29:3–10 alone. The phrase משכני בתוככם ("my dwelling in your midst") occurs in verse 11. Both שכן ("dwell") and -בתוך ("in the midst") are characteristic elements of redactional phrase one in table 8; the first term appears at least twice in TS 29:3–10 alone. ברית ("covenant") occurs eight times in Lev 26 (vv 9, 15, 25, 42 [*ter*], 44 and 45). Finally, the very significant phrase of Lev 26:12, והייתי לכם לאלהים ואתם תהיו לי לעם ("and I shall be your God, and you shall be my people") is echoed almost verbatim by TS 29:7.

Clearly, Lev 26 was influential in the redactor's thought generally, and it was specifically influential in what he said in col. 29. Given this fact, three observations are particularly relevant to the covenant of which 29:10 speaks:

> 1. Lev 26:9–12 reiterates the terms of the promises made to Jacob at Bethel. The chapter explicitly applies them not only to Jacob, but to all Israel. It thus sanctions the understanding that the covenant with Jacob involved all Israel—the "sons of Israel" which TS 29:3 addresses.

> 2. Lev 26:3–15 elaborates the condition of the promises found in Gen 28:15. There, the condition is simply that Jacob obey ("do what I say to you"). These verses further defines what that means, specifying that Israel must obey all God's statutes, commandments and ordinances, or be guilty of breaking the covenant. Verse 46 adds to this delineation by implying that the laws include all those given to Moses at Sinai. Those laws include, of course, all the sacrificial procedures, festival ordinances, and laws of cleanness and uncleanness. TS

---

11. Cols. 3–12 and 30–46 of the scroll contain the plans for such a place of worship.

12. Note col. 2 of the scroll, in which portions of Exod 34 and Deut 7 warning of foreign gods appear. Similar warnings against foreign gods and the religious practices associated with them recur throughout the scroll; cf. 48:7–10 and 51:19–21.

29:3–7a picks up this concept, making the promises which follow in 29:7b–10 conditional upon obedience to cultic commands.

3. Lev 26 as a whole is really about life in the land, and whether that life will be a life of blessings or curses (compare vv 1, 4, 6, 20, 32, 34 and 43). Consequently, the covenant to which the redactor appeals by his reference to the chapter is a covenant in which, as with the passages in Gen, the land takes pride of place. The verse which the redactor had in central focus, 26:42, connects four elements: the names of Jacob, Isaac, and Abraham, and the land.

As noted above, the names of all three patriarchs were also connected with the Gen covenant passages. Furthermore, the terms of the covenant with Jacob are the terms of God's covenant with Abraham and Isaac.[13] This fact, and the fact that in Lev 26:42 the name of Jacob is not, as might have been expected, the last name mentioned, but rather the first, directs attention back to 29:10 and to a possible textual restoration. At 29:10 the text breaks off, but it does not follow that the redactor's explanation of the covenant happened to end at the same juncture. In fact, that explanation continued for all or part of another twelve lines, since at 30:1 one encounters the redactional term ואקדש ("and I shall sanctify"). Taking into consideration the redactor's reference to Lev 26:42 and the connection of the covenant with all three patriarchs, the missing continuation may have read approximately as follows: כברית אשר כרתי עם יעקוב בבית אל [ועם יצחק בגרר ועם אברהם בחרן].[14] The chance misfortune that the text broke off, having mentioned only Jacob and Bethel, has frequently misled scholars in their efforts to explain the covenant.[15]

13. Cf. e.g., Gen 26:2–5 for Isaac and Gen 12:1–3 for Abraham (then Abram).

14. Note the reading of Targum Neofiti *ad loc.*

15. Thus Yadin's view of the referent of the term "covenant" is much narrower than in our interpretation. For him, the covenant is a covenant to create a future temple. He says, "The creation of the future Temple is the fulfillment of the promise pledged by the Lord in his covenant with Jacob at Bethel." (I, p. 184; cf. also II, p. 125). Yadin's interpretation has a major problem, of course; God does not promise to build a future temple when he talks with Jacob at Bethel. Therefore, Yadin turns to extrabiblical sources to find a promise to build such a temple. He believes that he has one in Jubilees chapters 31–32, especially the latter chapter. But, as Maier has noted, this chapter does not make such a promise; "it really concerns the installation of Levi as priest and the disposition of cultic tributes ... it is not so concerned with the building of the temple." (Maier, *The Temple Scroll*, p. 86. For another critique of Yadin's understanding, see J. Schwartz, "Jubilees, Bethel, and the Temple of Jacob," *HUCA* 56 [1985]: 69–72.) Yadin has overly restricted the referent of the ברית to the content of 29:9–10; he has not appreciated the significance of Lev 26 for the passage, nor considered the implications of the fact that the redactional passage does not end with the end of the column as preserved. In "Exegetische Erwägungen," Callaway has likewise concluded that the promise of the covenant is the creation of a new temple. He spends most of the article discussing the rabbinic concept of the "Grundstein," out of which arose heaven and earth. He argues that this concept must have guided the redactor's interpretation of Gen 28:22, where Jacob says, "This stone will become the house of God." If one does not see this concept in the redactor's interpretation of Gen 28, he says, no biblical basis exists for the creation of a temple by an act of God. But no such biblical basis is needed; the covenant is not about the creation of a temple but, as I relate here, the presence of God and the dwelling of Israel in the land. Cf. also A. Finkel, "God's Presence," p. 42: the scroll "reiterates in an interpolating way the Pentateuchal promise of God's indwelling in the Temple and among his people."

In essence, therefore, the term "covenant" of 29:10 signals the redactor's appropriation of the covenant made by God with the patriarchs. God promised them his presence and the land; in exchange they were to worship and obey him. The redactor saw this covenant as embracing all Israel by the authority of Lev 26. That text goes on to threaten a disobedient Israel with loss of the land and dispersal abroad. Contingent on their later repentance, says Lev 26:42, God would remember his covenant with Jacob, Isaac, and Abraham, and return them to the land. In the redactor's interpretation of history—assuming that he embraced the views expressed in CD—the promised return had yet to take place. When it did, the covenant of 29:3–10—a continuation of the ancient covenant with the patriarchs—would take effect. But the redactor apparently interpreted the covenant with the patriarchs as narrowly applicable in his day only to the CD community, the true "Israel" (and, perhaps, to similar groups),[16] and in the eschaton only to those obedient to the TS requirements.[17] It would be a covenant for life with God, a life in the land.

Other redactional portions underscore the fact that the redactor intended to compose a law for the land. The most frequently repeated "redactional phrase"[18] in the TS is כי אני יהוה שוכן בתוך בני ישראל ("for I, Yahweh, dwell in the midst of the sons of Israel") and its variants. This phrase is actually only one-half of a verse; judging from the fact that he repeats it eight times, it served the redactor as a primary conceptual guide when he shaped his work. The verse is Num 35:34: "And you shall not render impure the land which you are going to indwell, in whose midst I dwell, for I, Yahweh, dwell in the midst of the sons of Israel." The fact that the redactor returned so frequently to this verse indicates how central it was in his thinking. Again, one should not suppose that he was unaware of the first half of the verse, or that he did not presuppose its content every time he quoted the second half. In fact, once, at 48:10b–11a, he actually did insert the first half of Num 35:34 (in a slightly modified form). The importance of this verse in the TS, focusing as it does on the land, argues that the redactor wanted to create a law for the land.

The Redactional Relationship of the Temple Scroll to the Bible

That the redactor intended the scroll to serve as a law for the land is further evidenced by the scroll's relationship to the Hebrew Bible. As the *Appendix* shows, the scroll (in the form of

16. CD 8:17–18, speaking of the group itself, which it designates as the שבי ישראל ("the returnees of Israel," "the repentant of Israel," or, possibly, "the captives of Israel"), says להם ברית האבות, "the covenant with the patriarchs applies (only) to them." See also CD 3:1–5 and the comments of Ginsburg, *Unknown Jewish Sect*, pp. 204–8. Note especially his conclusion about CD and the patriarchs on p. 205: "In the view of our document, the covenant is vital for the survival of Israel, but it only benefits the elect, that is, the adherents of the sect." Note also the fundamental influence of Lev 26:42 and 26:45 on the concept of the covenant held by the CD community—see CD 1:4 and 6:2, and cf. R. Le Déaut, "Une citation de Lévitique 26,45 dans le Document de Damas I,4; VI, 2," *RQ* 6 (1967–68): 289–96.

17. This is the apparent meaning of 29:2–7: "These [you shall offer] ... according to the law of this ordinance ... *then* I shall accept them, and they shall be my people," etc. In other words, in the redactor's concept, God's promise of his presence and the other benefits of the covenant being affirmed depend on Israel's obedience to the TS's peculiar rules for offerings, and, presumably, to the other laws of the scroll as well.

18. See table 8 below for details on the use of redactional phrases.

the D source) quotes long portions of Deut beginning in col. 51. Since it does not do this with the other books of the Torah, the treatment of Deut must be meaningful.

This different treatment has given rise to a variety of scholarly explanations. Wacholder and Schiffman argue that the reason the scroll treats Deut differently is that the author of the scroll cared less about that book.[19] In this view, the TS is a sort of literary baker's dozen—having completed what he really wanted to say, the redactor "threw in" portions of Deut for good measure. Yet most scholars have rightly preferred the other alternative, recognizing that the Deut material actually held a greater attraction for the redactor than did other portions of the Torah. Arguing on this basis, Mink says that the TS represents an effort further to define the Deuteronomic legislation. By this effort, he goes on to explain, the author was not attempting to add another book to the Torah, nor did he intend the TS to take the place of Deut. Rather, the scroll is an explicit statement of the type of halakha which the Qumran community found "hidden" in the Hebrew Bible.[20] Stegemann goes along with Mink to a point, but in my view comes much closer to the truth when he says that the TS is a selection from, and a perfection of, the legal materials in Deut—particularly of the "Deuteronomic Law," the legal corpus of Deut 12–26.[21] In his view, cols. 3–47 of the scroll correspond to Deut 12, which commands Israel to worship God only in the "place" which he will chose. These columns of the scroll concern the matters involved with that worship—sacrifice, the temple, and the holy city. Columns 48–66 then correspond to Deut 13–23.

Stegemann is broadly correct. The TS begins to quote Deut at chapter 12 because that chapter begins the biblical "laws for the land." As table 7 demonstrates, the scroll has a special, redactionally shaped relationship to Deut; the redactor saw the scroll, like Deut 12–26, as a collection of laws for life in the land.

Table 7. The Redactional Shape of the Temple Scroll

Passage of Deut	Content	Temple Scroll Use
12:1–14	Laws of the land; *māqôm* of Deut = *miqdāš* (as the place where sacrifices occur)	51:15–16a; 53:10b; Temple Document
12:15–19	Laws of offerings	Replaced by Festival Calendar

---

19. Wacholder, *Dawn of Qumran*, p. 15.

20. H. Mink, "Use of Scripture," pp. 30, 46, and 48. Although he does not cite it, Mink apparently derives his concept of a "hidden" law as the object of community study from L. Schiffman, *The Halakhah at Qumran* (Leiden: Brill, 1975), esp. pp. 22–31.

21. H. Stegemann, "'Das Land'," pp. 157–58. He says,

> Was die Vorstellung vom "Land" in der "Tempelrolle" anbetrifft, so lässt sich dieses zunächst ganz grob charakterisieren als Aufnahme, Ausbau und Perfektionierung dessen, was sich im Deuteronomium findet, und zwar vor allem in dessen "Gesetzeskorpus" Dtn 12–26 … Den Ausführungen zur Einzigkeit der Opferstätte in Dtn 12 korrespondiert der grosse Anfangsblock der "Templerolle," Kolumnen 3–47, wo es um den Tempel, die Opfer und die heilige Stadt geht, während die anschliessenden Kolumnen 48–66 weithin Dtn 13–23 in der Reihenfolge der Stoffe entsprechen.

Table 7. The Redactional Shape of the Temple Scroll (*cont.*)

Passage of Deut	Content	Temple Scroll Use
12:20–28	Eating offering in city gate if chosen "place" is too far away	53:2–53:10a
12:29–30	General prohibition of idolatry	Subsumed under 54:5b–55:14
13:1–19	Detailed commands on idolatry	54:5b–55:14
14:1–3	Prohibition of heathen practices	48:7b–10b (interpolated into "laws" portion)
14:4–21	Clean and unclean animals	48:1–7 (combined with Lev 11)
14:22–27	Second tithe	43:3, 12b–15a (interpolated into Temple Document)
14:28–29	Tithe of the third year	Omitted
15:1–18	Release from debt and slavery at the end of seven years	Omitted
15:19–23	Consecration of firstlings	52:9b–12a
16:1–17	Feasts of Passover, Weeks, and Booths	Replaced by Festival Calendar
16:18–20	Administration of justice	52:11–16a
16:21–22	Bans on Asherah, sacred trees, and sacred pillars	52:20 (redactional, paraphrased); 52:01–0? (probably–lost)
17:1	Prohibition of blemished sacrifice	52:3b–5a
17:2–13	Administration of justice	55:15–56:11
17:14–20	Commands about the king ++ (++ = "additional material")	56:12–57:06 (56:22–57:06 lost); Additional material from MD 57:6–59:20

Table 7. The Redactional Shape of the Temple Scroll (*cont.*)

Passage of Deut	Content	Temple Scroll Use
18:1–5	Priestly and levitical portions	60:2–5, 6–9a, 10b–11 Mostly replaced by MD
18:6–8	The rustic levite	60:12–15
18:9–13	Ban on witchcraft	60:16–21a
18:14–22	True and false prophets	60:21a–61:5 (mostly lost)
19:1–13	The cities of refuge	Omitted; replaced by midrashic application to separate areas for impure persons 46:16–18, 48:11b–14b
19:14	The law of the boundary mark	Omitted
19:15–20	Laws of testimony	61:6–12a
20:1–9	Military exemptions, holy war	61:12b–62:5a
20:10–20	Rules of warfare	62:5b–63:04 (63:01–04 lost)
21:1–9	Expiation for a murder by an unknown murderer	63:05–63:8 (63:05–07 lost)
21:10–14	Marriage to captive women ++	63:10–64:02 (64:01–02 lost); Purity law added
21:15–17	The man with two wives—one loved, the other unloved	64:03–07 (reconstructed)
21:18–21	The rebellious youth	64:2–6a
21:22–23	The sin worthy of death—hanging on a tree	64:6b–13 Replaced by MD
22:1–4	A neighbor's ox or sheep	64:13b–65:04 (65:01–04 lost)
22:5	Prohibition of transvestism	65:05 (restored)

Table 7. The Redactional Shape of the Temple Scroll (*cont.*)

Passage of Deut	Content	Temple Scroll Use
22:6–7	Prohibition of taking a mother and her young	65:2–5a
22:8	Roofing a new house	65:5b–7a
22:9	Sowing a vineyard with two kinds of seed	65:06–07 (restored)
22:10	Plowing with a yoke of a donkey and an ox	52:13b
22:11–12	Laws of garments	65:07 (restored)
22:13–21	The questionable virgin	65:7b–66:04 (66:01–04 lost)
22:22	Adultery	65:04–07 (restored)
22:23–27	The rape of a betrothed virgin	66:08–66:6
22:28–29	The rape of a virgin who is not betrothed	66:8b–11a
23:1	Incestuous marriage ++	66:11b–12a Additional midrashic laws
23:2–9	Exclusion from the assembly	Replaced by laws interpolated at 39:5, 40:6; = exclusion from the sanctuary
23:10–15	Laws of camp for holy war	Replaced by laws for holy city 45:7b–10, 50:3b–4a, 50:14b–16a, 46:13–16a, 47:2
23:16–17	Laws for regulation of slavery	Omitted
23:18–19	Laws on cult prostitution	Omitted
23:20–21	Laws on interest for loans	Omitted
23:22–24	Laws of vows	53:11–14a

Table 7. The Redactional Shape of the Temple Scroll (*cont.*)

Passage of Deut	Content	Temple Scroll Use
23:25–26	Eating a neighbor's grapes or grain	Omitted
24:1–4	Laws of divorce	Omitted (no divorce-cf. King's Law)
24:5	The newlywed man exempt from war	Omitted; content covered by 61:12b–62:5a
24:6	Taking a handmill as pledge	Omitted
24:7	Kidnap and sale of a fellow Israelite punished by death	Omitted
24:8–9	Laws on leprosy	Replaced by laws based on Lev; 45:17–46:?, 46:16–18, 48:14–15
24:10–13	Laws of loans and pledges	Omitted
24:14–15	Loans on hired servants and *gērîm*	Omitted
24:16	Death penalty to be suffered only by the guilty party	Omitted; law on death penalty at 64:6b–13a; note 64:6 and wording here, בחטאו יומתו
24:17–22	Laws of justice and gleaning for *gērîm* and others	Omitted
25:1–3	Scourging of a wicked man	Omitted
25:4	The threshing ox	52:12b
25:5–10	Levirate marriage	Omitted; potential polygamy, contrary to 57:18–19
25:11–12	Wife touching the genitals of her husband's enemy during fight	Omitted

Table 7. The Redactional Shape of the Temple Scroll (*cont.*)

Passage of Deut	Content	Temple Scroll Use
25:13–16	Just weights	Omitted; subsumed under 52:15 צדק צדק תרדוף—here יהיה לך
25:17–19	The curse of Amalek	Omitted—nonlegal
26:1–11	Offering first fruits	Omitted
26:12–15	The law of third year tithes	Omitted
26:16–19	Israel a consecrated people	Omitted—nonlegal

The Temple Scroll as an Eschatological Law

That the scroll has a special relationship to Deut 12–26, the biblical "laws for the land," is virtually certain in light of the fact that the scroll accounts for every portion of that legal code. The redactor represented every single portion of Deut 12–26 in one of three ways: he either took it over complete, replaced it with a new formulation (or source), or deleted it—all in accordance with a discernible ideology. This ideology centered on providing an eschatological law for the land. Table 7 examines the redactor's treatment of each portion of Deut 12–26.

The table reveals a substantial and, perhaps, initially surprising number of omissions. Indeed, it may be difficult to believe that, with all these portions missing, the redactor really intended to present a complete and carefully structured new Deut 12–26. But most of these omissions are explicable on the basis of three simple principles which the redactor has applied programmatically and reasonably consistently.

The First Principle Governing Omissions

The omission of some portions of Deut can be explained by the redactor's desire to eliminate repetition—which is, of course, a form of harmonization. Motivated by the prospect of a simplified code, the redactor deleted Deut 12:29–30. He preferred to allow the more detailed commands of Deut 13:1–19 to speak on the subject of idolatry. By reason of simplification Deut 24:5, on the newly married man's exemption from war, also disappears, because Deut 20:7 (at TS 62:1) covers the subject. In each case where the redactor has eliminated repetition, he has retained the more detailed passages on a topic. It is, of course, possible—indeed likely—that this harmonizing process had already been carried out in the course of the topical organization which produced the D source; presumably the source was attractive to the redactor in the first place in part because of this format.

The Second Principle Governing Omissions

The second principle guiding the redactor's omissions was his abhorrence of זנות. The CD community to which he belonged regarded זנות, "improper marriage," as one of the "three nets of Belial" which afflicted Israel during the present wicked era.[22] CD provides two examples of זנות: marrying a second wife while the first wife is alive, and niece marriage.[23] It is striking that the redactor has incorporated extrabiblical laws to deal with precisely these two situations.[24] Concomitantly, he has eliminated from D all passages which explicitly concern divorce or polygamy.[25] Therefore, Deut 24:1–4 and Deut 25:5–10 do not appear in the scroll. Another omission to be explained by the concept of זנות is that of Deut 23:18–19. This passage explicitly refers to the זֹנָה, "prostitute," and connects her to the temple. Presumably any connection of the two was unthinkable for the redactor.

The Third Principle Governing Omissions

The vast majority of the omissions are explicable on the basis of the third principle: the TS is an eschatological law. The redactor left out all portions of D which would cease to function in the "end of days." One could easily deduce this principle on the basis of the pattern of omissions in the scroll alone, but this deduction is happily reinforced by another of the DSS, 4Q174. This scroll appears to be related to CD by its messianic concept, and it plainly expresses one legal consequence of the shift from wicked era to eschaton. Since its expression of this consequence is so clear, it is best to begin the discussion of the eschatological intentions of the TS with this subject.

The Evidence of 4QFlorilegium

4Q174 (also called 4QFlorilegium) takes as its topic the eschatological era and the temple which men will build for that time.[26] Brooke, the author of the fullest study of the text, has

---

22. CD 4:15–18.

23. CD 4:20 and 5:8–9.

24. TS 57:17–19 and 66:12b–17.

25. As discussed in chapter 2, however, he has not always omitted passages which touch on these topics only tangentially or implicitly. It should also be noted that the redactor did not necessarily hold that divorce was impermissible here and now; in fact, CD 13:17 has the word מגרש in a broken context. This word can be read in two ways, either as *mĕgārēš*, "divorced man," or as *migrāš*, "open land." The broken context allows either understanding depending on what is restored in the lacunae. Even if the first option should prove preferable, however, and the CD community did countenance divorce, the redactor is here urging that it not occur in the eschaton for which the TS would serve.

26. For the *editio princeps,* see J. Allegro, *DJDJ* V, pp. 53–57, and plates 19–20. See also Strugnell, "Notes en marge," pp. 220–25, and Brooke's monograph, *4Q Florilegium.* Of particular relevance to the TS and its possible relationship to the text are the studies of the nature of the temple described by Florilegium. See my forthcoming study, "4QFlorilegium and the Temple of Adam," *RQ,* and for other views D. Dimant, "4QFlorilegium and the Idea of the Community as Temple," in *Hellenica et Judaica: Hommage à Valentin Nikoprowetzky,* pp. 165–89; M. Ben-Yasher, "Noch zum miqdaš ʾādām in 4Q Florilegium," *RQ*

listed eleven terms and phrases which in his opinion connect it to CD, particularly to CD 3:12–8:20.[27] His argument is perhaps not fully compelling, but taken with the common messianic scheme apparently held by CD and Florilegium, one may affirm the connection between the two texts. It seems likely that Florilegium was composed by the CD community, or at least incorporates ideas known and espoused by that group. Accordingly, it is plausible to suggest that the redactor knew either the work or the general ideas which it develops.

A comparison of 4Q174 1:2b and 3b–4 with the pattern of omissions in the TS is very instructive, and helps to demonstrate the eschatological character of the TS. These lines read:

1:2b   הואה הבית אשר [יבנו] ²⁸לוא באחרית הימים

1:3b–4   הואה הבית אשר לוא יבוא שמה [   ] [ועלם ועמוני ומואבי וממזר ובן נכר וגר עד עולם

> 1:2b   It is the House which [they will build] for him in the end of days …
>
> 1:3b–4   It is the House into which shall not enter [for]ever and the Ammonite and the Moabite and the bastard and the foreigner and the *gēr* forever.

Lines 1:3b–4 paraphrase Deut 23:3–5, but Florilegium makes two significant interpretive adjustments to the biblical text. First, while the biblical portion is concerned with the congregation (קהל), Florilegium applies the text to the eschatological sanctuary (בית). As Deut is establishing legislation regarding those who are forever barred entry into the "assembly of Israel," the ban comes in Florilegium to apply to entry into the temple. Second, Florilegium adds two new categories to the list of excluded parties: the גר (*gēr*—"sojourner" or "proselyte")[29] and the בן נכר ("foreigner").

---

10 (1979–81): 587–88, and D. R. Schwartz, "The Three Temples of 4Q Florilegium," *RQ* 10 (1979–81): 83–91.

27. Brooke, *4Q Florilegium*, pp. 206–9. Although he lists eleven connections between the two texts, some are not very remarkable and might be explained without theorizing any connection between the texts. Those which are more persuasive include יחפשו לבליעל, 1:9 and CD 4:16–18; דורש התורה, 1:11 and CD 6:7, 7:18 ("A" text)—the term appears nowhere else in DSS literature as a formal title; אחרית הימים, 1:2,12 and CD 4:4, 6:11—the phrase appears nowhere else but the Pesharim and 1QS^a as a title for the eschaton; בני צדוק (unqualified use), 1:17 and CD 4:3; and, most important for the present discussion, גר, 1:4 and CD 6:21, 14:4–6—and nowhere else in the DSS nonbiblical materials except for TS 40:6.

28. Read לו. Brooke has restored יבנה. It seems equally possible, on the basis of 43.366 fragment 1, line 6, to restore יבנו.

29. The question of the correct translation of the term is a difficult one for the period in which the texts we are discussing were composed. The term גר could take either meaning by the third century B.C.E. at the latest. Already in the text of the Hebrew Bible, the term, which originally had meant "protected foreigner, permanent alien," shows an evolution in which it comes to mean essentially "proselyte." In the Levitical legislation, "the *ger* is regarded largely as a proselyte." (*TDOT*, s.v. גר, p. 446; cf. e.g., Lev 18:6–17 on marriage laws, and 18:18–23 on sins of unchastity.) The translators of the LXX, working on the Pentateuch in the third century B.C.E., (thus S. Jellicoe, *The Septuagint and Modern Study* [Oxford: Oxford University Press, 1968], pp. 47–73) nearly always render גר with προσήλυτος; the equation applies 77 of 91 times for the LXX as a whole. The deviations in the translation result from the fact that for the translators of the Greek Bible, the term גר was a religious term; for those instances in the Bible where "proselyte" could not make sense, they translated instead with the terms πάροικος or ξένος

Baumgarten has discussed these two additions at some length.[30] Dealing first with the foreigner, he argues that their exclusion has a double explanation. An exegetical rationale is provided by Ezek 44:9.[31] In addition, Baumgarten seeks to prove that the foreigner was the legal equivalent of the *Netînîm* described in rabbinic literature, and that the same equivalence was in the mind of the author of Florilegium. Since, according to Qiddushim 4:1, the legal status of the *Netîn* is equivalent to that of the bastard (ממזר)—a category which Deut 23 specifically excludes from the assembly—the *Netîn* (= foreigner) suffers the same fate. Thus, if Baumgarten is right, a process of association reinforces Ezek's exclusion of the foreigner. To my mind, however, the passage in Ezek fully suffices for the explanation, without recourse to rabbinic literature, particularly in view of the direction Baumgarten is then forced to take with the *gēr*.

("protected alien" and "stranger," respectively; see *TDNT*, s.v. προσήλυτος and πάροικος). That the term προσήλυτος in the LXX must mean "proselyte" is shown by the translation of the Hebrew verb from which *gēr* derives, גור. For example, Lev 20:2 מִן הַגֵּר הַגָּר becomes ἀπὸ τῶν γεγενημένων προσηλύτων. The latter phrase can only mean "out of those who have become proselytes" (as noted by T. J. Meek, "The Translation of *Ger* in the Hextateuch and its Bearing on the Documentary Hypothesis," *JBL* 49 [1930]: 178–79). Thus in 4QFlorilegium, whose date of composition, while uncertain, almost surely postdates the third century, the word could theoretically mean either "proselyte" or, harking back to the biblical text, "alien sojourner." In the literature of the DSS the term occurs but rarely. At CD 14:4–6, it appears twice in an explicitation of the order for the mustering of the community's members at the meeting of the "camps." The members are apparently to be mustered according to their status in the community, in the order priests, Levites, the children of Israel, and, last, הגר (the *gēr*). Since the text here is speaking only of those who adhere to the teaching of the community, it is hard to see how the meaning could be other than "proselyte." The term occurs again at CD 6:21, in a list of those whom the community is to help. The text reads "to strengthen the hand of the poor and needy and the *gēr*." Conceivably this use could be interpreted in a sociological sense, as listing the disadvantaged segments of society. If so, the meaning of *gēr* would probably be "sojourner," since the sojourner did not have full rights in ancient society and required special consideration. But 6:21 is apparently further explicated by the parallel at 14:14, where the phrase "strengthen the hand of the poor and needy" recurs. The context there is that of the community almsgiving system whereby each member would contribute about eight percent of his income towards "all the work of the corporation" (כל עבודת החבר). The implication seems to be that only the needy members of the community itself would be helped. If this is the correct interpretation, then once again the term *gēr* must mean "proselyte." Outside of TS 40:6, which I discuss below, the term appears in only one other text of the DSS, 4QpNah 3–4 II 9. The text reads, "the interpretation concerns the deceivers of Ephraim who ... will deceive many, their kings and princes, priests and people, with the *gēr* who joins" (גר נלוה). The latter phrase appears to be an allusion to Isa 14:1, "and the *gēr* will join them" (ונלוה הגר). The context is of a future idealistic restoration of Israel in the land. The use of נלוה to describe the *gēr* is also reminiscent of Esther 9:27, which speaks of the Jews and "all those joining (הנלוים) themselves to them." Given that the Jews are not in their land in Esther, the reference cannot be to sojourners; the meaning must be "those who converted to Judaism." If, as it seems, the author of 4QpNah had these texts in mind, he would be referring not to sojourners, but to proselytes. Hence outside of Florilegium and the TS all DSS occurrences of the term *gēr* appear to refer to proselytes.

30. J. Baumgarten, "The Exclusion of Netinim and Proselytes in 4Q Florilegium," *RQ* 8 (1972–74): 87–96. This article has been reprinted in idem, *Studies in Qumran Law* (Leiden: Brill, 1977), pp. 75–87, to which I refer here. For another helpful study, see G. Blidstein, "4Q Florilegium and Rabbinic Sources on Bastard and Proselyte," *RQ* 8 (1972–74): 431–35.

31. The text says, כול בן נכר ... לא יבוא אל מקדשי, "no foreigner ... shall enter my sanctuary."

Baumgarten attempts to show that the *gēr* also enjoys a lower legal status than other Jews in the Qiddushim passage.[32] He therefore concludes that in adding the foreigner and "proselyte" (as he understands the term in Florilegium) to the list of Deut 23, Florilegium parallels rabbinic legal tradition. Foreigners and "proselytes," he says, had a secondary status; they "were part of the general congregation, but not of the congregation of the Lord."[33]

Baumgarten's case regarding the added exclusions of Florilegium is suggestive, but clearly has some weak points. A basic fault is that he never considers the problem of defining the term *gēr*. The meaning of the term in 4QFlorilegium could well be "sojourner," but Baumgarten simply assumes that it has the same meaning in both the rabbinic materials and in 4Q Florilegium. This is a dubious assumption. Granted, the term certainly means "proselyte" in the rabbinic materials; but that it bears this meaning in Florilegium is, in my view, improbable. The other groups in the text's list of exclusions are united by their status as foreigners. (The bastard, since he was of unknown or uncertain paternity, was liable to the suspicion that his father might be a foreigner.) And Jewish tradition has generally recognized the proselyte as no longer foreign, but as a full Jew. Taking into account the linguistic possibilities and the exegetical context, it seems better to understand the term as "sojourner" in Florilegium. The sojourner would simply be another foreign element added to those already barred from entering the eschatological temple.

An even more formidable obstacle for Baumgarten's view than the problem of definition is Ezek 47:21–22. That text stipulates that in the eschatological future *gērîm* (or, possibly, their progeny, depending on how the verses are interpreted[34]) will inherit the land with Israel. It reads, "and you shall divide this land among the tribes of Israel ... and the *gērîm* who sojourn among you who have born children in your midst. They shall be for you as a native-born Israelite; with you they shall have a portion among the tribes of Israel."[35] This text from Ezek is one of two in that book which concern proselytes (for thus do scholars understand these

---

32. Baumgarten, "Exclusion," p. 81.

33. Ibid., p. 82. He refers to 1QS[a] for a parallel. According to 2:9–10, those with bodily afflictions were ineligible to enter the exclusive קהל of those called to the "Council of the Yaḥad" (cf. 2:4). They could, however, present inquiries by messenger. It is not clear that this is a cogent parallel.

34. Yet a third problem with Baumgarten's understanding of *gēr* in Florilegium becomes somewhat clearer as this discussion progresses. It is the fact that TS 40:6 groups the *gēr* who has been born in the land with women (and unknown others, lost in a lacuna). These groups are not to enter the middle court of the temple, where cultically qualified Israel worships. They must remain in the outer court. (Cf. 1QS[a] 1:4, where the congregation [קהל] includes women and children. The "congregation" is less restrictive than the עדה הקודש ["company of holiness"], which includes only men aged twenty and above, according to 1:9.) Baumgarten has recognized the problem the TS poses for his interpretation, and in his "Exclusions from the Temple: Proselytes and Agrippa I," *JJS* 33 (1982): 215–25, he has attempted an explanation. I am not persuaded; he has not recognized that the TS uses the term in both its meanings. For more detailed discussion see M. O. Wise, "The Eschatological Vision of the Temple Scroll," *JNES* 49 (1990): 155–72.

35. The Hebrew reads:

וחלקתם את הארץ הזאת לכם לשבטי ישראל ... ולגרים הגרים בתוככם אשר הולידו בנים

בתוככם והיו לכם כאזרח בבני ישראל אתכם יפלו בנחלה בתוך שבטי ישראל

verses; they do not concern sojourners).[36] It is evidently the intention of the biblical text to include proselytes as fully Israelite in the future restoration of the nation. Since Florilegium 1:2b states that it is describing that time (the "end of days") and since (as Baumgarten shows) it applies Ezek 44:9 in excluding the foreigner, it seems probable that Florilegium also presupposes Ezek 47:21–22. It tacitly incorporates all proselytes as Israelites, while explicitly excluding sojourners as alien. One need only consider texts such as Jubilees[37] or Psalms of Solomon[38] to find more or less contemporary parallels for Florilegium's xenophobic attitude. And, of course, that attitude was rooted in the ideas and attitudes of the immediate postexilic situation, at the time of Ezra 4 and the reforms of Ezra and Nehemiah.

Thus Baumgarten's case for *gēr* is not as convincing as is his case for the exclusion of the alien. Understanding the term *gēr* to mean "sojourner," 4QFlorilegium provides explicit support for the understanding that the TS is intended for the eschaton. Just as Florilegium allows no aliens or sojourners to enter the eschatological sanctuary, so the TS excludes both groups from its law for the eschaton.[39] These classes would not inhabit Israel in the "end of days." Those portions of Deut which dealt with them would accordingly not function in that period; they were always meant only for the wicked era.

The Evidence of the Temple Scroll

On this basis one can explain the omission of the following passages which deal with the גר. Deut 24:14–15 and 24:17–23 specifically concern this class; they are not in the TS. Deut 14:28–29, on the tithe of the third year, mentions the גר, although only in passing. The redactor cut the passage simply because the word appears. He likewise removed 15:8–18, which is about releasing slaves at the end of seven years of service. Although this passage speaks only of the עבד ("slave"), there is a parallel passage on the jubilee year, in Lev 25:47–54. Here גר appears. The redactor, apparently convinced that these two passages were about the same situation, cut the Deut portion from his eschatological law.

36. *TDOT*, s.v. גר.

37. Jubilees 16:25 specifies that when Abraham celebrated Tabernacles, aliens were excluded from participating.

38. Baumgarten actually refers to the *Psalms of Solomon* to support his contention that Florilegium excludes both foreigners and proselytes. The text of Psalm 17:28 reads καὶ πάροικος καὶ ἀλλογενὴς οὐ παροικήσει αὐτοῖς ἔτι. In fact, however, this text does not support the exclusion of proselytes. It should be translated "and sojourner and foreigner shall not dwell among them anymore." It is significant that the translator of the Psalm, which is thought to date to the first century B.C.E. (see R. B. Wright, "Psalms of Solomon," in *The Old Testament Pseudepigrapha*, ed. J. H. Charlesworth [Garden City: Doubleday, 1983–85] 2:640–41), did not use the term προσήλυτος, but instead chose πάροικος. This choice of terms appears to reflect the differentiation found in the LXX (note 29 above). Baumgarten's understanding of πάροικος as "proselyte" is overwhelmingly contradicted by the LXX evidence.

39. Cf. D. Altschuler, "Classification of Judaic Laws," p. 10: "The net effect of these omissions and deletions is to make the TS even more cult-centered and exclusivist than the Torah upon whose legal passages it generally is based."

In the same way the excision of 23:25–26 is based on the mention of the גר in a parallel passage, Deut 24:19–21. Both passages concern gleaning, and since the second mentions the גר, neither appears in the TS.[40] Also, contrary to the suggestions of several scholars that social or economic changes led to the exclusion of 26:1–11 (the so-called הודית המעשר), it is rather the mention of גר which led the redactor to pass it over.[41] Finally, because 26:12–15 also includes the term, the passage disappears from the scroll.

Passages which contain the term נכרי, "foreigner," were also excised from the TS. Deut 15:1–7, on release from debt at the end of every seven-year period, mentions that the debts of Israelites are to be forgiven, but not those of the foreigner. Deut 23:20–21 is about whether it is permissible to charge interest on loans (it is permitted only to charge the alien). The redactor excluded both passages. And another of the redactor's ideas about the eschaton evidently confirmed his decision to exclude them.

It was the redactor's belief that during the eschaton, Israel would neither borrow nor lend. Or, more precisely, that no Israelite would borrow, and her people would lend only to non-Israelites. He found this idea in Deut 28. The first fourteen verses of Deut 28 expatiate the blessings that Israel would enjoy in the land if the people kept the law of Deut 12–26. For the redactor, as I discuss below with regard to CD's ideology of the land, when Israel once again dwelled in the land, per definition they would be obedient to these laws. Therefore, the redactor understood Deut 28:1–14 as descriptive of the eschatological period. In 28:12 he read, והלוית גוים רבים ואתה לא תלוה, "and you shall lend to many peoples, but you shall not borrow." On the authority of this verse he excised from the TS all passages which relate to Israelites borrowing or pledging, or lending to other Israelites. Deut 15:1–7 would not be practical in the eschaton, since there is no need to release anyone from debt when no one borrows. Deut 23:20–21, about interest on loans to Israelites, would not be needed in the end of days. Thus these two passages mention both lending to Israelites, and the alien; the mention of either would have resulted in their exclusion.

Other portions of Deut which presuppose lending to Israelites also disappear from the TS. Taking of pledges, such as a handmill, would not arise in the society which the redactor envisioned. He therefore removed Deut 24:6. He also found no use for 24:10–13, which explicitly treats laws for pledges and loans.

Other eschatological ideas apparently explain additional omissions. The redactor decided to omit 19:14, the law which forbids moving a boundary mark, because he believed the law would not be necessary in the eschaton, and that it only applied to the wicked era. CD uses two terms in describing the present era, sitting on the cusp of the eschaton. קץ הרשע "the wicked era," is the blanket term, while קץ חרבן הארץ, "the era of the destruction of the land," applies to

---

40. It may be relevant that 4Q159 apparently linked 23:25–26 with 14:28–29. The latter's mention of the *gēr* may have been a factor in the elimination of the former. The connection of the two passages may have been a traditional exegesis of the CD community. See 4Q159 1 ii 3–4 and Weinert, "Legislation," pp. 183 and 190–91.

41. Luria, "הערות," pp. 381–86 and Rokeah, "The Temple Scroll, Philo, Josephus and the Talmud," pp. 518–19. On economic motives in general for related laws during the Second Temple period, cf. e.g., Sharvit, "טומאה וטהורה" p. 23, and more fully S. Zeitlin, "Prosbul," *JQR* 37 (1947): 341–62.

a point near the beginning of the present wicked era, when God visited his wrath upon apostate Israel. In CD 5:20 one reads ובקץ חרבן הארץ עמדו מסיגי הגבול, "and in the era of the destruction of the land the 'movers of the boundary mark' arose."[42] Evidently this rather colorful expression came to connote those who made changes in the traditional laws, leading to the widespread apostasy of the community's own day. As a member of the CD community, the redactor may have shared this somewhat metaphorical understanding of the law in Deut. Since the "movers of the boundary mark," whether literal or metaphorical, were active in the wicked era, he thought 19:14 inappropriate for his eschatological law.

Laws on slavery would also become dysfunctional in the end of days, according to the redactor's ideology. Therefore, he excised 23:16–17 and 24:7. His logic was straightforward. First, no Israelites would become slaves during the period which the TS covers, since there would be no poor among the people (debt was the only way an Israelite could become a slave to another Israelite according to the Hebrew Bible).[43] He knew this fact on the basis of Deut 28:3–6, 8, and 11. Second, no foreigners would become slaves to Israel. This situation was, of course, connected to the exclusion of foreigners generally. With no foreigners dwelling in eschatological Israel, there could accordingly be no foreign slaves.

Another factor served to reinforce the omission of 24:7. The redactor apparently held to a common eschatological concept known from many texts of the Second Temple period: few, if any, wicked men would inhabit the land in the "end of days." The passage at 4QpPs 37 ii 6–7 is a representative expression of such a vision. According to this portion there would be no "wicked man" in the period of the "end of days."[44] As another example, 1QS contains no legislation on assault among members of the community it describes. The absence of such legislation is notable, since in the many codes of guilds and religious associations of the Greco-Roman period with which 1QS is largely comparable, laws about members fighting are nearly always present.[45] The lack of rules and penalties for assault in this text must be idealistic; it is perhaps a reflection of the idea in 4QpPs 37. Psalms of Solomon 17:27 describes the eschaton thus: "He [the Davidic messiah] will not tolerate unrighteousness even to pause among them, and any person who knows wickedness will not live with them."[46]

---

42. Cf. CD 8:3.

43. See de Vaux, *Ancient Israel*, vol. 1, *Social Institutions*, pp. 82–83.

44. The passage in 4QpPs reads ולוא ימצא כול איש באָרץ רשע, "and no wicked man will be found in the land." For the *editio princeps*, see J. Allegro, *DJDJ* V, pp. 42–50 and plates 16–17, esp. p. 43. On this passage see also Strugnell, "Notes en marge," pp. 211–18; D. Pardee, "A Restudy of the Commentary on Psalm 37 from Qumran Cave 4 (Discoveries in the Judaean Desert of Jordan, vol. V, no 171)," *RQ* 8 (1972–74): 174–75; and Horgan, *Pesharim*, pp. 205–6.

45. M. Weinfeld, *The Organizational Pattern and the Penal Code of the Qumran Sect* (Göttingen: Vandenhoeck & Ruprecht, 1986), p. 36, "A conspicuous difference in the statutes of the Qumran sect as against the Demotic statutes, is that in the sect's statutes there is no section on assault. This offense is much discussed in the statutes of the associations which we are dealing with here." Weinfeld compares 1QS to 17 codes, ranging in time from the third century B.C.E. to the second century C.E., and coming from Greece, Egypt, and Syria.

46. Translation by Wright (see note 38 above).

This idealistic concept of the end of days apparently motivated the redactor's excision of Deut 25:1–3 and Deut 25:11–12. The first concerns the scourging of the wicked man,[47] and the second is a law about fighting. On this basis also the redactor removed and replaced Deut 19:1–13, as cities of refuge would not be required in the TS period. Probably the concept of an eschatological Israel inhabited only by the law-abiding righteous also explains the omission of Deut 24:16 in the TS. Another possibility is that neither 24:7 nor 24:16 were part of the D source, and hence did not come to be a part of the final form of the TS. In any case, it must be admitted that the redactor was less consistent in his excisions based on this idea than he was in other cases. He allowed some laws to remain which would presumably not be needed in a purely righteous society. For example, he retained Deut 21:1–9, on expiation for an unknown murderer; 21:18–21, on the stoning of a rebellious youth; and portions concerned with adultery and rape (22:22–29). He also kept—and even added—laws concerned with righteousness in judgement, which would seem unnecessary in a sinless community. Several considerations must be kept in mind in the face of these apparent inconsistencies. First, not only is inconsistency normal and expected in all human endeavors, but it is a recognized trademark of eschatological writings in particular. Often such works are attempting to reconcile scarcely reconcilable concepts derived from different portions of the Hebrew Bible. Further, the redactor's concept of eschatological righteousness evidently was not governed by any abstract notion of "righteousness;" he allowed for occasional individual aberrance from the ideals which would characterize the nation as a whole. And, the redactor may have retained some such portions precisely in order to emphasize the righteous character of the period and land he envisioned. For example, his insistence on a king who is righteous in judgement serves to underline that monarch's enviable character, and to draw attention to an ideal quality which was frequently a central focus in descriptions of eschatological or messianic figures.[48]

Conclusion on Omissions

Thus three basic principles can explain the great majority of the scroll's omissions of portions from Deut 12–26. The redactor eliminated repetitious portions, choosing only the more detailed of parallel passages (unless, as noted, they were already removed during the preparation of the D source). He deleted biblical portions which explicitly provide for divorce or improper marriage. And, because he shaped the TS as an eschatological code, he omitted portions of Deut which would no longer function when the "end of days" dawned. Consequently, no biblical passages which concern sojourners (גרים), the foreigner (איש נכרי), loans and pledges by Israelites, or slavery appear in the TS. On the same note the redactor deleted most portions which imply wickedness and violence. Of course, other portions he removed not because they were useless, but because he wanted to replace them with new formulations. To such instances I now proceed.

---

47. It is also possible that the redactor thought that God would carry out any necessary "scourging." See CD 4:7 and Rabin's note in *Zadokite Fragments, ad loc.*

48. See my discussion of this point in "Eschatological Vision."

Redactional Additions and Substitutions

It is not necessary to dwell very long on the redactional additions and substitutions, as table 7 can be consulted for any individual case. Substantial portions of Deut—or, strictly speaking, D—were removed in order to replace them with more detailed laws from other portions of scripture. For example, Deut 12:1–14 briefly sets down some laws regarding the "place" where God will dwell and will be worshipped. The redactor replaced this portion, as noted already, with the much more detailed temple description here called the Temple Source. The laws of offerings found in Deut are not nearly as specific and detailed as those in Num and Lev; wanting those details, and wanting to modify even those with certain extrabiblical prescriptions, the redactor added the Festival Calendar source. Then he no longer needed Deut 12:15–19 or 16:1–17. Not needing the laws regarding the cities of refuge at Deut 19:1–13 either, the redactor substituted a new, midrashic formulation concerned with ritual purity.

Concerns for ritual purity motivated other substitutions and additions as well. For example, the Deuteronomic laws on leprosy at 24:8–9 were not sufficient to cover certain foreseeable situations in the temple city. Thus the redactor substituted new laws, derived from his community's legal heritage, and based on the more detailed Levitical laws on leprosy. The addition to the "Law of the Beautiful Captive" at 63:14–15 is not really a marriage law *per se,* but a purity law. It represents the community's views on purity (טהרה), and the time required for the "absolute outsider" to become ritually pure.[49] Operating from the equation "wilderness camp = temple (city)," the redactor moved the Deut law on exclusion from the assembly to the appropriate points in the scroll, and applied it in modified form to exclude certain groups from the temple. The laws for the holy war camp contained in Deut 23:10–15 were also handled in part through the device of this equation. The redactor added purity laws gathered from various sources—many of the "laws" discussed in chapter 5—applying them to the holy city, while excising the now otiose portion from Deut 23.

In terms of additions pure and simple, these perhaps reflect more clearly even than his omissions the things of greatest importance to the redactor. For example, by adding a portion from MD at the beginning of col. 60, he showed his extremely high valuation of the Levites.[50] As already noted, he added laws in relation to זנות at 66:11b–12 and in the form of TM's law on royal marriage.

The mention of this law raises the problem of the reason for adding TM. I earlier remarked on the peculiar mix of the mundane and the ultramundane in these columns. The idea of a 12,000-man bodyguard having as a principle objective the prevention of royal sin is ultramundane—eschatological— in the same way as the idea that in the Israel ruled by the scroll there would be no assaults. Yet there are many more ordinary aspects to TM as well.

---

49. Cf. CD 12:3–6, on the man who profanes the Sabbath or one of the festivals. By this act the person sets himself at maximal distance from the community, but can return after *seven years* of proper behavior. Note also the permission clause of the law in CD, formally identical to that of the additional law on the "beautiful captive."

50. See especially J. Milgrom, "Studies in the Temple Scroll," pp. 501–3.

(And one could include in that evaluation the whole of the source MD; 64:6b–13, for example, which provides for the crucifixion of political criminals, is an extract from that source.) What is the explanation for the oddly mixed character of the "King's Law," and for what purpose did the redactor add it?

Perhaps a few lines from 4QpIsa[a] can serve as an entrée into these questions.[51] At lines 15–24 of fragment 8–10, there is a discussion of a royal messianic figure, the צמח דויד ("Branch of David"). This figure is to arise in the "end of days," and the priests will instruct him in the Torah.[52] I draw particular attention to lines 23–24:

.23 [וכאשר יורוהו כן ישפוט ועל פיהם
.24 [עמו יצא אחד מכוהני השם ובידו בגדי]

Translation

23.] and as they instruct him, so shall he judge. And by their permission ...
24.] with him will go out (to war?) one of the priests of God. And he will have in his hand cloth[es ...

These fragmentary lines seem to indicate that the Davidic king would rule in accordance with priestly direction. Line 24 apparently concerns a situation where the king "goes out" to war (יצא). A priest is to accompany him, evidently to direct certain aspects of this endeavor.

These lines are, of course, strongly reminiscent of portions of TM. It will be recalled that according to 56:20, the king of the TS is to read in a book of the Torah which the priests, as his instructors, write for him. When deciding whether and when to wage war, the king is expected to act as directed by the high priest. The wording and concept of TS 58:19 is especially close to that of lines 23–24 above: על פיהו יצא ועל פיהו יבוא, "and by his [the high priest's] permission he [the king] will go out [to war], and by his permission he will come in."

The point of these parallels is to suggest that TM was intended to instruct a messianic king (or kings?) who would rule an earthly kingdom during the eschaton. Although the precise relationship of 4QpIsa[a] to the TS and the CD community is still to be decided, it is nevertheless true that in the present form of CD, at 7:18–20, there is evidence for an expectation of a future, apparently messianic, royal figure.[53] And there are substantial parallels to the description of TM's king to be found in approximately contemporary literature which is more conventionally eschatological in its expression—texts such as Psalms of Solomon 17 and 1QS[b].[54] If this

---

51. Edited by J. Allegro, *DJDJ* V, pp. 11–15 and plates 4–5. Consult also Strugnell, "Notes en marge," pp. 183–86.

52. *Si vera lectio.* Allegro reads ב[   ]ה[תורה in line 18, but Strugnell, "Notes en marge," p. 185, tentatively suggests ב[רוח נ]בורה.

53. Cf esp. השבט הוא נשיא כול העדה, "The 'sceptre'—this is the 'Prince' of the whole congregation." The term "Prince" evidently derives from Ezekiel, where the future ruler of the restored state is called by this title rather than "king." This portion of CD is not a part of the earliest form of the work, so one must be careful about attributing its ideas to the earlier period when, presumably, the redactor flourished.

54. For a more detailed consideration of these parallels see my "Eschatological Vision."

suggestion is correct, it would explain both the peculiar character of TM and the redactor's purpose in adding it to the biblical laws on the king. TM was not intended to regulate any king in the here and now; it was to guide the ruler of a millennial kingdom. The character of the kingdom itself, a purified national Israel in the midst of often hostile gentile nations, explains the mixed character of the instruction for the king. The restored Israel of the latter days in the prophets of the Hebrew Bible is the model for this millennial concept. The biblical concept itself is simultaneously "realistic" (i.e., there are births and deaths and battles to be fought) and "idealistic" (i.e., the people are purified and righteous; they live to patriarchal ages).

The Redactional Plan of the Temple Scroll

I mention at several junctures that more than one scholar has thought that the TS is organized along the lines of the Pentateuch; that the redactor's plan was to present his material in the same general order as it occurs in those books of the Bible. Thus he begins with Exod 34 in col. 2, proceeds to sacrificial laws based on Lev and Num, and closes with laws selected from Deut. Now, a quick perusal of the *Appendix* suffices to put the lie to this suggestion. True enough, the scroll begins in col. 2 with material from Exod, but in that same column also appear portions from Deut 7. And so it goes—a detailed refutation of this superficial approach to the scroll would occupy unwarranted space. The TS mixes and matches portions drawn from the latter four books with no real regard to the order of books in the Torah. The real basis for the scroll's redactional plan is quite different. Put simply, the redactor had in mind the production of a new Deut—that is, of the legal portions—but he chose to organize that material in terms of concentric circles of holiness. As Maier has noted, the TS has arranged its material in terms of eleven circles of holiness, beginning with the Holy of Holies and working outward to the land.[55] The redactor has rearranged material from the D source in accordance with the circle to which it applies, and added his other sources according to the same plan. Always, however, he had in mind the production of a new Deut, so he accounted for every portion of the relevant laws. Accordingly, he added the Festival Calendar source at the time he was discussing the circle to which it was relevant—the circle surrounding the altar and inner portions of the inner court. He removed the laws on the second tithe from Deut 14:22–27, which one might have expected to find in TS col. 51 or 52, and, replacing them with a more satisfying midrashic application, inserted the equivalent at TS 43:3 and 12b–15a. This is the appropriate point in the scroll, for it is here that it describes the court of the temple where those tithes would be consumed. The redactor cut out the laws on exclusion from the assembly of Deut 23, as noted, and interpolated them into cols. 39 and 40, where they applied; here the scroll discusses who is excluded from the second and third courts, respectively. The laws on the camp during holy war were replaced, as noted above, by midrashic constructs, and inserted at cols. 45–47 (applying to the city of the sanctuary) and at col. 50 (applying to the cities of the land). These examples should suffice to make my point; table 7 and the *Appendix* provide the details and many additional examples, all adding up to the redactional pattern I describe. This

55. Maier, *The Temple Scroll*, pp. 5–6.

method of arrangement was dictated, of course, by the redactor's dual constraints: overriding concern for ritual purity, and his belief that one should base an eschatological law for the land on the biblical law for the land which begins at Deut 12.

The Redactor's Identity

As determined in the previous chapter, the redactor of the TS was a member of the CD community. It is appropriate here to examine more carefully the data of the TS, seeking to ascertain which portions the redactor wrote himself. It is from such portions, of course, that one may expect to learn most about the redactor's ideology and *Sitz im Leben*. I explain in chapter 5 my methodology for determining which are "redactional phrases," beginning with the redactional seams in 29:3–10 and 51:5b–10. Table 8 shows the distribution of the six basic redactional phrases, and suggests a seventh. Column 1 gives the form of the phrase found in cols. 29 and 51, while col. 2 lists the variants which occur elsewhere in the scroll.

As table 8 illustrates, redactional phrases tend to cluster at certain points in the TS. Chapter 5 contains a discussion of the significance of their frequency in columns 45–51, where the redactor has interpolated laws. They also appear in col. 3 three times, if the restorations are correct. It is not surprising that such should be the case, since col. 3 is the seam where the Temple Source begins. One expects seams to show pronounced redactional activity. Indeed, it would not be surprising if the end of col. 2 and the beginning of col. 3 comprised an explanatory redactional composition similar to those in cols. 29 and 51. Another column where these phrases cluster is col. 47. According to table 8, within a space of only fifteen lines redactional phrases occur eight times.

It is further significant that the redactional phrase in 47:3–4 cannot be removed without damage to the sense, because it is therefore unlikely that the phrase is an interpolation. Since in addition to these considerations, the column is entirely "free composition" (see the *Appendix*), col. 47 is almost certainly a redactional composition. It is therefore a potential source of information about the redactor.

The topic of the column is the entry of animal skins into the holy city. According to the redactor, the only skins which can be used to bring items into the city are those which come from clean animals, and then only from those which have been sacrificed in Jerusalem. The skins of clean animals which have been butchered in other cities cannot enter the city, for they are ritually unclean. As several scholars have pointed out, col. 47 is in its concerns strikingly reminiscent of a portion of Josephus' *Antiquities*.[56]

56. Baumgarten, review of מגילת המקדש, p. 12; Levine, "Aspects," pp. 15–16; McCready, "Sectarian Status," pp. 188–89; Milgrom, "Further Studies," p. 98, and Yadin, I, pp. 308–11. Note also that the entry of skins into Jerusalem was apparently an issue at the time that 4QMMT was composed; see Schiffman, "Systems of Jewish Law," p. 246.

Table 8. Redactional Phrases in the Temple Scroll

Phrase and Locus	*Variants and Loci*
1. אשר אשכין שמי עליו 29:3–4[1] אשר אשכין עליו את כבודי 29:8–9	1. לשום שמי עליו 3:4 2. אשר אשכין שמי בה 45:12 3. לשכין שמי ... בתוכה 47:4 4. אנוכי משכן את שמי ... בתוכה 47:10 5. אנוכי מקדש לשום שמי בתוכה 52:19–20
2. ושכנתי אתמה 29:8 כי אני יהוה שוכן בתוך בני ישראל 52:7–8	1. אשר אני שכן בתוכה 45:13–14 2. כי אני יהוה שוכן בתוך בני ישראל 45:14 3. אשר א[נ]י שוכ[ן בתוכם 46:4 4. אנוכי שוכן בתוכמה 46:12 5. וש[כנתי אני בתוכ]מה[2] 47:3 6. אשר אנוכי שוכן בתוכה 47:18
4. ואקדשה את מקדשי בכבודי 29:8	1. [והקדשתי בי]ח (?) 3:4 2. [ואקדש] 30:1 3. והעיר אשר אקדיש 47:3–4 4. עירי אשר אנוכי מקדש 52:19–20
5. לעולם ועד 29:8 כול הימים 29:10 לעולם 29:7	1. יהיה קודש קודשים לעולם ועד 35:9 2. כי אני יהוה שוכן ... לעולם ועד 45:14 3. ולוא יטהרו עוד עד לעולם (?) 50:19 4. לעולם ועד כול הימים 46:3–4 5. כ]ול הימים (?) 3:4 6. ש[כנתי [לעולם 47:3
6. כתורת המשפט הזה 29:4	1. כחוק המשפט הזה 50:6–7 2. כמשפט התורה הזואת 50:7 3. כמשפט התורה הזואת 50:17
7. אשר אני מגיד לכה בהר הזה 52:6–7	1. ועשה ככול אשר אנוכי מדבר אליכה 31:9

[1]In addition to the clear redactional use of this phrase, it is noteworthy that it appears several times in quotations from Deut where it does not occur in MT. Since at these junctures it does appear in the LXX, presumably these occurrences represent textual variants. Cf. 53:9–10 and 56:5.

[2]Yadin suggested only וש[כנתי ... בתוכ]מה at II, p. 302. I suggest restoring אני. The lacuna is large enough for only three letters, and this restoration results in a text similar to 29:9.

Ant. 12.138–146 comprises two documents: a proclamation, and an excerpt from an edict (πρόγραμμα), both issued by the orders of Antiochus III about the year 200 B.C.E. The first document is a letter from the Seleucid monarch to one Ptolemy, the *strategos* of Coele Syria, in favor of the Jews and their temple.[57] It bestows rewards upon the Jews for supporting Antiochus in the recent Fifth Syrian War. The second portion, the edict, legislates to protect the ritual purity of Jerusalem.[58] The following is an extract:[59]

> Nor shall anyone bring into the city the flesh of horses or of mules or of wild or tame asses, or of leopards, foxes or hares or, in general, of any animals forbidden to the Jews. Nor is it lawful to bring in their skins or even to breed any of these animals in the city. But only the sacrificial animals known to their ancestors and necessary for the propitiation of God shall they be permitted to use. And the person who violates any of these statutes shall pay to the priests a fine of three thousand drachmas of silver.

The parallels between this legislation and TS 47 are patent, and the fact that no similar law is known from any other source highlights their commonalities. Both take as a point of departure the need to distinguish between clean and unclean skins. While the πρόγραμμα prohibits the entry only of impure animals' skins, the TS excludes the skins even of pure animals, unless they come from temple sacrifices. The effect of the TS passage is thus to extend the application of the earlier law.[60] And the TS expands the geographical extent of the ban as well.[61]

Another point emerges from a comparison of TS 47 with Antiochus' edict. It involves the purposes of the legislation. In the case of the edict, the aims are explicit. Although the concern for the purity of the city is prominent, equally noteworthy is the substantial monetary benefit

57. On this proclamation, see E. J. Bikerman, "La charte séleucide de Jerusalem," *REJ* 100 (1935): 4–35. Drawing on his exact knowledge of Hellenistic and Roman sources, Bikerman proves that the proclamation is genuine. For a historical overview of scholarly approaches to this portion of Josephus, and a full bibliography, see Marcus, *Josephus VII*, pp. 743–60, and V. Tcherikover, *Hellenistic Civilization and the Jews*, trans. S. Applebaum (New York: Atheneum, 1982), pp. 82–84. For related correspondence consisting of six letters between the royal chancellery and Ptolemy, see Y. H. Landau, "A Greek Inscription Found Near Hefzibah," *IEJ* 16 (1966):54–70.

58. On the edict, see E. J. Bikerman, "Une proclamation séleucide relative au temple de Jerusalem," *Syria* 25 (1946–48): 67–85, esp. pp. 75–76; Marcus, *Josephus VII*, pp. 761–64; and Tcherikover, *Hellenistic Civilization*, pp. 84–87. All of these discussions will require adjustments in the light of TS 47.

59. The translation of this portion, *Ant.* 12.146, is that of Marcus.

60. Cf. Yadin, I, pp. 310–11.

61. This latter extension may not be obvious at first glance. Although one gains the impression that the edict banned the entry of skins into the entire city of Jerusalem, in fact this impression is false. It results from the present context into which Josephus has introduced the πρόγραμμα. Josephus himself was deceived as to the nature of the source he was using. As Bikerman shows ("Une proclamation," p. 83), the source of Josephus' misunderstanding was the word πρόγραμμα. Because he thought the Greek term the equivalent of the Latin *edictum*, Josephus inferred that the document was published "throughout the entire kingdom" (κατὰ πᾶσαν τὴν βασιλείαν), as were Roman edicts. Josephus then further adorned the source with the character of a proclamation. Yet as a πρόγραμμα, the document was probably posted only at the entrance to the temple precincts; it was neither published abroad, nor stood at the entrance to Jerusalem. (It was usual to post προγράμματα in a public location proximate to the area affected.) It follows that the redactor of the TS, knowing of this traditional law, has extended the original application from the temple precincts to all of the holy city. This sort of extension is consistent with his method of redacting legal materials, as I attempt to show in chapter 5.

which promises to accrue to the priests as a penalty for infraction of the skins law. The effect of TS 47 would be similar. Essentially, it grants the priests a monopoly on all skins used for commerce with the capital city. All merchants who wished to carry goods in skins would have to purchase the skins from the temple priests. Parchment, shoes, bedcoverings, and other leather products used in Jerusalem would also bring profits to the temple coffers. Consonant with its eschatological setting in the scroll, I do not believe that the TS passage has primarily an economic motivation *as now presented;* but if, as with other TS "laws," it derives from present-time or "wicked era" legislation of the CD community, it is clear that economics would have been involved originally.

Seen in this light, the analogy between TS 47 and the edict implies that both were intended to benefit the same group. The edict explicitly declares its beneficiary: the priesthood, particularly the elite. Because the redactor evidently wrote col. 47, it must express his concerns directly. Since the concerns of the column are, as the analogy reveals, those of the priestly elite, one may conclude that the redactor was probably a member of that elite. I elaborate upon this point in the discussion of the dating of the TS below.

It may be possible to be a great deal more specific about the identity of the redactor by comparing the redactional shape of the TS with the typology of eschatological expectations held by his community. In the ideology of CD, God has a legal case (ריב) against Israel, because they have not been obedient to his commandments, and have forsaken him.[62] Only a remnant has remained faithful to him and have been true to the covenant he made with the patriarchs or "first ones" (ראשונים). This remnant constitutes a "root" (שורש) which, according to CD 1:8, ultimately will inherit the land.[63] Its present inhabitants are for the most part those whom God has rejected.

The covenant which the community upheld was in their view, as we saw above, one and the same as the one God made with the patriarchs; but it includes some esoteric laws which Israel as a whole has either never known or has now forsaken. CD 3:14–15 contains the most explicit statement of what the covenant included. God had made known to them "hidden things" (נסתרות), comprising legal ordinances for the proper observance of the Sabbath, the festivals of the holy calendar, and in general a proper relationship with God. CD calls these ordinances variously "precepts" (יסורים 7:5), "statutes" (חוקים 7:9), and "the exact interpretation of the Law" (פרוש התורה 4:8, 6:14). The community underwent instruction in these gnostic laws (התוסרו 4:8); yet they did not think that they would all be eternally valid. They would be in force only for the duration of the "wicked era" (קץ הרשע).[64] This term embraced the period from the inception of God's lawsuit in the sixth century B.C.E. until the present and beyond, into the future (but, presumably, not too far into the future).

---

62. CD 1:2–4.

63. See also 8:14, and cf. H. W. Huppenbauer, "Zur Eschatologie der Damaskusschrift," *RQ* 4 (1963–64): 573. In his analysis, he points out that the community's expectations were "genährt vom Gedenken des 'heiligen Restes,' den Gott übrig gelassen hat."

64. Cf. CD 6:10, 6:14, 12:23–13:1, 15:6–7, and probably the broken 15:10.

By obeying these laws the community hoped to persuade God to end his lawsuit with Israel and grant the land to the righteous once again.[65] In their view, the cessation of the lawsuit, the granting of the land, and the end of the wicked era would all coincide with the beginning of the eschaton, which they called the "end of the days" (אחרית הימים 4:4).

The crucial clue for the relationship of these ideas to the redactional shape of the TS is found in CD 6:9–11. There it is said that the community should observe the laws (להתהלך במה), first clarified in the past by the "Staff" (מחוקק), "for the entire wicked era ... until there shall arise a 'Teacher of Righteousness' at the end of days."[66] From the author's perspective, the coming of the Teacher of Righteousness (T of R) is clearly still in the future. But to what stage of the redaction of CD does the statement belong?

It was Murphy-O'Connor's opinion that this portion of CD, known as the "Well Midrash," is a secondary addition, added after 1:1–6:1 was complete.[67] His reasons for this assignment were threefold. First, God's action toward the community is motivated in 6:2 by his remembering the covenant of the first ones, while in 3:12–13 it is motivated by the community's fidelity to his commandments. Second, the midrash assigns a major role to a single historical figure, the "Staff," while the earlier portion of CD deals only with a faithful remnant. Third, the midrash associates Israel and Aaron, while the earlier portion does not make this connection. None of these reasons is particularly compelling, as Murphy-O'Connor has apparently since realized himself. In his most recent treatment of CD, he concedes that he has been persuaded by Davies that the Well Midrash is not a later addition, but is an intrinsic part of the original CD.[68]

Indeed, Davies makes a good case for this position.[69] The centerpiece of his argument is a literary comparison between 6:2–11 and (the undoubtedly original) 3:12–4:4a, wherein he shows that a clear parallelism exists between these two portions, both in concept and vocabulary. Thus:

1. Covenant with the remnant of the destruction 3:12b–13a = 6:2a–3a
2. Divine revelation 3:13b–16a = 6:3a
3. Halakha of the remnant (well) 3:16b–17a = 6:3b–7a
4. Biblical midrash applied to the community's constituents 3:21–4:4a = 6:3b–9
5. Eternal nature of the new community 3:19–20 = 6:10–11a

Davies concludes that this parallelism proves that the "Well Midrash" must have been a part of the original CD, just as was 3:12–4:4, and this conclusion is difficult to dispute. It is perhaps still possible that CD 6:2–11a are secondary; but if so, the function of these lines is

65. Davies, *Damascus Covenant*, pp. 66–67, 128.

66. The Hebrew reads בכל קץ הרשיע ... עד עמד יורה הצדק באחרית הימים.

67. Murphy-O'Connor, "Damascus Document VI, 2–VIII, 3," pp. 228–32.

68. Idem, "Damascus Document Revisited," p. 232.

69. Davies, *Damascus Covenant*, pp. 121–25.

only further refinement of ideas already inherent in the original CD.[70] Whether the lines are original, as seems most probable, or secondary, they describe an element of the original CD community's expectations.

According to CD 6:11, the following situation thus obtained. The T of R would arise at the end of the wicked era and give a new law. He would be a kind of second Moses. This new law would be connected to the return of the land to the righteous and, hence, it would be a new law of the land for the "end of days."

The analysis of the purpose of the TS carried out above can now be compared with the typological scenario depicted by CD 6:11, as follows:

CD community expectations	*Redactional shape of the TS*
1. New laws for the eschaton	1. Consists of new laws for the eschaton
2. Laws will function in newly inherited land	2. Laws will function in land
3. Author will be Teacher of Righteousness	3. Identity of redactor?

The redactor of the TS was a member of the CD community. Presumably, therefore, he accepted their basic doctrine about the "end of days." The relationship between the typology of CD and the shape of the TS makes it very difficult to resist the conclusion that the redactor of the TS was the T of R whom the CD community had been awaiting.

It appears that somehow the redactor came to believe that he was the Teacher whom his community expected.[71] He came to believe, also, that the era of the wickedness was ending. Why? It is impossible to know for certain, but his idea may have been connected to the eschatological speculation for which there is evidence in CD. The end was calculated to be at hand.[72] The redactor, the Teacher, saw himself as the long-awaited "prophet like unto Moses," a role which, typologically, required him to present a law just as did the first Moses.

70. For example, the laws are said to function only during the wicked era, an idea consistent with the original charter for the "Laws" of columns 9–14 (cf. CD 6:11b and 6:14 with 12:23–13:1 and 15:6–7). If 6:7–11 are secondary and speak from the perspective of a period after the appearance of the T of R—a period represented, as noted in chapter 5, by columns 19–20—these lines would function to describe what the putative expectation of the earlier community once was. In such a case they would implicitly advance the claim that the expectation has been fulfilled, and that any person or group which knew of this expectation, but still rejected the Teacher in the face of its manifest fulfillment, is the more culpable.

71. Cf. Davies, "Eschatology at Qumran," *JBL* 104 (1985): 54, "The arrival of one claiming that title [Teacher of Righteousness] would entail a claim that the eschaton was imminent and that the law of the [CD] community was no longer operative. Those accepting the claims of this figure would regard themselves as the true community; excommunicate those who rejected the 'Teacher;' and prepare themselves, under a new dispensation given by the 'Teacher,' for the eschaton." Davies does not connect this idea to the TS, however.

72. CD contains evidence of such a scheme, which may have been the motivation for the return of the community from the diaspora to Judaea. See most recently Davies, *Behind the Essenes,* p. 34, where he refers to his discussion in his earlier work, and to Murphy-O'Connor's being persuaded by him on this point.

The idea that the T of R was viewed by his followers as a new Moses, as the promised Mosaic prophet, is not new. Numerous scholars have propounded the view in the past, although not in connection with the TS.[73] The typology of CD seems to require this conclusion, but there is additional evidence which is equally pertinent.

The Qumran text known as 4QTestimonia (4Q175)[74] consists of a selection of passages which apparently witness to eschatological expectations held by the CD community (or, perhaps, by their descendents). As usually interpreted, the four selections describe the Mosaic prophet, the two messiahs—priestly and royal—which the CD community awaited, and one or more anti-messianic figures. The text has relevance both for eschatological expectation and for the polemics the community hurled at its opponents.[75] In terms of identifying the T of R as the expected prophet, the first portion is all that need be considered. It reads:

1. וידבר ... אל מושה לאמור שמעת את קול דברי
2. העם הזה אשר דברו אליכה היטיבו כול אשר דברו
3. מי יתן ויהיה לבבם זה להם לירא אותי ולשמור את כול
4. מצוחי כול היומים למעאן יטב להם ולבניהם לעולם
5. נבי אקים לאהמה מקרב אחיהמה כמוכה ונתתי דברי
6. בפיהו וידבר אליהמה את כול אשר אצונו והיה האיש
7. אשר לוא ישמע אל דברי אשר ידבר הנבי בשמי אנוכי
8. אדרוש מעמו

73. See M. Delcor, "Contribution à l'étude de la législation des sectaires de Damas et de Qumran," *RB* 61 (1954): 545–53; J. Giblet, "Prophétisme et attente d'un Messie-prophète dans l'ancien Judaïsme," in *L'attente du Messie,* eds. L. Cerfaux, et al. (Louvain: Desclée de Brouwer, 1954), pp. 127–28; J. Jeremias, "Μωυσῆς," in *TDNT* IV, pp. 848–73, esp. pp. 858–59; H. Teeple, *The Mosaic Eschatological Prophet.* JBL Monograph Series vol. 10 (Philadelphia: SBL, 1957), pp. 49–68; G. Vermes, *Discovery in the Judaean Desert* (New York: Desclee, 1956), p. 221; idem, *The Dead Sea Scrolls: Qumran in Perspective* (Philadelphia: Fortress Press, 1977), pp. 185–86 and 195; idem, *Jesus the Jew* (Philadelphia: Fortress Press, 1973), pp. 94–96; N. Wieder, "The 'Law Interpreter' of the Sect of the Dead Sea Scrolls: The Second Moses," *JJS* 4 (1953): 158–75; and P. Winter, "Notes on Wieder's Observations on the דורש התורה in the Book of the New Covenanters of Damascus," *JQR* 45 (1954): 39–47. Davies' critical analysis of CD requires a complete reassessment of the basis for the arguments of Delcor and Wieder. Although, as noted, none of these scholars had the TS in mind when making their remarks, Teeple deserves credit for "prophetic" foresight, as he wrote in 1957 (p. 25 of *The Mosaic Eschatological Prophet)* regarding the "covenanters:"

> [They], on the other hand, may have thought that in the messianic period the *new laws would not come through interpretation of the Torah by the Prophet, but rather through direct utterances of God speaking through this Prophet.* If so, the new laws could be independent of the old Torah. It is hoped that future publication of Qumran material will throw more light on this problem. (emphasis mine)

74. For the preliminary publication see J. Allegro, "Further Messianic References in Qumran Literature," *JBL* 75 (1956): 182–87 and plate 4. The *editio princeps* is idem, *DJD* V, pp. 57–60 and plate 21. The secondary literature devoted specifically to this text is not extensive; see M. Treves, "On the Meaning of the Qumran Testimonia," *RQ* 2 (1959–60): 269–71, and note 75 below.

75. So J. Lübbe, "A Reinterpretation of 4QTestimonia," *RQ* 12 (1985–87): 187–98.

Translation

> And ...[76] spoke to Moses, saying, "Do you hear the words which this people has spoken to you? All that they say is to their credit. Would that they would always have this attitude, to fear me and to obey all my commands forever; that would guarantee their welfare, and that of their children, forever. From their midst I shall raise up for them a prophet like you, and I shall put my words in his mouth, and he shall speak to them everything which I order him to speak. And everyone who does not obey my words which the prophet will speak in my name—I myself shall judge such a person."

This portion combines Deut 5:28–29 (through line 4) with Deut 18:18–19. It may be that it was an *ad hoc* combination conceived by the author of Testimonia, for the effect of the first quotation is to guarantee a blessing for those obedient to the coming prophet, and, not less significant, to establish that it is from among those obedient to God's commands that the prophet would arise. As the CD community regarded themselves and those who espoused their views as the only such people, juxtaposing these portions from Deut amounts to a claim that the Mosaic prophet would be one of their own. But perhaps it would be unwise to press this observation too far, as the same combination of biblical portions is apparently found in 4Q364–365[77] (an "expanded Torah" text), and the quotation here may therefore have a textual rather than literary explanation—although, of course, the author of Testimonia may have preferred quoting such an expanded text for precisely the same reasons that might have led him to combine the portions. In any case, the basic message of the first eight lines of Testimonia is that the prophet will have absolute authority, speaking the very word of God; that obedience to his words will result in eternal blessing; and that failure to heed will be punished by God himself. In the light of these claims, it is instructive to see how the T of R, his friends and his foes are characterized by those Qumran texts which speak of the Teacher.

CD 1:11 states that God "raised up for them a Teacher of Righteousness," (ויקם להם מורה צדק) using the same Hebrew verb to describe the Teacher's appearance on the scene as Testimonia uses for the prophet's. 1QpHab 2:2–3 records that the Teacher's words came from God's mouth (מפיא אל), a transparent claim that the T of R was a typological Moses, since according to Num 12:6–8 God spoke only to Moses "mouth to mouth," and confined his revelations to other prophets to the media of dreams and visions. Several lines later, in 1QpHab 2:8, one reads that God put in the Teacher's heart the understanding which enabled him to decipher the hidden meanings of the prophets—including, presumably, Moses, who is called a prophet in Hos 12:13. A similar claim is made in 1QpHab 7:4–5; it seems that the Teacher had a special relationship to the prophets of old, and through new revelation could divine the true import of their statements. Both 2:8 and 7:4–5 claim that the Teacher was taught by God so he would know what to say; this is exactly what is written in Exod 4:12 about Moses. These parallels would not have been unintentional. It seems clear that the Teacher's community

---

76. The scribe has omitted the name of God, evidently out of reverence.

77. I owe this information to H. Stegemann (private communication).

regarded him as a new Moses, and characterized him in terms deliberately reminiscent of the Testimonia passage (or, perhaps, of the biblical passages associated there).

As for those followers, they are often described as "listening" or "obeying" the Teacher. The passages often use the same verb (שמע) that Testimonia uses for positive response to the coming prophet. Thus CD 20:28 states that they "listened (וישמעו) to the voice of the Teacher." That passage goes on to say that they "gave ear (האזינו) to the voice of the Teacher of Righteousness and did not reject the righteous statutes when they heard them (בשמעם); they shall be happy and rejoice...and prevail over all earthly men" (20:32–34). The portion thus promises the Teacher's followers an eschatological dominion, i.e., an eternal blessing, just as promised those obedient to the Mosaic prophet in Testimonia. 1QpHab 8:1–3 relates "all those obedient to the Law in the House of Judah [a cipher for the community], for [God] will deliver them from judgement because of their effort on behalf of, and faithfulness to, the Teacher of Righteousness." Here the community is blessed by virtue of their attitude of obedience to the Teacher. Conversely, the passage implies that those outside that group, those refusing to obey, await only judgment. Other passages explicitly declare that the Teacher's enemies will be judged precisely for their failure to heed his divine word, thus refusing his teaching.[78] As Testimonia characterizes those obedient and disobedient to the prophet in identical terms, presumably the passages describing the Teacher's followers and enemies were informed by Testimonia's claims and the belief that the Teacher was the prophet. Everything depended on one's reception of the prophet—acceptance meant eternal blessing, while rejection meant the wrath of God's judgment. The texts which speak of the T of R and the response to him therefore corroborate the typology of CD: the Teacher was the prophet like Moses.

That the CD community should await such a figure is not at all surprising, nor is it surprising that someone should claim for himself this office. This period in Jewish history was charged with eschatological speculations and hopes. Josephus describes a succession of would-be prophets who arose in the century before the destruction of the temple. Many of these men made promises or attempted actions which are explicable only if they were claiming to be a new Moses. For example, there was the Samaritan who promised to reveal the hidden sacred vessels from the Solomonic temple, and led thousands to Mt. Gerizim. His action and the Roman response, which recognized the political nature of his claims, ultimately caused the downfall of Pontius Pilate (*Ant.* 18.85–89). One Theudas led a large group of Jews to the Jordan, promising to divide it en route to the desert (*Ant.* 20.97–99). The so-called "Egyptian" was a messianic pretender who led his followers through the desert by a circuitous route, presumably mimicking the desert wanderings (*Ant.* 20.169–72; *BJ* 2.261). And there were others, often seeking to take their followers into the desert in imitation of the Mosaic period. Thus the typology which looked back to the ideals of a golden age, and guided the CD community as it looked to the future, was by no means particularly unusual. True, it is more

---

78. E.g., 1QpHab 2:1–3, 5:11–12, 4QpIsa[b] II 6–7, and CD 1:12–16. In this connection, note the final word of the passage of Testimonia under consideration, מעמו. This might easily be vocalized to mean "his people," or "his followers." In terms of the polemics which apparently divided the CD community at one point in their existence (cf. CD cols. 1–2 and 20), this may have been their understanding of the word.

clearly developed than that motivating those groups Josephus describes, but if their literature had survived, doubtless there would be many substantial parallels.

Compared with the new Moses, the CD community's expectation of a new Torah for the eschaton is rather difficult to parallel in approximately contemporary Judaism. W. D. Davies, who has done a full scale study of the question,[79] suspects that many such ideas did exist, but did not survive the destruction of the Second Temple. Rabbinic literature contains only a few hints of such expectations, he says, in part because these ideas were deliberately suppressed in the face of Christian claims. Also, the rabbis were heirs of only one stream among many in Second Temple Judaism, and he believes that the Pharisees may have had fewer such speculations than some other groups who perished.[80] Still, he finds evidence of expectations for important changes in the Torah; some passages expect the cessation of festival regulations, for example, while others look forward to changes in the purity laws. In the context of the TS, these expectations are suggestive, for much of the scroll is concerned with precisely these matters. And there are a very few portions which seem to go beyond mere change, and expect a whole new Law. The most unambiguous to which Davies can point is *Yalqut Shimoni* on Isa 26. The text reads:[81]

> The Holy One, blessed be He, will sit in Paradise and give instruction, and all the righteous will sit before him and all the hosts of Heaven will stand on His right and the sun, and the stars on His left; and the Holy One, blessed be He, interprets to them the grounds of a new Torah which the Holy One, blessed be He, will give to them by the hand of King Messiah.

Of course, *Yalqut* is an early medieval collection, and one cannot be at all certain—as Davies is careful to point out—that these very ideas were circulating in the period of our interest. Yet the analogy of the Gospel of Matthew, with its clear depiction of Jesus as a new Moses, is enough to prove that some circles in ancient Judaism expected a Law sufficiently changed from that of Moses to be called new. Further, the Gospel ties its promulgation to the arrival of a Mosaic prophet. So here, too, the CD community was not unique; their new Moses simply showed up first.

Obviously, if correct, this analysis has important implications for the understanding of the TS and how it was viewed. Following Yadin and Wacholder, many scholars have concluded that the author of the TS was perpetrating a pseudepigraphon; with this scroll, he was claiming to have found a lost book, written by Moses, but hidden for centuries.[82] In my view, however, the TS is not pseudepigraphic. The redactor was not claiming to have found a book written by the "old" Moses. He was much more audacious. He wrote in his own behalf as the new Moses. The reason that so much of the TS recapitulates the first Mosaic Law is simply that

79. W. D. Davies, *Torah in the Messianic Age and/or The Age to Come. JBL* Monograph Series vol. 7 (Philadelphia: SBL, 1952).

80. For a summary of these arguments see ibid, pp. 86–92.

81. Davies, p. 74 (his translation).

82. Yadin, *Hidden Law*, pp. 226–28, and Wacholder, *Dawn of Qumran*, pp. 112–19.

he believed in the verity of that revelation. From his perspective, it was only natural that, when God vouchsafed a new revelation for life in the land, much of the first revelation would remain in force. In this way he conceived of the Torah as eternal.

A Date for the Temple Scroll

Table 8 shows another column with signs of considerable redactional activity, col. 52. This column contains redactional phrases of types 1 and 4. Within this column, I focus on lines 13b–21. Like col. 47, this part of col. 52 is "free composition." These lines are either a redactional composition, or, perhaps more likely in view of the discussion of this portion in chapter 5, a substantial reworking of earlier laws.

Column 52 shares a number of commonalities with col. 47. Both aim at forcing people to participate in the temple economy. Both have the effect of bringing people to the temple, thereby improving the temple economy. But the importance of col. 52:13b–21 is greater than simply to corroborate the information gleaned about the redactor from the earlier column. It contains important evidence for a possible date for the final form of the TS.[83]

In this regard the most important sentence in 52:13b–21 is in lines 13–14. The portion here reads: לוא תזבח שור ושה ועז טהורים בכול שעריכה קרוב למקדשי דרך שלושת ימים כי אם בתוך מקדשי תזבחנו, "You shall not butcher a ceremonially clean ox or sheep or goat within any of your gates within a three-day journey of my temple. Rather, you shall sacrifice it at my temple." This is an extrabiblical prescription unknown from any other source, rabbinic, apocryphal, or pseudepigraphic. And it is directly connected with 43:12–13, which concerns the second tithe. As I discuss in chapter 3, col. 43 requires all second tithes to be consumed in the holy city. Their consumption is to be only on "holy days," which the scroll lists in 43:2–4. Thereafter, 43:12–13 reads, והיושבים מן המקדש דרך שלושת ימים כול אשר יוכלו להביא יביאו, "Those who dwell within a distance of a three-day journey from the temple must bring all that they are able to bring" (i.e., without converting the tithe to money).

Taking these two passages together, the following picture emerges. Any Jew living within a three-day journey of Jerusalem must have his livestock slaughtered in the temple. He is also required to journey to the holy city for the purpose of the second tithe, being permitted to do so

---

83. Before the discussion of this passage below, however, I indicate other portions of the TS, beyond those discussed above, which seem to be redactional compositions. I discuss above cols. 29, 51, 52, 43, and 48:10b–17. I also include as redactional compositions 46:11b and 51:19–21. The first passage cannot be assigned with certainty, but it has a style very different from the rest of the Temple Document. It reads, "and they shall not profane it. They shall sanctify my temple, and they shall fear my temple, for I dwell in their midst." This passage features an antithesis between קדשו and יחללוהו reminiscent of 51:5b–10. 51:19–21 reads: "You shall not do within your land as the nations do; in every place they sacrifice and plant for themselves Asheroth, and erect for themselves pillars, and set up figured stones, in order to bow down to them; and they build ..." Three factors suggest that this is a redactional composition. First, the phrase לוא תעשו כאשר הגואים is virtually identical to 48:11, a redactional composition. Second, these lines are distinct from D composition critically. They paraphrase a portion of Deut which D later provides as a verbatim quote; they serve thus as an anticipatory summary for what follows. Third, the reference to Lev 26:1 is significant in view of that chapter's evident influence on the redactor in 29:3–10.

on any of about seventy-three occasions.[84] Common sense would dictate combining the two trips if possible. In this way a man could bring along his livestock and other tithes, celebrate a festival, have his livestock butchered, eat the second tithe, and return home.

In this construction of the scroll's implications, certain questions arise. Why should the consumption of the second tithes be connected to the holy days? Why should the redactor stipulate a three-day journey's distance as that which pilgrims must be willing to travel? As Yadin notes,[85] no logical connection between these elements is apparent—yet the redactor certainly had a motive. The search for a connection between the tithe and the holy days, which can also encompass the scroll's mandate of a three-day pilgrimage, leads to 1 Maccabees 10.

1 Macc 10 is set early in the context of the Maccabean revolt. According to 10:1, the material in the chapter dates to 152 B.C.E. At that time, two men were contending for the Seleucid throne, Demetrius I and Alexander Balas. Each required the assistance of the Jews, and especially of their leader, Jonathan, if he were to make good his claim to power. The Jews controlled vital military positions and territory. 1 Macc 10 comprises letters from these two men (contrary to appearances, only one from each) to Jonathan or the Jews.[86] The letter from

---

84. The total is that of the "holy days" mentioned or implied in col. 43. It is the sum of 52 sabbaths, 12 New Moons, and 9 other occasions of the calendar. The last figure is uncertain, as discussed in chapter 5.

85. Yadin, I, p. 115.

86. In the course of an inquiry into the history of the period ca. 180 B.C.E. to 150 B.C.E., J. G. Bunge has subjected this chapter to a searching analysis. His study ("Zu Geschichte und Chronologie des Untergangs der Oniaden und des Aufstiegs der Hasmonaër," *JSJ* 6 [1975]: 1–46, esp. pp. 27–43) shows that the letter of 1 Macc 10:25–45, the apparent "second letter" from Demetrius to the Jews, is full of contradictions with its present literary setting. The most important internal contradictions which Bunge points out are:

1. According to 10:4–5, Demetrius decided to send a letter to make peace with Jonathan. By writing first, he hoped to win him over before his rival Alexander Balas did the same. It is surprising, then, that in 10:46–47 Jonathan and the Jews are said to reject this overture precisely because Alexander was the first to seek peace with them.

2. One gains the impression from the present shaping of the chapter that Demetrius wrote the second letter as a consequence of Jonathan receiving the high priesthood from Alexander (10:21–22). How is one to explain, then, that this letter makes no attempt to outbid Alexander by offering Jonathan the high priesthood plus additional perquisites? In fact, the content of the second letter seems to assume that Alexander had not yet attempted to win Jonathan over.

3. In his "first letter" Demetrius granted Jonathan the power to recruit and equip troops (10:6). It is strange, then, that Jonathan waited until much later to exercise this important power; in fact, he waited until he had made an alliance with Alexander (10:21). Then in the second letter Jewish troops are once again at issue (10:36).

4. In his second letter Demetrius offered to pay for the rebuilding of Jerusalem's walls (10:45). But Jonathan had already begun to rebuild as a result of the first letter—which, however, makes no mention of any rebuilding (10:10–11).

5. The reason that Demetrius wrote the second letter, according to the editorial remark in verses 22–25a (see K. D. Schunk, *Die Quellen des I. und II. Makkabäerbuches* [Halle: Max Niemeyer Verlag, 1954], pp. 43 and 65, on the sources of 1 Macc 10) was to offset Jonathan's alliance with Alexander. How, then, is verse 27 to be understood? Part of the letter itself, it assumes that the Jewish leader has been loyal all along.

Demetrius to the Jews, which begins at 10:25, occupies our attention. After promising various general and specific boons and exemptions to the recipients of the letter, Demetrius grants what one reads in 10:34–35:[87]

καὶ πᾶσαι αἱ ἑορταὶ καὶ τὰ σάββατα καὶ νουμηνίαι καὶ ἡμέραι ἀποδεδειγμέναι καὶ τρεῖς ἡμέραι πρὸ ἑορτῆς καὶ τρεῖς ἡμέραι μετὰ ἑορτὴν ἔστωσαν πᾶσαι [αἱ] ἡμέραι ἀτελείας καὶ ἀφέσεως πᾶσιν τοῖς Ἰουδαίδοις τοῖς οὖσιν ἐν τῇ βασιλείᾳ μου, καὶ οὐχ ἕξει εξουσίαν οὐδεὶς πράσσειν καὶ παρενοχλεῖν τινα αὐτῶν περὶ παντὸς πράγματος.

(34) And all the festivals and sabbaths and New Moons and appointed days, and the three days before a festival and the three days after a festival—let all the days be days of freedom from sales taxes[88] and exemption from custom duties and tolls[89] for all the Jews in my kingdom. (35) And no one shall have the power to exact anything from them or annoy any of them about any particular.

From the phrase ἡμέραι ἀποδεδειγμέναι (not used in Hellenistic sources for pagan festivals, yet here apparently coming from the Seleucid chancellery), one surmises that Demetrius was seeking to grant requests the Jews have made to him. The phrase has a Hebraic cast, corresponding to מועדים. The most reasonable explanation for such wording is that

---

Bunge shows that the assumption that Demetrius wrote only one letter, not two as the chapter's present editorial shaping makes it appear, solves all these contradictions. The one letter must antedate Jonathan's alliance with Alexander Balas by some two years. The date given in 1 Macc 10:1, 152 B.C.E., should be understood as the date of Demetrius' letter; thus Alexander's missive of verses 18–20 dates to approximately 150. In the present literary setting, the contents of Demetrius' letter appear in the putative second letter, at 10:25–45. The editor of 1 Macc has summarized these contents in the verses which comprise the putative first letter (10:6, 10–11). Bunge's analysis raises an interesting, if very speculative, point in regard to the date of the TS. In his scheme, Jonathan could not have become high priest by Alexander's bequest until 150. Yet the letter which Demetrius wrote, dated at 152, mentions a high priest in verses 32 and 38. Since this man could not have been Jonathan, when Demetrius granted a three-day grace period on taxation for pilgrims in verses 34–35, he was not aiming to please Jonathan, but another. This nameless high priest is perhaps connected to the redactor of the TS. Who was this nameless figure? Bunge, following certain suggestions made by H. Stegemann, thinks that the he was the T of R. For an analysis of the evidence upon which this suggestion is based, see my forthcoming study, "The Teacher of Righteousness and the High Priest of the Intersacerdotium: Two Approaches," in *RQ*.

87. The critical edition of the Greek text is W. Kappler, ed., *Septuaginta. Vetus Testamentum Graecum Auctoritate Academiae Litterarum Gottingensis editum. Vol. IX Maccabaeorum Libri I-IV. Fasc. 1 Maccabaeorum Liber I* (Göttingen: Vandenhoeck & Ruprecht, 1967).

88. The word ἀτελεία has diverse meanings in different fiscal contexts (E. J. Bikerman, *Institutions des Séleucides.* Bibliothèque Archéologique et Historique no. 26 [Paris: Librairie Orientaliste Paul Geuther, 1938], p. 115). One cannot be certain here if it means custom duties alone, or includes other taxes as well. See Goldstein, *1 Maccabees,* p. 401, and F.-M. Abel, *Les livres des Maccabées* (Paris: J. Gabalda, 1949), p. 189, for the present translation of the term.

89. This translation of ἀφέσεως follows Goldstein, *1 Maccabees,* p. 401. Like many such terms, its meaning is uncertain. Abel believes it means "franchise." See Abel, *Maccabées,* p. 188, and F.-M. Abel and J. Starcky, *Les livres des Maccabées* (Paris: Éditions du Cerf, 1961), p. 164.

Demetrius had Jewish advisors.[90] This surmise garners additional support in the full list of holidays in verse 34, which is suspiciously biblical for a Seleucid document.[91] The list clearly betrays Jewish influence. Presumably these advisors, well aware of circumstances in Jerusalem, informed Demetrius of the measures which would be especially pleasing to official priestly circles there. Taking their advice, the monarch granted these beneficences, thus paying in the appropriate coin for Jewish support .

Commentators on 1 Macc agree that 10:34–35 have to do with pilgrims.[92] Exorbitant taxes on goods they might bring along, such as tithes or livestock, would often discourage potential pilgrims from coming to Jerusalem. Since these taxes were assessed not only upon entrance to the city, but also each time the traveler passed a toll post, they could add up to a significant sum. The pilgrim might be assessed as much as ten percent of the value of his goods each time he paid the tax.[93] Understandably, this situation was a concern for the priestly elite in Jerusalem. With reduced taxes, more pilgrims would make the journey, resulting in more income for the temple economy. And, in all likelihood, they had more purely religious motives for encouraging Jewish pilgrimage to the temple as well.

Communicating this concern to Demetrius, they made their support conditional upon its alleviation. He responded by rescinding the appropriate taxes for three days before and after each major occasion of the Jewish calendar. But what induced the Jewish advisers to request this particular time span from the king?[94]

With but a single exception, commentators on 1 Macc pass over this question in silence. Only Goldstein has tried to explain the time period. He comments, "Evidently, there was an established practice to declare freedom from sales taxes and tolls at privileged places during the week surrounding an imperial festival."[95] For this suggestion, however, there is no evidence elsewhere. Seeking to bolster his case, Goldstein turns to the Mishnah and Tosephta, but here, also, convincing parallels are lacking.[96] In fact the only convincing parallel is with the portions of TS 43 and 52.

---

90. Goldstein, *1Maccabees*, p. 409. For a less satisfactory explanation, see S. Tedesche and S. Zeitlin, *The First Book of Maccabees* (New York: Harper & Bros., 1950), pp. 173–74.

91. Such lists occur several times in the Hebrew Bible. Cf. Ezek 45:17, 1 Chr 23:31, 2 Chr 2:3, 8:13, 31:3, and Neh 10:34.

92. Abel, *Maccabées*, p. 188, "assignés sans doute au voyage d'aller à Jérusalem et de retour." Agreeing are J. C. Dancy, *A Commentary on 1 Maccabees* (Oxford: Basil Blackwood, 1954), p. 145; J. R. Bartlett, *The First and Second Books of the Maccabees* (Cambridge: Cambridge University Press, 1973), p. 137; and Abel and Starcky, *Maccabées*, p. 164.

93. Bikerman, *Institutions*, pp. 115–16, on the τέλη.

94. Perhaps one might suggest that the time period they were requesting was really a week—three days, a sabbath, and three more days for the return. This supposition falters, however, when one further considers that a number of the holidays of the Jewish calendar are more than one day long, and do not necessarily, or even often, fall on a sabbath.

95. Goldstein, *1 Maccabees*, p. 409.

96. For a detailed critique of Goldstein's views, see M. O. Wise "A Note on the 'Three Days' of 1 Maccabees X 34," *VT* 60 (1990):116–22.

Comparing 1 Macc 10:34–35 and TS 43 and 52, what emerges is the following. Both deal with pilgrimages. Both stipulate a three-day pilgrimage. Both reflect the desires of the temple elite—the redactor on the one hand, and Demetrius's Jewish contacts on the other. And again, legislation mandating or encouraging three-day pilgrimages as normative appears in no other source, classical or Jewish. Two points are especially significant regarding the festal lists in the two documents. First, both are blanket lists, covering all the festal occasions of the calendar. Second, they agree in urging many more pilgrimage occasions than the biblical and later Tannaitic texts. In those sources only the three feasts of Passover, Pentecost, and Tabernacles required a pilgrimage to the temple.[97]

In view of these strong commonalities, it is reasonable to conclude that the two texts are in some way connected. It is entirely possible, since he was one of the temple elite, that the redactor of the TS was an advisor in the concessions which 1 Macc reports. At any rate it is clear that he would have favored them. The parallels between the two texts strongly suggest that they may be contemporary; and, conveniently, one of them (the letter of Demetrius) is a reliable historical source complete with date—152 B.C.E. Of course, it cannot be ruled out that the idea of a three-day pilgrimage for many festival occasions was widespread, perhaps a general tenet of the period's priestly mentality. In the face of our ignorance of the detailed history of this period, one should certainly not rely overmuch on this parallel between the two texts when seeking to date the final form of the TS. Yet this parallel is strikingly corroborated by another way of dating the scroll, namely, that of dating the T of R.

The date of the T of R is a matter which has so often been discussed that no detailed consideration is necessary here.[98] It suffices to note that broad scholarly consensus locates him in the middle of the second century B.C.E., in conflict with at least one early Hasmonean high priest. A date of ca. 150 B.C.E. is therefore consonant with previous conclusions. That this date or one slightly earlier should be sought for the TS would seem requisite in light of the eschatological ideology of the CD community. They expected that a "Teacher of Righteousness" would be raised up at the inception of, or just prior to, an eschatological era in which they would inherit the land. And this figure was expected to deliver a new law to regulate that period. If, then, a man appeared on the scene who actually claimed to be the Teacher, he would presumably make good his claim in part precisely by the promulgation of that new law. If I am right in identifying the TS as exactly that, then the T of R would have produced it at or near the time that he arose to make his claim. The nature of the evidence on the date of the TS is obviously not the sort which allows mathematical precision, but in agreement

---

97. This understanding arises from Exod 23:27, Exod 33:23, and Deut 16:16, and assumes that ἑορταί is in 1 Macc 10 the equivalent of the biblical מועדים. In biblical usage, the מועדים are Passover, Pentecost, the Day of Remembrance (Rosh Hashanah), the Day of Atonement, Tabernacles, and the Eighth Day of Assembly. See Goldstein, *1 Maccabees*, p. 409, for a discussion of the meaning of ἑορταί and ἡμέραι ἀποδεδειγμέναι. For a discussion of Tannaitic concepts of pilgrimage, see S. Safrai, "Relations Between the Diaspora and the Land of Israel," in *The Jewish People in the First Century. Compendia Rerum Iudaicarum ad Novum Testamentum*, 2 vols. ed. S. Safrai and M. Stern (Philadelphia: Fortress Press, 1974–1976), 1:191, and idem, "The Temple," in idem, 2:898.

98. For a recent and very judicious discussion see Callaway, *History of the Qumran Community*, esp. pp. 199–210.

with all the facts a date of ca. 150 B.C.E. results from these two independent lines of reasoning.

Conclusions

In this chapter I argue that the redactor of the TS was a member of the priestly elite connected with the temple at Jerusalem, based on comparison of col. 47 (apparently a redactional composition) with a portion of Josephus' *Antiquities*. I further argue that the redactor was the man known by CD as the T of R. Comparing redactional portions of cols. 43 and 52 with the letter of Demetrius I contained in 1 Macc 10, I suggest a date for the scroll of approximately 150 B.C.E. This approach to dating the scroll is fortified by another method, which relies on the data of CD, the pesharim, and Josephus to date the T of R. The principles governing the redactional shaping of the scroll reveal that its purpose was to serve as a law for remnant Israel during an earthly eschatological age, until God himself should usher in the "Day of Creation."[99] At that time history would have come full circle and all things would begin anew.[100]

---

99. TS 29:9.

100. This "two-tiered" view of eschatology, in which a millennial period of earthly rule by the righteous is followed by a new heaven and a new earth, was rather widespread in the late Second Temple period. See D. S. Russell, *The Method and Message of Jewish Apocalyptic* (Philadelphia: Westminster Press, 1964), pp. 291–97, and E. Schürer, *History*, 2:488–554, esp. pp. 529–38. Schürer's comment on p. 536 is especially apt: "Often, however, the glory of the messianic kingdom is not regarded as final and supreme. An even higher heavenly bliss is looked for, with the result that only a limited duration is ascribed to the rule of the Messiah."

7

SUMMARY AND CONCLUSIONS

This study is concerned with four interrelated questions about the TS: What can be determined about the composition of the scroll?, When was it written?, Why was it written?, and What was the provenance of the TS—was it "sectarian?" A summary of the suggestions regarding these four questions is in order here; only the reader can decide whether light is shed on its enigmas or whether the TS should remain a confident sphinx.

The Composition of the Temple Scroll

The argument made here is that a redactor drew together four basic sources in composing the present form of the TS. To these he added legal materials drawn from the resources of his own community, which he interpolated into the other sources as dictated by his overarching design. I call the four basic sources the Deuteronomy Source (D), the Temple Source, the Midrash to Deuteronomy (MD), and the Festival Calendar.

That the redactor of the TS did not excerpt Deut itself, but instead relied upon a source which was based on that biblical book, is indicated by four considerations. First, the use of the divine name; it is inconsistent in a way which is hard to explain if the redactor were carefully weighing each biblical portion while deciding whether or not to use it. This inconsistency is more easily explicable if the redactor took over an existing source which consistently used the tetragrammaton. The redactor then changed many of the occurrences of יהוה to a first person pronoun or verb, but was unconcerned to be completely consistent in this process.

Second, the TS includes additions to the text of Deuteronomy which apparently do not promote the redactor's concerns. These are best explained as belonging to a source which included legal material not found in Deut. D was an attempt to harmonize the legal portions of the Torah, using Deut as the base text. These additions testify to the character of D as a separate legal source.

Third, the TS includes portions of legal material from Deut and elsewhere which implicitly sanction divorce and polygamy. The redactional shape of the scroll, however, and the "King's Law" which the redactor added, make it clear that the redactor himself opposed these ideas.

That they are found in the scroll is support for the view that the redactor took over an existing source, apparently without perceiving these implicit sanctions.

Fourth, the 43.366 fragments require a D source separate from the book of Deut. These fragments include one portion which is incontestably part of the TS (fragment 3), but also two other portions which are not found in the present form of the scroll. Of these two, fragment 1 seems to be a Deuteronomic form of Lev 23, with extrabiblical additions. The most economical way to explain the connection of fragments 1 and 2 with fragment 3 is to postulate the existence of a D source. Fragment 1 is comparable in its "Deuteronomized" character to portions of the present TS, such as col. 2 and col. 48:1–10. Such "Deuteronomized" literature did exist, and is not merely an abstract possibility, as evidenced by 1Q22, the "Words of Moses." Further, D must once have been longer, perhaps substantially longer, than what appears in the TS.

As for the Temple Source, it seems clearly to be related to the Aramaic New Jerusalem text known from several of the caves near Qumran. This relationship seems certain, based upon the texts' use of the same programmatic numbers, their description of similar or identical structures and rituals—especially the named gates—and certain general phenomena. I also argue that the NJ text must antedate the Temple Source. The Temple Source drew its temple complex either from the NJ text or from common ancestral traditions.

The decision to write the New Jerusalem in Aramaic was purposeful. Its goal was to publicize broadly the programmatic architectural vision which the text's author(s) believed would someday be realized. The inference follows that this program may have been well known among the Jews some time before the TS appeared on the scene.

I also explore the relationship between the Temple Source and the book of Jubilees, and conclude that even where a direct literary relationship might seem to exist—between TS 43 and Jubilees 32—in fact none does. Instead, the best explanation is that both used a common earlier source. No certain indication can be found that either text knew the other, a somewhat unfortunate state of affairs for one seeking to secure at least a relative date for the Temple Source by means of Jubilees. Because the two texts both agree and disagree on various important ideas, it is apparent that the TS and Jubilees are simply the products of related circles within a wider Judaism. They do not stem from the same group, at least not at the same point in time.

I suggest in chapter 4 that the redactor used a Midrash to Deut. The reasons for seeing the designated portions (57:1–59:21, 60:2–11, 64:6b–13a) as excerpts from a single source are fourfold. First, the portions have in common their composition critical method, not found elsewhere in the TS. Second, they are exegetically interrelated. Third, they use in common unusual phrases unknown elsewhere among the DSS or from the Bible. Fourth, their ideas are at odds with those of D, in which they are imbedded. MD was apparently either a commentary on Deut, or a political treatise (based on the biblical text); similar political treatises were common in the Hellenistic period.

The last major source was the Festival Calendar. The redactor's principle reason for including it was to replace Deut 16 in the "New Deuteronomy" which is the TS. It contains many more details about biblical festivals than any biblical festal calendar, and adds several new festivals. It is interesting to observe that these new festivals evidence the same concern for "symmetry" that one finds in the Temple Source and the NJ. For example, the New Year of the seventh month in the biblical law is balanced by a New Year of the first month. The First Fruits of Wheat known from the biblical text finds a counterpart in a new First Fruits of Barley.

The Festival Calendar served two additional functions in the TS. It furnished a statement of the "exact rules" (פרוש) for sacrifice which the CD community possessed, apparently in contradistinction to other groups among the Jews. It also staked a claim, given the nature of the TS itself, for divine authority for its calendar.

I examine in chapter 5 Wilson and Wills' idea of a "Purity Source," and conclude that no such source exists. Rather than a single source, the laws of purity, marriage, and entry into the temple represent diverse sources. It is observable that many of the purity laws, especially those in cols. 49–50, originally dealt with communal eating in levitical purity. Incorporating them into the TS, the redactor applied them to a new situation. While they had originally been particularistic, his ideal was that they should now apply to all Israel. The explanation for their use in the TS was that the redactor advocated the equation "purity for eating = purity for entry into the Temple City (and other cities)."

Some of the laws as they appear in the TS are incomplete; it is therefore problematic how they could ever be applied. Since these laws were not complete, they presumably could not have been new to their audience. The text's readers or hearers must have known where to find the information necessary to fill out the incomplete portions. This realization led to a search for possible sources for the TS laws. I demonstrate the possibility that the redactor drew them from the larger corpus of legal material which made up the heritage of the CD community. In this connection I suggest sources or explanations for some of the TS laws based on the "Laws" of CD (cols. 9–16) and the unpublished portions of CD from cave 4, 4QD^a and 4QD^b. Other potential sources are 4Q159, 4Q512, PAM 42.408 (still unpublished), 4Q513 and 4Q514. (The latter two texts may well be additional exemplars of 4Q159.)

With regard to dating, only two of these sources for the TS yielded possible parameters. D was apparently the oldest source, dating between 300 and 190 B.C.E. The *terminus post quem* was dependent on the date of the final form of Nehemiah, while the *terminus ad quem* was the combination of D with the Temple Source. The Temple Source can be assigned a very rough date by reason of both its relationship to the NJ text and the suggested date for the final redaction of the TS. Thus I conclude that it dated to ca. 190 B.C.E. D and the Temple Source were combined at about the turn of the second century to form a "proto-Temple Scroll." It was this earlier literary work which the redactor of the TS modified by addition and excision. He added the Festival Calendar, which yielded only a tentative relative date: it seemed to be dependent on the Temple Source, and therefore must date between 190 and 150. The redactor also added the laws and MD, neither of which could be dated.

The following chart compares my conclusions on the source criticism of the TS to those of Wilson and Wills.

Wilson and Wills	*Present analysis*
1. Temple and Courts source 2:1–13:8, 30:3–47:18	1. Temple Source 3:1–13:8, 30:3–31:9a, 31:10–34:12a, 34:15–35:9a, 35:10–39:5a,

Wilson and Wills	*Present analysis*
	1. Temple Source (*cont.*) 39:11b–40:5, 40:7–43:12a, 44:1–45:7a, 46:1–11a, 46:13–47:2
2. Calendar source 13:9–30:2	2. Festival Calendar 13:8–29:2
3. Purity Laws source 48:1–51:10	3. Laws (diverse sources) 34:12b–14, 39:5–11a, 40:6, 45:7b–18, 49:1–51:5a, parts of 52:13b–21, 63:14b–15, 66:12b–17
4. Laws of Polity source 51:11–56:21, 60:1–66:17	4. D source 2:1–15, 48:1–10a, 51:11–18, 52:1–12, 53:1–56:21, 60:12–63:14a, 64:1–6a, 64:13b–66:9a, 66:10–12a
5. Torah of the King source 57–59	5. MD source 57:1–59:21, 60:2–11, 64:6b–13a
6. Redactional passages 29:2–30:2, 51:5b–10	6. Redactional compositions 29:2–30:2, 31:9b, 35:9b, 43:12b–17, 46:11b–12, 47:3–18, 48:11–17, 51:5b–11, 51:19–21, 52:13b–21 (incorporating legal sources), 66:9b

The Date of the Present Form of the Temple Scroll

While many scholars have suggested ideas about the date of the scroll, not many have produced detailed discussions. Yadin was one who did. He based his date of ca. 134 B.C.E. on the paleography of the 43.366 fragments, the form of Hebrew found in the scroll, and the rings mentioned in col. 34. I do not believe that any of these elements withstands scrutiny.

The 43.466 fragments are not a copy of the TS; therefore they cannot provide a paleographical basis for dating the scroll, even if the validity of that method for precise dating of Hebrew MSS were less open to question. Yadin's argument that the appearance in the TS of Mishnaic lexical items secures his dating is likewise flawed, since many such words may have been a part even of SBH vocabulary. They have simply not been preserved in the limited corpus of that language which we possess. Further, it is not at all certain, as Yadin claimed, that MH developed no earlier than the end of the second century B.C.E. And Yadin's connection of the rings of col. 34 with Talmudic texts which mention that John Hyrcanus installed rings is problematic. The Talmudic sages did not understand the earlier Tannaitic text upon which they based their assertion that Hyrcanus was responsible for the rings. As none of Yadin's arguments is convincing, his date of 134 B.C.E. does not compel assent.

I examine in chapter 4 other attempts to date the TS. Hengel, Charlesworth, and Mendels argued for a date in the reign of Alexander Jannaeus (103–76 B.C.E.). Their analysis derived almost entirely from what they considered the "King's Law," TS cols. 56–59. Although they produced seven reasons for their dating, only three were really independent arguments.

Perhaps their strongest argument was based on textual variants in col. 56 as compared to the MT of Deut 17. In their view, these reflected criticism of the policies of Jannaeus. I show that, on the contrary, these variants had a text critical explanation, and that there was evidence in other texts and versions for these same variants.

Hengel *et al.* also believed that col. 58 contained three or four different scenarios for defensive wars. This emphasis on defense, they said, reflected the harsh political realities of Jannaeus' reign, and the TS author's feeling that Jannaeus was not doing enough to insure the safety of Judaea when he sallied forth to war. In my view, however, col. 58 does not suggest defensive war stratagems, since it does not distinguish between defensive and offensive warfare. Thus it cannot be criticizing the defensive shortcomings of Alexander Jannaeus.

Again, Hengel and his coauthors held that the absence of any priestly role for the king portrayed in TS 56–59 reflected the issue over the unity of the priesthood and the monarchy in the single person of Jannaeus. Because the author of the TS did not approve of this arrangement, he denied any priestly role to his ideal king. I counter that a better explanation for the absence of such a role for the king is that the role was absent in the biblical texts which served as the model for the TS—Deut 17 and 1 Sam 8.

Without these three arguments for a foundation, the other evidence which Hengel and his collaborators adduced cannot stand. Their effort to date the TS using TM was unsuccessful. Others, however, have argued for a date in the reign of Jannaeus on other grounds.

A scholarly consensus attempts to date the TS to this king's reign based upon col. 64:6b–13a. This consensus focuses on two points. First, it holds that the author of the TS had inverted the order of the key verbs "die" and "hang" as they appear in the biblical text, Deut 21:22–23, upon which this portion of the scroll was based. The intent of this reversal was to prove that Jannaeus' hanging of 800 opponents had biblical sanction. Second, the consensus position urges that, since the TS was a sectarian text, and since 4QpNah was likewise a sectarian product and described crucifixion, they were describing the same historical situation. Since all agree that the pesher described Jannaeus' execution of his Pharisaic adversaries, it follows that the TS described this event as well. It therefore must date from the time of that occurrence, or shortly thereafter.

In fact, however, the supposed intentional reversal of the two verbs is more likely to be a mere textual variant. This variant can be traced through LXX MSS, the Peshitta, and Philo. As for the relationship of the TS and 4QpNah, I maintain that the assumed common origin of the pesher and the TS is problematic at best. Further, I argue that the consensus position had not sufficiently reckoned with the literary character of the TS text. It is "midrash;" it does not "describe" any historical event. This portion of the TS simply interprets the Bible. Nevertheless, for the sake of argument, I explore the assertion that both the TS and the pesher describe historical crucifixions. The likelihood that they were describing the same events is not great, since hanging or crucifixion was a relatively common method of execution in Palestine beginning in the Hellenistic period. Thus the TS cannot be dated to the time of Jannaeus using 64:6b–13a.

I suggest an entirely different basis for dating the present form of the scroll. Based on a redaction critical analysis of the scroll, I first isolate those portions which were redactional compositions. Several of these portions then combine to provide important clues. TS 47 shows that the redactor was probably numbered among the priestly elite in Jerusalem, attached to the temple there, and concerned with its economy. TS 52 and 43 contained requirements for pilgrimages to Jerusalem for all who dwelt within a distance of a three-day journey. These pilgrimages were to be connected with the celebration of holy occasions in the festal calendar. The same requirement for frequent three-day pilgrimages underlies 1 Macc 10:34–35, and there, also, it involves the priestly elite. Further, the TS and this portion of 1 Macc share other elements known from no other Second Temple text. This relationship may provide an approximate date for the scroll's final redaction, since the 1 Macc sources are historically reliable and are dated. Thus emerges a date of approximately 150 B.C.E. for the TS. And this is corroborated by a second approach, that of dating the scroll's redactor, the T of R.

The Purpose of the Temple Scroll

My argument is that the TS was intended as a new Deut, one for the eschaton. The redactor apparently expected it to take effect soon. This man conceived of himself as a new Moses; hence the TS is, properly speaking, not a pseudepigraphon. The redactor was not writing in the name of a long-dead hero of the faith, claiming that he had discovered a lost writing which that hero had produced. Rather, his claim was to the same relationship with God that Moses had had. As Moses had produced a "Law for the Land," so, too, did he—one which had been modified from the Mosaic original in light of its eschatological application.

This view of the scroll's purpose is borne along by the confluence of three streams of evidence. The first is the redactional analysis of the relationship between the TS and the biblical Deut. The second is the relationship between the shape of the scroll and a typology of the eschatological expectations of the CD community. And the third is the provenance of the temple complex found in the TS.

In the course of a redactional analysis of the scroll, I first show that it is likely to be largely complete as we have it. It lacks neither a beginning (probably) nor an end (almost certainly); thus any analysis can legitimately rely upon what has been preserved, without postulating missing portions. It thus emerges that *grosso modo,* the TS is supposed to replace Deut 12–26, the biblical "law of the land." Where the Bible is concerned with the מקום ("place"), the TS substitutes the מקדש ("temple"). Virtually every portion of Deut 12–26 which the TS then omits is explicable on the basis of three principles:

1. The scroll omits everything which the redactor regarded as repetitious.

2. The scroll omits every biblical portion which could be construed as sanctioning זנות, "illicit marriage."

3. The scroll omits every portion which would not function in the אחרית הימים, "the end of the days."

Regarding the third principle, I show that 4Q174 (Florilegium) makes explicit the eschatological significance of the TS omission of all references to the *gēr* and the foreigner.

Just as 4QFlorilegium denies those classes entry into its eschatological temple, so the TS tacitly denies them a place in the land during the eschaton. Portions of the biblical text which deal with violence between fellow Israelites, borrowing, and slavery were likewise omitted as nonfunctional for the eschaton.

The redactor also replaced some nonfunctional portions of Deut with new legal formulations. For example, where Deut 23:2–9 speaks of exclusion from the assembly (קהל), the redactor substituted laws on exclusion from the temple courts (TS 39:5–12 and 40:6). Where Deut 19:1–13 commanded the creation of cities of refuge, the redactor substituted commands for burial areas—one for each four cities of the eschatological land—and quarantine areas for each city (TS 48:11–17). In other cases, his additions served to reinforce his omissions. Thus, the marriage laws in 66:12–17 dealt with illegitimate forms of marriage as defined by the redactor's concept of זנות.

The second stream of evidence revealing the purpose of the TS is a typology of the eschatological expectations of the CD community, of which the redactor was a member. The community believed that they were living in the wicked era (קץ הרשיע [*sic*]). In their understanding this period encompassed the time of God's lawsuit with Israel. During this era, the community lived under certain laws intended only "for the duration." They believed that when the lawsuit ended, so would the wicked era; simultaneously, the righteous (including themselves) would receive back the land, and there would arise a long-awaited "Teacher of Righteousness." This figure would modify or eliminate some of the laws which had served for the era of wickedness, and the eschaton would begin. Although CD does not explicitly connect the reception of the land to the changes in the community's laws, the connection is implicit. They expected a new law when they once again took possession of the land—a new law for a "new land." This typology fits the phenomena of the TS so precisely that it is hard to believe there is no connection, *a fortiori* as its author was demonstrably a member of the CD community. Therefore, the scroll was intended as an eschatological law for the land, a new Deut.

The third confluent stream proving the intended purpose of the TS is its temple complex. This complex derived from a wider program for an enormous city, a program part of which is found in the NJ text. The NJ text in turn is a modification of Ezekiel's vision of a New Jerusalem, which was believed by Second Temple Jews to describe the eschatological era. Since the redactor drew his complex from an eschatological program, it follows that he thought of his temple as an eschatological one. Consequently, his law must also apply to that period.

The Provenance of the Temple Scroll

In the first chapter I state that most scholars writing on the scroll believe that it was a sectarian product. I also note that within the context of the scholarly discussion as it has evolved, the term "sectarian" has meant "a product of the Qumran community." This community is identified with the יחד or brotherhood of 1QS and many of the pesharim. Thus these scholars mean by designating the TS as a sectarian product that it was written by one or more members of the יחד.

The evidence given here shows that the designation of the TS as a sectarian product is certainly wrong unless further nuanced, and may be just plain wrong. The TS was not a product of the יחד. Rather, it's author was a member of the CD community. That the two communities were not identical has been shown by Davies and Murphy-O'Connor. People designating themselves as the יחד apparently took up and reworked the Damascus Covenant, as can be seen in CD 19–20. Therefore, as the term has been used in scholarly discourse on the TS, it is not a "sectarian" writing. But in saying this I do not mean that it has no possible sectarian connections.

Frankly, I am not sure that it is helpful to describe the scroll as the product of a "sect." That is like saying that a cat is an animal. Second Temple Judaism of the period in question was a welter of sects, and therefore almost any writing of that period is the product of a sect. But if the term must be applied, we would first do well to find a better definition of "sectarian" than simply "a product of the Qumran community."[1] Sociological studies on modern sectarianism may provide a more useful definition of the concept. B. R. Wilson has described a sect as follows:[2]

> It is a voluntary association; membership is by proof to sect authorities of some claim to personal merit—such as knowledge of doctrine, affirmation of a conversion experience, or recommendation of members in good standing; exclusiveness is emphasized, and expulsion exercised against those who contravene doctrinal, moral or organizational precepts; its self-conception is of an elect, a gathered remnant, possessing special enlightenment; personal perfection is the expected standard of aspiration, in whatever terms this is judged; it accepts, at least as an ideal, the priesthood of all believers; there is a high level of lay participation; there is opportunity for the member spontaneously to express his commitment; the sect is hostile or indifferent to the secular society and to the state.

Many of the elements of this definition find a response in CD and the TS. For example, the concept of טהרה, which dominates the legislation of the TS in particular, is one which applies levitical dietary standards to all the members of the community whence the laws derive. Here then is the idea of the priesthood of all believers. Indeed, one could easily cite portions of CD or the TS which correspond to most of the elements of Wilson's definition. In the terms of this broader definition, one could certainly describe the TS as a sectarian product.

But it may be suggestive for future research that not all the elements of Wilson's definition fit what can be deduced about the TS. The last element, for example, that of hostility to the

---

1. The predilection for applying the appellation "sectarian" generally derives from the outmoded but still widely held view that there existed a "normative Judaism" already in this period, and that it was represented by the Pharisees. For a discussion of this perspective on the period, see D. Goodblatt "The Place of the Pharisees in First Century Judaism: The State of the Debate," *JSJ* 20 (1989): 12–30.

2. B. R. Wilson, "An Analysis of Sect Development," in *Patterns of Sectarianism,* ed. B. R. Wilson (London: Heinemann, 1967), pp. 23–24.

state, may not apply. The TS is a program *for* the state during the period of the eschaton.[3] It is not concerned with a sectarian separation from broader society—rather, it mandates what the "establishment" is to be. Therein we may perhaps find a clue to the relationship between the community which produced the TS, and the יחד to which most scholars are so eager to consign it.

We know that the יחד redacted CD. It is only reasonable to infer that it was meaningful to them; their redaction doubtless proves that they saw it as somehow applicable to themselves. Indeed, the implication of CD 19–20 is that the members of the יחד saw themselves in continuity with the original members of the CD community, the members of the ברית הראשונים, "covenant of the first ones." The present analysis of the TS suggests a possible linkage, in the person of the author of the TS. I argue in the last chapter that the author or redactor was the person known as the Teacher of Righteousness.

Here then is a possible approach to the relationship of the CD community to the יחד. Since sects often develop when a charismatic leader arises and claims a new revelation from God,[4] or as the consequence of internal schism within existing sects,[5] perhaps the יחד was descended from that part of the CD community which accepted the claims of the charismatic Teacher inherent in the TS. In other words, it may be that the TS itself catalyzed, or was at least a strong contributing factor in, the formation of a sect. If so, however, in the strictest sense the TS was not the product of that group, and, if one wishes to identity that second group as the "Qumran community," then the conclusion has to be that the TS was not a product of that community.

---

3. Of course, I recognize that one could argue that simply by producing an alternate view of the state, the author of the TS manifested hostility toward the present state of affairs.

4. B. R. Wilson, "Introduction," in *Patterns of Sectarianism*, pp. 11–12.

5. Ibid., p. 17.

APPENDIX

A COMPOSITIONAL ANALYSIS OF
THE TEMPLE SCROLL

Methodology

General Comments

In this appendix, I present the results of a compositional analysis of the TS. Since these results are closely tied to methodology, a description of that method is necessary here. On one level, my method can be stated very simply: I have investigated the relationship of the TS to the Hebrew Bible, line by line. Yet in the process, it has been necessary to make many decisions about which verse or portion of a verse was in the author's mind, and about the nature of the relationship between the text of the scroll and that portion.

Perhaps it is easiest to characterize such decisions by contrasting my procedure with that of the two earlier efforts to describe the relationship between the biblical text and the TS. Both Yadin and Brin attempted similar analyses.[1] Two important differences of method distinguish my study from these earlier analyses. These differences concern, first, the question of influence, and, second, the textual relationship of the TS to the MT.

By the question of influence, I mean the problem of whether or not to see in a given portion of the TS the influence of biblical passages which are not clearly reflected in the wording of the scroll. In general, I take a minimalist position on this question, preferring to err, if necessary, on the side of caution. For this reason, a comparison of my chart of the scroll's use of biblical texts with Yadin's usually shows his listing to be longer.

One example which clarifies the difference in our procedures on this point is furnished by TS 47:5b–8.

Turning first to lines 5b–6, one reads: כול אשר בתוכה יהיה טהור וכול אשר יבוא לה יהיה טהור. Yadin commented, "The use of לה (after the verb בוא) in the sense of אליה betrays the clear

---

1. Yadin I, pp. 46-70. He also discussed the question throughout his notes to the text, column by column. For Brin, see "המקרא," *passim,* and also his "Uses of the Bible in the Temple Scroll."

influence of the language in Deut xxiii:3; Jer li:48; Zech ix:9 …"[2] The biblical passages to which he referred read as follows:

לא יבא ממזר בקהל יהוה גם דור עשירי לוא יבא לו בקהל יהוה	Deut 23:3
כי מצפון יבוא לה השודדים נאם יהוה	Jer 51:48
הנה מלכך יבוא לך צדיק ונושע הוא	Zech 9:9

The reason that Yadin suggested the influence of these verses is obvious—these are the only biblical portions which combine the elements of בוא plus ל with a reference to Zion, Jerusalem, the congregation, or the like. (Although, actually, only two of these passages illustrate Yadin's point. The passage in Deut is an example of the "ethical dative"—לו does not function here in the sense of אליו.[3])

In citing the other two passages, Yadin apparently did not consider the tendency of LBH to use ל with verbs of motion rather than the אל of SBH. A Second Temple Jew would most naturally express the idea of TS 47:5–6 with the verb-preposition combination found in the scroll.[4] Thus Yadin overstated the case when he called the relationship between the text of the scroll and the biblical portions "clear." One has no way to know whether the author of this portion of the TS was thinking specifically of any of these biblical portions, or simply writing in the fashion most natural to him. In any case, it seems most unlikely that he was thinking simultaneously of all three passages.

Yadin also commented on the following lines of the TS: "לוא יביאו לה in l. 8 points to the impact on the passages of the language that we find in references to the buying of offerings and holy things, e.g. Lev xvii:9, xxiii:14f; Exod xxxv:5; 1 Kings x:25; 2 Chron xxxi:10, etc."[5] But a check of these references shows that none of them actually contains all three elements of line eight's wording. All that can be said is that the verb בוא appears in the *Hiphil,* and that in each portion there is some connection with gathering or bringing offerings to God. Does this commonality really show the "impact" on the TS lines of the stated passages, as Yadin argued? How would one expect the author to express the idea of "bring"—is there a more obvious choice than הביא?

In the case of situations like these, I do not list the passages in Yadin's manner. Failing clearer evidence of "influence" (which, by its very nature, is notoriously difficult to ascertain), I choose the minimalist position. For the sake of brevity, I do not catalogue disagreements with Yadin's analysis item by item.

A second problem with earlier approaches is the assumption that the author of the TS was working with a text of the Hebrew Bible essentially identical to that of the MT. While, from time to time, Yadin did refer to versional texts such as the LXX or, much less frequently, the Peshitta, he tended to minimize the possibility that the authors of the TS used variant Hebrew

---

2. Yadin, II, pp. 202-3.

3. GKC §§ 119s, 135i.

4. Cf. Brin, "הערות לשוניות," p. 24.

5. Yadin, II, p. 203.

texts. He argued instead that, where there are differences with the MT, they reflect either the influence of other biblical portions on the portion in question, or deliberate changes of the biblical text in response to contemporary sectarian polemics.[6] Of course, these are legitimate possibilities, and each case must be examined on its own merits; in general, however, when faced with variant texts, I prefer text critical solutions.

During my research for this study I constantly faced the problem of how to categorize the data. Several problems in this regard are especially noteworthy. For one, when reading the text it is often impossible to distinguish the following three situations from one another: (1) combination of two or more short biblical portions; (2) versional texts; and (3) quotation from "faulty" memory. While one cannot disallow the possibility of the last-mentioned situation (in fact it was usual in antiquity to quote from memory, since references were often hard to locate in unwieldy scrolls), neither can one discern it.

For practical purposes, therefore, I operate on the assumption that one of the first two options obtains. In deciding between them, I consider the character of the scroll portion under investigation. For example, the Temple Source has very few references to the biblical text, so I do not feel free to suggest versional texts in analyzing that source. Because the evidence does not allow one to gauge the text critical character of the source, I choose "option one." On the other hand, in the case of D, many of its variants also appear in the LXX or the Peshitta. Its underlying text often does not agree with the MT. Therefore, when I encounter a portion in this source which includes an unattested variant, I frequently choose "option two."

Another problem I face is how to characterize a short biblical quote or paraphrase whose possible biblical sources cannot be narrowed to a single text. For example, in 59:7b one reads ואסתיר פני מהמה. Three different biblical verses contain phrases similar to this, Deut 31:18a, Ezek 39:23b, and Ezek 39:24b. To which portion was the author referring, if any? I have decided on Deut 31:18, because other parts of col. 59 quote or paraphrase this chapter. Thus, in deciding such questions, I choose the biblical portion which the author has already referred to in the immediate context, while listing the other possibilities in parentheses.

Categories of Analysis

When analyzing any text which is heavily dependent on a known source or group of sources, it is possible to construct a continuum which describes the relationship of any part of the text to its source(s). The continuum ranges from the extreme of extensive verbatim quotation, on the one hand, to the point where no relationship is discernible, on the other. I divide this continuum into gradations, and somewhat arbitrarily assign names to each division. In this analysis of the relationship of the TS to the biblical text, I designate the following categories:

6. Brin, "המקרא," takes the same approach. Cf. e.g., his discussion of the "Beautiful Captive" on p. 194. He allows very little room for the author's natural use of the Hebrew language—every nuance of the scroll is a response to the biblical text. It is possible that he is correct, of course; the nature of the evidence is such that one cannot reject his assertions out of hand. It is more natural to assume, however, that the author's ability to write Hebrew went beyond this "mixing and matching" of verses.

1. v: extensive verbatim quotation
2. vo: extensive verbatim quotation from a version other than the MT
3. vph: verbatim quotation of a short phrase
4. vd: verbatim quotation with a significant deletion
5. vr: verbatim quotation with the elements of the quotation in a rearranged order
6. pq: paraphrase of a verse or portion including a short quotation
7. p: paraphrase without quotation
8. h: halakhic "exegesis," which may include nonbiblical elements
9. m: midrashic usage where the elements are clear by reason of quotation
10. me: midrashic complexes where the elements are not readily identifiable
11. fc: free composition

These categories were not simply decided upon at the outset, but only after comparison of the scroll's text with the Hebrew Bible was completed. It was important to find a balance in this matter; one must have sufficient categories to reflect accurately the nuances of the compositional methods which appear in the scroll. But at the same time it is important to capture true commonalities, and thus not to have too many categories. Of course, the categories will necessarily shade into one another; they cannot be made entirely discrete. Difficult decisions thus arise. Some of the decisions I made in applying these categories require comment.

One decision involves the term "verbatim." I use it to describe obvious cases, of course; but consider the relationship of 35:7b–8a to Lev 22:11a. The text of the TS reads לשאת עון אשמה. The text of Leviticus says והשיאו אותם עון אשמה. One encounters the same word order and the same verbal root, but not the same verbal form. I place cases such as this in one of the "verbatim" categories. Another type of usage appears in the relationship between 43:14b–15a and Deut 14:23. The TS has דגן ויין ושמן ובקר וצאן. The biblical text reads בקרך וצאנך דגנך ותירושך וצהרך. In two instances here the scroll uses synonyms for biblical terms. Also, the second person possessive suffixes of the biblical verse do not infiltrate the scroll. Instances of this type of usage I also call "verbatim." Thus "v" is not always an exact quotation, but merely a situation which approaches such.

At least three different types of situation qualify for the category of "paraphrase." First, there are instances in which the scroll refers to a biblical portion which concerns the same topic as the scroll itself is discussing. It is not difficult to categorize such instances. But there is also a second type of paraphrase, wherein the scroll applies a biblical idea to a different situation. It interprets by "principalizing" the biblical text. In general, the scroll operates by a process of analogy. Nonbiblical additions, usually a phrase of three words or less, may appear. For example, in 43:12 Exod 29:34 is applied in this manner. Exod speaks of the sacrificial offerings for Aaron's ordination ceremony, mandating that they are not to be consumed after a certain period of time. The scroll applies this category, the נותר, to the "left-over" portions of the second tithe. In such cases it is difficult to say that this type of paraphrase is distinct from what I call "midrashic application" (m). Accordingly, in such cases I record both categories. A third type of paraphrase is conceivable, wherein the scroll uses a biblical portion stylistically, without reference to its ideas. As noted above, I have not discovered a way to tell whether possible examples of this sort of usage are really references to the biblical text, or simply the result of a late Second Temple author's attempt at writing "biblical Hebrew." I do not record such usages.

I use the term "midrash" to describe certain types of use of the biblical text in the TS. As noted in chapter 4, I understand midrash to refer to "an edifying and explanatory genre closely tied to Scripture, in which the role of amplification is real but secondary and always remains subordinate to the primary religious end, which is to show the full import of the work of God, the Word of God."[7] The term can also be used to refer to the attempt to find scriptural justification for particular beliefs. I prefer "midrash" to "pesher" because of the very specific connotation which the latter term apparently bore in its milieu, to judge by its use in the DSS.[8] That connotation is not appropriate to the TS usages to which I assign the term "midrash," itself known from the DSS with an appropriately general meaning.[9] It has often been particularly difficult to decide to which of the several categories of midrashic usage a given TS portion should be assigned.

The midrashic category which stands closest to a "literal" use of the biblical text is "halakhic exegesis." In 43:12b, for example, I see a "halakhic exegesis" of Deut 14:24b. The scroll reads והיושבים במרחק מן המקדש דרך שלושת ימים. The text of Deut says simply כי ירחק ממך המקום. The clear congruity between the TS מרחק and the biblical ירחק, and the substitution of "temple" for "place," show that the scroll is explicating the passage from Deut. It is answering the question, how far is "too far?" The distance of a "three-day journey" derives from analogy to texts such as Exod 3:18.

In this example, the relationship of the scroll's text to that of the Hebrew Bible is one which modern exegetes might appreciate as a genuine attempt to determine what the Bible meant. Although the scroll is engaged in midrash, it sticks very close to the biblical text. The TS paraphrases the biblical text, with quotes. It then adds nonbiblical portions, or biblical portions derived from elsewhere, to complete its understanding of the text.

The category "free composition" embraces those portions of the scroll which do not have a clear verbal relationship to some text of the Hebrew Bible. I do not mean by such a designation that biblical influence is in no way discernible. For example, the Temple Source has a general relationship to those portions of Ezek which describe a new temple. Nevertheless, no extended verbal relationship can be discovered, wherein one can point to a particular verse of Ezek as the basis of an architectural detail in the scroll's description. I do not feel that such general influence is particularly significant for compositional analysis, and I do not record it.

---

7. R. Bloch, "Midrash," p.29.

8. Cf. the definition given by Horgan in her study of all the pesharim (*Pesharim*, p. 229): "pesher is an interpretation made known by God to a selected interpreter of a mystery revealed by God to the biblical prophet concerning history." Using this definition, no instance of a pesher occurs in the TS.

9. E.g. 1QS 6:24, 8:15, 8:26; CD 20:6.

The Data

Part One: Line by Line Analysis of the Scroll

This analysis includes the following information. In the left column I indicate the topic of the scroll. In the right column I break the scroll's discussion into lines and portions of lines. In almost every case, it is possible to break the lines into no more than two divisions, "a" and "b." I do not mean by this designation that the line in question has two equal parts; sometimes "a" is six words long, and "b" only a single word. Rather, I divide the lines according to the way the lines of the scroll relate to the biblical text. The right column indicates to which verse(s) of the Hebrew Bible the scroll is referring, and which category of usage the lines of the scroll represent.

I also indicate how the particular line of the TS handles the divine name, if it occurs. The treatment of the divine name is an important indication of source divisions in the scroll, as noted in the first chapter. Thus, "Yahweh" means that this name of God appears unchanged. "I" means that the biblical text represents God speaking in the first person, and the scroll has taken it over unchanged. It also designates those instances when the scroll represents God speaking in the first person in nonbiblical (free composition) portions. "*I" means that the scroll has turned a biblical third person divine referent into a first person verbal or nominal form. "-I" means that the scroll has not changed a third person form into a first person form; of course, I use it only in those portions of the scroll where the lack of change is anomalous.

		Column 2		
General Statement		1	=	Exod 34:10b [v, I]
Removal of Canaanites		2–4a	=	Exod 34:11b [vo]
Warning Not to Make a Covenant		4b–5a	=	Exod 34:12 [vo]
Command to Tear Altars Down		5b–8a	=	Exod 34:13 [vo]
		8b–9a	=	Deut 7:25b [vo, *I]
		9b–11a	=	Deut 7:26 [v]
Command Not to Worship Idols		11b–12a	=	Exod 34:14 [vo, -I]
Results of Making Covenant with Canaanites		12b–13a	=	Exod 34:15 [vo]
		13b–15	=	Exod 34:16 [v]
		Column 3		
Collection of Materials for Temple		1	=	[too fragmentary]
		2	=	[fc (?)]
		3	=	[fc]
		4	=	[fc, I]
		5–7	=	[fc]

	Column 3 (*cont.*)		
Command to Build Ark and Vessels	8	=	2 Chr 4:9 [p (?)]
Command to Build Mercy Seat	9	=	Exod 25:17 [p (?)]
Command to Build Altar of Incense and Tables for Bread of Presence	10	=	[fc]
Command to Make Temple Vessels	11	=	[fc]
	12	=	[fc] or Exod 25:29 [p (?)]
	13a	=	[fc]
Command to Make Lampstand and Vessels	13b	=	[fc] or Exod 35:14 // 30:27 [p (?)]
Command to Build Altar of Burnt Offering	14	=	Exod 31:9 [p or fc (?)]
	15	=	Exod 35:16 [p or fc (?)]
	Column 4		
Command to Build Temple Wings (?)	1–2	=	[too fragmentary]
	3–5	=	[fc]
	6	=	[too fragmentary]
Dimensions of the Temple (?)	7	=	[fc (?)]
Dimensions of the Vestibule (?)	8	=	[fc (?)]
	9	=	[fc] or 1 Kngs 6:3 [p (?)]
	10	=	Ezra 6:3 [p (?)]
	11–12	=	[fc]
Dimensions of the Holy of Holies (?)	13	=	[fc] or 1 Kngs 6:20 [p] or 2 Chr 3:8 [p (?)]
	14–17	=	[too fragmentary]
	Columns 5–6 (Overlap)		
Uncertain Commands	1–4	=	[too fragmentary]
The Upper Chamber of the Heikhal	5–11	=	[fc]
Blank line	12	=	[blank]
Command to Build a Stoa	13	=	[fc]
	14	=	[too fragmentary]
	Column 7		
The "Tablets" (Boards?)	1–5	=	[fc]
Fragmentary portions	6–7	=	[too fragmentary]

	Column 7 (*cont.*)		
Command to Build Ark and Mercy Seat	8	=	Exod 25:10 [p] or Exod 37:1 [p (?)]
	9–10a	=	Exod 25:21 [p (?)]
Command to Fashion Cherubim	10b	=	Exod 25:18 [p (?)]
	11	=	Exod 24:19 [p (?)]
	12	=	Exod 25:20 [p (?)]
Command to Fashion Veil	13–14	=	Exod 26:31 [pq]
	Column 8		
Fragmentary Portion	1–4	=	[too fragmentary]
Table of the Bread of the Presence	5	=	Exod 25:23 [v (?)]
	6	=	Exod 25:23–24 [v (?)]
	7	=	[too fragmentary]
Bread of the Presence	8	=	Lev 24:5 [v (?)]
	9	=	Lev 24:6–7a [p]
	10	=	Lev 24:7 [pq]
	11	=	[fc]
	12	=	Lev 24:7 [p]
	13	=	Lev 24:4 [p (?)] + Lev 24:9 [p]
	14	=	[fc]
	Column 9		
The Menorah	1	=	[too fragmentary]
	2	=	Exod 25:31 [v] // Exod 37:18
	3	=	Exod 25:32a [p]
	4	=	Exod 25:32b [p]
	5	=	[fc]
	6–7	=	[too fragmentary]
	8–10	=	[fc]
	11	=	Exod 25:38–39 [p]
	12	=	Exod 25:37 [p] + Exod 40:5 [p]
	13	=	1 Kngs 7:49 [v (?)] + Exod 40:24 [v (?)] + Exod 27:21b [p]
	14	=	Lev 24:3 [v]
	Column 10		
Fragmentary Portions	1–7	=	[too fragmentary]
	8	=	[fc (?)]
Construction of a Screen or Curtain	9–12	=	[fc (?)]

	Column 11		
Fragmentary Portions	1–8	=	[too fragmentary]
General Occasions for Sacrifice	9	=	[fc]
Feasts of Unleavened Bread and Omer	10	=	[fc]
First Fruits Wheat	11	=	[fc]
Feasts of New Oil and Wood Offering	12	=	[fc]
Feast of Booths, Eighth-Day Convocation	13	=	[fc]
	Column 12		
Fragmentary Portions	1–7	=	[too fragmentary]
The Stone Altar (?)	8–11	=	[fc]
	12–13	=	[too fragmentary]
Vessels for the Altar (?)	14	=	[too fragmentary]
	15a	=	[fc]
Command for a New Structure	15b	=	[fc]
	Column 13		
The Four Pillars (?)	1	=	[too fragmentary]
	2–3	=	[fc (?)]
	4	=	[fc]
	5	=	[fc] or 2 Chr 3:17 [p]
	6	=	[fc]
	7	=	[fc (?)]
Fragmentary Portions	8–10	=	[too fragmentary]
The Tamid Offerings	10b–11a	=	Num 28:3 [v (?)]
	11b–12a	=	Num 28:5b [v (?)]
	12b–13a	=	Num 28:6 [vd, **Yahweh**]
	12א	=	Num 28:7a [vo]
	13b–14a	=	Lev 7:8 [pq (?)]
	14b–15	=	Num 28:8 [v (?), **Yahweh**]
	16	=	[fc (?)]
Sabbath Offerings	17	=	Num 28:9a [vo (?)]
	Column 14		
Sacrifices for the First Day of the Month	1	=	[lost]
	2–3	=	Num 28:12a [vr]
			+ Num 15:9b [vr (?) + fc]
	4	=	[fc]

	Column 14 (*cont.*)		
Sacrifices for the First Day of the Month (*cont.*)	5–6	=	Num 28:13a [v] + Num 15:5 [vr]
	7–8	=	Num 15:13b [v] + Num 28:11a [v (?) **Yahweh**]
Sacrifices for the New Year of the First Month	9–10a	=	Exod 12:2 [pq + fc]
	10b–11	=	Num 29:1b [v + fc] + Num 29:5b [pq]
	12	=	Num 29:2 [vr]
	13	=	Num 29:6a [v (?)]
	14	=	Num 15:9 [pq] + Num 15:10 [pq]
	15	=	Num 15:6b [vr]
	16–17	=	Num 15:7a [v] + Num 29:14 [vr]
	18	=	[too fragmentary]
	Column 15		
Sacrifices for New Year of the First Month (*cont.*)	1b–2	=	Num 29:2–29:6 [p]
The Ordination Ceremony	3	=	Exod 29:35 [p] + Exod 29:2, 15 [p] // Lev 8:33b + Lev 8:18, 22
	א3	=	Exod 29:2–3, 23 [p] // Lev 8:3, 26 [p]
	4	=	[fc]
	5	=	[fc, **Yahweh**]
	6a	=	[fc]
	6b	=	Lev 3:9b [v (?)]
	7	=	Lev 3:10 [v]
	8a	=	Lev 3:9b [v]
	8b	=	Lev 3:10b [v]
	9a	=	Num 29:6 [v]
	9b–10	=	Lev 8:26 [v]
	11	=	Exod 29:22 [p] + Exod 29:21a [p]
	12–13	=	Exod 29:24b [vr] + Exod 29:25b [vr] [(**Yahweh**),**Yahweh**]
	14	=	Exod 29:35 [p]
The High Priest's Ordination	15–16	=	[fc] + Lev 16:32b [v] + Lev 21:10a [v, **Yahweh**]
	17	=	Lev 16:23 [vr]
	18	=	Lev 4:15a [v]

	Column 16		
Sacrifice of the First Bull	01–02a	=	[fc] + Exod 29:11b [v] // Lev 4:15
	02b	=	[fc] + Exod 29:2a [v, (**Yahweh**)]
	03	=	Exod 29:12b [v] + Ezek 43:20 [vr]
Lost Portions	04–1	=	[lost]
Application of Sacrificial Blood	2	=	Exod 29:20a [v (?)]
	3	=	Exod 29:20b [v] + Exod 29:21a [v (?)]
Holiness of High Priest	4–5	=	Exod 29:21b [v] +Lev 21:11 [v] + Lev 21:7b [vr, (**Yahweh**)]
Sacrificial Portions of First Bull	6–8a	=	Exod 29:13b [p] + Lev 8:16 [vd]
	8b–10a	=	Lev 3:10b [v] + Exod 29:25b [vr] + Num 29:6 [v, (**Yahweh**)]
Disposal of Sacrificial Wastes	10b–11	=	Exod 29:14 [vr]
	12	=	Lev 4:12 [p]
	13	=	Lev 4:11b [v + fc]
	14a	=	Lev 4:24b [v]
Procedures for Second Bull	14b	=	Lev 16:15a [pq] + Lev 16:33b [vr]
	15a	=	[fc]
	15b	=	Lev 4:20b [v]
	16	=	Exod 29:12 [vr]
	17a	=	Ezek 45:19 [v]
	17b–18	=	Lev 4:19a [v + fc] + Lev 4:19b [v] + Lev 4:21b [v]
	Column 17		
Summary for Eighth Day of Ordination (?)	1	=	[fc]
	2	=	Lev 9:24 [p]
	3	=	Exod 12:14 [v]
	4	=	[fc]
Blank line	5	=	[blank]
Commands for Passover	6	=	Lev 23:5 [vr, (**Yahweh**)]
	7	=	[fc (?)]

Commands for Passover (*cont.*)	Column 17 (*cont.*)		
	8	=	Exod 30:14b [v]
			+ Exod 12:8 [v]
	9	=	Deut 16:7 [pq]
Commands for Unleavened Bread	10–12a	=	Lev 23:6 [vr] + Lev 23:7 [vr]
			// Num 28:17–18 [**Yahweh**]
	12b–14a	=	Lev 23:8 [v] + Num 28:19
			[vr, **Yahweh**]
	14b	=	Num 28:22a [v] + Num 28:20
			[v] +Num 28:24 [v + fc]
	15a	=	[fc]
	15b–16	=	Deut 16:8a [v] + Num 28:25b
			[v] // Lev 23:8b [**Yahweh**]
Waving of the Omer	Column 18		
	1	=	[too fragmentary]
	2	=	Num 28:27b [v (?)]
	3	=	[too fragmentary]
	4	=	Num 28:30 [v]
			+ Num 15:24 [v (?)]
	5–6	=	Num 29:6 [v]
			+ Num 15:4b–5a [v]
	7	=	Lev 16:33b [vr + fc]
	8–9a	=	Num 15:25 [v]
			+ Lev 23:14b [pq]
	9b–10a	=	[fc] + Lev 23:12a [pq]
Festival of First Fruits of Wheat	10b–11	=	Lev 23:15 [v]
	12–13a	=	Lev 23:16 [v, **Yahweh**]
	13b–15	=	Lev 23:17 [vr + fc, **Yahweh**]
	16	=	[fc]
Festival of First Fruits of Wheat —Further Commands	Column 19		
	1–3	=	[too fragmentary]
	4–5	=	Num 15:4b–5a [v]
			+ Lev 23:20a [v + fc]
	6–7a	=	[fc]
	7b–9a	=	Lev 23:21 [vr]
	9b	=	Num 28:26 [p + fc]
Blank Line	10	=	[blank]
Beginning of Commands for New Wine	11–13	=	Lev 23:15 [p, **Yahweh**]
	14–16	=	[fc, **Yahweh**]
Sacrifices for Feast of New Wine	Column 20		
	01–02	=	[too fragmentary]

	Column 20 (*cont.*)		
Sacrifices for Feast of New Wine (*cont.*)	03–04	=	Num 28:27b–28a [vr] + Num 28:30b [pq]
	04bis–05	=	Num 29:37 [vr]
	06	=	[fc, **Yahweh**]
	1	=	[fc]
	2	=	Num 29:13b [v (?)]
	3–4	=	[fc]
	5	=	Lev 3:9b [v]
	6–7a	=	Lev 3:10b [vr] + Lev 3:9b [vr]
	7b–9a	=	Lev 3:11 [pq, (**Yahweh**)]
	9b	=	Num 15:4–5a [pq]
	10a	=	Lev 7:10a [pq]
	10b–11a	=	Lev 2:2b [pq]
	11b–12	=	Lev 6:9 [vr] + Lev 2:11 [pq + fc]
	13–14a	=	Lev 2:13 [pq] + Num 18:19 [v, **Yahweh**]
	14b–15a	=	[fc]
	15b–16a	=	Lev 7:31b–7:32a [pq] + Deut 18:3b [vr]
	16b	=	[fc]
	Column 21		
Sacrifices for Feast of New Wine (*cont.*)	02	=	Lev 7:32–33 [pq]
	03	=	Deut 18:3a [v]
	04–2	=	[fc]
	3	=	[fc, **Yahweh**]
	4–7	=	[fc]
	8	=	[fc, **Yahweh**]
	9	=	Lev 3:17 [v + fc]
	10	=	Num 28:7b [pq, **Yahweh**]
Blank Line	11	=	[blank]
Beginning of Festival of New Oil	12–14	=	Lev 23:15–17a [v + fc]
	15–16	=	[fc, **Yahweh**]
	Column 22		
Sacrifices for New Oil	01	=	[too fragmentary]
	02	=	Lev 10:17b [pq (?)]
	03	=	Num 15:10 [pq]
	04	=	Exod 29:25b [vr]
	05–1	=	[fc, (**Yahweh**)]
	2	=	[fc]
	3	=	Num 29:13b [v + fc]
	4	=	[fc]
	5	=	Lev 3:2 [vr]

Sacrifices for New Oil (*cont.*)	**Column 22** (*cont.*)		
	6	=	Num 18:17b [vr + fc]
	7	=	[fc]
Priests Portion of Sacrifice	8–10a	=	[fc] + Lev 7:31b–32 [pq] + Deut 18:3b [pq, **Yahweh**]
	10b–11a	=	[fc]
Ritual of First Fruits of Oil	11b–13	=	[fc]
	14	=	Lev 3:17a [v] + Deut 15:20a [v, **Yahweh**]
	15–16	=	[fc, **Yahweh**]
Ritual of First Fruits of Oil (*cont.*)	**Column 23**		
	01	=	[fc]
Introduction to Festival of Wood Offering	02	=	[too fragmentary]
	03–3	=	[fc, **Yahweh**]
	4	=	Num 7:87b [v + (?)]
	5	=	Num 29:6 [v + (?)]
	6	=	Num 7:15 [v + (?)]
	7–8	=	[fc]
Procedures for the First Day of the Festival	9–10	=	[fc]
	11a	=	Lev 5:8 [pq + fc]
	11b	=	[fc]
	12	=	Lev 4:25 [v + fc]
	13–14a	=	Ezek 45:19 [v] + Exod 29:16b [v + fc]
	14b	=	Lev 4:26a [v]
	14c–17	=	Lev 3:14b–16 [vr, **Yahweh**]
Procedures for the First Day of the Festival (*cont.*)	**Column 24**		
	1–7	=	[too fragmentary]
	8–9	=	[fc, **Yahweh**]
Levi's and Judah's Offerings	10–11	=	[fc]
Offerings of Days 2–6	12–16	=	[fc]
The Day of Memorial of the Seventh Month	**Column 25**		
	1	=	[too fragmentary]
	2–3	=	Lev 23:14b [v]
	4–5a	=	Lev 29:2 [vr, **Yahweh**]
	5b–6a	=	Num 29:5a [vd]
	6b–7a	=	Num 29:6 [vr]
	7b–8	=	[fc] + Lev 23:14b [v, **Yahweh**]

	Column 25 (*cont.*)		
The Day of Memorial of the Seventh Month	9–10a	=	[fc] + Num 29:1a [vr] + Num 29:1b [pq]
The Day of Atonement	10b–11a	=	Lev 23:27 [vd]
	11b–12a	=	Lev 23:29 [vd]
	12b–13a	=	Num 29:8 [vd, **Yahweh**]
	13b–15a	=	Num 29:11 [vd + fc]
	15b–16	=	[fc]
	Column 26		
Sacrifices for the Day of Atonement	1–2	=	[too fragmentary]
	3	=	Lev 16:8a [v]
	4	=	Lev 16:8b [v, (**Yahweh**)]
	5	=	Lev 16:15a [v] + Lev 19:9b [v, (**Yahweh**)]
	6–7a	=	[fc] + Lev 16:15b [v]
	7b–8a	=	Lev 16:33 [vr] + Lev 16:35 [pq + fc]
	8b–9a	=	Exod 29:14a [v + fc]
	9b	=	Lev 4:21b [v] + Lev 11:33b [vr]
	10a	=	Lev 4:20b [v]
	10b–11a	=	Exod 29:19–20a [v]
	11b–13a	=	Lev 16:21 [vo (?)]
	13b	=	Lev 16:22a [v]
	Column 27		
Sacrifices for the Day of Atonement (*cont.*)	1	=	[too fragmentary]
	2	=	Num 15:25a [v]
	3–4a	=	Lev 16:24 [pq]
	4b–5a	=	[fc] + Lev 23:31b [v]
	5b	=	Lev 16:34a [v] + Exod 12:14a [v]
Summary for Day of Atonement	6a	=	Lev 23:31 [vr] +Lev 23:32a [v]
	6b–8a	=	Lev 23:29–30 [vr (deletions)]
	8b	=	Lev 23:32a [v] + Num 29:7a [v + fc]
Beginning of Tabernacles	9–10a	=	[fc] + Lev 23:31a [vr]
	10b	=	Lev 23:34b [vo]
	Column 28		
Tabernacles—Day One	1	=	[too fragmentary] (**Yahweh**)]
Tabernacles—Day Two	2b–3a	=	Num 29:17a [vd]
	3b	=	[lost]

	Column 28 (*cont.*)		
Tabernacles—Day Two (*cont.*)	4–5a	=	Num 29:17b [vd]+ Num 29:19a [v]+ Num 29:6a [v]
	5b–6a	=	Num 29:18a [v + fc] + Num 29:6b [vr]
Tabernacles—Day Three	6b–7	=	Num 29:20 [vd, **Yahweh**]
	8a	=	Num 29:22a [vo (?)]
	8b–9a	=	Num 29:21 [vr + fc]
Tabernacles—Day Four	9b–10	=	Num 29:23 [vd]
	11	=	Num 29:25a [v] + Num 29:24a [v]
	Column 29		
Conclusion to Tabernacles	1	=	[too fragmentary]
	2–3a	=	Num 29:39 [vr (?), (**Yahweh**)]
Redactional Insertion	3b–4a	=	[fc, I (bis)]
Final Summary to Festivals	4b	=	Lev 23:37 [pq + fc]
	5–6a	=	[fc] + Lev 23:38b [pq, I]
Israel and the Covenant	6b–7a	=	Exod 28:38 [pq, I]
	7b–8a	=	Ezek 37:23 [v + fc, I]
	8b–10	=	[fc, I (bis)]
	Column 30		
Israel and the Covenant (*cont.*)	1	=	[fc (?), I]
	2	=	[blank]
The Staircase Tower	3	=	[too fragmentary]
	4–10	=	[fc]
	Column 31		
Fragmentary Portion	1–5	=	[too fragmentary]
Command to Bridge Staircase Tower	6–7	=	[fc]
Command to Guild Staircase Tower	8–9	=	[fc, I]
The House of the Laver	10–13	=	[fc]
	Column 32		
Fragmentary Portion	1–5	=	[too fragmentary]
Items for House of Laver	6–8a	=	[fc]

	Column 32 (*cont.*)		
Wall Cabinets in House of Laver	8b–10a	=	[fc]
	10b–11a	=	Ezek 43:14 [p + fc]
	11b–12a	=	Exod 28:42 [p + fc]
Conduit for Waste Water	12b–15	=	[fc]
	Column 33		
Fragmentary Portion	1–4	=	[too fragmentary]
Conclusion of House of Laver	5	=	[fc]
	6	=	[too fragmentary]
	7	=	[fc]
The House for Temple Utensils	8–15	=	[fc]
	Column 34		
Design of the Slaughtering House	1–2	=	[fc (?)]
	3–4	=	[fc]
Slaughter and Sacrificial Procedure	5–7	=	[fc]
	8a	=	Lev 1:5b [v]
	8b–10a	=	Lev 1:6 [p]
	10b	=	Lev 2:13a [p]
	10c–11a	=	Lev 1:9a [p + fc]
	11b–12a	=	Lev 1:12b [vd]
	12b–13a	=	[fc]
	13b–14a	=	Lev 1:5b [v, **Yahweh**]
	14b	=	Lev 1:9b [v]
	15	=	[fc]
	Column 35		
Those Forbidden to Enter Sanctuary	1–5	=	[too fragmentary]
	6–7a	=	Exod 28:41b [p]
			+ Exod 28:43 [pq]
	7b–8a	=	Lev 21:13b [v]
			+ Lev 22:16a [v + fc]
	8b–9	=	Exod 40:10 [pq]
Stoa for Offerings	10–15	=	[fc]
	Column 36		
Command to Build Inner Court	1–3	=	[too fragmentary]
	4–14	=	[fc]
	Column 37		
Procedures for Consumption of Sacrifices	1–3	=	[too fragmentary]
	4	=	[fc]
	5	=	Lev 10:14b [v + (?)]
	6	=	[too fragmentary]

	Column 37 (*cont.*)		
Procedures for Consumption of Sacrifices (*cont.*)	7	=	[fc]
Buildings for Priestly Consumption of Prebends	8–12	=	[fc]
Stoves	13	=	[fc]
	14	=	Ezek 26:23b [pq + fc]
	Column 38		
Use of Inner Court by Priests	1–3	=	[too fragmentary]
	4	=	[fc]
	5	=	[lost]
	6–10	=	[fc]
Blank Line	11	=	[blank]
Construction of Middle Court	12–15	=	[fc]
	Column 39		
Doors and Elements of Middle Court	1	=	[too fragmentary]
	2–4	=	[fc]
Who May Enter Middle Court	5	=	[fc]
	6–7a	=	[fc, I]
	7b–8a	=	[fc]
	8b–9	=	Exod 30:12b [v] + Exod 30:13 b [v] + Lev 3:17 [pq] + Exod 30:16b [v] + Exod 30:13b [v, **Yahweh**]
	10–11a	=	Exod 30:13b [v] + Exod 30:14b [v+ fc, I]
Gates of the Middle Court	11b–12a	=	Ezek 48:31a [pq]
	12b–15	=	[fc]
	Column 40		
Directions for Priestly Clothing	1–3	=	Ezek 42:14 // 44:19 [p (?)]
	4	=	[fc]
Construction of Outer Court	5	=	[fc]
	6	=	Deut 23:9 [pq]
	7–15	=	[fc]
	Column 41		
Measurements for Gates	1–11	=	[fc]
Specifications for Individual Gates	12–17	=	[fc]

Column 42

Number and Dimensions of Chambers	1–6	=	[fc]
Stairs and Dimensions of Upper-level Chambers	7–10a	=	[fc]
Command to Build Framework for Sukkot	10b–17	=	[fc]

Column 43

When the Second Tithe May Be Eaten	1	=	[too fragmentary]
	2–3	=	[fc]
	4–5a	=	[fc] + Lev 7:15 [pq]
	5b	=	Deut 14:22b [h] + Exod 12:11a [pq]
	6–10	=	[fc]
Disposal of Unused Portions	10b–12a	=	Exod 29:34 [m (= pq)]
Who Must Bring the Tithe	12b–13a	=	Deut 14:24b [h]
	13b–14a	=	[fc] + Deut 14:24a [h] + Deut 14:25a [h (= pq)]
	14b–15a	=	Deut 14:26a [p] + Deut 14:23b [v + fc]
Summary of Eating of Portions	15b–17	=	Deut 26:14a [h]
		=	Deut 26:14a [v + fc] + Lev 27:30b [v + fc, (Exod 29:34b possible?)]

Column 44

Fragmentary Portion	1–2	=	[too fragmentary]
Allocation of Rooms by Tribe	3–16	=	[fc]

Column 45

Allocation of Rooms by Tribe (*cont.*)	1	=	[fc]
Changing of the Courses	2	=	[fc (?)]
	3–7a	=	[fc]
Laws on Entry into the City	7b–10	=	Deut 23:11–12 [m]
		=	Deut 23:11 [vrd] + Deut 23:12a [pq] + Exod 19:10–11 [vd] + Deut 23:12b [v + fc, I]
	11–12a	=	Lev 15:18 [m]
		=	Lev 15:18a [vr + fc] + Exod 19:11 [p]

	Column 45 (*cont.*)		
Laws on Entry into the City (*cont.*)	12b–14	=	Lev 21:17–23 [m]
		=	2 Sam 5:8b [pq + fc] + Lev 21:23b [p + fc, I (bis)]
	15–16a	=	Lev 15:13 [v + fc]
	16b–17a	=	[fc]
	17b	=	Num 5:2 [h]
	17c–18a	=	Num 5:2 [h]
	18b	=	Lev 14:12 [h]
	Column 46		
Spikes for Unclean Birds	1	=	[fc, (I) (?)]
	2–3	=	[fc, I]
	4	=	[fc, I]
Command to Build a רובד	5–8	=	[fc, I]
Command to Build a Dry Moat	9	=	[fc]
	10–11a	=	[fc] + Num [pq]
		=	Num 4:2a [m, I]
	11b	=	[fc] + Lev 29:5b [v, I]
	12	=	[fc, I]
Command to Build a Latrine	13–16a	=	Deut 23:13–15 [m]
		=	Deut 23:13 [pq + fc] +Deut 23:15b [pq + fc]
Command to Provide Quarantine Areas	16b–17	=	[fc]
	18	=	Num 5:2b [pq + fc]
		=	Lev 13:46 [m]
	Column 47		
Summary of Quarantines	1	=	[too fragmentary]
	2	=	Deut 23:13a [vr (?) + (?)]
	3a	=	[fc, (I)]
Clean and Unclean Animal Skins	3b–18	=	[fc, I (7x)]
	Column 48		
Unclean Animals	1	=	Deut 14:18 [v (?)]
	2	=	[too fragmentary]
	3–4a	=	Lev 11:22 [vo]
	4b–5a	=	Lev 11:21 [vo]
Corpses of Animals	5b–6a	=	Deut 14:21a [vo]
	6b–7a	=	Deut 14:3 [v] + Deut 14:21b [v, -I]
Forbidden Mourning Practices	7b–9a	=	Deut 14:1 [v, -I]

	Column 48 (*cont.*)		
Forbidden Mourning Practices (*cont.*)	9b–10a	=	Lev 19:28 [vd, -I]
	10b	=	Deut 14:2a [v]
General Command Not to Defile Land	10c–11a	=	Num 35:34a [v]
Command for Burial Areas	11b–14a	=	Deut 19:1–2 [m]
		=	[fc] + Deut 19:2 [p + fc]
Command to Quarantine Lepers and Others	14b–17a	=	[fc]
Procedure for Lepers' Sacrifice	17b	=	[fc (?)]
	Column 49		
Summary of Leper Purification	1–3	=	[too fragmentary]
	4	=	[fc]
Uncleanness of a Dead Man's House	5–7a	=	Num 19:14 [m]
		=	Num 19:14a [pq + fc] + Num 19:14b [pq]
	7b–8a	=	Lev 11:34 [m]
		=	Lev 11:34 [pq]
	8b–9a	=	Lev 11:33 [pq + fc]
	9b–10	=	Num 19:15 [pq + fc]
Procedures for Purification of People and Items in the House	11–13	=	[fc]
	14	=	Num 19:18 [p + fc]
	15	=	Num 31:20–23 [m]
		=	Num 31:20 [pq] + Num 31:22 [pq]
	16a	=	Lev 11:32a [m]
		=	Lev 11:32a [pq] + Num 31:24a [p]
	16b–17	=	Num 19:14 b [m]
		=	Num 19:14b [pq] + Exod 19:10 [p]
	18–19a	=	Num 31:19–20 [m]
		=	Num 31:19–20 [pq] + Exod 19:10b–11a [pq]
	19b–20	=	Num 19:19 [pq] + Num 31:20 [p]
	21	=	[fc]
	Column 50		
Uncertain Purification Procedure (For Lepers?)	1–3a	=	[too fragmentary]
	3b–4a	=	Num 19:19 [pq] + Deut 23:12 [pq]
The Corpse in an Open Field	4b–7a	=	Num 19:16 [h]

The Corpse in an Open Field (*cont.*)	Column 50 (*cont.*)		
		=	Num 19:16a [vrd] + Num 19:13a [p] + Lev 17:14 // Deut 12:23 [p + fc]
	7b–8a	=	Num 19:13b [pq + fc]
	8b–9	=	Num 19:22 [pq]
Woman with a Dead Fetus	10–11a	=	[fc]
	11b–12a	=	Num 19:14 [m]
	12b	=	Num 19:22 [pq]
	13a	=	Num 19:14b [pq]
	13b–14a	=	Exod 19:10 [pq]
	14b–16a	=	Num 19:19 [m] + Deut 23:12 [m]
	16b–17a	=	Num 31:20 [m]
		=	Num 31:20 [pq + fc]
	17b–19	=	Lev 11:33 [m]
		=	Lev 11:33 [pq + fc]
	20–21	=	Lev 11:21a [pq] + Lev 11:29b [vr] + Lev 11:31v [pq]
Purification Procedure for One Touching Body of a Creeping Thing	Column 51		
	1a	=	[too fragmentary]
	1b–3a	=	Lev 11:35b [v] + Lev 11:43b [v] + Lev 11:31b [v]
	3b	=	Num 19:19b [v] + Lev 21:7a [v]
Touching Bones of a Creeping Thing	4–5a	=	Lev 11:25 [pq + fc] + Num 19:19b [v] + Lev 21:7a [v]
Redactional Summary and Transition	5b–6a	=	Lev 15:31a [vo]
	6b–7a	=	Lev 11:43b [v + fc] + Lev 11:43b [v, I, **Yahweh**]
	7b–8a	=	Num 35:34b [v]
	8b–10	=	[fc] + Lev 11:43a [v] + Lev 20:25b [v + fc, I]
Command for Judges and Officials	11–12a	=	Deut 16:18 [vo]
	12b–14a	=	Deut 16:19 [vo]
	14b–15a	=	[fc]
	15b–16a	=	Deut 16:20 [vo] + Deut 12:1b [v, I]
	16b–18	=	Deut 18:22b [vo]
Idolatry	19–20a	=	[fc]
	20b	=	Deut 16:21a [pq] + Deut 16:22a [pq]
	21	=	Lev 26:1a [pq + fc (?)]

	Column 52		
Idolatry (*cont.*)	1	=	[too fragmentary]
	2–3a	=	Deut 16:22 [v]
			+ Lev 26:16 [v, *I]
Use of Animals for Sacrifice and Work	3b–5a	=	Deut 17:1 [vo (?), *I]
	5b	=	[fc]
	6–7a	=	Lev 22:28 [v]
			+ Deut 22:6b [vo (?)]
	7b–9a	=	Deut 15:19 [v, *I]
	9b–12a	=	Deut 15:20 [v] + Deut 15:21 [v] +Deut 15:22 [vo] + Deut 15:23 [vo, *I (bis)]
	12b–13a	=	Deut 25:4 [v]
			+ Deut 22:10 [v]
	13b–20a	=	[fc, I (7x)]
	20b–21a	=	Lev 4:25b [pq]
	21b	=	Lev 4:26a [pq]
	Column 53		
Eating Clean Meat in the Cities of the Land	1	=	[too fragmentary]
	2–3a	=	Deut 12:20b [v]
	3b–4a	=	Deut 12:21b [vo, *I]
	4b–6a	=	Deut 12:22b [vo] + Deut 12:23a [v] + Deut 12:24 [vo]
	6b–8	=	Deut 12:23b [vo]+ Deut 12:25 [vo, *I, -I]
Command to Bring Offerings to Chosen Place	9–10	=	Deut 12:26 [vo]
			+ Deut 12:11 [p, *I (bis)]
Laws Concerning Vows	11–12	=	Deut 23:22 [v]
			+ Deut 23:23 [v, *I]
	13–14a	=	Deut 23:24 [vo]
	14b–16a	=	Num 30:3 [vo, *I]
	16b–19a	=	Num 30:4 [vo]
			+ Num 30:5 [vo, *I]
	19b–21	=	Num 30:6 [vo, *I]
	Column 54		
Laws Concerning Vows (*cont.*)	1	=	[too fragmentary]
	2–3a	=	Num 30:14 [v]
	3b	=	Num 30:13a [vo]
			+ Num 30:13b [v, *I]
	4–5a	=	Num 30:10 [v]
			+ Num 30:3b [pq]
			(or Num 30:10 [vo] ?)
The False Prophet or Seer	5b–7	=	Deut 13:1 [vo, *I]

Column 54 (*cont.*)

The False Prophet or Seer (*cont.*)	8–9a	=	Deut 13:2 [v]
	9b–10a	=	Deut 13:3 [vo]
	10b–13a	=	Deut 13:4 [vo, *I, -I]
	13b–15a	=	Deut 13:5 [vo, -I]
	15b–18	=	Deut 13:6 [vo, *I (bis), -I]
	19–21	=	Deut 13:7 [vo]

Column 55

| Fragmentary Portion | 1 | = | [too fragmentary] |

A City Led into Idolatry	2–3a	=	Deut 13:13 [vo, *I]
	3b–4	=	Deut 13:14 [vo]
	5–6a	=	Deut 13:15 [vo]
	6b–8a	=	Deut 13:16 [vo]
	8b–10a	=	Deut 13:17 [v, -I]
	10b–12	=	Deut 13:18 [v, *I]
	13–14	=	Deut 13:19 [vo, *I, -I]

Individual Idol Worshipers	15–17a	=	Deut 17:2 [v, *I]
	17b–18	=	Deut 17:3 [v, *I]
	18b–20a	=	Deut 17:4 [vo]
	20b–21	=	Deut 17:5 [vo]

Column 56

Authority of the Priestly Torah	1–2	=	Deut 17:9 [vo]
	3–6a	=	Deut 17:10 [vo, *I]
	6b–8a	=	Deut 17:11 [vo]

| Disrespect for Priestly Authority | 8b–10a | = | Deut 17:12 [vo, *I] |
| | 10b–11 | = | Deut 17:13 [vo] |

| The King's Parentage | 12–13 | = | Deut 17:14 [*I] |
| | 14–15a | = | Deut 17:15 [vo, *I] |

| Restriction on Return to Egypt | 15b–18 | = | Deut 17:16 [vo, *I] |

| Prohibition of King's Polygamy | 18b–19 | = | Deut 17:17 [vo, *I |

| King Commanded to Copy Law | 20–21 | = | Deut 17:18 [vo] |

Column 57

| Session, Conscription, and Appointment | 1–5a | = | midrashic composition of Deut 17:18, 1 Sam 8:11, Lev 27:3, and Deut 1:15 // Exod 18:21; cf. also Num 1:3, 1 Sam 8:12, and 1 Sam 22:7 |

	Column 57 (*cont.*)	
The Body Guard	5b–11a =	midrashic composition of 1 Sam 8:16, 2 Sam 17:1, Num 31:4, Num 31:5, 1 Kngs 10:26, Exod 18:21, Exod 18:25, Cant 3:7–8, and 2 Kngs 11:8; cf. also 2 Sam 11, 2 Sam 12:1–12, 1 Sam 15:8, 1 Kngs 20:13–21, 1 Sam 24:1–7, 1 Sam 26:6–12, 2 Kngs 14:1–14, Jer 34:8, Jer 38:23, Ezek 21:28, Ezek 21:29, and Psalm 10:2
The Royal Council	11b–15a =	midrashic composition of Num 1:44, 2 Chr 19:8, and Deut 17:9, 20
The Queen	15b–19a =	midrashic composition of 1 Sam 8:13, 1 Kngs 11:1–2, Lev 21:13–14 (versional), Lev 18:18, and Deut 17:7; cf. also Deut 7:3, Ezek 9:12, Neh 10:31, Neh 13:25, and Ezek 26:5–6
The King as Judge	19b–21 =	midrashic composition of 1 Sam 8:5, Deut 16:18–19, 1 Sam 8:14, and Micah 2:2; cf. also Micah 3:2, Prov 19:14, and Jer 34:8
	Column 58	
Fragmentary Portion	1–2 =	[too fragmentary]
The Enemy Raid—1/10 of Army Mustered	3–6a =	midrashic composition of Judges 20:9–10, 2 Sam 22:9–10, 1 Chr 14:8, 1 Chr 27:1–4; cf. also 2 Sam 23:13 and 1 Chr 14:10, 14
A Great Army—1/5 of Army to War	6b–7a =	midrashic composition of Jos 1:4 and Jos 10:1–7; cf. also Deut 2:21, Jos 11:4, Joel 2:2, 9, and 2 Chr 32:4
A King, Horses and Great Army— 1/3 of Army to War	7b–9 =	midrashic composition of Deut 20:1, 2 Sam 18:2, 1 Sam 11:11, Judges 9:43, Judges

A King, Horses and Great Army— 1/3 of Army to War (*cont.*)	**Column 58** (*cont.*) 7:16, 2 Kngs 11:4–6, Deut 19:3, 2 Kngs 5:2 and 1 Sam 30:23; cf. also 2 Kngs 6:23, 1 Sam 7:13, and 2 Kngs 2:32	
The Battle in Danger of Being Lost	10–11a =	midrashic composition of 2 Sam 10:9–13, Zech 14:2, 2 Sam 19:41 and 1 Sam 30:24–5
The Division of Booty	11b–15a =	midrashic composition of Deut 17:17, Num 31:27–30, 1 Sam 30:24–5, 1 Sam 8:10, Gen 14:20; cf. also Judges 8:24–5 and 1 Sam 30:20
Rules for Large-Scale Combat	15b–17 =	midrashic composition of Deut 23:10. and Deut 23:14
Command to Seek God's Oracle	18–21 =	midrashic composition of Num 27:21, 2 Chr 26:5, and 2 Chr 24:20
Curses on a Disobedient People	**Column 59** 1 =	[too fragmentary]
	2 =	Deut 28:64a [p] + Deut 28:37a [v] + 1 Kngs 12:11a [v] (// 2 Chr 10:11)
	3 =	Deut 28:48b [v] + Deut 4:28a [v] + Psalm 135:15a [v] (// Psalm 105:4)
	4a =	Lev 26:31 [pq] + Jer 25:9 [v]
	4b–5a =	Lev 26:33b [pq]
	5b–6a =	Exod 2:23b [pq] + 1 Kngs 12:11a [v]
	6b–7a =	Zech 7:13b [v] + Jer 11:11b [pq] + Jer 21:11b [v] (// Jer 26:3b; Deut 28:20b) + Deut 31:18 [v] (// Ezek 39:23b; Ezek 39:24b) [I (bis)]
	7b–8 =	Ezek 34:8b [pq] + 2 Kngs 21:14b [v] + Jer 44:3a [v] + Jer 31:32b [v, I]
	9–10 =	Lev 26:43b [vo (?)] + Hos 5:15b [pq] + Hos 3:5a [v] + Deut 30:2b [v] (// Deut 4:29b) + Deut 17:19b [v, I, *I]
	11–12 =	Judges 2:18b [v] + Jer 15:21b

		Column 59 (*cont.*)
Curses on a Disobedient People (*cont.*)		[v] + Deut 31:21b [pq] + Zech 10:8b [pq] + Deut 28:63a [pq, *I (bis)]
Curses on a Disobedient King	13a =	Lev 26:12 [v, I]
	13b–14a =	Num 15:39b [p, *I]
	14b–15 =	Jer 33:17 [p] + Jer 33:18b [v] + 2 Chr 7:18b [p, I]
Blessings on an Obedient King	16–18a =	1 Kngs 6:12 [pq] + Deut 6:18a [p] + 1 Kngs 9:5 [pq, *I, I]
	18b–19a =	Judges 2:18b [p] + Jer 42:30b [p, I]
	19b–20a =	Deut 28:7 [pq] + Deut 15:6b [pq, *I]
	20b–21 =	Deut 28:13a [vd] + Deut 17:20b [v, *I]
		Column 60
Fragmentary Portion	1 =	[too fragmentary]
Priestly Portions	2–5 =	midrashic composition of Deut 18:1 ?, Num 18:11, Lev 27:26, Exod 13:12, Num 18:8, Lev 19:24, Num 31:41, and Num 31:28–9 [I]
Levitical Portions	6–9a =	midrashic composition of Deut 18:3, Num 31:30, Neh 10:38, Neh 13:5, Num 18:21, and 2 Chr 31:5 [I]
Postscript: Priestly Portions	9b–10a =	Num 31:30 [m, *I]
Reasons for Portions	10b–11 =	Deut 18:5 [vo, *I]
The Rustic Levite	12–14a =	Deut 18:6 [vo, *I]
	14b–15 =	Deut 18:7 [vo] + Deut 18:8 [vo, *I]
Prohibition of Heathen Divination	16–17a =	Deut 18:9 [vo, *I]
	17b–18a =	Deut 18:10 [v]
	18b–19a =	Deut 18:11 [vo]
	19b–20 =	Deut 18:12 [vo, *I]
	21a =	Deut 18:13 [v, -I]
	21b =	Deut 18:14a [v + (?)]

	Column 61		
The False Prophet	1–2a	=	Deut 18:20b [vo, *I]
	2b–3a	=	Deut 18:21 [v, -I]
	3b–5	=	Deut 18:22 [vo, *I, -I]
The False Witness	6–7a	=	Deut 19:15 [vo]
	7b–8a	=	Deut 19:16 [v]
	8b–9a	=	Deut 19:17 [vo, *I]
	9b–10a	=	Deut 19:18 [vo]
	10b	=	Deut 19:19 [vo]
	11a	=	Deut 19:20 [vo]
	11b–12a	=	Deut 19:21 [vo]
Going to War	12b–14a	=	Deut 20:1 [v, *I]
	14b–15a	=	Deut 20:2 [v]
	15b	=	Deut 20:3a [v]
	Column 62		
Fragmentary Portion	1–2	=	[too fragmentary]
Preparations for War	3–4a	=	Deut 20:8b [vo]
	4b–5a	=	Deut 20:9 [vo]
The Conquest of a Distant City	5b–6a	=	Deut 20:10 [v]
	6b–8a	=	Deut 20:11 [v]
	8b–9a	=	Deut 20:12 [v]
	9b	=	Deut 20:13 [vo, *I]
	9c–11a	=	Deut 20:14 [v, *I]
	11b–13a	=	Deut 20:15 [vo]
The Conquest of a Nearby City	13b–14a	=	Deut 20:16 [vo, *I]
	14b–15a	=	Deut 20:17 [vo, *I]
	15b–16	=	Deut 20:18a [vo]
	Column 63		
Expiation for an Unknown Murderer	1	=	too fragmentary
	2	=	Deut 21:4b [vo]
	3–4a	=	Deut 21:5 [vo, *I]
	4b–5a	=	Deut 21:6 [vo]
	5b–6a	=	Deut 21:7 [v]
	6b–7a	=	Deut 21:8 [v, -I]
	7b–8	=	Deut 21:9 [vo, -I]
Blank Line	9	=	blank
The Beautiful Captive	10	=	Deut 21:10 [vo, *I]
	11	=	Deut 21:11 [vo]
	12a	=	Deut 21:12 [vo]
	12b–14a	=	Deut 21:13 [vo]

	Column 63 (*cont.*)		
The Beautiful Captive (*cont.*)	14b–15	=	[fc]
	Column 64		
The Rebellious Child	1	=	[too fragmentary]
	2–3a	=	Deut 21:18 [v]
	3b–4a	=	Deut 21:19 [v]
	4b–5a	=	Deut 21:21 [v]
	5b–6a	=	Deut 21:21 [vo]
The Sin Worthy of the Most Shameful Death	6b–13a	=	midrashic composition of Lev 19:16 + 2 Kngs 8:12 + Deut 17:6–7 + Deut 21:22a + Exod 22:27 + Jer 26:11, 16 + Deut 21:23 [*I]
Lost Livestock	13b–14a	=	Deut 22:1 [vo]
	14b–15	=	Deut 22:2a [v]
	Column 65		
Prohibition on Taking Mother Bird with her Young	2–4a	=	Deut 22:6 [vo]
	4b–5a	=	Deut 22:7 [v]
Command to Build a Parapet with a New House	5b–7a	=	Deut 22:8 [vo]
The Questionable Virgin	7b–9a	=	Deut 22:13 [vo] + Deut 22:14 [vo]
	9b–10a	=	Deut 22:15 [vo]
	10b–11a	=	Deut 22:16 [vo]
	11b–13a	=	Deut 22:17 [vo]
	13b–14a	=	Deut 22:18 [vo]
	14b–15	=	Deut 22:19a [v]
	Column 66		
Rape of a Compliant Espoused Woman	1–4a	=	Deut 22:24 [vo]
Rape of an Unwilling Espoused Woman	4b–5	=	Deut 22:25 [vo]
	6–7a	=	Deut 22:26 [vo]
	7b–8a	=	Deut 22:27 [vo]
The Rape of a Seduced Woman	8b–10a	=	Exod 22:15a [v] + Deut 22:28 [v + fc]
	10b–11a	=	Deut 22:29 [v]
Illicit and Incestuous Marriages	11b–12a	=	Deut 23:1 [v]
	12b–13	=	midrash of Deut 23:1 + Lev 20:21 + Lev 20:17

Illicit and Incestuous Marriages (*cont.*)

Column 66 (*cont.*)

14a	=	midrash of Deut 23:1 + Lev 20:7 + Lev 20:13
14b–15a	=	midrash of Deut 23:1 + Lev 20:19 + Lev 20:14; cf. also Lev 18:12–13, 17
15b–17a	=	midrash of Deut 23:1 + Lev 18:13 + Lev 20:13
17b	=	[too fragmentary]

Part Two: The Hebrew Bible in the Temple Scroll

Presented here is an analysis of which portions of the Hebrew Bible appear in the TS, and of how the scroll has used them. The left column indicates the book and verse of the Bible. The right column tells where in the TS the verse of the Bible appears, and the method of its use.

Genesis	TS	Exod (cont.)	TS
14:20	58:11b–15 [me]	29:2	15:3b [pq]
		29:2–3	15:א3 [p]
Exodus		29:11a	16:01 [v]
		29:12	16:16 [vr]
12:2	14:9b–10a [pq]	29:12a	16:02b [v]
12:8	17:8b [v]	29:12b	16:03 [v]
12:11a	43:5b [p (?)]	29:13b	16:6–8a [p]
12:14	17:3 [v]	29:14	16:10b–11 [vr]
12:14a	27:5 [v]	29:14a	26:8b–9a [v]
13:12	60:2–5 [me]	29:15	15:3b [p]
18:21	57:5b–11a [me]	29:16b	23:13 [v]
18:25	57:5b–11a [me]	29:19–20a	26:10b–11a [v]
19:10	49:16b–17 [m]	29:20a	16:2 [v (?)]
19:10	50:13b–14a [m]	29:20b	16:3 [v]
19:10b–11a	49:18–19a [m]	29:21a	16:3 [v]
22:15	66:8b–10a [v (phrase)]	29:21b	16:4–5 [v]
22:27	64:6b–13a [me]	29:21–22	15:11 [pq]
25:10	7:8 [p (?)]	29:23	15:א3 [p (?)]
25:17	3:9 [p (?)]	29:24b	15:12b [vr]
25:18	7:10b [p (?)]	29:25b	15:13a [vr]
25:19	7:11 [p (?)]		16:8–10a [vr]
25:20	7:12 [p (?)]		22:04 [vr]
25:21	7:9 [p (?)]	29:34	43:10b–12a [pq]
25:23	8:5 [v (?)]	29:35	15:14 [p]
25:23–24	8:6 [v (?)]	29:35b	15:3b [p (?)]
25:29	3:12 [p (?)]	30:12b	39:8b–9 [v]
25:31	9:2 [v]	30:13b	39:8b–9 [v (phrase)]
25:32a	9:3 [p (?)]		39:10–11a [v]
25:32b–33	9:4 [p (?)]	30:14b	17:8a [v]
25:37	9:12 [p]		39:10–11a [v]
25:38–39	9:11 [p]	30:16b	39:8b–9 [v (phrase)]
26:31	7:13–14 [pq]	30:27	3:13b [p (?)]
27:21b	9:13 [p]	31:9	3:14 [p (?)]
28:28	29:6b–7 [pq]	34:8b	59:7b–8 [pq]
28:41b	35:6–7a	34:10b	2:1 [v]
28:42	31:12a [p]	34:11b	2:2–4a [vo]
28:43	35:6–7 [pq]	34:12	2:4b–5a [vo]

Exod (cont.)	TS	Lev (cont.)	TS
34:13	2:5–8a [vo]	4:25b	52:20b–21a [pq]
34:14	2:11b–12a [vo]	4:26a	23:14b [v]
34:15	2:12b–13a [vo]		52:21b [pq]
34:16	2:13b–15 [vo]	5:8	23:11a [pq]
35:14	3:13b [p (?)]	6:9	20:11b–12 [vr]
35:16	3:15 [p (?)]	7:8	13:13b–14a [pq (?)]
37:1	7:8 [p (?)]	7:10a	20:10a [pq]
40:5	9:12 [p (?)]	7:15	43:4–5a [pq]
40:10	35:8b–9 [p]	7:31b	20:15b–16a [pq]
40:24	9:13 [v (?)]	7:31b–32a	22:8 [pq]
		7:32a	20:15b–16a [pq]
Leviticus		7:32–33	21:02 [pq]
		8:3	15:א3 [pq]
1:5b	34:8a [v]	8:16	16:6–8a [vr]
	34:13b–14a [v]	8:18	15:3b [pq]
1:6	34:8b–10a [p]	8:22	15:3b [pq]
1:9a	34:10a–11a [p]	8:26	15:א3 [p (?)]
1:9b	34:14b [v]		15:9b–10 [v]
1:12b	34:11b–12a [vd]	8:33b	15:3b [pq (?)]
2:2b	20:10b–11a [pq]	9:24	17:2 [p]
2:11	20:11b–12 [p]	10:14b	37:5 [v]
2:13	20:13–14a [pq]	10:17b	22:02 [pq (?)]
2:13a	34:10b [p]	11:21	48:4b–5a [vo]
3:2	22:5 [vr]	11:22	48:3–4a [vo]
3:9b	15:6b [v (?)]	11:23	51:4–5a [pq]
	15:8a [v]	11:29a	50:20–21 [pq]
	20:5 [v]	11:29b	50:20–21 [vr]
	20:6–7 [vr]	11:31b	50:20–21 [pq]
3:10	15:7 [v]		51:1b–3a [v]
	16:8–10a [v]	11:32a	49:16a [m]
3:10b	15:8b [v]	11:33	49:8b–9 [pq]
	20:6–7a [vr]		50:17b–19a [m]
3:11	20:7b–9a [pq]	11:34	49:7b–8a [m]
3:14b–16	23:14b–17 [vr]	11:35b	51:1b–3a [v]
3:17	21:9 [v]	11:43a	51:8b–10 [v]
	39:8b–9 [pq]	11:43b	50:1b–3a [v]
3:17a	22:14 [v]		51:6b–7a
4:11b	16:13 [vr]	14:12	45:18b [h]
4:12	16:12 [p]	15:13	45:15–16a [h]
4:15a	15:18 [v]	15:18	45:11–12a [h]
4:19	16:17b–18 [v]	15:31	51:5b–6a
4:20b	16:15b [v]	16:8a	26:3 [v]
	26:10a [v]	16:8b	26:4 [v]
4:21	16:17b–18 [v]	16:15a	16:14b [pq]
4:21b	26:9b [v]		26:5 [v]
4:24	16:14a [v]	16:15b	26:6–7a [v]
4:25	23:12 [v]	16:21	26:11b–13a [vo (?)]

Lev (*cont.*)	TS	Lev (*cont.*)	TS
16:22a	26:13b [v]	23:27	21:10b–11a [v]
16:24	27:3–4a [p]	23:29	25:11b–12a [vd]
16:25	26:7b–8a [pq]	23:29–30	27:6b–8a [vr]
16:32b	15:15–16 [v]	23:31	27:4b–5a [v]
16:33	26:7b–8a [vr]		27:6a [vr]
16:33b	15:17 [vr]	23:31a	27:9–10a [vr]
	16:14b [vr]	23:32	27:6a [v]
	18:7 [vr]	23:32a	27:8b [v]
	26:9b [vr]	23:34b	27:10b [vo (?)]
18:13	66:15b–17a [m]	23:37b	29:4b [pq]
18:18	57:15b–19a [me]	23:38b	29:5–6a [pq]
19:9b	26:5 [v]	24:3	9:14 [v]
19:16	64:6b–13a [me]	24:4	8:13 [p]
20:13	66:14a [m]	24:5	8:8 [v (?)]
	66:15b–17a [m]	24:6–7a	8:9 [p]
20:14	66:14b–15a [m]	24:7	8:10 [v]
20:17	66:12b–13 [m]		8:12 [p]
	66:14a [m]	24:9	8:13 [p]
20:19	66:14b–15a [m]	26:1a	51:21 [pq]
20:21	66:12b–13 [m]	26:1b	52:2–3a [v]
20:25b	51:8b–10 [v]	26:12	59:13a [v]
21:7a	51:3b [v]	26:31	59:4a [pq]
	51:4–5a [v]	26:33	59:4b–5a [pq]
21:7b	16:4–5 [v]	26:43b	59:9–10 [vo (?)]
21:10a	15:15–16 [v]	27:3	57:1–5a [me]
21:11	16:4–5 [v]	27:26	60:2–5 [me]
21:13b	35:7b–8a [v]	27:30b	43:15b–17 [v]
21:13–14	57:15b–19a [me]		
21:16a	35:7b–8a [v]	**Numbers**	
22:28	52:6a [v]		
23:5	17:6 [vr]	1:44	57:11b–15a [me]
23:6	17:10–12a [vr]	1:52	57:1–5a [me]
23:7	17:10–12a [vr]	4:20	46:10–11a [m]
23:8	17:12b–14a [v]	5:2	45:17b–18a [h]
23:12a	18:9b–10a [pq]	5:2b	46:18 [pq]
23:14b	18:8–9a [pq]	7:15	23:6 [v]
	25:7b–8 [v]	7:87b	23:4 [vd]
23:15	18:10b–11 [v]	15:4–5a	20:9b [pq]
	19:11–13 [v]	15:4b–5a	18:5–6 [v]
23:15–17a	21:12–14 [v]		19:4–5 [v]
23:16	18:12–13a [vr]	15:5	14:5–6 [vr]
23:17	18:13b–15 [vr]	15:6b	14:15 [vr]
23:20a	19:4–5 [v]	15:6–7a	20:02 [pq (?)]
	19:12a [v (phrase)]	15:7a	14:16–17 [v]
23:21	19:7b–9a [v]	15:9	14:14 [pq]
23:24a	25:2–3 [v]	15:9b	14:2–3 [vr]

Num (*cont.*)	TS	Num (*cont.*)	TS
15:10	14:14 [pq]	28:27b	18:2 [v (?)]
	22:03 [pq]	28:27b–28a	20:03–04 [vr]
15:13b	14:7–8 [v]	28:28	19:13 [v (phrase)]
15:24	18:4 [v (?)]	28:30	18:4 [v]
15:25	18:8–9a [v]	28:30b	20:03–04 [pq]
15:25a	27:2 [v]	29:1a	25:9–10a [vr]
15:39b	59:13b–14a [p]	29:1b	14:10b–11 [v]
18:8	60:2–5 [me]	29:2	14:12 [vr]
18:11	60:2–5 [me]	29:2–6	15:1b–2 [pq]
18:17b	22:6 [vr]	29:5a	25:5b–6a [vd]
18:19	20:13–14a [vr]	29:5b	14:10b–11 [pq]
18:21	60:6–9a [me]	29:6	15:9a [v]
19:13b	50:7b–8a [pq]		16:8b–10a [v]
19:14	49:5–7a [m]		18:5–6 [v]
	50:11b–12a		23:5 [v]
19:14b	49:16b–17 [p]		25:6b–7a [v]
	50:13a [m]	29:6a	14:14 [v (?)]
19:15	49:9b–10 [pq]		28:4–5a [v]
19:16	50:4b–7a [h]	29:6b	28:5b–6a [vr]
19:18	49:14 [p]	29:7a	27:8b [v]
19:19	49:18–19a [pq]	29:8	25:12b–13a [vd]
	49:19b–20 [pq]	29:11	25:13b–15a [vd]
	50:3b–4a [pq]	29:13a	28:2a [v]
	50:14b–16a [m]	29:13b	20:2 [v (?)]
	51:4–5a [v]		22:3 [v]
19:19b	51:3b [v]	29:14	14:16–17 [vr (?)]
19:22	50:8b–9a [pq]	29:16	25:9–10a [pq]
19:22	50:12b [pq]	29:17a	28:2b–3a [vd]
19:28	48:9b–10a [vd]	29:17b	28:4–5a [v]
27:21	58:18–21 [me]	29:18a	28:5b–6a
28:3	13:10b–11a [v (?)]	29:19a	28:4–5a [v]
28:5b	13:11b–12a	29:20	28:6b–7 [vd]
28:6	13:12b–13a [vd (?)]	29:21	28:8b–9a [vr]
28:7a	13:12a [vo]	29:22a	28:8a [vo (?)]
28:7b	20:10 [pq]	29:23	28:9b–10 [vd]
28:8	13:14b–15 [v (?)]	29:24a	28:11a [v]
28:9a	13:17 [vo (?)]	29:25a	28:11a [v]
28:11a	14:7–8 [v (?)]	29:37	20:04bis–05 [vr]
28:12a	14:2–3 [vr]	29:39	29:2–3a [vr (?)]
28:13a	14:5–6 [v]	30:3	53:14b–16a [vo]
28:14b	14:7–8 [v]	30:3b	54:4–5a [v (?)]
28:19	17:12b–14a [vr]	30:4	53:16b–17a [vo]
28:20	17:14b [v]	30:5	53:17b–19a [vo]
28:22a	17:14b [v]	30:6	53:19b–21 [vo]
28:24	17:14b [v]	30:10	54:4–5a [v]
28:25b	17:15b–16 [v]	30:13	54:3b [v (phrase)]
28:26	19:9b [pq]	30:14	54:2–3a [v]

Num (*cont.*)	TS	Deut (*cont.*)	TS
31:4	57:5b–11a [me]	14:1	48:7b–9a [v]
31:5	57:5b–11a [me]	14:2a	48:10b [v]
31:19–20	49:18–19 [m]	14:3	48:6b–7a [vr]
31:20	49:19b–20 [m]	14:18	48:1 [v]
	50:16b–17a [m]	14:21a	48:5b–6a [vr (?)]
31:20–23	49:15 [m]	14:21b	48:6b–7a [v]
31:24	49:16a [m]	14:22b	43:5b [pq]
31:27–30	58:11b–15a [me]	14:23	43:3 [pq]
31:28–29	60:2–5 [me]	14:23b	43:14b–15a [h]
31:30	60:6–9a [me]	14:24a	34:12b–13a [h]
	60:9b–10a [m (?)]	14:25a	43:13b–14a [h]
31:41	60:2–5 [me]	14:26a	43:14b–15a [p]
35:34a	48:10b–11a [v]	15:6b	59:19b–20a [pq]
35:34b	51:7b–8a [v]	15:19	52:7b–9a [v]
		15:20	52:9b [vo]
Deuteronomy		15:20a	22:14 [v]
		15:21	52:9b–10a [v]
1:15	57:1–5a [me]	15:22	52:10b–11a [vo]
4:28a	59:3 [v]	15:23	52:11b–12a [vo]
6:18a	59:16–18a [p]	16:7	17:9 [pq]
7:25b	2:8b–9a [vo]	16:8a	17:15b–16 [v]
7:26	2:9b–11a [vo]	16:9	19:12b [v (phrase)]
12:1b	51:15b–16a [v]		57:19b–21 [me]
12:11	53:10b [p]	16:18	51:11–12a [vd]
12:20b	53:2–3a [v]		57:19b–21 [me]
12:21b	53:3b–4a vdo	16:19	51:12b–14a [vo]
12:22b	53:4b–5a [vo]	16:20	51:15b–16a [vo]
12:23a	53:5b [v]	16:21a	51:20b [pq]
12:23b	53:6b [vo]	16:22	52:2 [v]
12:24	53:5b–6a [vo]	16:22a	51:20b [pq]
12:25	53:7–8a [vo]	17:1	52:3b–5a [vo (?)]
12:26	53:9–10a [vo]	17:2	55:15–17a [v]
13:1	54:5b–7 [vo]	17:3	55:17b–18 [v]
13:2	54:8–9a [v]	17:4	55:18b–20a [v]
13:3	54:9b–10a [vo]	17:5	55:20b–21 [vo]
13:4	54:10b–13a [vo]	17:6	64:6b–13a [me]
13:5	54:13b–15a [vo]	17:7	64:6b–13a [me]
13:6	54:15b–18 [vo]	17:9	56:1–2 [vo]
13:7	54:19–20 [vo]	17:10	56:3–6a [vo]
13:13	55:2–3a [vo]	17:11	56:6b–8a [vo]
13:14	55:3b–4 [vo]	17:12	56:8b–10a [vo]
13:15	55:5–6a [vo]	17:13	56:10b–11 [vo]
13:16	55:6b–8a [vo]	17:14	56:12–13 [vo]
13:17	55:8b–10a [v]	17:15	56:14–15a [vo]
13:18	55:10b–12 [v]	17:16	56:15b–18a [vo]
13:19	55:13–14 [vo]	17:17	56:18b–19 [vo]

Deut (*cont.*)	TS	Deut (*cont.*)	TS
17:17 (*cont.*)	57:15b–19a [me]	20:17	62:14b–15a [vo]
	58:11b–15a [me]	20:18a	62:15b–16 [vo]
17:18	56:20–21 [vd]	21:4b	63:2 [vo]
	57:1–5a [me]	21:5	63:3–4a [vo]
17:19b	59:9–10 [v]	21:6	63:4b–5a [vo]
17:20	57:11b–15a [me]	21:7	63:5b–6a [v]
17:20b	59:20b–21 [v]	21:8	63:6b–7a [v]
18:1	60:2–5 [me]	21:9	63:7b–8 [vo]
18:3	60:6–9a [me]	21:10	63:20 [vo]
18:3a	21:03 [v]	21:11	62:11 [vo]
18:3b	20:14b–15a [vr]	21:12	63:12a [vo]
18:5	60:10b–11 [vo]	21:13	63:12b–14a [vo]
18:6	60:12–14a [vo]	21:18	64:2–3a [v]
18:7	60:14b–15 [vo]	21:19	64:3b–4a [v]
18:8	60:14b–15 [vo]	21:20	64:4b–5a [v]
18:9	60:16–17a [vo]	21:21	64:5b–6a [vo]
18:10	60:17b–18a [v]	21:22a	64:6b–13a [me]
18:11	60:18b–19 [vo]	21:22b	64:6b–13a [me]
18:12	60:19b–20 [vo]	21:23	64:6b–13a [me]
18:13	60:21a [v]	22:1	64:13b–14a [vo]
18:14a	60:21b [v]	22:2a	64:14b–15 [v]
18:20b	61:1–2a [vo]	22:6	65:2–4a [vo]
18:21	61:2b–3a [v]	22:7	65:4b–5a [v]
18:22	61:3b–5 [vo]	22:8	65:5b–7a [vo]
18:22b	51:16b–18 [vo]	22:10	52:13a [v]
19:1–2	48:11b–14a [m]	22:13	65:7b–9a [vo]
19:3	58:7b–9 [me]	22:14	65:7b–9a [vo]
19:15	61:6–7a [vo]	22:15	65:9b–10a [vo]
19:16	61:7b–8a [v]	22:16	65:10b–11a [vo]
19:17	61:8b–9a [vo]	22:17	65:11b–13a [vo]
19:18	61:9b–10a [vo]	22:18	65:13b–14a [vo]
19:19	61:10b [vo]	22:19a	65:14b–15 [v]
19:20	61:11a [vo]	22:24	66:1–4a [vo]
19:21	61:11b–12a [vo]	22:25	66:4b–5 [vo]
20:1	61:12b–14a [v]	22:26	66:6–7a [vo]
	58:7b–9 [me]	22:27	66:7b–8a [vo]
20:2	61:14b–15a [v]	22:28	66:8b–10a [v]
20:3a	61:15b [v]	22:29	66:10b–11a [v]
20:8b	62:3–4a [vo]	23:1	66:11b–12a [v]
20:9	62:4b–5a [vo]		66:12b–13 [m]
20:10	62:5b–6a [v]		66:14a [m]
20:11	62:6b–8a [v]		66:14b–15a [m]
20:12	62:8b–9a [v]		66:15b–17a [m]
20:13	62:9b [vo]	23:9	40:6 [pq]
20:14	62:9b–11a [v]	23:10	58:15b–17 [me]
20:15	62:11b–13a [vo]	23:11–12	45:7b–10 [h]
20:16	62:13b–14a [vo]	23:12	50:3b–4a [m]

Deut (*cont.*)	TS
23:12 (*cont.*)	50:14b–16a [m]
23:13–15	46:13–16a [m]
23:13a	47:2 [vr (?)]
23:14	58:15b–17 [me]
23:22	53:11–12a [v]
23:23	53:12b [v]
23:24	53:13–14a [vo]
25:4	52:12b [v]
26:14a	43:15b–17 [h]
28:7	59:19b–20a [pq]
28:13a	59:20b–21 [vd]
28:29	59:7b–8 [v]
28:37a	59:2 [v]
28:48b	59:3 [v]
28:63	59:11–12 [pq]
28:64	59:2 [v]
30:2b	59:9–10 [v]
31:18a	59:6b–7a [v]
31:21b	59:11–12 [pq]

Joshua	
1:4	58:6a–7a [me]
10:1–7	58:6a–7a [me]

Judges	
2:18b	59:11–12 [v]
	59:18b–19a [p]
7:16	58:7b–9 [me]
9:43	58:7b–9 [me]
20:9–10	58:3–6a [me]

1 Samuel	
8:5	57:19b–21 [me]
8:10	58:11b–15a [me]
8:11	57:1–5a [me]
8:13	57:15b–19a [me]
8:14	57:19b–21 [me]
8:16	57:5b–11a [me]
11:11	58:7b–9 [me]
18:1	57:1–5a [me]
30:23	58:7b–9 [me]
30:24–25	58:10–11 [me]
	58:11b–15a [me]

2 Samuel	TS
5:8b	45:12b–14 [h]
10:9–13	58:10–11 [me]
17:1	57:5b–11a [me]
18:2	58:7b–9 [me]
19:41	58:10–11 [me]
22:9–10	58:3–6a [me]

1 Kings	
6:3	4:9 [p (?)]
6:12	59:16–18a [pq]
6:20	4:13 [p (?)]
7:49	9:13 [v (?)]
9:5	59:16–19a [pq]
10:6	57:5b–11a [me]
11:1–2	57:15b–19a [me]
12:11a	59:2 [v]

2 Kings	
5:2	58:7b–9 [me]
8:12	64:6b–13a [me]
11:4–6	58:7b–9 [me]
21:14b	59:7b–8 [v]

Jeremiah	
11:11b	59:6b–7a [pq]
15:21b	59:11–12 [v]
21:11b	59:6b–7a [pq]
25:9b	59:4a [v]
26:11	64:6b–13a [me]
26:16	64:6b–13a [me]
31:32	59:7b–8 [v]
33:17	59:14b–15 [p]
38:18b	59:14b–15 [v]
42:30b	59:18b–19a
44:3a	59:7b–8 [v]

Ezekiel	
26:23b	37:14 [pq]
37:23	29:7b–8a [v]
42:14	40:1–3 [p (?)]
43:14	32:10b–11a [p]
43:20	16:03 [vr]

Ezek (cont.)	TS	Canticles	TS
44:19	40:1–3 [p (?)]	3:7–8	57:5b–11a [me]
45:19	16:17a [v]		
	23:13 [v]	**Ezra**	
48:31	39:11b–12a [pq]		
		6:3	4:10 [p (?)]
Hosea			
		Nehemiah	
3:5a	59:9–10 [v]		
5:15b	59:9–10 [pq]	10:38	60:6–9a [me]
		13:5	60:6–9a [me]
Micah			
		1 Chronicles	
2:2	57:19b–21 [me]		
		14:8	58:3–6a [me]
Zechariah		27:1–4	58:3–6a [me]
7:13b	59:6b–7a [v]	**2 Chronicles**	
10:8b	59:11–12 [pq]		
14:2	58:10–11 [me]	3:8	4:13 [p (?)]
		4:9	3:8 [p (?)]
Psalms		7:18b	59:14b–15 [p]
		24:20	58:18–21 [me]
135:15a	59:3 [v]	26:5	58:18–21 [me]

LITERATURE CITED AND ADDITIONAL BIBLIOGRAPHY

Abel, F.-M.

1949   *Les Livres des Maccabées*. Paris: J. Gabalda.

Abel, F.-M. and Starcky, J.

1961   *Les Livres des Maccabées*. Paris: Éditions du cerf.

Alexander, Philip S.

1983   "Notes on the 'Imago Mundi' of the Book of Jubilees." In *Essays in Honour of Yigael Yadin*, pp. 197–213. Edited by G. Vermes and J. Neusner. Totowa, New Jersey: Allenheld, Osmun & Co.

Allegro, John

1956   "Further Messianic References in Qumran Literature." *Journal of Biblical Literature* 75: 174–87.

1961   "An Unpublished Fragment of Essene Halakhah (4Q Ordinances)." *Journal of Semitic Studies* 6: 71–73.

1968   *Discoveries in the Judaean Desert of Jordan* V: *Qumran Cave 4 I (4Q 158–4Q 186)*. Oxford: Clarendon Press.

Altschuler, David

1982–83 "On the Classification of Judaic Laws in the Antiquities of Josephus and the Temple Scroll of Qumran." *Association for Jewish Studies Review* 7–8: 1–14.

Ammassari, A.

1981   "Lo statuto matrimoniale del re di Israel (Dt 17,17) secondo l'esegesi del
            'Rotolo del Tempio.'" *Euntes Docete* 34: 123–27.

Andreassen, Andreas

1968   "Tempel-Rullen." *Kirke og Kultur* 73: 262–67.

Avigad, Nahman and Yadin, Yigael

1956   *A Genesis Apocryphon: A Scroll From the Wilderness in Judaea.* Jerusalem:
            Magnes Press and Heikhal ha-Sefer.

Avi-Yonah, Michael

1966   *The Holy Land from the Persian to the Arab Conquest (536 B.C.–A.D. 640): A
            Historical Geography.* Grand Rapids: Baker Book House.

Baillet, M.

1955   "Fragments araméens de Qumrân 2: description de la Jérusalem nouvelle."
            Revue Biblique 62: 222–45.

1982   *Discoveries in the Judaean Desert* VII: *Qumran Grotte 4 III (4Q 482–4Q 520).*
            Oxford: Clarendon Press.

Baillet, M., Milik, J. T., and Vaux, R. de

1962   *Discoveries in the Judaean Desert of Jordan* III: *Les Petites Grottes de Qumran.*
            Oxford: Clarendon Press.

Barker, M.

1989   "The Temple Measurements and the Solar Calendar." In *Temple Scroll Studies,*
            pp. 63–66. Edited by G. J. Brooke. Sheffield: *JSOT* Press.

Barthélemy, O. P. and Milik, J. T.

1955   *Discoveries in the Judaean Desert* I: *Qumran Cave I.* Oxford: Clarendon Press.

Bartlett, John

1973   *The First and Second Books of the Maccabees.* Cambridge: Cambridge University Press.

Basser, H. W.

1982–84   "The Rabbinic Citations in Wacholder's 'The Dawn of Qumran.'" *Revue de Qumran* 11: 549–60.

Baumgarten, Joseph M.

1972a   "Does TLH in the Temple Scroll Refer to Crucifixion?" *Journal of Biblical Literature* 91: 472–81.

1972b   "The Exclusion of Netinim and Proselytes in 4Q Florilegium." *Revue de Qumran* 8: 87–96.

1976a   "4Q Halakah[a] 5, the Law of Hadash, and the Pentecontad Calendar." *Journal of Jewish Studies* 27: 36–46.

1976b   "The Duodecimal Courts of Qumran, Revelation, and the Sanhedrin." *Journal of Biblical Literature* 95: 59–78.

1977   *Studies in Qumran Law.* Leiden: Brill.

1978   Review of *The Temple Scroll,* by Yigael Yadin. In *Journal of Biblical Literature* 97: 584–89.

1980   "The Pharisaic-Sadducean Controversies about Purity and the Qumran Texts." *Journal of Jewish Studies* 31: 157–70.

1982a   "Hanging and Treason in Qumran and Roman Law." *Eretz Israel* 16: 7*– 16*.

1982b   "Exclusions from the Temple: Proselytes and Agrippa I." *Journal of Jewish Studies* 33: 215–25.

1984   "Critical Notes on the Non-literal Use of Maʿăśēr/Dekatē." *Journal of Biblical Literature* 103: 245–51.

1985a   "Halakhic Polemics in New Fragments from Qumran Cave 4." In *Biblical Archaeology Today,* pp. 390–99. Edited by J. Amitai. Jerusalem: Israel Exploration Society.

1985b   "The First and Second Tithes in the Temple Scroll." In *Biblical and Related Studies Presented to Samuel Iwry,* pp. 5–15. Edited by Ann Kort and Scott Morschauer. Winona Lake: Eisenbrauns.

1987a   "The Calendars of the Book of Jubilees and the Temple Scroll." *Vetus Testamentum* 37: 71–78.

1987b   "The Laws of ʿOrlah and First Fruits in the Light of Jubilees, the Qumran Writings, and Targum Ps Jonathan." *Journal of Jewish Studies* 38: 195–202.

Baumgartner, Walter

1968   "Eine neue Qumranrolle." *Universitas* 23: 981–84.

Bean, Philip B.

1987   "A Theoretical Construct for the Temple of the Temple Scroll." M. Arch. thesis, University of Oregon.

Beattie, D. R. G.

1985a   "The Targum of Ruth—18 Years On." *Hermathena* 138: 57–61.

1985b   "The Targum of Ruth—A Sectarian Composition?" *Journal of Jewish Studies* 36: 222–29.

Beckwith, Roger

1984   "The Feast of New Wine and the Question of Fasting." *Expository Times* 95: 334–35.

Ben-Hayyim, Zeʾev

1978   "ישנים גם חדשים מן צפוני מדבר יהודה." *Leshonenu* 42: 278–93.

Benoit, P., Baillet, M., Milik, J. T., Cross, F. M., Jr., Skehan, P. W., Allegro, J. M., Strugnell, J., Starcky, J., and Hanzinger, C.-H.

1956a   "Editing the Manuscript Fragments from Qumran." *Biblical Archaeologist* 19: 75–96.

1956b   "Le travail d'édition des fragments manuscrits de Qumrân." *Revue Biblique* 63: 49–67.

Benoit, P., Milik, J. T., and Vaux, R. de

1961   *Discoveries in the Judaean Desert* II: *Les Grottes de Murabba'at.* Oxford: Clarendon Press.

Ben-Yashar, M.

1979–81   "Noch zum miqdaš ʾādām in 4Q Florilegium." *Revue de Qumran* 10: 587–88.

Bernstein, Moshe

1979   "Midrash Halakhah at Qumran? 11Q Temple 64:6–13 and Deuteronomy 21:22–23." *Gesher* 7: 145–66.

1983   "כי קללת אלהים תלוי (Deut 21:23): A Study in Early Jewish Exegesis." *Jewish Quarterly Review* 74: 21–45.

Betz, Otto

1980   "מותו של חוני-חוניו לאור מגילת המקדש מקומראן." In *Jerusalem in the Second Temple Period,* pp. 84–97. Edited by A. Oppenheimer, U. Rappaport, and M. Stern. Jerusalem: Yad Izhak Ben-Zvi / Ministry of Defense.

Beyer, Klaus

1984   *Die Aramäischen Texte vom Toten Meer.* Göttingen: Vandenhoeck & Ruprecht.

Bikerman [Bickermann], E. J.

1935   "La charte séleucide de Jerusalem." *Revues des Études Juives* 100: 4–35.

1938   *Institutions des Seleucides.* Bibliothèque Archéologique et Historique 26. Paris: Librairie Orientaliste Paul Geuthner.

1944   "The Colophon of the Greek Book of Esther." *Journal of Biblical Literature* 63: 339–62.

1946–48   "Une proclamation séleucide relative au temple de Jérusalem." *Syria* 25: 67–85.

1976   "The Septuagint as a Translation." In *Studies in Jewish and Christian History* 1: 167–200. Leiden: Brill.

Blidstein, Gerald

1974   "4Q Florilegium and Rabbinic Sources on Bastard and Proselyte." *Revue de Qumran* 8: 431–35.

Bloch, Renée

1978   "Midrash." Translated by Mary Howard Callaway. In *Approaches to Ancient Judaism: Theory and Practice,* Brown Judaic Series no. 1, pp. 29–50. Edited by William Scott Green. Missoula: Scholars Press.

Bogaard, L. van der

1982   "Le Rouleau du Temple: quelques remarques concernant les 'petits fragments.'" In *Von Kanaan bis Kerala,* pp. 285–94. Edited by W. C. Delsman, J. T. Meliz, J. R. T. M. Peters, W. H. Ph. Römer, and A. S. van der Woude. Kevelaer: Butzon and Bercker.

Bright, John

1965   *Jeremiah.* 2nd Ed. Anchor Bible vol. 21. Garden City: Doubleday & Co.

Brin, Gershon

1979   "הערות לשוניות למגילת המקדש." *Leshonenu* 43: 20–28.

1980   "המקרא במגילת המקדש." *Shnaton* 4: 182–225.

1985–87   "Concerning Some of the Uses of the Bible in the Temple Scroll." *Revue de Qumran* 12: 519–28.

Brooke, Alan E. and McLean, Norman, eds.

1911   *The Old Testament in Greek According to the Text of Codex Vaticanus, Supplemented From Other Uncial Manuscripts, with a Critical Apparatus Containing the Variants of the Chief Ancient Authorities for the Text of the*

Septuagint. Volume I. *The Octateuch.* Part III. *Numbers and Deuteronomy.* Cambridge: Cambridge University Press.

Brooke, George

1984   "The Feast of New Wine and the Question of Fasting." *The Expository Times* 95: 175–76.

1985   *Exegesis at Qumran: 4Q Florilegium in its Jewish Context.* Journal for the Study of the Old Testament Supplement Series 29. Sheffield: *JSOT* Press.

1988   "The Temple Scroll and the Archaeology of Qumran, 'Ain Feshka and Masada." *Revue de Qumran* 13: 225–38.

1989   "The Temple Scroll and the New Testament." In *Temple Scroll Studies,* pp. 181–99. Edited by G. J. Brooke. Sheffield: *JSOT* Press.

Brooten, Bernadette

1982   "Konnten Frauen in alten Judentum die Scheidung betreiben?" *Evangelische Theologie* 42: 65–80.

Broshi, Magen

1978   "Le Rouleau du Temple." *Le Monde de la Bible* 4: 70–72.

1987   "The Gigantic Dimensions of the Visionary Temple in the Temple Scroll." *Biblical Archaeology Review* 13: 36–37.

Brown, Francis, Driver, S. R., and Briggs, Charles A.

1977   *A Hebrew and English Lexicon of the Old Testament.* Oxford: Clarendon Press.

Brownlee, William

1979   *The Midrash Pesher of Habakkuk.* Society of Biblical Literature Monograph Series 24. Missoula: Scholars Press.

Bruce, F. F.

1986   Review of *The Temple Scroll,* ed. by Yigael Yadin. In *Palestine Exploration Quarterly* 118: 76.

Bunge, J. G.

1975   "Zu Geschichte und Chronologie des Untergangs der Oniaden und des Aufstiegs der Hasmonäer." *Journal for the Study of Judaism* 6: 1–46.

Burgmann, H.

1989   "11QT: The Sadducean Torah." In *Temple Scroll Studies,* pp. 257–63. Edited by G. J. Brooke. Sheffield: *JSOT* Press.

Busink, T. A.

1970–80   *Der Tempel von Jerusalem von Salamo bis Herodes.* 2 vols. Leiden: Brill.

Callaway, Philip

1982–84   "The Translation of 11Q Temple LI, 5b–10." *Revue de Qumran* 11: 585–86.

1985   Review of *The Dawn of Qumran: The Sectarian Torah and the Teacher of Righteousness,* by B. Z. Wacholder. In *Journal of the American Academy of Religion* 53: 133–34.

1985–86a   "Exegetische Erwägungen zur Tempelrolle XXIX, 7–10." *Revue de Qumran* 12: 95–104.

1985–86b   "Source Criticism of the Temple Scroll: The Purity Laws." *Revue de Qumran* 12: 213–22.

1985–86c   "'BRYH in the Temple Scroll XXIV, 8." *Revue de Qumran* 12: 269–70.

1988a   *The History of the Qumran Community: An Investigation.* Sheffield: *JSOT* Press.

1988b   "The Temple Scroll and the Canonization of Jewish Law." *Revue de Qumran* 13: 239–50.

1989   "Extending Divine Revelation: Micro-Compositional Strategies in the Temple Scroll." In *Temple Scroll Studies,* pp. 149–62. Edited by G. J. Brooke. Sheffield: *JSOT* Press.

Caquot, André

1973   "Information préliminaire sur le 'Rouleau du Temple' de Qumrân." *Bulletin de la Société Ernest-Renan* 22: 1 and 3–4.

1977–78   "Le Rouleau du Temple de Qoumrân." *Annuaire du College du France* : 577–80.

1978   "Le Rouleau du Temple de Qoumrân." *Etudes Theologiques et Religieuses* 53: 443–500.

1980   "Le Rouleau du Temple." *Le Monde de la Bible* 13: 34–35.

1987   "Rouleau du Temple." In *La Bible: écrits intertestamentaire,* pp. 61–132. Edited by A. Dupont-Sommer and L. M. Philonenko. Paris: Éditions Gallimard.

Charles, R. H.

1895   *The Ethiopic Version of the Hebrew Book of Jubilees.* Oxford: Clarendon Press.

1984   "Jubilees." Translation revised by Chaim Rabin. In *The Apocryphal Old Testament,* pp. 1–139. Edited by H. F. D. Sparks. Oxford: Clarendon Press.

Charlesworth, James H.

1984   Review of *The Dawn of Qumran: The Sectarian Torah and the Teacher of Righteousness,* by B. Z. Wacholder. In *Religious Studies Review* 10: 405.

1985   "The Date of Jubilees and of the Temple Scroll." In *SBL 1985 Seminar Papers,* pp. 193–204. Edited by Kent Richards. Atlanta: Scholars Press.

Chmiel, J.

1969   "Nowe rekopisy z Qumran." *Ruch Biblijny i Liturgiczny* 22: 302–3.

Clarke, E. G.

1984   *Targum Pseudo-Jonathan of the Pentateuch: Text and Concordance.* Hoboken, New Jersey: Ktav.

Cohen, Shaye J. D.

1987   *From the Maccabees to the Mishnah.* Philadelphia: Westminster Press.

Colella, Pasquale

1968   "Nuovi manoscritti del Mar Morto." *Revista Biblica Italiana* 16: 214–15.

Collins, John J.

1973a   "The Date and Provenance of the Testament of Moses." In *Studies on the Testament of Moses,* pp. 15–32. Edited by G. W. E. Nickelsburg. Cambridge, MA : Society of Biblical Literature.

1973b   "Some Remaining Traditio-Historical Problems in the Testament of Moses." In *Studies in the Testament of Moses,* pp. 38–43. Edited by G. W. E. Nickelsburg. Cambridge, MA : Society of Biblical Literature.

1985   Review of *The Damascus Covenant: An Interpretation of the "Damascus Document,"* by P. R. Davies. In *Journal of Biblical Literature* 104: 530–33.

Colson, F. H., trans.

1937   *Philo VII.* Loeb Classical Library. Cambridge: Harvard University Press.

Cook, Johann

1984   Review of *The Dawn of Qumran: The Sectarian Torah and the Teacher of Righteousness,* by B. Z. Wacholder. In *Bibliotheca Orientalis* 41: 708–11.

Coulet, Claude

1985   Review of *The Dawn of Qumran: The Sectarian Torah and the Teacher of Righteousness,* by B. Z. Wacholder. In *Revue des Sciences Religieuses* 59: 271.

Dancy, J. C.

1954   *A Commentary on I Maccabees*. Oxford: Basil Blackwell.

Davies, Philip R.

1977   *1QM, the War Scroll from Qumran: Its Structure and History*. Rome: Biblical Institute Press.

1982   *Qumran*. Grand Rapids: Eerdmans.

1983a   *The Damascus Covenant: An Interpretation of the "Damascus Document."* Journal for the Study of the Old Testament Supplement Series no. 25. Sheffield: *JSOT* Press.

1983b   "The Ideology of the Temple in the Damascus Document." In *Essays in Honour of Yigael Yadin*, pp. 287–302. Edited by G. Vermes and J. Neusner. Totowa, New Jersey: Allenheld, Osmun & Co.

1984   Review of *The Dawn of Qumran: The Sectarian Torah and the Teacher of Righteousness*, by B. Z. Wacholder. In *Expository Times* 95: 155–56.

1985a   "Eschatology at Qumran." *Journal of Biblical Literature* 104: 39–55.

1985b   Review of *The Dawn of Qumran: The Sectarian Torah and the Teacher of Righteousness*, by B. Z. Wacholder. In *Palestine Exploration Quarterly* 117: 79–80.

1985c   Review of *The Dawn of Qumran: The Sectarian Torah and the Teacher of Righteousness*, by B. Z. Wacholder. In *Journal for the Study of the Old Testament* 31: 128.

1987   *Behind the Essenes: History and Ideology in the Dead Sea Scrolls*. Brown Judaic Studies no. 94. Atlanta: Scholars Press.

1988   "How Not to Do Archaeology: The Story of Qumran." *Biblical Archaeologist* 51: 203–7.

1989   "The Temple Scroll and the Damascus Document." In *Temple Scroll Studies,* pp. 201–10. Edited by G. J. Brooke. Sheffield: *JSOT* Press.

Davies, W. D.

1952   *Torah in the Messianic Age and/or The Age to Come. JBL* Monograph Series 7. Philadelphia: SBL.

Deichgräber, R.

1964–66   "Fragmente einer Jubiläen-Handschrift aus Höhle 3 von Qumran." *Revue de Qumran* 5: 415–22.

Delcor, Mathias

1954   "Contribution à l'étude de la législation des sectaires de Damas et de Qumran." *Revue Biblique* 61: 533–53.

1979   "Qumran. Rouleau du Temple." In *Dictionaire de la Bible, Supplement.* Volume 9, pp. 943–50. Edited by L. Pirot, A. Roberti, H. Cazalles, and A. Feuillet. Paris: Letouzey & Ané.

1981   "Le statut du roi d'apres le Rouleau du Temple." *Henoch* 3: 47–68.

1981–82   "Explication du Rouleau du Temple de Qoumrân." *Annuaire École Pratique des Hautes Études* 90: 229–35.

1982–83   "Explication du Rouleau du Temple de Qoumrân." *Annuaire École Pratique des Hautes Études* 91: 257–64.

1983–84   "Explication du Rouleau du Temple de Qoumrân." *Annuaire École Pratique des Hautes Études* 92: 245–51.

1984   Review of *The Dawn of Qumran: The Sectarian Torah and the Teacher of Righteousness,* by B. Z. Wacholder. In *Bulletin de Littérature Ecclésiastique* 85: 81–83.

1985–87   "Réflexions sur la fête de Xylophorie dans le Rouleau du Temple et les textes parallèles." *Revue de Qumran* 12: 561–70.

1986   "Réflexions sur l'investiture sacerdotale sans onction à la fête du Nouvel An d'après le Rouleau du Temple de Qumran (XIV 15–17)." In *Hellenica et Judaica: Homâge à Valentin Nikoprowetzky,* pp. 155–64. Edited by A. Caquot, M. Hadas-Lebel, and J. Riaud. Leuven-Paris: Éditions Peeters.

1988   "La description du Temple de Salomon selon Eupolémus et le problème de ses sources." *Revue de Qumran* 13: 251–72.

1989   "Is the Temple Scroll a Source of the Herodian Temple?" In *Temple Scroll Studies,* pp. 67–89. Edited by G. J. Brooke. Sheffield: *JSOT* Press.

Delcor, Mathias and García-Martínez, Florentino

1982   *Introduccion a la literatura esenìa de Qumran.* Madrid: Ediciones Cristiandad.

Denis, Albert-Marie

1970   *Fragmenta Pseudepigraphorum Quae Supersunt Graeca.* Pseudepigrapha Veteris Testamenti Graece vol. 3. Leiden: Brill.

Dimant, Devorah

1982   "ירושלים והמקדש בחזון החיות (חנוך החבשי פה–צ) לאור השקפות כת מדבר יהודה." *Shnaton* 5–6: 177–93.

1984   "Qumran Sectarian Literature." In *Jewish Writings of the Second Temple Period,* pp. 483–550. Edited by Michael Stone. Philadelphia: Fortress Press.

1986a   Review of *The Dawn of Qumran: The Sectarian Torah and the Teacher of Righteousness,* by B. Z. Wacholder. In *Zion. A Quarterly for Research in Jewish History* 41: 246–50.

1986b   "4QFlorilegium and the Idea of the Community as Temple." In *Hellenica et Judaica: Homâge à Valentin Nikoprowetzky,* pp. 165–89. Edited by A. Caquot, M. Hadas-Lebel, and J. Riaud. Leuven-Paris: Éditions Peeters.

Dion, Paul-E.

1979   "Le 'Rouleau du Temple' et les Douze." *Science et Esprit* 31: 81–83.

Driver, G. R.

1965   *The Judaean Scrolls.* Oxford: Basil Blackwood.

Dupont-Sommer, A.

1972 "Observations nouvelles sur l'expression 'suspendu vivant sur le bois' dans le Commentaire de Nahum (4Q pNah II 8) a la lumière du Rouleau du Temple (11Q Temple Scroll LXIV, 6–13)." *Académie des Inscriptions et Belles-Lettres: Comptes Rendus des Séances:* 709–20.

Eisenman, Robert

1983 *Maccabees, Zadokites, Christians and Qumran: A New Hypothesis of Qumran Origins.* Studia Post-Biblica no 34. Leiden: Brill.

1986 *James the Just in the Habakkuk Pesher.* Leiden: Brill.

1989 "The Historical Provenance of the 'Three Nets of Belial' Allusion in the Zadokite Document and BALLᶜ/BELAᶜ." *Folia Orientalia* 25: 51–66.

Elgvin, Torleif

1985a "Tempelrollen fra Qumran." *Tidsskrift for Teologi og Kirke* 1: 1–21.

1985b "The Qumran Covenant Festival and the Temple Scroll." *Journal of Jewish Studies* 36: 103–6.

Emerton, J. A.

1987 Review of *The Temple Scroll: An Introduction, Translation, and Commentary,* by Johann Maier. In *Vetus Testamentum* 37: 242.

1988 "A Consideration of Two Recent Theories About Bethso in Josephus' Description of Jerusalem and a Passage in the Temple Scroll." In *Text and Context: Old Testament and Semitic Studies for F. C. Fensham,* pp. 93–104. Edited by W. Claasen. *JSOT* Supplemet Series 48. Sheffield: *JSOT* Press.

Falk, Zeev

1978 "מגילת המקדש והמשנה הראשונה." *Sinai* 83: 30–41.

1979 "The Temple Scroll and the Codification of Jewish Law." *Jewish Law Annual* 2: 33–44.

Farmer, William Reuben

1956   *Maccabees, Zealots and Josephus: An Inquiry into Jewish Nationalism in the Greco-Roman Period.* New York: Columbia University Press.

Finkel, Asher

1983   "The Theme of God's Presence and the Qumran Temple Scroll." In *God and His Temple: Reflections on Professor Samuel Terrien's The Elusive Presence: Toward a New Biblical Theology,* pp. 39–47. Edited by Lawrence E. Frizzell. South Orange, New Jersey: Seton Hall University.

Finkelstein, Louis

1923   "The Book of Jubilees and the Rabbinic Halaka." *Harvard Theological Review* 16: 39–61.

Fischer, B., Gribomont, J., Sparks, H. F. D., and Thiele, W., eds.

1969   *Biblia Sacra Iuxta Vulgata Versionem.* Stuttgart: Württembergische Bibelanstalt.

Fitzmyer, Joseph A.

1967   *The Aramaic Inscriptions of Sefire.* Biblia et Orientalia 19. Rome: Pontifical Biblical Institute.

1969   "A Bibliographical Aid to the Study of the Qumran Cave IV Texts 158–186." *Catholic Biblical Quarterly* 31: 59–71.

1970   "The Languages of Palestine in the First Century A.D." *Catholic Biblical Quarterly* 32: 501–31.

1971   *The Genesis Apocryphon of Qumran Cave I: A Commentary.* 2nd ed. Rome: Biblical Institute Press.

1976   "The Matthean Divorce Texts and Some New Palestinian Evidence." *Theological Studies* 37: 197–226.

1978   "Crucifixion in Ancient Palestine, Qumran Literature, and the New Testament." *Catholic Biblical Quarterly* 40: 493–513.

1984a   Review of *The Dawn of Qumran: The Sectarian Torah and the Teacher of Righteousness,* by B. Z. Wacholder. In *Theological Studies* 45: 556–58.

1984b   "The Ascension of Christ and Pentecost." *Theological Studies* 45: 409–40.

1986   Review of *The Temple Scroll,* by Yigael Yadin. In *Catholic Biblical Quarterly* 48: 547–49.

Fitzmyer, Joseph A. and Harrington, Daniel J.

1978   *A Manual of Palestinian Aramaic Texts (Second Century B.C.-Second Century A.D.).* Biblica et Orientalia 34. Rome: Pontifical Biblical Institute.

Flusser, David

1979a   Review of מגילת המקדש, ed. by Yigael Yadin. In *Numen* 26: 271–74.

1979b   Review of מגילת המקדש, ed. by Yigael Yadin. In *Immanuel* 9: 49–52.

Fohrer, Georg

1979   Review of *Die Tempelrolle vom Toten Meer,* by Johann Maier. In *Zeitschrift für die Alttestamentliche Wissenschaft* 91: 150–51.

Ford, J. Massyngberde

1976   "'Crucify him, crucify him' and the Temple Scroll." *Expository Times* 87: 275–78.

Freedman, David Noel and Mathews, K. A.

1985   *The Paleo-Leviticus Scroll (11Q paleoLev).* Contribution by R. S. Hanson. Winona Lake: Eisenbrauns.

García-Martínez, Florentino

1977   "El Rollo del Templo." *Estudios Biblicos* 36: 247–92.

1979–80   "4QpNah y la Crucifixion: Nueva hipótesis de reconstrucción de 4Q 169 3–4 i, 4–8." *Estudios Biblicos* 38: 221–35.

1983   Review of *The Damascus Covenant: An Interpretation of the "Damascus Document,"* by P. R. Davies. In *Journal for the Study of Judaism* 14: 189–94.

1984   "El Rollo del Templo y la halaká sectaria." In *Simposio Bíblíco Español,* pp. 611–22. Edited by N. F. Marcos, J. T. Barrera, and J. F. Vallina. Madrid: Editorial de la Universita Complutense.

1986a   Review of *The Temple Scroll: An Introduction, Translation, and Commentary,* by Johann Maier. In *Journal for the Study of Judaism* 17: 108–9.

1986b   Review of *The Temple Scroll: The Hidden Law of the Dead Sea Sect,* by Yigael Yadin. In *Journal for the Study of Judaism* 17: 124–25.

1986–87   "El Rollo del Templo (11Q Temple): Bibliografía Sistemática." *Revue de Qumran* 12: 425–40.

Garner, Gordon

1979   "The Temple Scroll." *Buried History* 15: 1–16.

Gevirtz, Stanley

1987   "Asher in the Blessing of Jacob." *Vetus Testamentum* 37: 154–63.

Giblet, J.

1954   "Prophétisme et attente d'un Messie-prophète dans l'ancien Judaïsme." In *L'attente du Messie,* pp. 85–130. Edited by L. Cerfaux, et al. Louvain: Desclée de Brouwer.

Ginzberg, Louis

1970   *An Unknown Jewish Sect.* 2nd ed., rev. and updated. New York: Jewish Theological Seminary of America.

Golb, Norman

1980   "The Problem of Origin and Identification of the Dead Sea Scrolls." *Proceedings of the American Philosophical Society* 124: 1–24.

1985a   "Who Hid the Dead Sea Scrolls?" *Biblical Archaeologist* 48: 68–82.

1985b   "Les manuscrits de la Mer Morte: une nouvelle approche du problème de leur origine." *Annales Économies Sociétés Civilisations* 5: 1133–49.

1987   "Who Wrote the Dead Sea Scrolls?" *The Sciences* 27: 40–49.

Goldstein, Jonathan

1976   *I Maccabees.* The Anchor Bible vol. 41. New York: Doubleday & Co.

1983   "The Date of the Book of Jubilees." *Proceedings of the American Academy of Jewish Research* 50: 63–86.

Good, Robert

1983   *The Sheep of His Pasture: A Study of the Hebrew Noun ʿAm(m) and its Semitic Cognates.* Harvard Semitic Monographs no. 29. Chico: Scholars Press.

Goodblatt, D.

1989   "The Place of the Pharisees in First Century Judaism: The State of the Debate." *Journal for the Study of Judaism* 20: 12–30.

Goranson, Stephen

1985   Review of *The Temple Scroll: The Hidden Law of the Dead Sea Sect,* by Yigael Yadin. In *Biblical Archaeologist* 48: 127.

Gordon, R. P.

1985   Review of *The Dawn of Qumran: The Sectarian Torah and the Teacher of Righteousness,* by B. Z. Wacholder. In *Vetus Testamentum* 35: 512.

Greenfield, Jonas

1969   "The Small Caves of Qumran." *Journal of the American Oriental Society* 89: 128–41.

1974   "Standard Literary Aramaic." In *Actes du Premier Congrès International de Linguistique Sémitique et Chamito-Sémitique. Paris 16–19 juillet 1969,* pp. 280–89. Edited by André Caquot and David Cohen. The Hague: Mouton.

1978   "Aramaic and its Dialects." In *Jewish Languages: Themes and Variations,* pp. 29–43. Edited by H. Paper. New York: n.p.

1988   "The Words of Levi son of Jacob in Damascus Document IV, 15–19." *Revue de Qumran* 13: 319–22.

Halperin, David

1981   "Crucifixion, the Nahum Pesher, and the Rabbinic Penalty of Strangulation." *Journal of Jewish Studies* 32: 32–46.

Hamerton-Kelly, R. G.

1970   "The Temple and the Origins of Jewish Apocalyptic." *Vetus Testamentum* 20: 1–15.

Hammond, N. G. L. and Scullard, H. H., eds.

1970   *The Oxford Classical Dictionary.* Oxford: Clarendon Press.

Hatch, Edwin and Redpath, Henry

1954   *A Concordance to the Septuagint.* 2 volumes. Graz: Akademische Druck und Verlaganstalt. Photomechanical reproduction of the 1897 Oxford Press edition.

Hengel, Martin

1977   *Crucifixion.* Translated by John Bowden. Philadelphia: Fortress Press.

1984   *Rabbinische Legende und frühpharisäische Geschichte.* Heidelberg: Carl Winter Universitätsverlag.

Hengel, M., Charlesworth, J. H., and Mendels, D.

1986   "The Polemical Character of 'On Kingship' in the Temple Scroll: An Attempt at Dating 11Q Temple." *Journal of Jewish Studies* 37: 28–38.

Horgan, Maurya P.

1979   *Pesharim: Qumran Interpretation of Biblical Books.* Catholic Biblical Quarterly Monograph Series 8. Washington: Catholic Biblical Association of America.

1986   Review of *The Damascus Covenant: An Interpretation of the "Damascus Document,"* by P. R. Davies. In *Catholic Biblical Quarterly* 48: 301–3.

Houtman, C.

1981   "Ezra and the Law: Observations on the Supposed Relation Between Ezra and the Pentateuch." *Oudtestamentische Studiën* 21: 91–115.

Howard, G. and Shelton, J. C.

1973   "The Bar-Kochba Letters and Palestinian Greek." *Israel Exploration Journal* 23: 100–1.

Huppenbauer, H. W.

1963–64   "Zur Eschatologie der Damaskusschrift." *Revue de Qumran* 4: 567–73.

Isaac, Benjamin and Oppenheimer, Aharon

1985   "The Revolt of Bar Kochba: Ideology and Modern Scholarship." *Journal of Jewish Studies* 36: 33–60.

Iwry, S.

1969   "Was there a Migration to Damascus? The Problem of שבי ישראל." *Eretz Israel* 9: 80–88.

Jacques, X.

1985   Review of *The Temple Scroll,* ed. Yigael Yadin. In *Nouvelle Revue Théologique* 107: 603–5.

Jastrow, Marcus

1982   *A Dictionary of the Targumim, Talmud Babli, Yerushalmi and Midrashic Literature.* Reprint. New York: Judaica Press.

Jellicoe, S.

1968   *The Septuagint and Modern Study.* Oxford: Oxford University Press.

Jeremias, Joachim

1969   *Jerusalem in the Time of Jesus*. Philadelphia: Fortress Press.

1967   "Μωυσῆς." In *Theological Dictionary of the New Testament*, vol. IV, pp. 848–73. Edited by Gerhard Kittel; edited and translated by Geoffrey W. Bromiley. Grand Rapids: William B. Eerdmans.

Jongeling, B.

1970a   "Publication provisoire d'un fragment provenant de la grotte 11 de Qumran (11Q Jér Nouv ar)." *Journal for the Study of Judaism* 1: 58–64.

1970b   "Note additionelle." *Journal for the Study of Judaism* 1: 185–86.

1979   "De 'Tempelrol.'" *Phoenix* 25: 84–99.

1981   "À propos de la colonne XXIII du Rouleau du Temple." *Revue de Qumran* 10: 593–95.

Kampen, John

1981   "The Temple Scroll: The Torah of Qumran?" *Proceedings of the Eastern Great Lakes Biblical Society* 1: 37–54.

Kapera, Z. J.

1989   "A Review of East European Studies on the Temple Scroll." In *Temple Scroll Studies,* pp. 275–86. Edited by G. J. Brooke. Sheffield: *JSOT* Press.

Kappler, Werner, ed.

1967   *Septuaginta. Vetus Testamentum Graecum Auctoritate Academiae Litterarum Gottingensis editum. Vol. IX Maccabaeorum libri I–IV. Fasc. 1 Maccabaeorum liber I*. Göttingen: Vandenhoeck & Ruprecht.

Kassowsky, Chaim Joshua

1956   אוצר לשון המשנה. Jerusalem: Massadah.

Kaufman, Stephen A.

1982   "The Temple Scroll and Higher Criticism." *Hebrew Union College Annual* 53: 29–43.

Kautzsch, E.

1978   *Gesenius' Hebrew Grammar.* Revised by A. E. Cowley. 2nd ed. Oxford: Clarendon Press, repr.

Kellerman, D.

1975   ".גּר" In *Theological Dictionary of the Old Testament*, pp. 439-49. Edited by G. J. Botterweck and H. Ringgren, translated by J. T. Willis. Grand Rapids: Eerdmans.

Kellerman, Ulrich

1968   "Erwägungen zum Esragesetz." *Zeitschrift für die Alttestamentliche Wissenschaft* 80: 373–85.

Keshishian, J. M.

1968   "Il più lungo manoscritto del Mar Morto." *Sapere* 59: 60–63.

Kida, Kenichi

1984   Review of *The Dawn of Qumran: The Sectarian Torah and the Teacher of Righteousness,* by B. Z. Wacholder. In *Annual of the Japanese Biblical Institute* 10: 101–4.

Kister, Menahem

1985–87 "Newly-Identified Fragments of the Book of Jubilees: Jub. 23:21–23, 30–31." *Revue de Qumran* 12: 529–36.

Kittel, Bonnie P.

1981   *The Hymns of Qumran.* SBL Dissertation Series 50. Chico: Scholars Press.

Knibb, M. A.

1986a   Review of *The Temple Scroll: An Introduction, Translation, and Commentary,* by Johann Maier. In *The Society for Old Testament Study Book List 1986:* 126.

1986b   Review of *The Temple Scroll: The Hidden Law of the Dead Sea Sect,* by Yigael Yadin. In *The Society for Old Testament Study Book List 1986:* 138–39.

1986c   Review of *The Temple Scroll,* ed. by Yigael Yadin. In *The Society for Old Testament Study Book List 1986:* 139.

1987   *The Qumran Community.* Cambridge Commentaries on Writings of the Jewish and Christian World 200 B.C. to A.D. 200. New York: Cambridge University Press.

Kuhn, Heinz-Wolfgang

1975   "Jesus als Gekreuzigter in der frühchristlichen Verkündigung bis zur Mitte des 2. Jahrhunderts." *Zeitschrift für Theologie und Kirche* 72: 1–46.

Kuhn, Karl Georg

1960   *Konkordanz zu den Qumrantexten.* Göttingen: Vandenhoeck & Ruprecht.

1968   "προσήλυτος." In *Theological Dictionary of the New Testament,* vol. VI, pp. 727–44. Edited by Gerhard Friedrich; edited and translated by Geoffrey W. Bromiley. Grand Rapids: William B. Eerdmans.

Kutscher, Eduard Yechezkiel

1957   "The Language of the Genesis Apocryphon." In *Scripta Hierosolymitana IV: Aspects of the Dead Sea Scrolls,* pp. 1–35. Edited by Chaim Rabin and Yigael Yadin. Jerusalem: Magnes Press.

1962   "לשונן של האיגרות העבריות והארמיות של בר כוסבה ובני דורו." *Leshonenu* 26: 7–23.

1964   "Mishnisches Hebräisch." *Rocznik Orientalistyczny* 28: 36–48.

1977   "לשון חז"ל." In *Eduard Yechezkiel Kutscher: Hebrew and Aramaic Studies,* pp. 73–87. Edited by Z. Ben–Hayyim, A. Dotan and G. Sarfatti. Jerusalem: Magnes Press.

1982   *A History of the Hebrew Language.* Edited by Raphael Kutscher. Jerusalem: Magnes Press.

Lacocoque, Andre

1979   *The Book of Daniel.* Atlanta: John Knox.

Lambin, Thomas

1978   *Introduction to Classical Ethiopic (Ge ʿez).* Missoula: Scholars Press.

Landau, Y. H.

1966   "A Greek Inscription Found Near Hefzibah." *Israel Exploration Journal* 16: 54–70.

Laperrousaz, E. M.

1968   "Presentation, a Jerusalem, du plus long des rouleaux—actuellement connus—provenant du Qumrân." *Revue de l'Histoire des Religions* 174: 113–15.

1981   "Note à propos de la datation du Rouleau du Temple et, plus généralement, des manuscrits de la Mer Morte." *Revue de Qumran* 10: 447–52.

1989   "Does the Temple Scroll Date from the First or the Second Century BCE?" In *Temple Scroll Studies,* pp. 91–97. Edited by G. J. Brooke. Sheffield: *JSOT* Press.

Lapide, Paul

1978   "Die Nachbarn der Urgemeinde." *Lutherische Monatshefte* 17: 273–75.

Leaney, A. R. C.

1984   Review of *The Dawn of Qumran: The Sectarian Torah and the Teacher of Righteousness,* by B. Z. Wacholder. In *The Journal of Theological Studies* NS 35: 493–97.

1985   Review of *The Damascus Covenant: An Interpretation of the "Damascus Document,"* by P. R. Davies. In *Journal of Theological Studies* 36: 195–98.

Le Déaut, R.

1967–68   "Une citation de Lévitique 26,45 dans le Document de Damas I, 4; VI, 2." *Revue de Qumran* 6: 289–96.

Lehman, Manfred

1978   "The Temple Scroll as a Source of Sectarian Halakhah." *Revue de Qumran* 9: 579–87.

1979–80   "מגילת המקדש כמקור להלכה כיתתית." *Beth Mikra* 26: 302–9.

1988   "אשת יפת תואר והלכות אחרות במגילת המקדש." *Beth Mikra* 34: 313–16.

1989   "The Beautiful War Bride (יפת תאר) and Other Halakhoth in the Temple Scroll." In *Temple Scroll Studies,* pp. 265–71. Edited by G. J. Brooke. Sheffield: *JSOT* Press.

Levine, Baruch

1978   "The Temple Scroll: Aspects of its Historical Provenance and Literary Character." *Bulletin of the American Schools of Oriental Research* 232: 5–23.

1980   "Preliminary Reflections on 'The Temple Scroll.'" Foreword to *A History of the Mishnaic Law of Holy Things Part Six: The Mishnaic System of Sacrifice and Sanctuary,* by Jacob Neusner. Leiden: Brill.

Levine, Étan

1973   *The Aramaic Version of Ruth.* Analecta Biblica 58. Rome: Biblical Institute Press.

Licht, Jacob

1961   "Taxo, or the Apocalyptic Doctrine of Vengeance." *Journal of Jewish Studies* 12: 95–103.

1979   "An Ideal Town Plan From Qumran—The Description of the New Jerusalem."
            Israel Exploration Journal 29: 45–59.

Liddell, H. G. and Scott, R.

1968   *A Greek-English Lexicon.* Revised and augmented by H. S. Jones with a
            supplement. Edited by E. A. Barber. 9th edition. Oxford: Clarendon Press.

Lifshitz, B.

1961   "The Greek Documents from Naḥal Ṣeelim and Naḥal Mishmar." *Israel
            Exploration Journal* 11:53–62.

1962   "Papyrus grecs du désert de Juda." *Aegyptus* 42: 240–56.

Liver, J.

1963   "The Half-Shekel Offering in Biblical and Post-Biblical Literature." *Harvard
            Theological Review* 56: 173–98.

Lübbe, J.

1985–87   "A Reinterpretation of 4QTestimonia." *Revue de Qumran* 12: 187–98.

Luria, Ben-Zion

1978   "הערות למגילת המקדש." *Beth Mikra* 24: 370–86.

Lust, J.

1984   Review of *The Dawn of Qumran: The Sectarian Torah and the Teacher of
            Righteousness,* by B. Z. Wacholder. In *Ephemerides Theologicae Lovanienses*
            60: 152–53.

1986   Review of *The Temple Scroll: An Introduction, Translation, and Commentary,*
            by Johann Maier. In *Ephemerides Theologicae Lovanienses* 62: 190.

Macho, Alejandro Díez

1978   *Neophyti I. Targum Palestinense Ms de la Biblioteca Vaticana. Tomo V:
            Deuteronomio.* Madrid: Consejo Superior de Investigaciònes Científicas.

Magen, I.

1984   "המסיבה' או 'בית המסיבה' של המקדש'." *Eretz Israel* 17: 226–35.

Maier, Johann

1978a   *Die Tempelrolle vom Totem Meer*. Munich: Ernst Reinhardt, 1978.

1978b   "Die sog. Tempelrolle von Qumran." *Zeitschrift für die Alttestamentliche Wissenschaft* 90: 152–54.

1979   "Aspekte der Kultfrömmigkeit im Lichte der Tempelrolle von Qumran." In *Judische Liturgie: Geschichte-Struktur-Wesen*, pp. 33–46. Freiburg: Herder.

1980   "Die Hofanlagen im Tempel-Entwurf des Ezechiel im Licht der 'Tempelrolle' von Qumran." In *Prophecy: Essays Presented to Georg Fohrer on his Sixty-Fifth Birthday*, pp. 55–67. Edited by J. A. Emerton. Berlin: de Gruyter.

1985   *The Temple Scroll*. Translated by John White. Sheffield: *JSOT* Press.

1989   "The Architectural History of the Temple in Jerusalem in the Light of the Temple Scroll." In *Temple Scroll Studies*, pp. 23–62. Edited by G. J. Brooke. Sheffield: *JSOT* Press.

Manns, P. Frédéric

1978   "Nouveautes in Librairie au sujet de Qumran." *La Terre Saint :* 74–75.

Marcus, R., trans.

1976   *Josephus* VII: *Jewish Antiquities* XII–XIV. Loeb Classical Library no. 365. Cambridge, MA: Harvard University Press, 1933. Reprinted.

Martin, Malachi

1958   *The Scribal Character of the Dead Sea Scrolls*. 2 vols. Louvain: University of Louvain.

Mason, S. N.

1989   "Was Josephus A Pharisee? A Reexamination of Life 10–12." *Journal of Jewish Studies* 40: 31–45.

Mayes, A. D. H.

1981   "Deuteronomy 4 and the Literary Criticism of Deuteronomy." *Journal of Biblical Literature* 100: 23–51.

McCarter, P. Kyle

1986   *Textual Criticism: Recovering the Text of the Hebrew Bible.* Philadelphia: Fortress Press.

McCready, Wayne O.

1982–84   "The Sectarian Status of Qumran: The Temple Scroll." *Revue de Qumran* 11: 183–91.

1985   "A Second Torah at Qumran?" *Studies in Religion/Sciences Religieuses* 14: 5–15.

McNamara, Martin

1983   *Intertestamental Literature.* Old Testament Message vol. 23. Wilmington: Michael Glazier.

Meek, Theophile James

1930   "The Translation of *ger* in the Hextateuch and its Bearing on the Documentary Hypothesis." *Journal of Biblical Literature* 49: 172–80.

Mendels, Doron

1979   "'On Kingship' in the 'Temple Scroll' and the Ideological Vorlage of the Seven Banquets in the 'Letter of Aristeas to Philocrates.'" *Aegyptus* 59: 127–36.

Metzger, Bruce M., ed.

1977   *The Apocrypha of the Old Testament.* Revised Standard Version. New York: Oxford University Press.

Meyer, R., Schmidt, K. L., and Schmidt, M. A.

1967   "πάροικος." In *Theological Dictionary of the New Testament*, vol. V, pp. 841–53. Edited by Gerhard Friedrich; edited and translated by Geoffrey W. Bromiley. Grand Rapids: William B. Eerdmans.

Milgrom, Jacob

1978a   "'Sabbath' and 'Temple City' in the Temple Scroll." *Bulletin of the American Schools of Oriental Research* 232: 25–27.

1978b   "Studies in the Temple Scroll." *Journal of Biblical Literature* 97: 501–23.

1978c   "The Temple Scroll." *Biblical Archaeologist* 41: 105–20.

1979   "הערות למגילת המקדש." *Beth Mikra* 25: 205–11.

1980a   "Further Studies in the Temple Scroll." *Jewish Quarterly Review* 71:1–17.

1980b   "Further Studies in the Temple Scroll." *Jewish Quarterly Review* 71: 89–106.

1981   "The Paradox of the Red Cow (Num. XIX)." *Vetus Testamentum* 31: 62–72.

1984   Review of *The Temple Scroll,* ed. Yigael Yadin. In *Biblical Archaeology Review* 10: 12–14.

1985   "Challenge to Sun-Worship Interpretation of Temple Scroll's Gilded Staircase." *Biblical Archaeology Review* 11: 70–73.

1989   "The Qumran Cult: Its Exegetical Principles." In *Temple Scroll Studies,* pp. 165–80. Edited by G. J. Brooke. Sheffield: *JSOT* Press.

Milik, J. T.

1957a   *Dix ans de découvertes dans le désert de Juda.* Paris: Éditions du cerf.

1957b   "Le travail d'édition des manuscrits du Désert de Juda." In *Supplements to Vetus Testamentum vol. 4 (Strasburg 1956),* pp. 17–26. Leiden: Brill.

1959   *Ten Years of Discovery in the Wilderness of Judaea.* Translated by John Strugnell. Studies in Biblical Theology 26. London: SCM Press.

1966   "Fragment d'une source du psautier (4Q Ps 89)." *Revue Biblique* 73: 94–106.

1973   "À propos de 11Q Jub." *Biblica* 54: 77–78.

1976   *The Books of Enoch: Aramaic Fragments of Qumrân Cave 4.* With the collaboration of Matthew Black. Oxford: Clarendon Press.

Milikowsky, Chaim

    1985–87   "Law at Qumran: A Critical Reaction to Lawrence H. Schiffman, 'Sectarian Law in the Dead Sea Scroll: [*sic*] Courts, Testimony, and the Penal Code'." *Revue de Qumran* 12: 237–50.

Millar, Fergus

    1987   "Empire, Community and Culture in the Roman Near East: Greeks, Syrians, Jews and Arabs." *Journal of Jewish Studies* 38: 143–64.

Mink, Hans Aage

    1979   "Præsentation af et nyt Qumranskrift: Tempelrullen." *Dansk Teologisk Tidsskrift* 42: 81–112.

    1982–84   "Die Kol. III der Tempelrolle: Versuch Einer Rekonstruction." *Revue de Qumran* 11: 163–81.

    1987   "The Use of Scripture in the Temple Scroll and the Status of the Scroll as Law." *Scandinavian Journal of the Old Testament* 1: 20–50.

    1988   "Tempel und Hofanlagen in der Tempelrolle." *Revue de Qumran* 13: 273–86.

Mishor, Mordechai

    1978   "עוד לנוסחה של 'מגילת המקדש'." *Tarbiz* 48: 173.

Moore, Cary

    1977   *Daniel, Esther and Jeremiah: The Additions*. Garden City: Doubleday.

Mor, Menachem

    1985   "The Bar-Kochba Revolt and Non-Jewish Participants." *Journal of Jewish Studies* 36: 200–9.

Moraldi, Luigi

    1971   *I manoscritti di Qumran*. Turin: Unione Tipografico-Editrice Torinese.

Mueller, James R.

1980   "The Temple Scroll and the Gospel Divorce Texts." *Revue de Qumran* 10: 247–56.

Murphy-O'Connor, Jerome

1970   "An Essene Missionary Document? CD II, 14–VI, 1." *Revue Biblique* 77: 201–29.

1971   "A Literary Analysis of Damascus Document VI, 2–VIII, 3." *Revue Biblique* 78: 210–32.

1972a   "Remarques sur l'exposé du Professor Y. Yadin." *Revue Biblique* 79: 99–100.

1972b   "The Critique of the Princes of Judah." *Revue Biblique* 79: 200–16.

1972c   "A Literary Analysis of Damascus Document XIX, 33–XX, 34." *Revue Biblique* 79: 544–64.

1974   "The Essenes and their History." *Revue Biblique* 81: 215–44.

1976   "Demetrius I and the Teacher of Righteousness." *Revue Biblique* 83: 400–20.

1985a   "The Damascus Document Revisited." *Revue Biblique* 92: 223–46.

1985b   Review of *The Damascus Covenant: An Interpretation of the "Damascus Document,"* by P. R. Davies. In *Revue Biblique* 92: 274–77.

1986   "The Judean Desert." In *Early Judaism and its Modern Interpreters,* pp. 119–56. Edited by R. A. Kraft and G. W. E. Nickelsburg. Philadelphia: Fortress Press.

Murray, R. P. R.

1984   Review of *The Dawn of Qumran: The Sectarian Torah and the Teacher of Righteousness,* by B. Z. Wacholder. In *The Society for Old Testament Study Book List 1984:* 139–40.

Naveh, Joseph, and Greenfield, Jonas

1984   "Hebrew and Aramaic in the Persian Period." In *The Cambridge History of Judaism, Volume I: Introduction; The Persian Period,* pp. 115–29. Edited by W. D. Davies and Louis Finkelstein. Cambridge: Cambridge University Press.

Nebe, G.W.

1982–84a   "אורשך 'Mass, Abmessung' in 11Q Tempelrolle XLI, 16." *Revue de Qumran* 11: 391–400.

1982–84b   "Addimentum zu אורשך in 11Q Tempelrolle." *Revue de Qumran* 11: 587–89.

Nelis, J.

1984   Review of *The Dawn of Qumran: The Sectarian Torah and the Teacher of Righteousness,* by B. Z. Wacholder. In *Tijdschrift voor Theologie* 24: 180–81.

Nobile, Marco

1984   Review of *The Dawn of Qumran: The Sectarian Torah and the Teacher of Righteousness,* by B. Z. Wacholder. In *Antonianum* 59: 662–64.

North, Robert

1980   Review of *Die Tempelrolle vom Toten Meer,* by Johann Maier. In *Biblica* 61: 116–17.

Oesch, J.

1981   Review of *Die Tempelrolle vom Toten Meer,* by Johann Maier. In *Zeitschrift für Katholische Theologie* 103: 200–1.

Pardee, Dennis

1972–74   "A Restudy of the Commentary on Psalm 37 from Qumran Cave 4 (Discoveries in the Judaean Desert of Jordan, vol. V, nᵒ 171)." *Revue de Qumran* 8: 163–94.

1989   Review of *The Dawn of Qumran: The Sectarian Torah and the Teacher of Righteousness,* by B. Z. Wacholder. In *Journal of Near Eastern Studies* 48: 72–74.

Patrich, Joseph

1986   "The Mesibbah of the Temple According to the Tractate Middot." *Israel Exploration Journal* 36: 215–33.

Paul, André

1986   Review of *The Dawn of Qumran: The Sectarian Torah and the Teacher of Righteousness,* by B. Z. Wacholder. In *Recherches de Science Religieuse* 74: 129–48.

Perrin, Norman

1969   *What is Redaction Criticism?* Philadelphia: Fortress Press.

Ploeg, J. van der

1978   "Une halakha inédite de Qumran." In *Qumrân: sa piété, sa théologie et son milieu,* pp. 107–14. Edited by J. Carmignac. Paris: Duculot.

1985–87 "Les manuscrits de la Grotte XI de Qumrân." *Revue de Qumran* 12: 3–16.

Polzin, Robert

1976   *Late Biblical Hebrew: Toward An Historical Typology of Biblical Hebrew Prose.* Harvard Semitic Monographs 12. Missoula: Scholars Press.

Qimron, E.

1978a   "לשונה של מגילת המקדש." *Leshonenu* 42 (1978): 83–98.

1978b   "New Readings in the Temple Scroll." *Israel Exploration Journal* 28: 162–71.

1978c   "מן העבודה במילון ההיסטורי." *Leshonenu* 42: 136–45.

1980   "למילונה של מגילת המקדש." *Shnaton* 4: 239–62.

1981   "שלוש הערות לנוסחה של מגילת המקדש." *Tarbiz* 51: 135–37.

1982–83 "כוננה = כלי מכלי המזבח." *Tarbiz* 52: 133.

1983   "הערות לנוסח מגילת המקדש." *Tarbiz* 53: 139–41.

1986a   Review of *The Damascus Covenant: An Interpretation of the "Damascus Document,"* by P. R. Davies. In *Jewish Quarterly Review* 77: 83–87.

1986b   *The Hebrew of the Dead Sea Scrolls*. Harvard Semitic Studies no. 29. Atlanta: Scholars Press.

1987   "Further New Readings in the Temple Scroll." *Israel Exploration Journal* 37: 31–35.

1988   "The Holiness of the Holy Land in the Light of a New Document from Qumran." In *The Holy Land in History and Thought,* pp. 9–13. Edited by M. Sharon. Leiden: Brill.

Qimron, E. and Strugnell, J.

1985   "An Unpublished Halakhic Letter from Qumran." *Israel Museum Journal* 4: 9–12.

1986   "An Unpublished Halakhic Letter from Qumran." *In Biblical Archaeology Today,* pp. 400–7. Edited by R. Amitai. Jerusalem: Israel Exploration Society.

Rabin, Chaim

1957   *Qumran Studies*. Oxford: Clarendon Press.

1958   *The Zadokite Documents*. 2nd rev. ed. Oxford: Clarendon Press.

1965   "The Historical Background of Qumran Hebrew." In *Scripta Hierosolymitana Volume IV: Aspects of the Dead Sea Scrolls,* pp. 144–61. 2nd ed. Edited by Chaim Rabin and Yigael Yadin. Jerusalem: Magnes Press.

1976   "Hebrew and Aramaic in the First Century." In *The Jewish People in the First Century. Compendia Rerum Iudaicarum ad Novum Testamentum, Section One, Vol. 2,* pp. 1007–39. Edited by S. Safrai and M. Stern. Philadelphia: Fortress Press.

Rahlfs, Alfred

1935   *Septuaginta*. 2 vols. Stuttgart: Württembergische Bibelanstalt.

Riesner, Rainer

1985   "Essener und Urkirche in Jerusalem." *Bibel und Kirche* 40: 64–76.

Rinaldi, Giovanni

1984   Review of *The Dawn of Qumran: The Sectarian Torah and the Teacher of Righteousness,* by B. Z. Wacholder. In *Bibbia e Oriente* 26: 62.

Rofe, Alexander

1965   "קטעים מכתב נוסף של ס. היובלים במערה 3 של קומראן." *Tarbiz* 34: 333–36.

Rokeah, David

1979–80   "הערות אסניות." *Shnaton* 4: 263–68.

1982   "הערת השלמה למאמר 'הערות אסניות' (שנתון כרך ד)." *Shnaton* 5–6: 231.

1983   "The Temple Scroll, Philo, Josephus, and the Talmud." *Journal of Theological Studies* 34: 515–26.

Rosen, Debra and Salvesen, Alison

1987   "A Note on the Qumran Temple Scroll 56: 15–18 and Psalm of Solomon 17: 33." *Journal of Jewish Studies* 38: 99–101.

Rosso, Liliana

1977   "Deuteronomio 21, 22: Contributo del Rotolo del Tempio alla valutazione di una variante medievale dei Settanta." *Revue de Qumran* 9: 231–36.

Russell, D. S.

1964   *The Method and Message of Jewish Apocalyptic.* Philadelphia: Westminster Press.

Sacchi, Paolo

1967   "Scoperta di una nuovo rotolo in Palestina." *Rivista di Storia e Letteratura Religiosa* 3: 579–80.

Safrai, S.

1974   "Relations Between the Diaspora and the Land of Israel." In *The Jewish People in the First Century. Compendia Rerum Iudaicarum ad Novum Testamentum,*

Section One, Vol. 1, pp. 184–215. Edited by S. Safrai and M. Stern. Philadelphia: Fortress Press.

1976   "The Temple." In *The Jewish People in the First Century. Compendia Rerum Iudaicarum ad Novum Testamentum, Section One, Vol. 2*, pp. 865–907. Edited by S. Safrai and M. Stern. Philadelphia: Fortress Press.

Saint-Blanqunt, H.

1968   "Le nouveau manuscrit de la Mer Morte." *Sciences et Avenir* 257: 582–89.

Sanders, James A.

1965   *Discoveries in the Judaean Desert of Jordan* IV: *The Psalms Scroll of Qumrân Cave 11 (11QPsª)*. Oxford: Clarendon Press.

1984   *Canon and Community: A Guide to Canonical Criticism*. Philadelphia: Fortress Press.

1985   Review of *The Dawn of Qumran: The Sectarian Torah and the Teacher of Righteousness*, by B. Z. Wacholder. In *Journal of the American Oriental Society* 105: 147–48.

Santos, Elmar

n.d.   *An Expanded Hebrew Index for the Hatch-Redpath Concordance to the Septuagint*. Jerusalem: Dugith.

Scharvit, Baruch

1980   "טומאה וטהרה לפי כת מדבר יהודה." *Beth Mikra* 26: 18–27.

Schedl, Claus

1984   "Zur Ehebruchklausel der Bergpredigt im Lichte der neu gefundenen Tempelrolle." *Theologisch-Praktische Quartalschrift* 130: 362–65.

Scher, T.

1968   "A kumráni Templomtekeres." *Világosság* 9: 636–37.

Schiffman, Lawrence

1975   *The Halakhah at Qumran.* Leiden: Brill.

1980   "The Temple Scroll in Literary and Philological Perspective." In *Approaches to Ancient Judaism* Volume II, pp. 143–58. Edited by William S. Green. Chico: Scholars Press.

1983   *Sectarian Law in the Dead Sea Scrolls: Courts, Testimony and the Penal Code.* Chico: Scholars Press.

1985a   "Exclusion from the Sanctuary and the City of the Sanctuary in the Temple Scroll." *Hebrew Annual Review* 9: 301–20.

1985b   Review of *The Temple Scroll: The Hidden Law of the Dead Sea Sect,* by Yigael Yadin. In *Biblical Archaeology Review* 11: 12–14.

1985c   Review of *The Temple Scroll,* ed. by Yigael Yadin. In *Biblical Archaeology Review* 11: 122–26.

1985d   "The Sacrificial System of the Temple Scroll and the Book of Jubilees." In *SBL 1985 Seminar Papers,* pp. 217–34. Edited by Kent Richards. Atlanta: Scholars Press.

1987   "The King, His Guard, and the Royal Council in the Temple Scroll." *Proceedings of the American Academy for Jewish Research* 54: 237–60.

1989a   "The Temple Scroll and the Systems of Jewish Law of the Second Temple Period." In *Temple Scroll Studies,* pp. 239–55. Edited by G. J. Brooke. Sheffield: *JSOT* Press.

1989b   "The Law of the Temple Scroll and its Provenance." *Folia Orientalia* 25: 89–98.

Schmid, Herbert

1978   Review of *Die Tempelrolle vom Toten Meer,* by Johann Maier. In *Judaica* 34: 187–88.

Schmidt, H. C.

1986   Review of *The Dawn of Qumran: The Sectarian Torah and the Teacher of Righteousness,* by B. Z. Wacholder. In *Zeitschrift für die Alttestamentliche Wissenschaft* 98: 316–17.

Schuller, Eileen M.

1986   *Non-Canonical Psalms from Qumran: A Pseudepigraphic Collection.* Atlanta: Scholars Press.

Schunk, Klaus Dietrich

1954   *Die Quellen des I. und II. Makkabäerbuches.* Halle: Max Niemyer Verlag.

Schürer, Emil

1973–87   *The History of the Jewish People in the Age of Jesus Christ (175 B.C.– A.D. 135).* 3 vols. Revised by G. Vermes, F. Millar, and M. Goodman. Edinburgh: T&T Clark.

Schwartz, David R.

1979–81   "The Three Temples of 4Q Florilegium." *Revue de Qumran* 10: 83–91.

Schwartz, Joshua

1985   "Jubilees, Bethel and the Temple of Jacob." *Hebrew Union College Annual* 56: 63–86.

Schwarz, Daniel.

1985   "מקוללי אלוהים ואנשים (מגילת המקדש סד 12)." *Leshonenu* 47: 18–24.

Segal, Moses H.

1907–08   "Mishnaic Hebrew and Its Relation to Biblical Hebrew and to Aramaic." *Jewish Quarterly Review* 20: 647–737.

1927   *A Grammar of Mishnaic Hebrew.* Oxford: Clarendon Press.

Sen, Felipe

1968   "El nuevo Manuscrito del Templo." *Cultura Bíblica* 25: 173–74.

Shanks, Hershel

1987   "Intrigue and the Scroll: Behind the Scenes of Israel's Acquisition of the Temple Scroll." *Biblical Archaeology Review* 13: 23–27.

Smalley, Stephen S.

1977   "Redaction Criticism." In *New Testament Interpretation: Essays in Principles and Methods,* pp. 181–95. Edited by I. Howard Marshall. Grand Rapids: Eerdmans.

Smith, Morton

1982   "Helios in Palestine." *Eretz Israel* 16: 199*–214*.

1984   "The Case of the Gilded Staircase." *Biblical Archaeology Review* 10: 50–55.

Smyth, Kevin

1985   Review of *The Dawn of Qumran: The Sectarian Torah and the Teacher of Righteousness,* by B. Z. Wacholder. In *Études Théologiques et Religieuses* 60: 292.

Soggin, J. A.

1978   *I manoscritti del Mar Morto.* Paperbacks civiltà scomparse 22. Rome: Newton Compton.

Starcky, J.

1977   "Jerusalem et les manuscrits de la Mer Morte." *Le Monde de la Bible* 1: 38–40.

Stauffer, Ethelbert

1957   *Jerusalem und Rom im Zeitalter Jesu Christi.* Munich: Francke Verlag.

Stegemann, Hartmut

1983a   "Die Bedeutung der Qumranfunde für die Erforschung der Apokalyptik." In *Apocalypticism in the Mediterranean World and the Near East: Proceedings of the International Colloquium on Apocalypticism,* pp. 495–530. Edited by K. Hellholm. Tübingen: J. C. B. Mohr.

1983b   "'Das Land' in der Tempelrolle und in anderen Texten aus den Qumranfunden." In *Das Land Israel in Biblischer Zeit,* pp. 154–71. Edited by G. Strecker. Göttingen: Vandenhoeck & Ruprecht.

1985   "Some Aspects of Eschatology in Texts from the Qumran Community and in the Teachings of Jesus." In *Biblical Archaeology Today,* pp. 408–26. Edited by Ruth Amitai. Jerusalem: Israel Exploration Society.

1986   "The Origins of the Temple Scroll." *Supplements to Vetus Testamentum* 40 (Congress Volume Jerusalem 1986): 235–56.

1987   "Is the Temple Scroll a Sixth Book of the Torah—Lost for 2,500 Years?" *Biblical Archaeology Review* 13: 28–35.

1989   "The Literary Composition of the Temple Scroll and its Status at Qumran." In *Temple Scroll Studies,* pp. 123–48. Edited by G. J. Brooke. Sheffield: *JSOT* Press.

Strugnell, J.

1970   "Notes en marge du volume v des 'Discoveries in the Judaean Desert of Jordan.'" *Revue de Qumran* 7: 163–276.

Suder, Robert

1985   Review of *The Dawn of Qumran: The Sectarian Torah and the Teacher of Righteousness,* by B. Z. Wacholder. In *Hebrew Studies* 26: 373–76.

Sukenik, E. L.

1954   אוצר המגילות הגנוזות שביד האוניברסיטה העברית. Jerusalem: Bialik Foundation and the Hebrew University.

Sweeney, Marvin A.

1983   "Sefirah at Qumran: Aspects of the Counting Formulas for the First-Fruits Festivals in the Temple Scroll." *Bulletin of the American School of Oriental Research* 251: 61–66.

1987a   "Midrashic Perspectives on the Torat Ham-Melek of the Temple Scroll." *Hebrew Studies* 28: 51–66.

1987b   Review of *The Temple Scroll,* by Johann Maier. In *Hebrew Studies* 28: 189–91.

Symmons-Symonolewicz, Konstantin

1970   *Nationalist Movements: A Comparative View.* Meadville: Maplewood Press.

Tcherikover, Victor

1982   *Hellenistic Civilization and the Jews.* Translated by S. Applebaum. New York: Atheneum.

Tedesche, Sidney and Zeitlin, Solomon

1950   *The First Book of Maccabees.* New York: Harper & Brothers.

Teeple, H. W.

1957   *The Mosaic Eschatological Prophet. JBL* Monograph Series 10. Philadelphia: Society for Biblical Literature.

Thiering, Barbara E.

1979   *Redating the Teacher of Righteousness.* Sydney: Theological Explorations.

1981   "Mebaqqer and Episcopos in the Light of the Temple Scroll." *Journal of Biblical Literature* 100: 59–74.

1989   "The Date of Composition of the Temple Scroll." In *Temple Scroll Studies,* pp. 99–120. Edited by G. J. Brooke. Sheffield: *JSOT* Press.

Thorion, Yohanan

1979–81a   "Zur Bedeutung von גבורי חיל למלחמה in 11QT LVII, 9." *Revue de Qumran* 10: 597–98.

1979–81b   "Zur Bedeutung von חטא in 11QT." *Revue de Qumran* 10: 598–99.

1982–84a   "Die Sprache der Tempelrolle und die Chronikbücher." *Revue de Qumran* 11: 423–26.

1982–84b   "Tempelrolle LIX, 8–11 und Bablî, Sanhedrin 98a." *Revue de Qumran* 11: 427–28.

1985–87   "Die Syntax der Präposition B in der Qumran Literatur." *Revue de Qumran* 12: 17–64.

Thorion-Vardi, Talia

1982–84   "Die Adversativen Konjunktionen in der Qumran Literatur." *Revue de Qumran* 11: 579–82.

1985–87a "The Personal Pronoun as Syntactical Glide in the Temple Scroll and in the Masoretic Text." *Revue de Qumran* 12: 421–22.

1985–87b "'t nominativi in the Qumran Literature." *Revue de Qumran* 12: 423–24.

Tigay, Jeffrey H.

1985 "The Stylistic Criterion of Source Criticism in the Light of Ancient Near Eastern and Post-biblical Literature." In *Empirical Models for Biblical Criticism,* pp. 149–73. Edited by Jeffrey H. Tigay. Philadelphia: University of Pennsylvania Press.

Tosato, Angelo

1984 "The Law of Leviticus 18:18: A Reexamination." *Catholic Biblical Quarterly* 46: 199–214.

Tov, Emanuel

1981 *The Text Critical Use of the Septuagint in Biblical Research.* Jerusalem: Simor.

1982 "מגילת המקדש' וביקורת נוסח המקרא." *Eretz Israel* 16: 100–11.

1985 "The Nature and Background of Harmonization in Biblical Manuscripts." *Journal for the Study of the Old Testament* 31: 3–29.

1986 "The Orthography and Language of the Hebrew Scrolls Found at Qumran and the Origin of these Scrolls." *Textus* 13: 31–57.

Trever, John C.

1972 *Scrolls from Qumran Cave I: The Great Isaiah Scroll, The Order of the Community, The Pesher to Habakkuk.* Jerusalem: The Albright Institute of Archaeological Research and the Shrine of the Book.

Treves, M.

1959–60 "On the Meaning of the Qumran Testimonia." *Revue de Qumran* 2: 269–71.

Tyloch, Witold

1980   "Le 'Rouleau du Temple' et les Esséniens." *Rocznik Orientalistyczny* 41 (1980): 139–43.

1983a   "L'importance du 'Rouleau du Temple' pour l'identification de la communaute de Qumran." In *Traditions in Contact and Change: Selected Proceedings of the XIVth Congress of the International Association for the History of Religions,* pp. 285–93. Edited by Peter Slater and Donald Wiebe. Winnipeg: Wilfrid Laurier University Press.

1983b   "Zwój swiatynny [The Temple Scroll]." *Euhemer* 27 no. 3 (129): 3–20.

1984a   "'Zwój swiatynny' najwazniejszy rekopis z Qumran i czas jego powstania [The Temple Scroll: The Most Important Manuscript from Qumran and the Period of its Composition]." *Studia Religioznawcza* 19: 27–38.

1984b   "Zwój swiatynny [The Temple Scroll]." *Euhemer* 28 no. 1 (131): 3–24.

1984c   "Zwój swiatynny [The Temple Scroll]." *Euhemer* 28 no. 2 (132): 11–28.

1984d   "Zwój swiatynny [The Temple Scroll]." *Euhemer* 28 no. 3 (133): 9–27.

1989   "La provenance et la date du Rouleau du Temple." *Folia Orientalia* 25: 33–40.

United Bible Societies

1979   *Syriac Bible*. Norfolk: Lowe and Brydone.

Vadja, G.

1979   Review of *Die Tempelrolle vom Toten Meer,* by Johann Maier. In *Revue des Études Juives* 138: 443.

VanderKam, James C.

1977   *Textual and Historical Studies in the Book of Jubilees*. Harvard Semitic Monographs 14. Missoula: Scholars Press.

1982–84   "Zadok and the SPR HTWRH HḤTWM in Dam. Doc. V, 2–5." *Revue de Qumran* 11: 561–70.

1984   Review of *The Dawn of Qumran: The Sectarian Torah and the Teacher of Righteousness*, by B. Z. Wacholder. In *Catholic Biblical Quarterly* 46: 803–4.

1985   Review of *The Dawn of Qumran: The Sectarian Torah and the Teacher of Righteousness*, by B. Z. Wacholder. In *Biblical Archaeologist* 48: 126–27.

1989   "The Temple Scroll and the Book of Jubilees." In *Temple Scroll Studies*, pp. 211–36. Edited by G. J. Brooke. Sheffield: *JSOT* Press.

Vargas-Machura, Antonio

1981   "Divorcio e indisolubilidad del matrimonio en la sgda. escritura." *Estudios Biblicos* 39: 19–61.

Vaux, Roland de

1965   *Ancient Israel,* vol. 1: *Social Institutions.* New York: McGraw Hill.

Veenhof, K. R.

1968   "Een nieuw handschrift van de Dode Zee: De 'Tempelrol.'" *Phoenix* 14: 186–88.

Vermes, Geza

1956   *Discovery in the Judean Desert.* New York: Desclee.

1973   *Jesus the Jew.* Philadelphia: Fortress Press.

1977   *The Dead Sea Scrolls: Qumran in Perspective.* Rev. ed. With the collaboration of Pamela Vermes. Philadelphia: Fortress Press.

1986a   Review of *The Temple Scroll: An Introduction, Translation, and Commentary*, by Johann Maier. In *Journal of Jewish Studies* 37: 130–32.

1986b   Review of *The Dawn of Qumran: The Sectarian Torah and the Teacher of Righteousness*, by B. Z. Wacholder. In *Journal of Jewish Studies* 37: 268.

1987   *The Dead Sea Scrolls in English.* 3rd ed. Sheffield: *JSOT* Press.

Wacholder, Ben Zion

1983   *The Dawn of Qumran: The Sectarian Torah and the Teacher of Righteousness.* Cincinnati: Hebrew Union College Press.

1985   "The Relationship between 11Q Torah (The Temple Scroll) and the Book of Jubilees: One Single or Two Independent Compositions." In *SBL 1985 Seminar Papers,* pp. 205–16. Edited by Kent Richards. Atlanta: Scholars Press.

1985–87 "The 'Sealed' Torah versus the 'Revealed' Torah: An Exegesis of Damascus Covenant V, 1–6 and Jeremiah 32, 10–14." *Revue de Qumran* 12: 351–68.

Weinert, Francis

1974   "4Q 159: Legislation for an Essene Community Outside of Qumran?" *Journal for the Study of Judaism* 5: 179–207.

1977–78 "A Note on 4Q 159 and a New Theory of Essene Origins." *Revue de Qumran* 9: 223–30.

Weinfeld, Moshe

1978–79a "חוקת המלך' במגילת המקדש והמצע הרעיוני של הסימפוסיונים באגרת אריסטיאס לפילוקרטס." *Shnaton* 3: 245–52.

1978–79b "'מגילת המקדש' או 'תורה למלך'." *Shnaton* 3: 214–37.

1980   "The Royal Guard According to the Temple Scroll." *Revue Biblique* 87: 394–96.

Wentling, J. L.

1989   "Unraveling the Relationship Between 11QT, the Eschatological Temple, and the Qumran Community." *Revue de Qumran* 14: 61–74.

Wevers, John William

1978   *Text History of the Greek Deuteronomy.* Abhandlungen der Akademie der Wissenschaften in Göttingen, Philologisch-Historische Klasse: Folge 3, no. 106. Göttingen: Vandenhoeck & Ruprecht.

White, R.

1985   Review of *The Damascus Covenant: An Interpretation of the "Damascus Document,"* by P. R. Davies. *Journal of Jewish Studies* 36: 113–15.

Wieder, N.

1953   "The 'Law Interpreter' of the Sect of the Dead Sea Scrolls: The Second Moses."
            Journal of Jewish Studies 4: 158–75.

Wilcox, Max

1977   "'Upon the Tree'—Deut 21:22–23 in the New Testament." *Journal of Biblical
            Literature* 96: 85–99.

Wilhelm, G.

1968–69   "Qumran ('Tempelrolle')." *Archiv für Orientforschung* 22: 165–66.

Wilk, Roman

1985   "יוחנן הורקנוס הראשון ומגילת המקדש." *Shnaton* 9: 221–30.

Williamson, H. G. M.

1985   *Ezra, Nehemiah.* Word Biblical Commentary vol. 16. Waco: Word Books.

Wilson, Andrew and Wills, Lawrence

1982   "Literary Sources for the Temple Scroll." *Harvard Theological Review* 75:
            275–88.

Wilson, B. R.

1967a   "Introduction." In *Patterns of Sectarianism,* pp. 1–21. Edited by B. R. Wilson.
            London: Heinemann.

1967b   "An Analysis of Sect Development." In *Patterns of Sectarianism,* pp. 22–47.
            Edited by B. R. Wilson. London: Heinemann.

Winter, P.

1954   "Notes on Wieder's Observations on the דורש התורה in the Book of the New
            Covenant of Damascus." *Jewish Quarterly Review* 45: 39–47.

Wintermute, O. S.

1983–85   "Jubilees: A New Translation and Introduction." In *The Old Testament Pseudepigrapha,* 2: 35–142. Edited by J. H. Charlesworth. Garden City: Doubleday & Co.

Wise, Michael O.

1988   "A New Manuscript Join in the 'Festival of Wood Offering' (Temple Scroll XXIII)." *Journal of Near Eastern Studies* 47: 113–21.

1989a   Review of *The Temple Scroll: An Introduction, Translation, and Commentary,* by Johann Maier. In *Journal of Near Eastern Studies* 48: 40–41.

1989b   "The Covenant of the Temple Scroll XXIX, 3–10." *Revue de Qumran* 14: 49–60.

1990a   "A Note on the 'Three Days' of 1Maccabees X 34." *Vetus Testamentum* 60: 116–22.

1990b   "The Eschatological Vision of the Temple Scroll." *Journal of Near Eastern Studies* 49.2: 155–72.

—   "4QFlorilegium and the Temple of Adam." *Revue de Qumran.* (In press).

—   "The Teacher of Righteousness and the High Priest of the Intersacerdotium: Two Approaches." *Revue de Qumran.* (In press).

Woude, A. S. van der

1971   "Fragmente des Buches Jubiläen aus Qumran XI (11Q Jub)." In *Tradition und Glaube: Das frühe Christentum in seiner Umwelt. Festgabe für Georg Kuhn zum 65. Geburtstag,* pp. 140–46. Edited by G. Jeremias and others. Göttingen: Vandenhoeck & Ruprecht.

1979   Review of *Die Tempelrolle vom Toten Meer,* by Johann Maier. *Journal for the Study of Judaism* 10: 106.

1980a   "De Tempelrol van Qumrân (I)." *Nederlands Theologisch Tijdschrift* 34: 177–90.

1980b   "De Tempelrol van Qumrân (II)." *Nederlands Theologisch Tijdschrift* 34: 281–93.

1983   "Een Gedeelte uit de Tempelrol van Qumrân." In *Schrijvend Verleden: Documenten uit het oude Nabije Oosten Vertaald en Togelicht,* pp. 387–91. Edited by K.R. Veenhof. Leiden: Leiden Terra.

1986   Review of *The Dawn of Qumran: The Sectarian Torah and the Teacher of Righteousness,* by B. Z. Wacholder. In *Journal for the Study of Judaism* 17: 120–24.

Wright, D. P.

1989   Review of *The Temple Scroll: An Introduction, Translation, and Commentary,* by Johann Maier. *Biblical Archaeologist* 52: 45.

Wright, R. B.

1983–85   "Psalms of Solomon." In *The Old Testament Pseudepigrapha,* 2:639–70. Edited by J. H. Charlesworth. Garden City: Doubleday.

Yadin, Yigael

1961   "Expedition D." *Israel Exploration Journal* 11: 36–52.

1962a   "Expedition D—The Cave of Letters." *Israel Exploration Journal* 12: 227–57.

1962b   *The Scroll of the War of the Sons of Light Against the Sons of Darkness.* Oxford: Oxford University Press.

1967a   "The Temple Scroll." *Biblical Archaeologist* 30: 135–39.

1967b   "Un nouveau manuscrit de la Mer Morte: 'Le Rouleau du Temple.'" *Académie des Inscriptions et Belles-Lettres: Comptes rendus des Séances:* 607–19.

1968a   "מגילת המקדש." In *Jerusalem Through the Ages: The Twenty-Fifth Archaeological Convention October 1967,* pp. 72–84. Jerusalem: Israel Exploration Society.

1968b   "What the Temple Scroll Reveals." *The Daily Telegraph Magazine,* 19 July, 15–17.

1969a   "De Tempelrol." *Spiegel Historiael* 4: 202–10.

1969b   *Tefillin from Qumran (XQ Phyl 1–4).* Jerusalem: Israel Exploration Society.

1971a   *Bar Kokhba*. London: Weidenfeld and Nicolson.

1971b   "Pesher Nahum (4QpNahum) Reconsidered." *Israel Exploration Journal* 21: 1–12.

1971c   "The Temple Scroll." In *New Directions in Biblical Archaeology,* pp. 156–66. Edited by David Noel Freedman and Jonas C. Greenfield. Garden City: Doubleday.

1971d   "Temple Scroll." In *Encyclopedia Judaica*, vol. 15, pp. 996–98. Jerusalem: Keter Publishing House.

1972a   "שער האיסיים בירושלים ומגילת המקדש." *Qadmoniot* 5: 129–30.

1972b   "L'attitude essénienne envers la polygamie et le divorce." *Revue Biblique* 79: 98–99.

1975   "The Gate of the Essenes and the Temple Scroll." In *Jerusalem Revealed: Archaeology in the Holy City 1968–1974*, pp. 90–91. Edited by Yigael Yadin. Jerusalem: Israel Exploration Society.

1977   *מגילת המקדש*. 3 vols. and supplementary plates. Jerusalem: Israel Exploration Society.

1978   "Le Rouleau du Temple." In *Qumrân: sa piété, sa théologie et son milieu,* pp. 115–20. Edited by J. Carmignac. Paris: Duculot.

1979   "Militante Herodianer aus Qumran." *Lutherische Monatshefte* 18: 355–58.

1981a   "האם מגילת המקדש היא יצירה כיתתיח?" In *Thirty Years of Archaeology in Eretz Israel*, pp. 152–71. Jerusalem: Israel Exploration Society.

1981b   "The Holy City in the Temple Scroll." In *Temples and High Places in Biblical Times*, p. 181. Edited by Avraham Biran. Jerusalem: Hebrew Union College-Jewish Institute of Religion.

1982   "Is the Temple Scroll a Sectarian Document?" In *Humanizing America's Iconic Book,* pp. 153–69. Edited by G. M. Tucker and D. A. Knight. Chico: Scholars Press.

1983   *The Temple Scroll.* 3 vols. and supplementary plates. Jerusalem: Israel Exploration Society.

1984   "The Temple Scroll—The Longest and Most Recently Discovered Dead Sea Scroll." *Biblical Archaeology Review* 10: 32–49.

1985   *The Temple Scroll: The Hidden Law of the Dead Sea Sect.* London: Weidenfeld and Nicolson.

Yeivin, Israel

1980   *Introduction to the Tiberian Masorah.* Translated and edited by E. J. Revell. Missoula: Scholars Press.

Zahavy, Tzvee

1979–81   "The Sabbath Code of Damascus Document X, 14–XI, 18: Form Analytical and Redaction Critical Observations." *Revue de Qumran* 10: 588–91.

Zeitlin, Solomon

1947   "Prosbul." *Jewish Quarterly Review* 37: 341–62.

1962   "Johanan the High Priest's Abrogations and Decrees." In *Studies and Essays in Honor of A. A. Newman,* pp. 569–79. Edited by M. Ben-Horin, B. D. Weinryb and S. Zeitlin. Leiden: Brill.

Zimmerli, Walter

1979–83   *Ezekiel.* 2 vols. Philadelphia: Fortress Press.

Zuckermandel, M. S.

1970   *Tosephta: Based on the Erfurt and Vienna Codices.* New ed. Jerusalem: Wahrmann Books.